BESTSELLER

BESTSELLER

A Century of America's Favorite Books

Robert McParland

ROWMAN & LITTLEFIELD
Lanham • Boulder • New York • London

Published by Rowman & Littlefield
An imprint of The Rowman & Littlefield Publishing Group, Inc.
4501 Forbes Boulevard, Suite 200, Lanham, Maryland 20706
www.rowman.com

Unit A, Whitacre Mews, 26-34 Stannary Street, London SE11 4AB

British Library Cataloguing in Publication Information Available

Library of Congress Cataloging-in-Publication Data

Names: McParland, Robert, author.
Title: Bestseller : a century of America's favorite books / Robert McParland.
Description: Lanham : Rowman & Littlefield, [2019] | Includes bibliographical references and index.
Identifiers: LCCN 2018029808 (print) | LCCN 2018033216 (ebook) | ISBN 9781538110003 (electronic) | ISBN 9781538109991 (cloth : alk. paper)
Subjects: LCSH: Best sellers—United States—History—20th century. | Best sellers—United States—History—21st century. | Books and reading—United States—History—20th century. | Books and reading—United States—History—21st century.
Classification: LCC Z1033.B3 (ebook) | LCC Z1033.B3 M37 2019 (print) | DDC 38/.4500209730904—dc23
LC record available at https://lccn.loc.gov/2018029808

Printed in the United States of America

CONTENTS

ACKNOWLEDGMENTS

This book provides a listing of bestselling books and recalls the contemporary context in which those books were situated. The bestseller list gives us an opportunity to see what people were reading at the time. In considering the list, we might think about reader interests, the pulse of culture, the development of the book publishing industry, or the creativity of popular writers. By consulting bestseller lists we can reopen some of these books for enjoyment and ask what they say about American life. The popular book, which is the subject of this volume, captures images of life, refracting them as in a stained-glass window. The popular book registers a kind of enthusiasm, a suggestion of private and public consciousness. The bestseller list gives us a glimpse of the people, dreams, fantasies, hopes, and concerns of America.

The responses of readers to popular fiction and nonfiction may be found in library-based reading groups, in oral history collections, and in the pages of magazines and newspapers where there are letters to the editor. Today some readers post their comments about books on websites like Goodreads, or on their own blogs. Such gestures remind us that reading is not only a private activity but also a social one. The author is thankful to the Rutgers University Oral History Project for permission to share a few comments from individuals that they have interviewed. Any other brief quotations from readers are available on public website postings.

Bestseller owes much to editor Stephen Ryan's creativity. Thanks also to Bob Batchelor for his enthusiasm for popular literature. My colleagues and students at Felician University continue to be a source of encouragement. On the home front, Debbie and Brian keep me in touch with popular films and television shows. For this book, there was a lot to read! No, I did not read *all* of this material. I made use of synopses, looked at reviews and comments by critics, and revisited many books I have read across the years. While reading Michael Crichton's *Dragon Teeth* or Senator Ben Sasse's *The Vanishing Adult*, there were journeys back through Grisham, King, Clark, Uris, Forsyth, Ludlum, Clancy, Grafton, Koontz, and many others. I dusted off my father's 1960 Allen Drury novels, the paperback of *Anatomy of a Murder* that was #1 on the list when I was born, my mother's paperback of Mary Jane Ward's *The Snake Pit*. I read Danielle Steel for the first time. Today, on the way downstairs, I pass by bookshelves where more books await—the familiar ones I have read and the yet to be read pages, like a vast ocean of wonder still to be explored. As a friend of mine, a literature professor, once said to me, "Well, you can't read everything." Yes, but you can try.

INTRODUCTION

Reaching the Top of the Shelf: Discovering a Century of Bestsellers

A bestseller is a book that has caught the imagination of many readers. It is a book that has energy and momentum in the market and is being successfully marketed by its publisher. In hardcover, paperback, or electronic form it has sparkled into life like a fireworks display and made its colorful dash across the sky. Bestsellers are plentifully available; selling briskly, they rise to the top of the list and many of them vanish quickly. You can buy a bestseller at that bookstore that you like. Bestsellers are in your local library too, or they soon will be. Yes, they are available online too. Press some buttons, include your payment, provide an address, and you will be getting that new book in a few days. (Or right away, if you order an electronic copy.) These days you can listen to books on CDs in your car while you are driving to work. You can download books onto your computer or smartphone. Or, you might go out for a drive down the road to try to find a copy.

Imagine that you are drifting down a road in Maine. On occasion the sky appears through the high branches and shadows. Someone has warned you about these desolate rural roads in Stephen King country: about the moose and the deer that could appear at any turn. There is strangeness and a chill, not only of the cold air, but from the Stephen King story you read last night, the one that kept you awake. The trees sway and seem to come to life near Route 222. Bangor becomes Derry,

Maine; it transforms in a fog: a fictional place where the roads become lost. You've read that Castle Rock has mad dogs and dead zones. The Mount Hope cemetery, ten miles east of Bangor, has a pet cemetery. You drive into town. The public library is surrounded by snow. It is a large building, stately and welcoming. The library has a quiet elegance, even if those three large windows to each side, their tops curved, might remind you of cemetery monuments. It has an austere beauty, like something out of a Henry James novel. Step inside and you can discover the bestsellers: Stephen King books, James Michener books, Agatha Christie books—romances and heroes and stories like an icy Maine winter that will chill you to the bone.

This book traces the path of hundreds of bestsellers that have seized the public imagination across the past one hundred years. Bestsellers reflect us. They hold the world in their pages. They are filled with dreams, drama and adventure, entertainment, information, and imagination. A book is a repository of culture, information, ideas, entertainment, expression, and style. Its popularity suggests that readers desire adventures, crave mysteries, or have a desire for self-improvement. These commercially successful books have enchanted and entertained millions. This book provides a composite of multiple bestseller lists, including the national lists produced by *Publishers Weekly* and the *New York Times*. (Another popular recent list is the Amazon bestseller list, which tracks books sold by Amazon.) Many major newspapers today have bestseller lists: the *Los Angeles Times*, the *Washington Post*, the *San Francisco Chronicle*, and *USA Today* among them. Sometimes these lists reflect regional preferences in book sales. Books suggest tendencies in American culture and provide an indication of our concerns at any given time. This book is necessarily a kind of history book. There is some discussion of U.S. culture insofar as it may be reflected in works of fiction and nonfiction.

Bestseller lists indicate that the general pattern of nonfiction book reader interests has remained consistent across the years. There have been books that have focused upon humor, self-help, amusement, diets, celebrities, or political scandals. There have been a variety of "serious" novels on the bestseller list, and it is clear that some popular novels can make a lasting impact. Other books are products of their time that have an ephemeral life: they quickly rise and fall and disappear.[1]

Publishers Weekly began developing its list early in the twentieth century. Founder Frederick Leypoldt, a bibliographer, sold the publication to R. R. Bowker in 1878. (Today Bowker provides the annual Books in Print database.) The *Bookman* was a literary journal that listed and surveyed books beginning in 1891 in London and 1895 in New York. The *Bookman* continued from 1895 to 1912. Harry Thurston Peck printed lists of the bestselling books in several cities. *Publishers Weekly* followed the *Bookman* by creating the first bestseller list in 1912. After a few earlier starts, the *New York Times* national bestseller list began on April 9, 1942, in the *New York Times Book Review* section. At that time, sales figures were gathered from city lists. The national market list that emerged was created based upon bookseller reports in twenty-two U.S. cities. In the 1950s, *Publishers Weekly* and *New York Times* bestseller lists became the central sources for booksellers across the United States who wished to track sales trends. Their lists continue to provide a gauge of consumer demand. They recognize reader interests and patterns of consumption. When a book arrives on a bestseller list, it will be advertised as a bestseller and that will boost sales further. This becomes a major marketing tool.[2] The bestseller lists chart books with sales figures that demonstrate their striking current appeal. Benedict Anderson once pointed out that one of the principles of order in a newspaper is the date and what he called "calendrical coincidence." This, he remarked, is the "essential literary convention of the newspaper."[3] The *New York Times Book Review* is date oriented and provides a chronological list. So too *Publishers Weekly* and various newspapers across the United States list bestsellers chronologically. The system by which the *New York Times* bestseller list is compiled remains about as secret as the recipe for Coca-Cola.

Today sales reports from independent bookstores, chain bookstores, and online sales contribute to the figures. (The Amazon list tracks online purchases and creates a rating system.) It is held that retail sales tend to correspond to book buyer purchases. So, wholesale volumes are likely not within the calculation. The *New York Times* has said that the list refers to the sales of currently popular works rather than "classic" works of fiction or nonfiction.[4] That tends to be true of *Publishers Weekly* also. *Publishers Weekly* is particularly helpful to readers, publishers, booksellers, and librarians. The *New York Times* book reviews appear in its Sunday newspaper. Its bestseller list has long been divided between works of fiction and nonfiction. In 2000, with the repeated success of the Harry

Potter series in 1999, "Children's Best Sellers" were separated out into their own category. In 2007, a paperback fiction list was divided into "trade" and "mass market." In 2011, attempts were made to record e-book sales. In 2017, the *New York Times* readjusted and trimmed the number of its lists.

Readers have responded to bestselling books for a variety of reasons: the expectation of entertainment, interest in a subject, familiarity with an author's previous work, or clever sales and marketing. Word of mouth sells books. However, it is difficult to gauge the reasons for a given book's popularity strictly by its sales. Sometimes a book may be purchased and left unread on a shelf or on the coffee table. In *The Great Gatsby*, "Owl Eyes" recognizes that the pages in the books in Jay Gatsby's library are uncut: they have not been turned. They have become like furniture, objects for display and for snob value. Some bestsellers may be like this. After all, how many people have taken the time to read through Stephen Hawking's *A Brief History of Time*? More likely the book collects cosmic dust and fills a black hole on the bookshelf. Books like this (while actually quite fascinating) may be purchased, sampled, and set aside. Other books are devoured by the reading public. They keep readers up at night.

A sociologist might point out that the list first appeared during the same era when consumer culture was emerging as a significant trend in America. The World War II period marks a change in American culture. It was a time of increased productivity, advertising, and a gradual improvement of the economy. Of course, to regard the book as a commodity to be sold as a means of profit by publishing companies was certainly nothing new. In the years before the mid-nineteenth century, publishers like Putnam, the Harper Brothers, and Ticknor and Fields balanced a gentlemanly tradition of publishing with tenacious commercial efforts. One hundred years later, publishers were looking to marketing devices from print and radio ads to the Book of the Month Club. Despite paper shortages, books were printed and reading was a popular pastime. The paperback series initiated by Penguin and the development of the Modern Library by Random House expanded the audience.

The bestseller list is a measure of popular interest. It is not a guarantee of lasting impact or importance. Some books are more like long-distance runners than sprinters: they achieve sustained sales while other books are ephemeral. The novel has always provided readers with a way to extend their lives imaginatively beyond the local. The story brings readers to places and people not previously experienced. Emily Dickinson recognized this when she wrote: "There is no frigate like a book to take us lands away." However, readers have different tastes and the bestseller list reflects this. E. L. James's *Fifty Shades of Grey* may offer erotic fantasy to some readers. Dan Brown's symbol-seeking Robert Langdon may intrigue others. Who knows whether those books will be read in the future or will soon disappear? Authors who have bid farewell to this world, like the thriller writers Robert Ludlum and Tom Clancy, have had an extraordinary afterlife on the bestseller list. Dr. Seuss still rhymes and charms us.

Even so, bestsellers can be ephemeral. A glance at the bestseller lists of the past one hundred years will remind us of that. Some of these books reach their sales peaks quickly and do not have much longevity. The popular rage of the day, the startling wonder of a few weeks, may be no longer in print. Yet, to look at books is "an approach to the past," as Leslie Howsam has pointed out.[5] Each book has its own history. Books are material artifacts, and the book changes from manuscript to print book or electronic book. The readers who read each book are situated in a historical time and place. It might be said that there is a "community" of readers who have some shared experience since they have read the same book, even though they have read it at quite different times. Those readers may also have read the same book in different ways. Meanwhile, people have made a living by producing this book, marketing it, responding to it, or managing its placement and circulation within a library. We may ask about the appetites of readers, what they desire to read. A book *happens* to the people who read it. Howsam writes: "The book can be a force for change and the history of the book documents that change."[6]

Literary works are a conversation. They offer the opportunity for an interaction, a space for discourse. Print culture is discovered through its audiences, particularly when a reader writes or speaks about his or her reading experience. A book's cultural significance lies in how readers recreate the texts they read and in what this means for their lives. We may ask what affects or shapes a reader's reception of a text, or the reader's reconstruction of it. We revisit the past through the lens of these books. Books by a single author become his or her bibliography, and they are artifacts that tell a story, which we can read historically. Bestseller lists are indications of social trends and exist as marketing tools, as Laura J. Miller points out.[7] The production and reception of a book may reveal a pattern and history of mentality. We may often think of reading as a solitary practice; however, as sociologist Elizabeth Long has recognized, reading is not only a matter of private life. Reading is also social.[8]

We can ask what the bestselling books of a given time may have to do with the culture and life of a nation. In June 2012, the Library of Congress listed its library staff's choices of the "Books That Shaped America." These culturally important books were not only productions of high culture. They included popular bestselling books. Among them are *Atlas Shrugged* by Ayn Rand; *How to Win Friends and Influence People* by Dale Carnegie; *The Great Gatsby* by F. Scott Fitzgerald; *Tarzan of the Apes* by Edgar Rice Burroughs; *Riders of the Purple Sage* by Zane Grey; *Gone with the Wind* by Margaret Mitchell; and *Stranger in a Strange Land* by science fiction writer Robert Heinlein.

At times, the bestseller relates the personal to the institutional, as Scott McCracken has pointed out.[9] For example, Danielle Steel's *Mixed Blessings* brings together concerns about fertility with medicine and legal adoption laws. Steel's novels often incorporate romance and relationship issues with Hollywood, television, retail business, and corporations. Arthur Hailey's novels connect personal lives with hotel management (*Hotel*), airports (*Airport*), or the automotive industry (*Wheels*). Several bestsellers are works of easily read prose in which a suspenseful tale is developed. McCracken observes that "the bestselling novels of Jackie Collins and Harold Robbins are composed of short passages of prose that leap from character to character so that the narrative is built up from internally coherent fragments, which invite the reader's imaginative intervention."[10] The bestseller often involves mystery, romance, or sex, as in the case of Jackie Collins, Harold Robbins, Jacqueline Susann, or the more recent *Fifty Shades of Grey*. Then there is the "thriller": Ian Fleming's James Bond stories, Frederick Forsyth's *The Day of the Jackal*, Daniel Silva's international spy novels featuring the Mossad agent Gabriel Allon. John Grisham has appeared on the bestseller list more than twenty times with legal thrillers. Sometimes these authors include commentary in their novels on the state of the nation and the world. Whereas *The Hunt for Red October* dealt with Cold War issues, Tom Clancy's *Debt of Honor* (1995) considered the United States "weaker" in a "new world order," and Jack Ryan, now the national security advisor, was earnestly determined to deal with that.

MAKING A BESTSELLER

Many attempts have been made to determine which books will become bestsellers. A book published in 2016, *The Bestseller Code: The Making of a Blockbuster Novel*, used computer models to analyze the elements that comprise a bestseller. In *Hit Lit*, James W. Hall claims that there is a formula. However, Ruth Franklin argues that "no generalization" can be made about the wide variety of books that have appeared on the bestseller lists.[11] Of course, having a good story, a hot topic, or a noted celebrity biography (the more scandalous the better) might prompt sales. Sex and violence sometimes works too. Publicity dollars, ads, book tours, and social media may help. However, even the professionals will tell you that, except for the big brand-name authors and books by celebrities with well-established public platforms, there is something intangible to the process. There are still surprises, like J. K. Rowling's first Harry Potter novel.

Frank Luther Mott, in *Golden Multitudes* in 1947, set forth criteria for the bestseller. In his view this is a book that sells a quantity equal to 1 percent of the population during the time that the book has appeared. "Bestseller" becomes a form of cultural capital. This designation of a work in the literary marketplace suggests value. If many other people are reading this book it must be good and worthy of one's time.[12] Of course, readers will have differing views about what is worth their time. When we read literature we are "communing with the mind of the author," as Martin Amis observed in an essay on Saul Bellow's stories in 1997. (Amis remarked that we should refer to the author as "Soul" Bellow.)[13] Literary critic Wayne Booth referred to this as "the company we keep." Each of us makes choices about the company we keep in life and what we read.

CRITICISMS OF POPULAR FICTION

Is there an unbridgeable chasm between the literary tradition and popular storytelling? In *The Bloomsbury Introduction to Popular Fiction*, Christine Berberich has some rather harsh criticism for popular fiction. Berberich calls it "manipulative" and a form of plagiarizing that pushes itself into people's lives through copycat productions. This popular fiction participates in "the plethora of seemingly mindless material we are fed on a

daily basis," she writes.[14] Other critics contend that popular fiction seduces readers and will bring an end to "serious" literature. From a literary
standpoint, it has been argued that popular fiction engages in a reduction
of writing to market requirements and profitability. These critics raise a
concern that literary standards will decline when economic value is
prized over artistic values.

Even so, writing bestselling popular fiction requires effort and persistence. Writers may rely upon formulas, or on tricks of the trade that they
have learned across the years. Yet, these same writers are productive.
They create sequels, work on deadlines and schedules, aim at entertainment, enter their stories with imagination, and practice their craft in ways
in which they develop a system of production. They do not wait for
inspiration but perhaps find it along the way. They develop the fortitude,
courage, and ability to write and to do it again.

Henry James once saw popular fiction and "Grub Street" as a potential
threat to literary quality. In "The Art of Fiction" (1884), James speaks of
the "vulgarization" of literature by this popular fiction. He points out that
the novel can be distinguished from the romance, or adventure fiction.
Other critics have more recently issued similar observations. Jonathan
Franzen, who rejected inclusion in Oprah's Book Club, commented in an
essay in *Harper's*, "Why Bother?" in 2003, that the dollar ought not to be
"the yardstick of cultural authority."[15] There are higher goals and purposes, other critics will say: aesthetic quality, reflection upon the human
condition, matters of art. Yet, one may also point to Robert Louis Stevenson's defense of popular fiction in "A Humble Remonstrance" in 1884.
There he asserted that "no art can compare with life." The novel is "not a
transcript of life," Stevenson said. It is an act of the imagination. Writing
on Walter Besant, Henry James, and William Dean Howells, he asserted
that the work he was engaged in was about "not so much making a story
true as making them typical." A story "may be great because it displays
the workings of a perturbed heart and the impersonal utterance of passion."[16] Stevenson wrote several adventure stories and regarded them as
sustained dramas with a controlled narrative structure. His stories were
"romances" that entertained readers.

Bestsellers circulate widely and often quickly among readers. Yet,
there are those critics who point out that "bestseller" may mean a lack of
artistic quality. Many works of commercial fiction are not about style,
finely worked sentences, or character development and psychological in-

quiry. They are engaged in suspenseful entertainment, romance, or humor. So, there remains a divide between art and commerce, between literary craft and formula. Of course, literary novels have reached the bestseller list. For example, some of Toni Morrison's novels have been listed among the nation's bestsellers. However, *Paradise* reached the top of the list largely because Oprah Winfrey had the vision to feature it in her book club. Danielle Steel's novels have repeatedly gone to #1, but her talent will not be honored by the Nobel Prize committee anytime soon.

Critics have frequently addressed the perceived gap between the aesthetic creations of art culture and those of popular culture. Lawrence Levine examined this in *Highbrow/Lowbrow*. Andreas Huyssen addressed what he referred to as "the great divide between high art and mass culture."[17] Other critics have examined "middlebrow" and have included the readers of popular fiction and nonfiction in their reflections. The criticisms of popular writing that have issued from cultural critics and literary critics are numerous. The Frankfurt school was critical of manipulation, and these critics argued that the popular bestseller was not of the people but rather was a matter of production by manufacturers. Popular books are cultural productions that are "manufactured more or less according to plan," says Theodor Adorno.[18] In Max Horkheimer's essay "Art and Mass Culture" (1941), he points to the popular book as part of an "amusement industry."[19] Walter Benjamin defended aspects of genre fiction and wrote on the detective story. However, Theodor Adorno injected scorn into his criticisms and expressed concern about popular culture. Meanwhile, literary critics distinguished between works of art and entertainments or commercial commodities.[20]

In the 1940s, Book of the Month Club reviewers Henry Seidel Canby and Dorothy Canfield Fisher represented a concern with literary quality in the midst of an organization that was connected with advertising and consumption. The Book of the Month Club promoted books its selection committee believed would satisfy readers. In doing so, it promoted some bestsellers. Joan Shelley Rubin points out that Canby expressed concern about "vulgarization" and "reading by excerpt."[21] The issues he was concerned with surrounded the idea of "taste." Behind this view were Matthew Arnold's notions of culture and literary inheritance and standards. Canby made a distinction between criticism and description of titles: "I am describing rather than criticizing *Gone with the Wind*," he wrote, asserting that "readers will make their own criticisms."[22]

In the 1970s, John Sutherland observed that "bestseller" was not a term that had figured much to that point in critical discussion. He wrote: "We have no critical vocabulary for applauding the ingenious polymorphic tie-ins of an otherwise poor novel (its media adaptability) or for congratulating a novelist who writes indifferently . . . but promotes his or her book with genius." He observed that "bestseller" had been used a pejorative term for books "literary criticism prefers not to discuss."[23]

Some critics continue to respond harshly to some varieties of the commercial bestseller. Ken Gelder cites a British review of James Patterson's *1st to Die* in which the reviewer calls Patterson a "thriller writer by numbers." The reviewer writes: "A computer could have written this. Maybe a computer did."[24] In recent years James Patterson has placed at least four novels onto the national bestseller lists annually by writing solo and with cowriters. In 2010, Jonathan Mahler in the *New York Times Magazine* observed that "since 2006, one out of every 17 novels bought in the United States was written by James Patterson." He called the writer "James Patterson Inc.," "the Henry Ford of books," and spoke of his work as a matter of "industrial production." The more than two dozen Alex Cross series novels started in 2003. There are four more series, one with the Women's Murder Club. That productivity continues with Patterson's collaborations with a variety of writers. He uses aspects of the detective mystery genre and promises new similar stories. Critics may say that the stories, while entertaining, are thin. Certainly, as Mahler points out, Patterson's books are unlike dense novels like Joyce's *Ulysses* or Garcia Marquez's *One Hundred Years of Solitude*, which require deliberate attention. Mahler calls Patterson an entertainer rather than a man of letters.[25] Other popular writers draw similar criticism. Literary critic Harold Bloom has said that he finds it impossible to read the novels of John Grisham. Grisham writes "page-turners": entertaining novels that draw our sympathy for his characters and probe issues of justice. He is a writer who connects with readers.

What may be overlooked by some critics is the ingenuity, talent, and dogged persistence of writers whose works have become popular, marketable commodities. They work hard. They contribute to popular culture. The bestseller lists are dominated by the romances of Danielle Steel and the mastery of the suspense genre by Dean Koontz or Mary Higgins Clark. Michael Crichton's stories are marked by scientific curiosity, science fiction mishaps, and sense of adventure. Bestseller lists are filled with brand-name authors like these. Readers turn to the expansive and encyclopedic range of a James Michener novel and to the remarkable imagination of Stephen King—and his ability to scare the hell out of us.

There are also many writers who find that middle ground somewhere between the literary novel and the popular novel: John Irving, E. L. Doctorow, and Anne Tyler have been among those writers. Some literary luminaries have had a book reach the coveted number one spot on the bestseller list, including Ernest Hemingway and Saul Bellow. Toni Morrison, Philip Roth, Cormac McCarthy, Don DeLillo, and John Updike are writers who would appear on most anyone's list of "literary" authors whose works have appeared on the bestseller list. These writers have appeared on multiple bestseller lists, from the *Wall Street Journal* to the *Chicago Tribune*. When Sam Tanenhaus of the *New York Times* circulated a questionnaire to writers and critics, those authors' names frequently appeared as some of America's "best." Novels they cited included Morrison's *Beloved*, DeLillo's *Libra* and *Underworld*, Roth's *American Pastoral*, Marilynne Robinson's *Housekeeping*, McCarthy's *Blood Meridian*, and Updike's Rabbit Angstrom novels. There was no mention of the commercial accomplishments of *New York Times* #1 bestselling authors like Danielle Steel, Tom Clancy, Dean Koontz, Nora Roberts, Sue Grafton, Sidney Sheldon, or Janet Evanovich.

LITERATURE IN SOCIETY

Bestsellers have received increasing critical attention since the 1970s. There have been impressive studies of romance fiction, science fiction, horror fiction, and detective mystery fiction. Ken Gelder recognizes that popular fiction is "a highly differentiated field." Scott McCracken says that popular fiction "can tell us much about who we are and about the society in which we live." Laura J. Miller observes: "The bestseller list is actively participating in the doings of the book world rather than just passively recording it."[26] The bestseller list is a dynamic process that is engaged in launching books and bringing people to read them. The bestseller encourages us to look at "literature in society," to use Raymond Williams's phrase.[27] It tells us something about the book trade, the marketplace, and the popularity of books among readers.

Critics have argued that the various bestseller lists correspond to sales in any particular week, rather than to overall sales. A book may sell more copies at a slower pace across a longer period of time. If wholesale is counted with retail and there is overlap, some titles may be counted twice. It has also been claimed that authors with sizable bank accounts have purchased large quantities of their own books, inflating the ratings of their books. Donald Trump was accused of inflating sales figures for his book *The Art of the Deal* by sending people out to buy it in large quantities, something that he fiercely denied. It has been documented that Wayne Dyer bought numerous copies of *Your Erroneous Zones* and actively toured the country in speaking engagements. Jacqueline Susann inflated sales of *The Valley of the Dolls*. The Gannett Foundation bought two thousand copies of CEO Al Neuharth's book *Confessions of an S.O.B.*[28] William Peter Blatty brought a lawsuit when he believed that his new novel should have been on the bestseller list like his chilling novel *The Exorcist*.

Yes, popular fiction bestsellers entertain us. Whether they serve a social, moral, or didactic function is quite another question. A correlation between the development of empathy and the reading of literary fiction was found in a study by Emanuel Castano and David Kidd of the New School in New York that was first reported in *Science*, October 4, 2013. Researchers at the University of Toronto have reported similar findings. In an article by Julianne Chiaet in *Scientific American*, the assertion was made that much popular fiction does not encourage this reflection in readers. Literary fiction tends to explore character and "disrupts expectations" of readers more often than popular fiction, which one of the researchers calls "predictable." Their sample of readers appeared to them to have gained more from a literary novel by Louise Erdrich than from a pop novel by Danielle Steel.[29] The literary novel tends to explore character more deeply than the popular commercial novel. In its attention to sentences, to language, and to craft, the literary novel is a work of art.

PULP FICTION: MYSTERIES AND THRILLERS

Bestsellers are usually genre fiction. Most are romances, thrillers, or mysteries with detectives who become series characters. The genres of romance and science fiction participate in a community of readers who are often familiar with the themes and recognizable features of the genre. These fans create a genre-based experience. The genre of science fiction is engaged in a discussion among its fans and includes a variety of clubs and fanzines. These readers are well prepared for the stories that extend the science fiction field and develop what Hans Robert Jauss has called a "horizon of expectation." (Theorists refer to this as the social action of a genre.) They are familiar with a variety of stories in the genre, and they become a discourse community familiar with and conversant about many novels in the field. Writers who work within these genres know the conventions of the genre and make use of intertextuality: the references and resources available to them that arise from their intimate acquaintance with previous genre fiction.

Pulp fiction is associated with the cheap magazine productions of the 1920s and 1930s. Pulp refers to cheap paper. The hardboiled detective was a popular staple of pulp fiction. He faced evil. He was surrounded by murder and deception. The Black Mask writers like Dashiell Hammett and Raymond Chandler transformed the genre. The pulps also offered adventure stories, westerns, and science fiction. Following the heyday of these magazines, the mass-market paperback brought cover designs with the lure of the sensational. As Paula Rabinowitz points out, novels by modernists like Faulkner and Hemingway were mixed in with these pop paperback covers. She points to a New American Library cover by Tony Varaday for *Double Indemnity* (1947) by James M. Cain that reflects an image from Paramount Pictures. She describes this as featuring a man with his leg extending over railroad tracks and a blond female "in a yellow blouse with a plunging neckline."[30] As she begins her study of pulp fiction, Paula Rabinowitz tells the story of a reader whose account she read in the New American Library files at New York University's Fales Library. That this reader picked up a paperback on the way home from choir practice suggests a kind of spontaneous form of book buying, and that the reader recalls becoming "immersed" all day long in the story speaks to the appeal of paperback fiction.[31]

Paperbacks, from the days of pulp fiction to the present day, have appeared in supermarkets, drugstores, train stations, and airports. With them silent reading enters public spaces. In 1950, New American Library world literature books sold for twenty-five or thirty-five cents.[32] Today you can expect to spend close to ten dollars for one of the larger-format paperbacks. Anchor Books introduced trade paperbacks in 1953, and Vintage, an imprint at Alfred A. Knopf, published quality paperbacks beginning in 1954. These productions utilized paper of better quality, and with them the industry moved past the pulp of the previous period. These books were connected with college texts and the increase in college education with the GI Bill following the Second World War.

ROMANCE FICTION

Romance originally meant tales in the vernacular. Romance was composed of stories about the meeting and experiences of lovers, or medieval courtly romances. They had their basis in folktales and were expressed in the chansons de geste of the knight-hero, or in the *lais* of Marie de France. There are a variety of predecessors to the contemporary romance, including gothic fiction and the novel of manners. Ann Radcliffe and the Brontës gave their readers gothic wildness and melodrama. In their fiction, romance was sometimes a solution, a way out, a resolution for their heroines. The heroines of several contemporary romances are, in part, a recasting of the protagonists devised by Jane Austen. *Pride and Prejudice* by Jane Austen is a fundamental text for romance. It is a social comedy of manners that focuses upon Elizabeth Bennet's experiences. It emphasizes the restrictions that society placed upon young women of her time more than the perils of a dramatic plot. Stephenie Meyer's *Twilight* (2005) adapts Jane Austen's *Pride and Prejudice*. Melissa Nathan's *Persuading Annie* (2004) adapts Austen's *Persuasion*. Debra White Smith's *Amanda* (2006) adapts Austen's *Emma*.

In the past few decades, considerable scholarship has been devoted to studies of popular romance fiction. The investigation of readers of popular romance began in earnest with Janice Radway's study *Reading the Romance* (1984). Radway's analysis of romance readers is a reader-response study in which she discusses the perspectives of readers whom she interviewed in a place she calls "Smithton." Radway shows that romance novels contribute to the lives of their most enthusiastic readers. She looks at the publishing industry's output of romance novels and recognizes the "mediating process" that includes production and distribution.[33] In the second section of her book, Radway reports on the community's readers and how reading romances is significant in their lives. She asks them what a good or bad romance novel is and what romance novels mean to them. She notes their familiarity with many romance novels and acknowledges the importance of word-of-mouth recommendations of books among these readers. Radway discusses the conventions of romance novels and the impact of the language of romance novels upon their readers. These books are usually written in a simple style with "cliché . . . standard syntax" and engage techniques that are associated with the nineteenth-century realist novel, Radway observes. She points out that romance novel readers "rely on standard cultural codes correlating signifiers and signifieds that they accept as definitive. It has never occurred to them that those codes might be historically or culturally relative." Radway writes that "Dot and her friends accept without question the accuracy of all statements about a character's personality."[34]

Other critics have probed the popular romance novel through the lenses of various feminist perspectives. The *Journal of Popular Romance Studies* regularly publishes articles that explore the field of romance writing. These essays range across popular fiction, classics, Regency romances, paranormal romance, soap operas, and many other topics. Filled with book reviews, the journal provides excellent coverage of books in the field of romance fiction studies.[35]

READERS OF POPULAR BOOKS

The phenomenon of the bestseller encourages us to ask questions about readers. Which books do they read and why? Through the bestseller list we can begin to trace the record of quantities of books sold. This does not tell us about how these books were read. The bestseller list is about readers. Yet, it continues to be difficult to gauge how readers interpret their reading. To do so we need their comments in autobiographies, in reading group records, in letters. For some readers, popular novels are a diversion for while they are traveling on a plane or on a train to a distant location. For others, the books that people can buy online, or take home from the library, promise an enjoyable evening of reading.

In 1850, Charles Dickens recommended popular entertainment in his essay "Amusements of the People" in *Household Words*. He acknowledged that British workers was among the hardest-working people in the world and that they deserved the variety of popular activity that could be offered to them. A few years later, his friend Wilkie Collins wrote an essay addressing the rise of a wide "unknown public" of common readers. An *Atlantic Monthly* reviewer, in 1879, wrote that story paper and dime novel literature "is an enormous field of mental activity, the greatest movement in bulk, of the age and worthy of very serious consideration in itself." The writer, a man named Bishop, wrote: "Disdained as it may be by the highly cultivated for its character, the phenomenon of its existence cannot be overlooked."[36] That remains true of the popular fiction of our own time.

Is it possible to distinguish most literary reading from other kinds of reading? Scholars like David S. Miall ask: What are the effects of books on readers?[37] Looking back upon readers of the past, Robert Darnton once pointed out that "our relation to those texts cannot be the same as that of readers in the past."[38] That is true of any assessments that we may make today of reading in the 1940s and 1950s, or at any earlier time. We live in our time and culture, and it is possible that we may impose upon these books of the past our own inclinations. Our interpretation is affected by our cultural situation. Reading remains a fascinating subject for historical scholarship. Roger Chartier recognized that readers do "read between the lines" and "subvert the lessons imposed on them." He asserted that our great works "have no stable fixed universal meanings."[39] Pierre Bourdieu points out that "a work of art has meaning and interest only for someone who possesses the cultural competence, that is, the code into which it is encoded." This is true of genre readers of mystery or thrillers or romances. Jonathan Rose, in 1992, asked: "How do texts change the minds and lives of modern readers?"[40] That is a lively question that will be taken up here amid the listings of bestselling books.

Most readers who make meaning from their reading today have had ongoing exposure to other media: television, radio, computer. What influence have these media had on reading styles? How do people choose their reading? Do they learn about books that they will read via word of mouth, advertising, a film or television adaptation? Popular fiction is a type of production and a means by which to look at culture and society insofar as these works "embody social consciousness," as Raymond Williams has observed.[41] To consider books and readers within their cultural context is to explore the spirit of an age. This book will list one hundred years' worth of titles and describe some of those creations so that we can speculate about how they may reflect our culture.

The bestselling book is a popular commodity: it is tangible, visible, and marketable. A good story is the primary appeal of the fiction bestseller. However, there are a variety of other appeals: the promise of entertainment, the reliability of the established and familiar author—the brand name, the power of conversation among readers, the attractiveness of a book's cover, advertising dollars and active marketing, and the bestseller list itself and the visibility that it gives a book.

Clearly, this is an industry that aims at profitability. The collaborations by James Patterson and Clive Cussler with other writers trade on their familiar brand names to make money by entertaining, Writers like Danielle Steel and John Grisham continue to gain and gather fans. The "brand-name" author continues to sell thousands of books. Readers rightly come to expect entertainment from these writers and are assured that they are in good hands. Even so, what readers get from these creative and often prolific authors is usually more of the same—although perhaps with a twist. Some critics will say that the same character types and the same plot devices are pulled out again and again and that formula, rather than innovation, is the hallmark of the fiction bestseller. Others will point to the ingenuity and the hard work of these writers and their ability to engage and hold their readers with clever stories.

One ought not to underestimate the effort or the craft of a popular writer. That writer may be quite concerned about form and structure, characterization, pace, and narrative design. Readers who pick up a book generally hope to be entertained, to participate in the drama or romance of a story. Plot-driven entertainments appeal to imagination and our craving for story. These are the contemporary storytellers who regale us with the myths and legends of our times. They are writers whose imaginations peek into the dark corners and unexpected possibilities of ordinary life. Their stories lift us, inspire us, frighten us, or soothe us. They shake up the mundane world with imagination and restore wonder, tug at our hearts, or reaffirm our sense of life.

I

BIRTH OF THE BESTSELLER

The 1890s to the 1930s

To the cities of America for work they came: small-town adventurers, dreamers, waves of immigrants on hopeful and determined journeys. They entered the factories, the offices, the tenements, and they watched the buildings go up. They imagined heights, magnificent motion: the skyscraper, the motor car, and the possibility that man could fly. Industry welded steel, unearthed the coal, planned and designed and made things. The news of the world came to them in print, and the books that they read informed them. Books offered them entertainment and escape and lifted their spirits.

In 1900 America was reading the historical novel: Winston Churchill gave them *Richard Carvel* and Edward Noyes Westcott provided *David Harum*. They read *When Knighthood Was in Flower*, Charles Major's historical novel, and soon were reading Churchill's *The Crisis*, about the American Civil War. In someone's hands was *The Day's Work* by Rudyard Kipling, of which *Publishers Weekly* a year before had written: "The volume has taken on the lead in bestselling books."[1] Perhaps they arrived at work by trolley, pulled along by horses, or by hansom cab: a horse-drawn carriage. In the first years of the twentieth century, the nation was recovering from the McKinley assassination at the Pan-American Exposition and from the financial panic of 1901. There were ads in the newspapers that brought visibility to bestsellers like *Alice of Old Vincennes* (#2 in 1901) and historical romances like *To Have and to Hold* (#1 in

1900). So successful was *The Helmet of Navarre* (1901) in serialization in the *Century* magazine that the Century Company printed one hundred thousand copies.

In 1903, from a field in North Carolina, the first successful airplane flight by Wilbur and Orville Wright lifted into the sky. Today on an airplane you might read Danielle Steel's *The Cast* (#1 on June 3, 2018), James Patterson and Bill Clinton's *The President Is Missing*, Stephen King's *The Outsider*, or David Baldacci's *The Fallen*. If you are interested in history, you might have picked up Jake Tapper's *The Hellfire Club*, set in 1950s Washington. After all, it is a crossover fiction combining the intrigue of the thriller with politics and history, and Charlie Marder meets his wife in—of all places—a library. Back in 1905 one could transport a novel by motor car, announce it by wireless telegraphy, or adapt it to a silent movie. Bowen and Merrill of Indianapolis had become Bobbs-Merrill, a strong producer of bestsellers. The Century Company began producing a series of short dollar novels. Today we order on Amazon, go to Barnes & Noble, or venture into one of the dozens of lovingly tended bookstores or public libraries that still offer us bestselling books.

If we could go back, jettison time and turn back the clock, and pass through some black hole in the gravitational pull of heat and motion, we would see books on the shelves like *To Have and to Hold*, *Red Pottage*, and *Unleavened Bread* (#1, #2, and #3, respectively, in 1900). If we could go back to the excited wonder of the first Model T, we might still hear the *clip-clop* sound from the street of a horse's hooves or see a feathered hat and dark petticoat descending from the carriage. You might turn the page of a book as a little bell tinkles and a man steps through the door; by now his hair has gone gray, and beneath the searching eyes, the sturdy chin, the stiff, straight, shirt collar that sports a dark tie. R. R. Bowker steps into the book shop, and the clerk looks up and greets him. What will it be today, Mr. Bowker? The new book by Churchill, Winston Churchill. And surely you are confused. This is not the prime minister, the politician, whose book he seeks, but rather the American historical novelist of the same name. And the books that surround you on slightly sagging shelves are ones by authors of whom you have never heard: Mary Johnston, Maurice Thompson, Irving Bacheller, and Bertha Runkle.

One moment you were at Politics and Prose bookstore in Washington, D.C., listening to the physicist Carlo Rovelli claim that there is no time. Then down you went on that steep elevator, descending to the subway, going down. . . . The clerk wears a mustache. The papers say McKinley. Mr. Bowker of *Publishers Weekly*, a central figure in the book trade, stands before you. Surely, you have entered the Twilight Zone. To return home, could you tap your heels three times like Dorothy, or lift off in a hot air balloon like the wizard in that bestselling children's book of 1900, *The Wizard of Oz*?

History has long been a framework for novels. For readers at the turn of the twentieth century it was a favorite genre. The grand sweep of history came in romances and adventures, in epic recollections and family sagas. Readers were nostalgic. They took their time with big books. In the popular fiction of the first decades there is history everywhere one looks. A reader might go back in time in these pages, through images, characters, actions imagined, and stories that sustained the national imagination. Stories set in the past enchanted readers and spoke to their time, for the modern world was changing and the foundations were being shaken.

In the first decade of the twentieth century, Winston Churchill of New Hampshire dominated the bestseller lists. The British politician of the same name knew him. He sent the American Churchill a letter, declaring that he would sign his own books with his middle name, Spencer, to mark the distinction between them. *Richard Carvel* (1899), the U.S.-born Churchill's novel of the American Revolution, was #1 on *Publishers Weekly*'s list and sold two million copies among the seventy-six million people who lived in the United States at the time. During that period, he wrote the bestselling Civil War novel *The Crisis* (1901, #1) and a series of other top bestsellers: *The Crossing* (1904, #1), *Coniston* (1906, #1), *Mr. Crewe's Career* (1908, #1), *A Modern Chronicle* (1910, #2), *The Inside of the Cup* (1913, #1), *A Far Country* (1915, #2), and *The Dwelling Place of Light* (1917). Of *A Modern Chronicle*, Upton Sinclair wrote that he preferred Churchill's historical novels to this one on the modern woman and divorce in an industrialized world.

Winston Churchill the American novelist was born in St. Louis November 10, 1871. He attended to U.S. Naval Academy, graduating in 1894. Churchill ran for governor of New Hampshire in 1906 and again, as the Progressive candidate, in 1912. He was not elected. In 1917, Churchill wrote of the battlefields of the Great War upon visiting them. He took up landscape painting and stopped writing. Churchill's great-grandfather was born in New Hampshire; Edward Churchill, his grandfather, was a merchant in Maine. The writer lived in Cornish, New Hampshire, in a house that looked out over the Connecticut River. He named his house after his wife. Woodrow Wilson leased it as a summer residence in the years 1913 through 1915. In 1923, following a fire, Churchill moved to Plainfield, New Hampshire. If you drive on I-91 past Windsor in Sullivan County, you might turn off for Plainfield; there is a commemorative plaque to Churchill on Route 12-A some two hundred yards south of the Plainfield-Cornish town line.

THE VIRGINIAN

In 1902, *The Virginian* by Owen Wister (#1) began selling what would become a bestseller record for that time of 1,736,299 copies.[2] This tale of Wyoming would become the source for three films and a long-running television series western. It ushered in a sustained audience for the western, from the fifteen major bestsellers of Zane Grey (from 1912 to 1928) to Jack Schaefer's *Shane* (1954) and the fiction of Louis L'Amour. Owen Wister brought attention to the cowboy in western literature and to a land of open spaces. At the age of twenty-five, Owen Wister lay down on a counter at the general store, waiting for a train in Medicine Bow. So begins *The Virginian*. The young man could speak French, like his mother. His father wanted him to be a banker and sent him to Harvard, but he disliked that and chose law school instead. Wister was a classmate of Theodore Roosevelt at Harvard, and soon they shared a love of the outdoors and wild, open spaces. Under strain and in need of health, Wister traveled west to Wyoming. At Deer Creek, he fell in love with the land and the hearty life of the West. He began to keep a journal and he returned to Wyoming often: fifteen times between 1885 and 1900. He wrote stories: "Hank's Woman" (1892) and "Evolution of a Cow Puncher" (1895), featuring a cowboy.

The subtitle of *The Virginian* is *A Horseman on the Plains*. The cowboy of history and legend was a man with a moral code, a knight in dungarees with a cowboy hat and boots with spurs. The image has become imprinted upon the American mind, partly due to *The Virginian*, a book that sold more than two million copies across the twentieth century. The hero plays poker by the railroad tracks; he gazes out across the land. He stands for justice, honor, the protection and appreciation of women, and the strength of American individualism. Owen Wister took the literature of the West beyond the dime novel into descriptive eloquence and able storytelling, creating a mythical West of hope and nostalgia, an ideal of sturdiness and honesty. The novel does not always exhibit the Hollywood drama of a shoot-out with bandits or an intense cattle drive; Wister intersects the western with the novel of manners.

Much of Owen Wister's story emerged from the journals he kept, which offer keen observations of the West in Wyoming and the personalities he met there. At times they are rich in description: "The Tetons lifted their peaks pale and keen as steel through the high radiant air," he writes in "Hank's Woman." "I sat and looked down . . . at Wind River shrunk to map size, a basking valley, a drowsy country, tawny and warm," he writes in "The Gift Horse." In his notebook of 1895 that he marks with page numbers, he recalls a meeting with a Russian exile on a train between Deming and Wilcox. His account reads almost like a short story. "He is a strange person, more strange than almost any I have met," Wister writes of the Russian man. He is "torrentlike" and sincere, interesting but "erratic." He says that he changed his opinions about the assassination of the czar and left Russia when his estates were confiscated. He gives Wister his opinions about popular American literature: "He thinks nothing of Craddock, nothing of Cable. Too highly of Grace King, George Hibbard, and Bob Grant—and me! He also thinks 'Her First Appearance' by Dick Davis very fine, and [likes] Mrs. Eleanor Cuyler."[3] Wister's powers of observation and his ability to record conversation—including ones when trapped with a voluble exile—clearly were assets in his writing of *The Virginian*.

A reader begins Arthur Conan Doyle's *The Hound of the Baskervilles* (1902) with Sherlock Holmes at breakfast. Dr. Watson is challenged to determine the owner of a staff simply from its design and apparent use. He accomplishes this deductive puzzle well, and Holmes compliments him. James Mortimer has a manuscript from a family paper from Baskerville Hall in 1742: "the statement of a certain legend."[4] In chapter 3 the problem arises: On the night of Sir Charles's death, Barrymore makes the discovery of the footprints of a giant hound. Watson shivers and says: "I confess that at these words a shudder passed through me."

In 1905, Mrs. Humphrey Ward's *The Marriage of William Ashe* led the fiction bestseller list. At #4 on the list was *The Clansman* by Thomas Dixon, from which the film *Birth of a Nation* was derived. The #1 novel of 1906 was Winston Churchill's *Coniston*. The story, which is set in

New Hampshire in 1840 to 1870, offers us a fictionalized family history and a study of politics in the age of reform. The novel considers abolitionism and early days of industrialization. In it, Honora Leffingwell divorces her stockbroker husband to marry a man of social standing, only to discover that he is not what he seemed to be. *Lady Baltimore* by Owen Wister was #2.

The most enduring novels of 1906 were *The House of Mirth* by Edith Wharton (#9) and Upton Sinclair's *The Jungle* (#6). *The House of Mirth* is the story of Lily Bart, a woman who seeks her place in society and meaning in her life. *The House of Mirth* was #8 in 1905 and #9 in 1906. Lily Bart is confronted with the upper-class "duty" to marry well. Lily questions that role that society expects of her and the pretenses and expectations that they live by. Lawrence Selden encourages her to live beyond the crowd and to question the goals of her life. We begin the novel by meeting them: "Selden paused in surprise. In the afternoon rush of Grand Central Station, his eyes had been refreshed by the sight of Miss Lily Bart." We gain an image of Lily Bart from his perspective: "It was characteristic of her that she always roused speculation that her simplest acts seemed the result of far-reaching intentions."[5] Grand Central Station was new: begun in 1903, it was completed in 1913.

Upton Sinclair's *The Jungle* was a scathing indictment of food issues and worker conditions that led to reform and the Pure Foods and Drugs Act. We are given the story of Lithuanian immigrants Jurgis and Ona and the troubled labor and unsanitary conditions in the meatpacking industry of Chicago. The novel has been associated with the muckraking journalism of the time. It is a work of crisp storytelling supported by personal investigation. Upton Sinclair offers us a historical glimpse into the Progressive Era of American politics and industrialization. Among his many works are *The Brass Check* (1919), in which he critiqued yellow journalism. The novel examined the business interests of newspapers and included pointed jabs at William Randolph Hearst. It criticized press sensationalism and the invention of stories by newspapers to spark reader interest. Consequently, the novel raised attention to matters of press credibility that led to a code of journalistic ethics. Sinclair also wrote an industrial novel, *King Coal*, on working conditions in coal mining. A politically minded man, he ran unsuccessfully for the office of governor of California.

America struggled through the 1907 financial panic. The public elected William Howard Taft as U.S. president in 1909. *The Lady of Decoration* by Frances Little was #1 in 1907, and Winston Churchill's *Mr. Crewe's Career* was #1 in 1908. Basil King's *The Inner Shrine* was #1 in 1909, although his name was not on the book's cover.

1910–1920

Can a #1 novel be inspired by a song? *The Rosary* by Florence Barclay (1910, #1) was. Later in the century, the tenor Mario Lanza sang the song at a time when few remembered the novel. It is the romantic story of Jane Champion, friend to the handsome artist Garth Dalmain, who emphasizes that her character is beautiful although she is perhaps plain in appearance. In this sentimental novel, Jane is asked to sing "The Rosary" and Garth falls for her. The balcony is lit by the light of the moon. Jane is not sure what to make of Garth's ardor; unsure of herself, she rejects him and goes away to Egypt. Then she has second thoughts: Should she return to Garth?

In the January 15, 1910, issue of *Publishers Weekly* we see a full-page ad. By 1913 as many as five hundred copies of Barclay's novel had been sold. Frank Luther Mott's study of bestsellers, *Golden Multitudes*, puts the number at nine hundred thousand. Florence Barclay was married to an Anglican cleric, and she knew her theology well. She visited the Holy Land with her husband on their honeymoon, and they believed they had rediscovered the biblical Jacob's well. Her sister Maud was a Salvation Army Volunteers of America leader. Ill and bedridden in her forties, Florence Barclay wrote *The Wheels of Time* and *The Rosary*.

The Broad Highway by Jeffery Farnol (1910) was the #1 book of 1911. The story is set in a village in Kent and begins with some cues on how to make a bestseller. "As I sat of an early morning in the shade of a tree, eating fried bacon with a tinker, the thought came to me that I might someday write a book of my own." The narrator describes the country-side, and then the tinker remarks that trees aren't very interesting in a book. So what else have you got? I'm sure there is a highwayman, a pugilist, a one-legged soldier in my book, he says, and I'll put you in the book too. "I never read a novel with a tinker," the tinker replies, "and I've read a good many novels in my time." This tinker claims to be an avid reader and to know how to create a bestseller. "If you can put a little blood into your book, so much the better," he says. Add some duels and heiresses. "I've run off with them in the pages of novels," he declares. So, there must be a flight from desperate villains through the woodland, much melodrama and derring-do. Farnol's historical romance outpaced sales for all other novels that year.

The Harvester by Gene Stratton-Porter (1912, #1) is a romantic novel. David Langston lives in the country with his dog and sells herbs to a pharmaceutical company–medical drug supply firm. He builds a house in the woods. One day he sees a beautiful girl in a dream, and he ventures forth to meet her: she is Ruth Jameson, a young woman whose uncle treats her poorly. *The Harvester* is a sentimental novel that reflects how their love grows and how they must face her illness (much like Erich Segal's 1970 *Love Story*). Ruth Jameson is not likely to appeal to any contemporary reader who prefers a strong female character. The novel unfolds in an older style of narrative with lengthy phrasing. Gene Stratton-Porter also wrote the bestselling children's book *Freckles* (1904), which sold more than two million copies; *Laddie* (1913, #3) sold an estimated 1,586,529, according to Alice Payne Hackett's perusal of the records. *Michael O'Halloran* (1915, #3) was also a bestseller.

Basil King's fiction was also popular at the time. He was an Anglican clergyman from Prince Edward Island in Canada. King's *The Inner Shrine* (1909, #1) appeared anonymously. It was subtitled *A Novel of Today*. The frontispiece illustration shows a woman in a black dress and a hat who is evidently aboard a ship: "She stood watching the rise and dip of the steamer's bow." The novel begins with the introduction of a sense of time: "Though she had counted the strokes of every hour since midnight, Mrs. Eveleth had no thought of going to bed." We see her limping down the hallway, "listening for the sound of wheels." Yes, there are cars, and this one will bring her son George and his new wife Diane home from a night out. Yet, she has a "presentiment of disaster" that comes like "the first flicker of dusk across the radiance of an afternoon." The story is said to provide a picture of a brilliant but dissolute society caught up in trivial concerns. A reader is met with sentences that appear lengthy in comparison with those in today's bestsellers.

The Street Called Straight by Basil King (1912, #2) begins: "As a matter of fact, Davenant was under no illusions concerning the quality of the welcome his hostess was according him, although he found a certain pleasure in being at once in her company." This is a novel that ends with the words "I wonder! . . . I wonder!" and readers were held in wonder at a novel that seems to have possibilities in its first chapters. Chapter 2 begins: "The three men being left together, Davenant's conviction of inner excitement on the part of his host was deepened. It was as if, on the withdrawal of the ladies, Guion had less intention of concealing it. . . . 'So. Mr. Davenant, you've come back to us. Got here only this afternoon, didn't you? I wonder why you came. Having gotten out of a dull place like Waverton, why should you return to it?'" Indeed, perhaps Peter Davenant has come back home from the military because he fell in love with Guion nine years earlier. Readers looked for more from Basil King. *McClure's*, in volume 47, announced *The Lifted Veil* by Basil King (1917) with the James Montgomery Flagg illustration of a shrouded lady under a hat and a cleric who holds his hands behind his back as he gazes at her. The ad calls "the remarkable new serial to begin next month," August 9, in nine installments, "an event" in the history of the magazine.[6]

From sentimental fiction, Mr. King moved toward reflections on spiritualism. The Great War had an impact upon King, as well as upon his reading audience. The English public had once believed in a swift end to the war and expected its resolution in glorious victory; however, the fighting bogged down in a war of attrition in the muddy trenches. Those who were lost were a cause for grief. The esteemed scientist Oliver Lodge lost his son in battle in France; he was a member of the Society for Psychical Research in Britain and believed that he and his wife communicated with their deceased son in séances with Gladys Osborne Leonard. *Raymond* (1916) was a bestseller: a sure indication of the reading audience's concern with the war, thoughts on eternity, and desire for answers. King contributed his mystical considerations in *The Abolishing of Death* (1919) and *The Conquest of Fear* (1921). This was part of a trend, of course. A public battered by war and loss was interested in reflections on the possibility of the afterlife. *Theosophical Outlook* wrote: "Persons who work in bookshops can not doubt the extraordinary interest in the subject."[7] Historians have tended to focus their attention on spiritualism as a late Victorian and Edwardian cultural phenomenon. However, with the Great War there was a plethora of books on spiritualism: *The Reality of Psychic Phenomena* (1916), *On the Threshold of the Unseen* (1917), *Spiritualism: Its History, Phenomena, and Doctrine* (1919), and Arthur Conan Doyle's *The New Revelation* and *The Vital Message* (1918–1919) among them. The cover ad copy for Basil King's first book on spiritualism read: "Six months ago, Mr. King did not believe in messages from the dead. To-day he is not sure." The *Journal of the American Society for Psychical Research* listed the book at $1.25. The stories of Arthur Machen, collected in *The Bowman and Other Legends* (1915), also entered the speculations in fiction about the war.

Eyes of the World by Harold Bell Wright (1914) was a romance novel set in Southern California. It is a morality play about art and society that features a portrait painter, Aaron King, a violinist, a media critic, and a novelist named Conrad Lagrange. The wealthy Mrs. Taine insists that she has the power to make an artist's career, but Aaron's motives for creating art are pure. When Aaron arrives in California he meets Conrad Lagrange, who writes quickly drafted popular books, while Aaron is more painstaking with his art. He falls in love with Sibyl. The novel raises the question of whether he will become a sycophant to the wealthy of the art world or be a true artist. It was heavily advertised, with more than $100,000 (or roughly two million dollars today) spent to promote it. *Publishers Weekly* remarked: "The story has elements which make for popularity." Frank Luther Mott regarded it as a financial success but a story in which each character only represents a type, or a "quality."[8] The novel wanders, moving in and out of focus, as painterly descriptions drift along, going nowhere in particular.

Harold Bell Wright was born in Rome, New York, and was orphaned at age ten. He was sent to a farm to live and work. He became a house-painter and then an itinerant preacher, although he never went to any seminary. He went to Pittsburg, Kansas, and there he wrote *The Shepherd of the Hills*, which later became a John Wayne film. *Eyes of the World* begins in the winter weather from which the protagonist travels to California "in the greedy rush of those younger times." In chapter 2 he rides a train through the San Gorgonio Pass, which is, the narrator says, "the gateway to the scenes of my story."

Booth Tarkington's star rose with *The Turmoil* (1915, #1) and *Seventeen* (1916, #1). *The Gentleman from Indiana* (1899) was the first novel by Tarkington, one of the most prolific and popular of the bestselling novelists of the first decades of the twentieth century. One critic recognized the novelist would become a leading light of American popular fiction in the future. He wrote: "This young man seems to have the dramatic instinct and touch to a greater degree than any other American writer now before the reading public. *The Gentleman* is a promise rather than an achievement. But it is a very good promise."[9] That promise sparkled with *Penrod* (1914), the story of a twelve-year-old that sold well enough to reach #7 on *Publishers Weekly*'s annual list. *Penrod and Sam* (1916) was the sequel. *Seventeen* (1915) was serialized in *Metropolitan Magazine* from January 1915. *Harper's* published the novel in book form in 1916, and it became the #1 novel of the year. William Baxter is seventeen and infatuated with Lola Pratt, a popular girl from another town. He is a love-stricken courtly lover, a self-conscious adolescent Don Quixote who tries to appear cool to Lola, his dream girl, who acts childishly. The book sold an estimated 1,682,891, observed Alice Payne Hackett.[10] *The Turmoil* (1915) was volume 1 of a trilogy that included *The Magnificent Ambersons* (1918), which won the Pulitzer Prize. (He also won the Pulitzer for *Alice Adams* [1931].) In *The Turmoil*, Tarkington presents the life of the Sheridan family in Indianapolis. Bibbs Sheridan is the youngest son of industrialist Jim Sheridan's family. He has been at a sanitarium and is returning home after a nervous breakdown. His father had wanted him to follow in his footsteps, like his brothers; Tarkington describes the smoke of industry as "like a giant panting for more riches." Bibbs is a sensitive poet-dreamer, alienated and isolated. Mary Vertrees becomes his love interest. *The Turmoil* is surely a novel of its time. The United States was engaged in corporate and industrial development, with a rising middle class; big business had arrived in the Midwest. The images of old wealth and new wealth appear as features of the era, a bit like F. Scott Fitzgerald's contrast of them in East Egg and West Egg in *The Great Gatsby* (1925).

In 1914, the First World War erupted following the assassination of the Archduke Ferdinand on June 28 in Sarajevo. It was the year after Woodrow Wilson became president and Grand Central Station opened in New York, the year after Ford assembly lines were introduced, the year after Richard Nixon was born. Gandhi had been arrested. Armies assembled on the western front. The popular fiction of 1914 included *Penrod* by Booth Tarkington, *The Inside of the Cup* by Winston Churchill (#3), *Pollyanna* by Eleanor H. Porter (#2), and *The Eyes of the World* by Harold Bell Wright (#1). Less popular was *Dubliners* by James Joyce, found on no bestseller list and delayed until at last published that year. The year 1915 brought Einstein's *General Theory of Relativity* and a Nobel Prize for Physics awarded to the father-and-son team of W. H. and

W. L. Bragg. The war began to drag on through the brutal battles of Ypres and Gallipoli.

Mary Roberts Rinehart was the most popular American mystery novelist of her time. *K* (1915, #5) can be classified as a crime novel. It is set in Allegheny, on the north side of Pittsburgh. In the story, Sidney takes in a boarder who goes by the initial K., and the story proceeds suspensefully across 410 pages. A previous novel, *When a Man Marries* (1910), reached #10 on the *Publishers Weekly* bestseller list. Her bestsellers included *The Amazing Interlude* (1918, #3), *Dangerous Days* (1919, #4), *A Poor Wise Man* (1921, #7), *The Breaking Point* (1922, #6; 1923, #10), and *Lost Ecstasy* (1927, #6).

Ernest Poole's *The Harbor* (1915) likely would have won the Pulitzer Prize had there been one. He received the prize for *His Family* three years later. The committee was recalling *The Harbor*, wrote Dennis Drabelle in the *Washington Post* on January 13, 2012.[11] *The Harbor* was #8 on *Publishers Weekly*'s bestseller list of 1915. The novel has been reissued by Penguin Classics. It is regarded by some readers as protest fiction, a novel of the struggles of workers for rights, dignity, safe working conditions, and just wages. Billy likes the harbor in New York City; his family lives by the Brooklyn waterfront, and his father owns a warehouse. He watches the changes as the nineteenth-century clipper ships give way to steamboats. He becomes a journalist. It is a time of industrialism: Mr. Dillon will organize shipping firms and railroad lines, and efficiency is now the watchword of the day. Billy still admires the harbor; however, Joe Kramer calls the harbor a hell and points out the unsafe conditions for workers. As a journalist, Billy has a Whitman-like style in which he unfolds a spell of prose. Ernest Poole, who attended Princeton about a decade before F. Scott Fitzgerald, wrote in *The Harbor* a kind of urban history in well-crafted fiction that deserves to be rediscovered and read.

Mr. Britling Sees It Through by H. G. Wells (1917, #1) was among the great publishing successes of 1917. *The Outline of History* dominated the nonfiction market two years later. Wells had long been entertaining readers by looking forward into the future, as well as looking back in time. *Publishers Weekly* wrote on January 21, 1899: "H. G. Wells has completed another story of a fanciful nature which like 'Looking Backward' will picture life as it may be, in this case, a couple of hundred years hence. It is being published serially in *Harper's Weekly* under the title of *When the Sleeper Awakes*."[12]

The Light in the Clearing by Irving Bacheller was the #2 fiction book of 1917. *Red Planet* (1917, #3) is not to be confused with the Robert Heinlein science fiction novel of 1948. William John Locke's novel is his story of the Boer War and his narrator's story about a young man named Leonard. In 1902 the Boer War accounted for 5,724 British casualties. [13]

American readers escaped to the rugged and idyllic West of Zane Grey's adventures. Zane Grey's *The U.P. Trail* (1918, #1) is set in the 1860s as the Union Pacific is building the Transcontinental Railroad. Warren Neale is an engineer, and Larry King (not the TV host: he's not that old) is a gunslinging cowboy called Red. Allie Lee is the romantic interest. When Slingerland arrives, he needs help. Neale and Red assist when a wagon is attacked by Sioux Indians; Allie is among the group of people on the wagon, and she and her mother are spared. Neale falls for Allie. We are given melodrama, romance, and descriptions of the land of the West. Zane Grey helped readers to think about something else besides the war. In *The Man of the Forest* (1920, #1) Milt Dale lives in the forest where he has a pet cougar. The heir and nieces of a ranch (Helen and Bo) are in jeopardy: they may be kidnapped, because bandits seek to get the rancher's land. Milt will attempt to save them.

Meanwhile, the Third Battle of Ypres unfolded with the inevitability of a Greek tragedy, as one historian has said. American forces reached Britain on May 18, 1918. Soldiers followed, 1,308 of them, and landed on May 26. In France, discontent among the French troops resulted in a mutiny, desertion, and withdrawal to the rear of the line on the Chemin des Dames. General Pershing insisted that the U.S. enlist a million men to set sail for France. From the sky came the air war that H. G. Wells had prophesied: bombing from planes that grew harsher than that which had come from the zeppelins. On June 5, military draft registration began in the United States. On the Fourth of July, in a ceremony in Paris, Colonel Charles Stanton proclaimed triumphantly: "Lafayette, we are here!" [14]

The Four Horsemen of the Apocalypse by Vicente Blasco Ibáñez (1919, #1) had a biblical title that echoed the devastation of the war. The French and German sons-in-law of an Argentinian fight on opposing sides in the First World War.

1920–1930

Zane Grey's *The Man of the Forest* (1920, #1) took readers away from memories of the war. *This Side of Paradise* by F. Scott Fitzgerald sold briskly and launched the career of its author. The year 1921 brought *Main Street* by Sinclair Lewis (#1). It appeared destined for the Pulitzer Prize, but the award eventually was given to Edith Wharton for *The Age of Innocence*. In *The Age of Innocence*, Newland Archer is intrigued by Ellen Olenska, an immigrant from Europe. His wife May Welland knows about his affair with her cousin. Archer belongs to an upper-class society whose codes, expectations, and pretenses this story unsparingly examines.

So *Big* (1924, #1) by Edna Ferber was the first of her big bestsellers. It features Selina, who marries a Dutch farmer and has a child Dirk, who she calls "So Big." Babies have been bounced in parents' arms to that phrase ever after. Selina raises Dirk after Purvis, her husband, dies, and she runs the farm. Dirk becomes an architect but loses his commitment to that profession through an attraction to money. Roelf, her youthful protégé, becomes a sculptor after training in France. Dirk is left to try to figure out the meaning of his life. Ferber's next big novel, *Show Boat* (1926, #8), became a memorable musical.

Soundings by A. Hamilton Gibbs (#1) and *The Constant Nymph* by Margaret Kennedy (#2) led the fiction list in 1925. The #1 bestseller of 1926 was *The Private Life of Helen of Troy* by John Erskine, a Columbia University professor, musician, and proponent of the great books. The #2 novel was Anita Loos's popular *Gentlemen Prefer Blondes*. The year 1927 was marked by the Charles Lindbergh flight from Roosevelt Field to Paris, the floods of the Mississippi, and Babe Ruth's home run record. It was the year that the Literary Guild book club began. The #1 fiction bestseller was *Elmer Gantry*; following it on the list was *The Plutocrat* by Booth Tarkington. Warwick Deeping had both #3 *Doomsday* and #4 *Sorrell and Son*. Mary Roberts Rinehart and Edith Wharton both had novels in the top ten on the fiction list, and the nonfiction list was led by Will Durant's *The Story of Philosophy*. Lindbergh is also remembered because the kidnapping of his infant son became one of the sensational news stories of 1932. His wife Anne Morrow Lindbergh became a popular bestselling author. The late Philip Roth imagined Lindbergh as a presidential candidate whose election led toward Fascism in *The Plot against*

America (2004). A similar note of concern is sounded by Sinclair Lewis in *It Can't Happen Here* (1935).

Elmer Gantry (1927, #1) is a sharp satire from Sinclair Lewis, directed at the manipulations of a dubious evangelist. The novel unfolds in episodes, reflecting aspects of American culture before 1900. Elmer Gantry joins preacher Sharon Falconer and gives her poems. From sermons and songs have come his only knowledge of literature. Lewis gives us an account of Elmer Gantry's middlebrow reading: "two volumes of Conan Doyle, one of E. P. Roe, and a priceless copy of 'Only a Boy.,"[15] He has been schooled on McGuffey's Readers, stories featuring Nick Carter, the dime novel detective, and Bible stories. (E. P. Roe, a former pastor, was a writer of middle-class stories for middle-class readers.) Sharon Falconer gives him, perhaps, a sense of purpose and books from Mrs. Humphrey Ward, Winston Churchill, Dickens, and Scott, and *Main Street* by Sinclair Lewis, of which he says: "Lord, how that book of Lewis' *Main Street*, did bore me."[16] In contrast to Elmer Gantry, Frank Shallard is a good man, a learned preacher, a man of conscience whose mind is filled with theology. He is self-conscious, wondering if to be a preacher is to be not quite virile, or if his inclination toward study and his faith separates him and sets him apart from "the real desires of normal humanity."[17] He feels compassion and pity for those who come to the Church seeking help. Yet, he wonders why the Church is so imperfect. He questions contradictions he sees in the Bible but is determined to do his work of ministry.

Elmer Gantry takes his first sermon directly from the notable preacher Robert G. Ingersoll. He recites cliché phrases from books he was forced to read in school. He goes forth to preach with daydreams of being beloved by "hundreds of beautiful women [who sigh] with conviction and rush down to clasp his hand."[18] Meanwhile, Sharon Falconer insists that she is "above sin." Her voice is "a little husky, desperately alive." She claims to have visions and to hear the voice of God. She declares that she hates small vices of drinking and smoking, swearing and scandal, but can "love" the big ones: "murder, lust, cruelty, ambition."[19] She seduces Elmer Gantry. Later, when a fire threatens to consume the church, Elmer Gantry flees while she attempts to save the congregation. Frank Shallard decides that he might be better off in the army, with everyday young men. He is pushed from the Church and works for a charitable organization and then wanders to the West. Thus, Sinclair Lewis creates a satire rather than a portrait of religion in America. Of *Elmer Gantry*, H. L. Mencken wrote: "The story is beautifully designed, and it moves with the inevitability of a fugue. It is packed with observation, all fresh, all shrewd, all sound."[20] Lewis biographer Mark Schorer claimed that *Elmer Gantry* never reaches any level of conscience or change of awareness.[21]

In 1929, the sons of the bestselling mystery novelist Mary Robert Rinehart, Stan and Ted, joined with John Farrar to create the Farrar, Rinehart Publishing Company. In the 1930s they would see Mary Roberts Rinehart again on the fiction bestseller list with *The Door* (1930, #6) and *The Doctor* (1936, #9). They published *Young Man of Manhattan* by Katherine Brush (1930, #9), *Magnolia Street* by Louis Golding (1932, #4), and the Hervey Allen's monumental bestseller *Anthony Adverse* (1934, #1).

In *All Quiet on the Western Front* (1929) by Erich Maria Remarque (1929, #1) Paul Baumer tells the story of German soldiers and the harshness they experience in the fighting on the front. Fiction offers us a glimpse into trench warfare and the hearts of common soldiers. Paul Baumer at first approaches war as an adventure and then confronts the human face of a tragic war of attrition. Through Paul we witness the graphic images of destruction and learn of the trauma and mental repercussions of soldiers' experiences. The novel was viewed by some readers as holding a pacifist position. It was banned by Joseph Goebbels and the Nazi Party as unpatriotic. As a soldier, Erich Maria Remarque had seen the war firsthand. He laid barbwire, built bunkers, formed gun fortifications. On July 1917 he tried to save a fellow soldier and was wounded.

All Quiet on the Western Front was dramatic and controversial. An American critic wrote that Remarque's novel expressed "the whole modern impulse: the amalgamation of prayer and desperation, dream and chaos, wish and desolation." Alfred Bonadeo saw in it universal themes and likened it to English accounts of the war. Paul Fussell, writer of *The Great War and Modern Memory*, saw in the novel "the whole frenzied machinery of Gothic romance" and considered the story different from the English accounts of the war. For F. F. Hill, the novel had "the lean savagery of an Ibsen tragedy." Literary critic Joseph Krutch wrote: "Remarque tells his plain tale was a sort of naivete which is the result, not of too little experience but of too much."[22]

The reception of Remarque's novel and the context it emerged from is explored in an essay by Thomas Schneider in which he tells us how the novel entered interpretations of the First World War. [23] Initial publications on the war featured the fighting man as a soldier with the power to achieve victory. By the Battle of the Marne this image was contradictory: it was not consistent with the brutal reality of men stuck in trench warfare engaging in futile attacks on the enemy. The solider by this time was diminished, alienated, "de-individualized" by industrial warfare. As Ernest Hemingway wrote in *A Farewell to Arms* (1929), the word "heroism" seemed hollow, and sure words that spelled out concrete reality were needed. The German audience sought "authenticity." A soldier should have experienced the events of war personally. Rather than fiction, what was sought was autobiography. Schneider connects Remarque's novel with the fate of the Weimer Republic. Upon reviewing news accounts, book reviews, publicity materials, letters to editors, and other responses to *All Quiet on the Western Front*, he reflected upon the novel's place and impact upon culture and society. Remarque revised the story to sound like a personal account from a soldier, reduced his antiwar commentary, and made this Paul Baumer's story. Schneider found that 85 percent of the documents he perused indicated that readers believed that the war should continue to be discussed and only about 9 percent argued to end the discussion. [24] The publisher, Ullstein, regarded the novel as a new way of representing the war, giving it a documentary-like credibility. Some readers sought to find "facts" in the novel.

THE 1930s

The stock market crash of October 1929 and the Depression that followed prompted the central cultural forces of the 1930s in America. Despite the Depression, or perhaps because of it, Americans were avid readers. In 1930, Edna Ferber's *Cimarron* (#1) dramatized the land runs into the unsettled former Cherokee and Sioux territory of Oklahoma. It portrayed a period of American life in the crucible of change. Ferber drew upon her parents' stories of the West. Her reading audience obviously was interested in this historical novel of grand proportions. In the 1880s the U.S. government attempted to lease land for cattle ranchers, and the Cherokees rejected this. In 1886 the land was opened for settlement. In *Cimarron*, the prospects have brought Yancey Cravat and Sabra Cravat from Wichita. There are disputes between cattle ranchers and small ranchers who have claimed land; the story, as well as the film, recalls the 1889 land rush. By 1893 the land was open to homesteaders. Cherokee land holdings in Oklahoma were reduced by treaties, but the Cherokee nation remains a presence there. The 1930 novel was adapted and filmed at a cost of more than $125,000, a considerable amount of money at that time, despite the Great Depression. There was a remake of a *Cimarron* film in 1960.

The Good Earth (1931) by Pearl S. Buck (#1 in 1931 and #1 in 1932) generated a fascination with China. Buck was the daughter of Presbyterian missionaries in China. She was the first American woman awarded the Nobel Prize. In *The Good Earth* she offered Depression-era readers a story in which determination, effort, and hard work and integrity appealed to readers. The novel suggests hope despite adversity. In Anhwei, Wang Lung is to be married to O-Lan, a slave of the wealthy family of Hwang. The opium trade affects the Hwangs. Wang Lung and O-Lan have three sons and three daughters, one of whom is disabled because of famine and malnutrition. The difficulties of poverty prompt O-Lan to attempt to spare some of her children; one daughter is sacrificed. Wang Lung, seeking to move his family south, learns that they can travel by train. Wang Lung, who maintains a code of Confucian honor, pushes a rickshaw through the city, and the family lives in poverty. He dreams of returning to the land and bringing the family home. This poignant novel about a family's struggle unfolds gradually, without complex language or sentences. Yet its compelling story underscores the need of women for respect and dignity and for people to be good like the earth. Oprah featured the novel in her book club in 2004.

Willa Cather's *Shadows on the Rock* (1931, #2) is a historical novel set in Quebec in 1697 in which Cather's skill for characterization is clear. Cecile Auclair and her father Euclide have a close relationship and are well-rounded characters who seem quite real. Euclide arrived in Quebec as a physician and apothecary to Count de Frontenac. His wife has died. Cecile and Euclide go to see Mother Juschereau, who tells Cecile a story, and they travel to farms and vegetable sellers. We see Cecile as she goes to the governor Frontenac to seek shoes for Jacques. In the past, Bishop Laval had saved Jacques from a snowstorm. The reader of *Shadows on the Rock* follows Cecile and Euclide through their experiences.

Historical novels are often lengthy. *War and Peace* by Leo Tolstoy is 1,455 pages in paperback in the Signet Classics edition. *Anthony Adverse* by Hervey Allen (1933, #1; 1934, #1) was published at more than 1,224 pages. It has been suggested that *Anthony Adverse* primed the audience for *Gone with the Wind*. The story is an adventure that focuses upon the life and fortunes of its central character, Anthony. This expansive historical novel brings a reader across continents and the years of the French Revolution and the Napoleonic era. A book club selection, it was filled with sailors and slaves, pirates and politicians, ladies and gentlemen. The story provides a "you are there" experience, which may have been a useful imaginative escape from the pains of the Depression. Anthony Adverse begins his life journey as an orphan, and his adventures become a quest for meaning. Anthony is apprenticed to a merchant; on comes Napoleon's army. Off he goes on Captain Jordan's ship to Cuba, to Africa, to Spain, and on to New Orleans, where he meets Jean Lafitte, and then to Napoleon's France. The sensibility of Hervey Allen of Pittsburgh appears to have been grazed by the shell shock of war when he was a first lieutenant in France. Yet this man could return home to write one of the great historical epics of his time. The *Saturday Evening Post* called *Anthony Adverse* "a book likely to last."[25] Yet, it has not. Perhaps only the most adventurous of readers can navigate that wide, churning ocean of prose.

Lloyd Douglas led the bestseller list in 1935 with *Green Light*. *Vein of Iron* by Ellen Glasgow was #2; *Of Time and the River*, the posthumous novel by Thomas Wolfe, was #3. On the list also was *Time out of Mind* by Rachel Field (#4), and *Goodbye Mr. Chips* by James Hilton (#5).

In *Gone with the Wind* (1936, #1; #1937, #1) Margaret Mitchell could dream her story of the South, a story so evocative it brought echoes of a memory and the myth of a romantic imagined past. Mention *Gone with the Wind* to someone, and that person may recall Technicolor images of Vivien Leigh as Scarlett O'Hara and Clark Gable as Rhett Butler, or Olivia de Havilland as Melanie and Hattie McDaniel as Mammy, kerchief on her head. Yet, there was more than enough romance and drama in Mitchell's novel before Hollywood ever cast that epic film. *Gone with the Wind* was the #1 novel of 1936 and the #1 novel of 1937. It received the Pulitzer Prize and the National Book Award. Mitchell's South is a place of myth and imagination, a never-was that is now gone with the wind. That quixotic Tara of hoopskirts, plantation grace, and winding balustrades was a secure world dismantled by the scorched-earth campaign of

Sherman's troops. It was an idyllic landscape turned to tattered chimneys and the stone remnants of Civil War memory.

Margaret Mitchell wrote her story in the late 1920s through the early 1930s. She wrote stories as a child, eventually penning these into notebooks that were placed in boxes. Her brother Stephens went to Harvard and then to war. She became engaged to Clifford West Henry, who was killed in battle at Verdun weeks before the armistice. The flu epidemic of 1918 took her mother. Mitchell then married Berrien Red Upshaw, who had failed out of West Point and took up bootlegging whiskey in 1922, and she became a reporter in Atlanta from 1922 to 1926. Red evidently drank too much of the whiskey; their tempestuous marriage was dissolved, and she married the best man from their wedding, John March, an Associated Press copyeditor. Mitchell was fascinated by history and by erotica. Her husband, who collected books from the library for her, remarked: "Can't you write a book instead of reading thousands of them?" She began writing about "Pansy" O'Hara, a character whose name she later changed to Scarlett. Mitchell allegedly used reams of paper from her *Gone with the Wind* manuscript to prop up her couch.

Robert Penn Warren wrote of the lessons we "feel" from the Civil War. Frederick Douglass once spoke of national regeneration and the sacred significance of the war. He recognized that the Civil War would be a memory where slavery inevitably confronts us. As statues are withdrawn from public squares, national memory is distilled in a mixture of pride and loss, racial concern, and honor and criticism of Confederate legends. For history and memory are emotionally complicated, and in people's dreams live the ghosts that popular novelist James Lee Burke once imagined to be *In the Electric Mist with the Confederate Dead*. As James Baldwin once wrote: "History . . . does not refer merely to the past . . . history is literally present in all that we do." History and memory, says historian David Blight, represent "two streams of historical consciousness that must at some point flow together."[26] History is a reasoned construction of the past rooted in research and critical analysis. Memory is rich with stories and feeling, meaning and recollections. It is the "felt" heritage or identity of a community. *Gone with the Wind*, as a culture text, participates most certainly in the latter.

Marjorie Kinnan Rawlings's *The Yearling* (1938, #1) was a smash bestseller, edited by Maxwell Perkins at Scribner's. Perkins had rejected her first efforts and then took on this novel, after advising Rawlings to write a story that was close to her life experience. After all, it had certainly worked effectively for Scribner's notable authors Thomas Wolfe and F. Scott Fitzgerald. The novel became a Book of the Month Club selection and rose to #1, where it remained for twenty-three weeks. *The Yearling* sold more than 250,000 copies and became a film in 1943, a short-lived Broadway musical in 1965, and a television show in 1994. *The Yearling* is one of the great sentimental animal stories. It is the story of Jody Baxter's development and his attachment to his pet fawn, the yearling. Jody's family lives on a simple bit of land, and Jody would like a pet. One day Penny shoots a deer, leaving a fawn that is adopted by Jody. Meanwhile, Slewfoot hunts the bear that has been decimating the family's livestock. The story is filled with Jody's experiences, family times, and his relationship with the yearling and with friends. It is also a story of losses: of friends and of the yearling. The yearling grows and begins eating the corn crop that the family depends on for survival. So, Jody faces the hard task of bidding farewell to the yearling, ending its life. Torn by this, Jody runs away to face the world. In this story we have the struggle and resourcefulness of a family, a theme that clearly appealed to struggling and resourceful families facing the Great Depression. It was a theme that would be repeated in John Steinbeck's *The Grapes of Wrath*.

The Grapes of Wrath by John Steinbeck (1939, #1) has sold more than fourteen million copies. In 1967, Alice Payne Hackett set sales at 2,100,908 and said that bookstores sold three hundred thousand copies in the first year of publication.[27] A rare edition copy sold at auction in 2007 for $47,800. Steinbeck's novel was #1 in 1939 and #8 in 1940. *The Grapes of Wrath* was awarded the Pulitzer Prize, and the successful 1940 film is today regarded as an American classic. (Director John Ford received the Academy Award for his efforts, and Jane Darwell received the award for Best Supporting Actress. The film received five nominations in other categories, including one for Henry Fonda in his role as Tom Joad.) Steinbeck tells us the story of the troubled journey of the Joad family from dust bowl–ravaged Oklahoma west to California. The Joads are migrant famers, Americans on an arduous trek, who seek to take refuge and to find work in a land where they are ultimately exploited. The novel was both acclaimed and censored. *The Grapes of Wrath* was grounded in John Steinbeck's on-site observations in migrant camps. The novel emphasizes the values of family, democracy, and persistence, and it makes an ethical appeal to its readers regarding truth, justice, and compassion for less fortunate citizens. *The Grapes of Wrath* is a story that helps us to explore moral character. The story focuses on Tom Joad, whose growth we follow from parolee from prison to sturdy family supporter to sympathetic seeker for justice. At the core of the novel also is Ma Joad, the resilient center of the family who begins to see how all families struggling and enduring are much the same. They are the people who comprise the fabric of the American dream. Jim Casy, a doubt-filled former preacher, joins the family on their journey and eventually realizes his faith in a social gospel as a community organizer among the farmworkers. The novel's emphasis on social justice, family, and community relationships is summed up in Ma Joad's assertion of endurance: "We're the people that live!"

2

THE 1940s

All the Books Fit to Sell

The bestseller lists of 1942 can be largely characterized as alternating between books that looked squarely at the war in Europe and those that sought to provide nostalgia, romance, or entertainment, perhaps as an escape from it. These lists recorded the persistence in reading and book production despite paper shortages during the Second World War. *Publishers Weekly* maintained its honored tradition of listing bestselling books. In 1940, *How Green Was My Valley* and *Kitty Foyle* led its list just ahead of Ernest Hemingway's *For Whom the Bell Tolls*. America entered the war after December 7, 1941. Moving toward the top of the list in 1942 were Franz Werfel's *The Song of Bernadette* and John Steinbeck's *The Moon Is Down*. The first national *New York Times* list appeared on September 9, 1945. This included reports from twenty-two booksellers across the United States. Up to that point, the year's bestselling books had been tracked only in New York City by the *New York Times*. Book sales continued to be tracked nationally by *Publishers Weekly*. Their lists were particularly helpful to sectors of the publishing industry.

In a time of war, many readers turned to popular fiction for diversion and entertainment. World War II "increased demand for books out of a need for distraction," Jonathan Rose observes. Pocket Books sales reached some thirty-eight million paperbacks in 1940. *Time* reported that book sales in 1943 increased by about three hundred million. This created a mass popular audience.[1] The top fiction of 1938 and 1939 sustained public interest into the early 1940s. *The Grapes of Wrath* by John Stein-beck, a popular film in 1940, encapsulated the family and community dilemma of the Great Depression. *Rebecca* by Daphne du Maurier was adapted as an Academy Award–winning film. *The Yearling* by Marjorie Kinnan Rawlings became an enduring classic read by teens, young adults, and older adults. Richard Wright's *Native Son* appeared in 1940. The *Detroit Tribune*, Michigan's oldest African American newspaper, serial-ized *Native Son* in 1942. Installments of the novel could sometimes be found alongside the column "In Print," which appeared regularly in the *Detroit Tribune*. On October 23, 1942, the editor pointed out that the column had not appeared in more than six weeks but "has not faded out." In an adjacent article, the editor commented on "the art of the Negro in modern times."[2] Wright's voice would appear again in his autobiography *Black Boy*, which cast light on racism and issues in Chicago and through-out the nation.

In 1940, Mortimer Adler focused upon the great books tradition and instructed readers in *How to Read a Book*. The proponents of the great books tradition asserted that culture could be made available to people.[3] Mortimer Adler and Robert Hutchins sought a "great books" curriculum at the University of Chicago. *Great Books of the Western World* (pub-lished April 15, 1952) appeared courtesy of *Encyclopedia Britannica*. Simon and Schuster's *How to Read a Book* (1940) called the "great books" those that "elevate our spirit."[4] This book urged reading as a "discipline" to pursue knowledge rather than only information. There was "a quest for permanence and meaning in a world rendered transient and confusing by the Second World War," observes Joan Shelley Rubin. She points out that Hutchins believed that people would buy the books for display and did not have to presume to understand them.[5] Meanwhile, Clifton Fadiman, who wrote *Reading I've Liked* (1941), said that the books that people found worth rereading were those that contained some "magic" and "personality."[6] In his essay "Decline of Attention," Fadiman asserted that American culture had created "producers and consumers" and fewer "rational men." In his view, readers had to be sold words and thoughts.[7]

Readers of the great books, or of popular novels, developed the habit of reading as children in school in the 1930s and 1940s. Ruth Moncrief recalls her teacher, Mrs. Wilcox: "Oh, I loved my English teacher and she would get excited over Shakespeare, or whatever she was reading; her head would shake and her hairpins would fly." Hans Fisher, who was born in Germany, did not know English when he arrived in America as a child. He developed his ability to speak and write in English by reading books. In class a teacher read from *Alice in Wonderland*. "It is a very famous British book. There were very few books I had not read by the time I graduated from Vineland High School," he told an interviewer.[8]

Books were promoted on the radio in 1940. NBC featured "Best Books of the Month." In 1941, Edwin Seaver was Book of the Month Club publicity director and a radio reviewer for WQXR-Radio, where he offered scripts on *Books and Authors*.[9] "The Author Meets the Critics" premiered in 1943, and the Book of the Month Club became a sponsor in 1945. In 1946, the Literary Guild presented an "identical" show, *Books on Trial*.[10] Popular fiction brought *Lassie Come Home* by Eric Knight, a beloved children's classic, and lasting modern religious classics: *The Song of Bernadette*, *The Robe*, *The Keys of the Kingdom*. Most lasting novels are "big novels," as Michael Korda has pointed out. These include the historical family saga, what Korda calls "the ambitious novel of broad scope." This is a novel that is "big in concept, with a big, central moral conflict."[11] Although widely read in their time, many of these books are not often read today, even though they are well written and entertaining.

An overview of the books of the 1940s will show that several authors frequently returned with interesting books to the bestseller lists. Dale Carnegie's *How to Win Friends and Influence People* (1938) was followed by *How to Stop Worrying and Start Living* (1948). John Gunther's series of "Inside" books continued with *Inside Latin America* (1941). Curiosity about events in Europe led to many other nonfiction bestsellers in 1940 and 1941. Readers discovered William Shirer's *Berlin Dairy* (1941) and Winston S. Churchill's *Blood, Sweat and Tears* (1941). Authors like John P. Marquand (*Wickford Point*, 1939), Kenneth Roberts (*Northwest Passage*, 1938), A. J. Cronin (*The Citadel*, 1938), and Lloyd Douglas (*Disputed Passage*, 1939) remained bestselling authors through the 1940s. We see in the 1940s Kenneth Roberts's *Oliver Wiswell* (1940); J. P. Marquand's *H. M. Pulham, Esquire* (1941), *So Little Time* (1943), *B. F.'s Daughter* (1946), and *Point of No Return* (1949); A. J. Cronin's *The Keys of the Kingdom* (1941); John Steinbeck's *The Moon Is Down* (1942), *Cannery Row* (1945), and *The Wayward Bus* (1947). Lloyd Douglas's *The Robe* (1944) was a big bestseller, as was his novel *The Big Fisherman* (1949). A. J. Cronin produced *The Green Years* (1944) and

Shannon's Way (1948). Daphne du Maurier created the popular novel *The King's General* (1946). Perhaps reflecting a nostalgic interest, historical fiction was popular: Thomas B. Costain's *The Black Rose* (1945), Mika Waltari's *The Egyptian* (1949), and Ben Ames Williams's *House Divided* (1947) were bestsellers. Several female writers were popular: Elizabeth Gouge wrote *Pilgrim's Inn* (1948); Pearl S. Buck, focusing on China, wrote *Dragon Seed* (1942); Maria Davenport wrote *The Valley of Decision* (1943) and *East Side, West Side* (1947); Taylor Caldwell created *This Side of Innocence* (1946); and Frances Parkinson Keyes wrote *Dinner at Antoine's* (1949). There were the adventure tales of Samuel Shellabarger, like *Captain from Castile* (1945). There was the sexy and censored novel, *Forever Amber* (1944) by Kathleen Winsor. There were also literary novels like Ernest Hemingway's *For Whom the Bell Tolls* (1940) and W. Somerset Maugham's *The Razor's Edge* (1944).

The war novel did not truly come into its own until after the war. A few novels of this type were published during the war, including *A Bell for Adano* by John Hersey, which won the Pulitzer Prize. However, some of the most memorable novels—Norman Mailer's *The Naked and the Dead*, Irwin Shaw's *The Young Lions*, and James Jones's *From Here to Eternity*—appeared after the war. The war novels of Norman Mailer and Irwin Shaw appeared in 1948 and were followed by those of James Jones and Herman Wouk in 1951. Mailer and Shaw offered critiques of military powers, bureaucracy, and dehumanization and focused on ordinary enlisted men. James Gould Cozzens and Herman Wouk were more conservative in their approaches to military order.

Ernest Hemingway's *For Whom the Bell Tolls* brought the experience of war to readers. Hemingway's novel was written while Hemingway was in Cuba. His story is set during the Spanish Civil War and takes place across three days in late May 1937 in the Sierra de Guadarrama, mountains northwest of Madrid. Hemingway's character Robert Jordan has become the leader of a guerrilla group that enters enemy territory to blow up a bridge to keep the Fascists from using the road. Jordan has to wait until the enemy attack begins before he can destroy the bridge. Hemingway's novel is filled with drama and romance: There are love scenes between Jordan and Maria. Pilar, the leader of the guerrillas, plans strategy; we follow the guerrilla band and Jordan through the story. Jordan's relationship with Maria is opposed by Pilar and by Pablo. Enemy planes fly threateningly overhead. Jordan encourages himself to be a man of action. The introductory caption to the novel draws the reader's attention to the poet John Donne. We are all implicated in each other's lives, wrote Donne: "Ask not for whom the bell tolls, it tolls for thee." Scribner's records indicate that the company printed 210,192 sets of sheets of *For Whom the Bell Tolls* before the October 21 publication of the novel and issued 73,000. A film with Gary Cooper and Ingrid Bergman in 1943 stimulated further printings and book sales.

1942

We can see that there has been considerable overlap between the *Publishers Weekly* and *New York Times* bestseller lists across the years. The bestseller lists of 1942 listed *The Last Time I Saw Paris* by Elliot Paul at #1 in the spring of that year. This book provides a nostalgic look at prewar Paris at a time when the city is under German occupation. Paul focuses upon one area of Paris. *Publishers Weekly* listed it as the #3 nonfiction book of the year. *Victory through Air Power* by Alexander de Seversky was also on this first listing of bestsellers by the *New York Times*. He was a pilot who offered his strategy for fighting the enemy and achieving victory. Later that summer the civilian aviation expert William B. Ziff offered his strategy in *The Coming Battle of Germany* and joined Alexander de Seversky's book in the top positions on this somewhat limited bestseller list. W. L. White's *They Were Expendable* told the exploits and adventures of a war correspondent and later became a film. Marion Hargrove, also a war correspondent, offered a comic approach to army life in *See Here, Private Hargrove. Time* magazine commented that this was a book that "can build morale." *Publishers Weekly* listed the book as the #1 nonfiction book of the year. *Mission to Moscow* by Joseph E. Davies was #2.

There were three portrayals of courageous women simultaneously on the bestseller list. *And Now Tomorrow* by Rachel Field was the sentimental story of a girl who became deaf and determinedly struggled to hear again. Elizabeth Chevalier's *Drivin' Woman* was a historical romance set in Kentucky after the American Civil War. It was #5 on *Publishers Weekly*'s fiction list. *The Song of Bernadette* was Franz Werfel's deeply felt rendering of the life of Bernadette Soubirous, who is said to have miraculously encountered an appearance of the Virgin Mary at Lourdes. Werfel's own story is also a tale of wonder. As a Jew and an expressionist artist in Germany, he came under threat and fled from the Nazi regime. While passing through Lourdes, where a shrine draws pilgrims in search of healing, he determined to write the story of Bernadette's life. *Publishers Weekly* listed *The Song of Bernadette* at #1 for 1942. The *Moon Is Down* by John Steinbeck, a story of resistance to an occupying army, was the year's #2 fiction bestseller on *Publishers Weekly*'s list. Clearly the war brought nostalgic longing to some and the desire to fight and win to others. It also became a time ripe for the religious bestseller.

The Robe (1942) by Lloyd Douglas was perhaps the biggest seller of 1942. The Lutheran minister created the story of Marcellus, a Roman soldier, who gambles to win the robe of the crucified Jesus, and Marcellus's unexpected conversion. Marcellus witnesses the Crucifixion and believes that Jesus is innocent. He is accompanied by his Greek slave Demetrius. At a banquet for Pontius Pilate, Marcellus is coerced by a centurion to wear Jesus's robe; Marcellus has a nervous breakdown. While Marcellus recovers, Demetrius urges him to touch the robe and he is healed. Marcellus returns to Judea and meets the followers of Jesus. Douglas's novel held the #1 spot on the bestseller list from November 22 through the end of the year and into 1943.

1943

The United States was now actively engaged in the Second World War. *The Robe* by Lloyd Douglas was the #1 book in America on January 4, 1943. *The Robe* and Franz Werfel's *Song of Bernadette* suggests a nation at war that was seeking hope in stories of Christian faith. Novels were produced despite a reduction of paper supplies. Popular among readers also were domestic romances by Nancy Hale (*The Prodigal Woman*) and Marcia Davenport (*The Valley of Decision*). *The Robe* remained among the top five bestsellers through the first two months or so of 1943. *The Robe* would become #1 on *Publishers Weekly*'s annual fiction bestseller list.

The novel of manners set within a segment of American culture also attracted the attention of readers. Louis Bromfield's *Mrs. Parkington* was the novel that replaced *The Robe* atop the bestseller list on March 14, 1943. This was the story of the life of Mrs. Parkington in New York, from the time she was eighteen until her years as an elderly woman. As in the case of Chevalier's *Drivin' Woman*, Field's *And Now Tomorrow*, and Werfel's *The Song of Bernadette*, a book focusing upon the life of a female protagonist held the #1 place on the *Times* bestseller list. *The Robe* was followed on the list in May by *The Human Comedy* by William Saroyan and *The Forest and the Fort* by Hervey Allen. In June, a new novel by Sinclair Lewis, *Gideon Planish*, could be found at #4 on the list, alongside Daphne du Maurier's *Hungry Hill* and Howard Fast's *Citizen Tom Paine*. *The Robe* returned to #1 in June, in its thirty-fourth week on the list, and remained at #1 until August.

So Little Time, by John P. Marquand, was the book that displaced *The Robe* on August 30. *So Little Time* is narrated by a male character; however, his wife is conspicuously present, vocal, and quite interesting throughout the first chapters of that novel. The narrator appears to be successful but feels something lacking stirring inside of him. A war correspondent who returns from his past is outwardly successful and acclaimed but is rather a misfit. At the time, Marquand was a prolific writer whose attention was trained upon American middle-class life and upon the war in Europe. (*So Little Time* was #3 on *Publishers Weekly*'s annual bestseller fiction list. Marcia Davenport's *The Valley of Decision* was #2. *A Tree Grows in Brooklyn* was #4.)

A Tree Grows in Brooklyn by Betty Smith was also now on the list. It would become #1 on September 20 and September 27. *So Little Time* and *A Tree Grows in Brooklyn* alternated at #1 in October. Scholem Asch's *The Apostle* joined the top five along with *The Robe*. *A Tree Grows in Brooklyn* held the #1 spot, followed by *So Little Time* and *The Robe* until the end of the year. *A Tree Grows in Brooklyn* is the story of the Nolan family during the first decades of the twentieth century. Jonathan Rose observes a U.S. Marine's comments about the book in a May 1944 letter to author Betty Smith. The Marine remarked that he was deeply affected by reading *A Tree Grows in Brooklyn*. This reader recognized that the book was part of his healing process; it had helped him reclaim a sense of empathy after his difficult experience of war.[12]

The taste of readers for reports of hard-nosed combat and military strategy persisted. *Guadalcanal Diary* by Richard Tregaskis reached #1 on the list on March 7, 1943. At the end of April, Harry Emerson Fosdick's *On Being a Real Person* was one of the first the self-help books to capture reader interest. It was the #4 nonfiction book on the *Publishers*

Weekly annual bestseller list. Fosdick's work as a minister and counselor lay behind this encouragement to people about how to deal with their problems. He was one of the most prominent liberal ministers of the twentieth century. At first a Baptist preacher, he later served at Riverside Church on the Upper West Side in Manhattan. He had attended Union Theological Seminary, which is next door. He was called to the First Baptist Church in Montclair, New Jersey, and was an army chaplain in France during the First World War. Upon returning home to the United States he was assigned to the First Presbyterian Church. He broke with the fundamentalist reading of the Bible; following some controversy, he resigned from the Presbyterian Church and became pastor at Park Baptist Church. John D. Rockefeller, a parishioner, was instrumental in bringing him to Riverside Church, which opened October 1930.

With their attention on the war, readers bought books about it, or books concerning international affairs. Meanwhile, Wendell Willkie, the future presidential candidate, had returned from a trip around the world and had written about it. In *One World*, Willkie offered ideas on how to bring nations and people together after the Second World War. His message was one of global unity, and his book quickly went up the bestseller list to #1 on May 9 and stayed there for seventeen weeks. It was the #2 book on *Publishers Weekly*'s 1943 nonfiction bestseller list. Walter Lippmann's *U.S. Foreign Policy* was also on the list at the same time. It climbed to #1 on August 29. Lippmann's political commentary continued in the *New Republic* magazine.

In nonfiction, the year ended with *Under Cover*, John Roy Carlton's stirring tale of espionage. In *Under Cover*, Carlson talked about spies and Communist subversives. It was the #1 nonfiction book on *Publishers Weekly*'s 1943 list. This popular book preceded the McCarthy era by many years. *Burma Surgeon* by Gordon S. Seagrave was the #2 book on the list. *Here Is Your War* by the popular war correspondent Ernie Pyle was #3. Wendell Willkie's *One World* held the #1 spot from May through June 7; then in August, *Under Cover* rose to #1. It is rare that a volume of poetry appears on the bestseller list. *Western Star* by Stephen Vincent Benet was an exception. It reached #5 on August 2. Benet had died on March 13, and his lyrical tribute to America was awarded the Pulitzer Prize in 1943.

Readers of African American background in Detroit on June 6, 1942, could open to page 16 of the *Detroit Tribune* where William Sherrill encouraged reading "good books."[13] "When you find a small bookcase in a home you will rarely find a single book of readable worth," he wrote. In many homes, one will find that "Detective Story," "Snappy Stories," "True Romance" will "cover the reading matter." He encouraged parents: "Tell the children interesting stories that you have read in books." In the center of the page was an article by Associated Negro Press editor Carl Murphy that declared "You Can Abolish Prejudice." Readers were provided with an "In Print" column in the *Detroit Tribune*. The column went on a hiatus during the summer. On October 23, 1943, the upper left column announced that "In Print" had returned and "has not faded out."[14]

In downtown Detroit, book stalls were set inside public buildings to solicit donations of books for African American soldiers.[15] In July 1943, the Detroit Public Library attempted to respond to racial tensions in Detroit with a reading program. The *Detroit Tribune* carried an announcement for the new reading group: "Deplorable was the recent race riot; it has at least served to stimulate the Detroit Public Library to promote more cordial race relations through a program of reading and education" (July 24, 1943). The newspaper reported on September 11, 1943, that, according to a Houghton Mifflin announcement, Roi Ottley's book *New World A'Coming: Inside Black America* had achieved bestseller status, "making this the third time in history that a book by a Negro author" had entered the list.[16] The *New York Times* "Bestsellers of the Week" listed the book on September 6. Thousands of miles away, American troops were landing in Salerno, Italy, beginning a fierce military campaign in southern Italy.

Several American libraries actively stocked bestsellers. A new library in Rising Sun, Maryland, announced that "the library will offer to its readers the current bestsellers. . . . The trend is to keep a higher percentage of older best-sellers in fiction than newer ones."[17] The public library in East Orange, New Jersey, reported: "For the first time on record the library can report that the supply of mystery stories exceeds the demand." It called its staff that had discovered this "our library detective experts."[18] That summer the *Midland Journal* in Rising Sun, Maryland, serialized *See Here, Private Hargrove* by Marion Hargrove.[19]

1944

On July 20, 1944, in the forests of East Prussia, an attempt on Hitler's life had failed miserably. Some say that a table leg saved him. Had the bomb exploded closer to Hitler and with more force, what would have become of Germany? Would the Nazi Party have splintered? Would the nation have been led deeper into war by hard and cynical men like Hermann Goering and the wiry propagandist Goebbels? The bitter reality of the war continued.

The Time for Decision (1944) by Sumner Welles, a former secretary of state, reflected upon history since the First World War and provided plans keeping peace for after the war. Published by the World Publishing Company, this was a Book of the Month Club selection that was available to readers for three dollars. *A Tree Grows in Brooklyn* by Betty Smith topped the bestseller list for four months. *Strange Fruit*, Lillian Smith's interrogation of racism in the South, took the form of a novel about a relationship between a black girl and a white man. Social tensions surrounded this relationship. *Good Night, Sweet Prince* by screenwriter Gene Fowler was a celebrity book about actor John Barrymore. *Yankee from Olympus* by Catherine Drinker Bowen was a biography of Oliver Wendell Holmes, the Supreme Court justice. It was a Book of the Month Club selection, and that aided its push toward the top of the bestseller list for seven weeks, from June 18 through July 1944. *The Razor's Edge* by W. Somerset Maugham was the story of a World War I aviator who goes home and then sets off for Paris and then India. Maugham was a well-known literary writer who wrote many short stories along with his novels, notably *Of Human Bondage*. Elizabeth Goudge's romance *Green Dolphin Street* was the next big seller of the year. It is a story set in New Zealand in which two sisters fall in love with the same man.

The historical romance *Forever Amber* (1944) by Kathleen Winsor was a bawdy #1 bestseller. It was controversial and was censored in Boston and other locations. Winsor's story was set in Restoration England during the reign of Charles II. The titillating romance raised some sensual heat for its readers, and the book sold thousands of copies. A. J. Cronin also turned toward history for his novels. His novel *The Green Years* (1944) addressed the story of Robert Shannon, an orphan from Ireland who goes to Scotland and befriends his great-grandfather. It reached the #1 spot on December 17.

On D-Day, June 6, 1944, *Strange Fruit* by Lillian Smith was the #1 book on the bestseller lists. *The Razor's Edge* by W. Somerset Maugham was #2. *A Tree Grows in Brooklyn* was #3. These books were followed by John Hersey's story of the recent Allied forces' liberation of Italy, *A Bell for Adano*, and Lloyd Douglas's *The Robe*. On July 2 Upton Sinclair's *The Presidential Agent* entered the list at #5 and became #4 the next week. *Leave Her to Heaven* by Ben Ames Williams was #4 on July 30 and #3 on August 6. Toward the end of that month, Maugham's *The Razor's Edge* was #1 on August 20 and August 27, followed by *Strange Fruit*, at #2. *Publishers Weekly* placed *Strange Fruit* at #1 for the year. *The Robe* was #2, *A Tree Grows in Brooklyn* was #3. *Forever Amber* was #4, and *The Razor's Edge* was #5.

Comedian Bob Hope lightened up the nonfiction list with *I Never Left Home*, which became the #1 book on September 3. *I Never Left Home* (1944) brought readers his anecdotes about entertaining troops overseas. It was the #1 bestseller of the year on the *Publishers Weekly* nonfiction list. In the early 1940s, Bob Hope appeared in the films *The Ghost Breakers* (1940), *Road to Singapore* (1940), *Road to Zanzibar* (1941), *Road to Morocco* (1942), *My Favorite Blonde* (1942), and *The Princess and the Pirate* (1944). Joseph S. Pennell's *History of Rome* was #1 on September 10 and 17. In fiction, Aldous Huxley's *Time Must Stop* was #5 on September 24. *The Razor's Edge* and *Strange Fruit* alternated at the #1 spot, with *Strange Fruit* rising to #1 throughout October. That is when *Green Dolphin Street* and *Forever Amber* first appeared on the bestseller list. *Forever Amber* shot up to #1 on November 5, and *Green Dolphin Street* became the #2 book on the list. *Green Dolphin Street* looks back to the 1840s. Marianne and Marguerite are both interested in William Ozone. In an unlikely plot, William, settled in New Zealand, proposes by letter to Marianne, who is ready to go to become his wife. He then realizes that he put the wrong name on the letter. It should have been Marguerite.

By Christmas, *Forever Amber* was still #1 and *Green Years* by A. J. Cronin had climbed to #2, followed by *Green Dolphin Street* at #3. Readers turned again to Ernie Pyle, whose *Brave Men* was the #1 nonfiction book at the end of 1944. *A Time for Decision* by Sumner Welles, #1 on December 3, was now #3. *Lee's Lieutenants* by Douglas Southall Freeman, a fine historical study of the Confederacy, was #4 on the list.

SOLDIERS READING

Newspapers brought the news from war correspondents across the world to Americans at home. The popular war correspondent Ernie Pyle's observations from the front were widely distributed. His reports and anecdotes were collected in *Brave Men* (1944), which reached #1 on the bestseller list the week before Christmas. Ernie Pyle had recently died in combat when he was hit by Japanese machine-gun fire. Two more books that collected his articles were subsequently published. "Every soldier loved Ernie Pyle," Roland Winter, a soldier from New Jersey, recalled.[20] Soldiers read more than missives from the field by Ernie Pyle; during World War II, American servicemen were provided with cheap books to read during their leisure time. Armed Services Editions (ASE) paperbacks were distributed to soldiers. A "paperback revolution" began during the 1940s and followed the war.

Memories of reading were etched in the minds of veterans in New Jersey, New York City, and the Philadelphia area who responded to interviews about their lives from the 1980s to 2010. Their remarks appear in the Rutgers University Oral History Project. One of them, Alvin H. Fagon, recalled that in the quarters where the soldiers resided "there were tiers of bunks and they gave us paper books to read. I remember the first book I read was *God's Little Acre*. It was supposed to be a lascivious book at that time by, I think his name was John Robert Faulkner." (The novel is by Erskine Caldwell.) Fagon's father was born in czarist Russia, and his mother was from Bialystok, Poland. They were Jewish. He recalls growing up in Depression America and then going to "the Stanley or Fox movies for ten cents." He read one of William Shirer's books—probably *Berlin Diary*—although he recalled *The Rise and Fall of the Third Reich* during his interview. Recalling school, he said: "I studied Ernest Hemingway, F. Scott Fitzgerald, many of the great American literary icons. I remember one of the first books we had to read there was Ernest Hemingway." He says that he met Hemingway in Europe during the war and had a drink with him. There are no further thoughts on Hemingway. "I was just a drinker," he says.[21]

Reading was important for servicemen overseas during the Second World War. Before the D-Day invasion, June 6, 1944, one paperback book was distributed to each soldier along with cigarettes and candy. The *Saturday Evening Post* called this "the greatest book publishing project in history." Journalist A. J. Liebling reported of the troops that "most of them were reading paper-cover ASE books." The books played a role in boosting morale.[22]

The Council on Books in Wartime was the publishing industry's advisory group. Christopher Loos accounts for 122 million copies of 1,322 paperback titles. Eight thousand sets of Series C and D books were developed for distribution before D-Day. For ASE books, the Cameo Press, W. F. Hall, Street and Smith, Rumford Press, and Western Printing and Lithography Company printed pocket-sized books. Loos notes that the program "received uniformly sized, easy to ship first run bestsellers" at six cents or less per copy. This cost the U.S. government about eight million dollars. Loos points out that "serious titles often went unread."[23] Biographies of George Washington Carver, Frederick Douglass, and Joe Louis were received by African American soldiers while the military was still segregated. Fiction distributed to soldiers included Lillian Smith's *Strange Fruit* and George Lowther's *The Adventures of Superman*.[24]

The Razor's Edge by W. Somerset Maugham was among the top five or six books of the year on the *Publishers Weekly* list. It was at #2 on the *New York Times* list for multiple weeks and passed *Strange Fruit* on July 2, July 30, August 20, and September 24. Maugham's novel looks back to 1919. The narrator Elliott Templeton is invited to a luncheon in Chicago where he meets Louisa Bradley and Isabel, her daughter. Isabel's fiancé Larry Darrell is a pilot affected by his experience of World War I. The war has changed him, and he is engaged in a search for meaning. The writer weaves his narrative between the characters and occasionally inserts himself into the story. Larry is a point-of-view character, wounded in the war and traumatized. Larry delays marriage. He rejects materialistic occupations and, although offered a job, will not work as a stockbroker. When he moves to Paris, the woman he is supposed to marry cannot adopt that lifestyle, and she returns to Chicago where she marries a millionaire, but the 1929 stock market crash wrecks their fortune. Maugham contrasts spiritual search and materialism. Larry's quest for meaning leads him to India and then back to Paris. The Hindu Upanishads provide the title: "The sharp edge of a razor is difficult to pass on. . . . The wise say the path to Enlightenment is hard."

Forever Amber by Kathleen Winsor was the hottest historical novel of its day: a racy romance set in seventeenth-century England. It was 972 pages long. Amber St. Clare sleeps with men to gain prestige and position. Sometimes she marries them, sometimes not. In 1644 Judith Marsh is engaged to John Mainwaring, the heir to the Earl of Rosswood. Their families are on opposite sides of the English conflict, but they persist in their affair. Judith becomes pregnant. She becomes Judith St. Clare but dies in childbirth. Amber is born; her eyes are the same color as John's and she is named for that. Unaware of her origins, as she grows into womanhood she is attracted to Lord Bruce Carlton. She draws him into the woods for a romantic tryst. Pregnant from their sexual encounter, Amber is supported by Carlton, who becomes a privateer. With the assistance of Sally Goodman, Amber takes on the role of heiress. She meets Luke Channel and marries him. However, Sally and Luke are not what they seem to be. Amber is left alone in poverty and is sent to a debtor's prison. There she comes into contact with Black Jack Mallard, a highwayman, who breaks them out of the prison. Black Jack sneaks Amber away to the Whitefriars and his criminal cronies. She has a child, Bruce, whom she gives away to another woman to raise. Meanwhile, Jack uses Amber for his devious criminal plans. She will lure any dashingly handsome man so that Jack can rob him of his money. However, Jack's former lover is jealous. . . . Kathleen Winsor spent about five years researching and writing the novel while her husband was in the military. Michael Korda suggests that *Forever Amber* made possible Grace Metalious's *Peyton Place* and Jacqueline Susann's *Valley of the Dolls*. Winsor's novel is a precursor to *Peyton Place*, *Valley of the Dolls*, or *Fifty Shades of Grey*.

1945

The year 1945 began with *The Green Years* by A. J. Cronin at #1. *The Green Years* had first reached #1 on December 17, 1944. In January, *Forever Amber*, *Green Dolphin Street*, *Earth and High Heaven*, and Irving Stone's *The Immortal Wife* made up the rest of the top five on the *Publishers Weekly* and *New York Times* bestseller lists. In February, John Steinbeck's *Cannery Row* became #2 with a lighthearted story about a group of delightfully bumbling workers who attempt to give their marine biologist friend Doc a birthday party.

The Egg and I was a surprise bestseller in 1945—and a big one. Anne Elizabeth MacDonald's recollections of life on her farm and then in the mining districts of the West in America remained at the top of the best-seller list for a remarkable forty-three weeks. *So Well Remembered*, by the British writer James Hilton, was about George Boswell who was the mayor of the town. Hilton is best known as the writer of *Goodbye Mr. Chips* and *Lost Horizon*. Thomas B. Costain's *The Black Rose* concerned a British earl of the thirteenth century. Daphne du Maurier's *The King's General* immediately succeeded Costain's novel at #1 on February 6 and stayed there for six weeks. The French aviator Antoine de Saint-Exupery's *The Little Prince* was at #2 and also remained on the list. Daphne du Maurier was the English author of historical and sinister gothic sensation novels including *The King's General, Frenchman's Creek, Hungry Hill, Rebecca*, and *Jamaica Inn*, of which the latter two were adapted for Alfred Hitchcock films. One of her short stories was adapted for Hitchcock's film *The Birds*.[25]

In 1944, *A Tree Grows in Brooklyn* by Betty Smith and *Strange Fruit* by Lillian Smith rivaled A. J. Cronin's novel *The Green Years* for the top spots on the *New York Times* and *Publishers Weekly* bestseller lists. *A Tree Grows in Brooklyn* stood at #1 from January 1 through May 7, 1944. *Strange Fruit* spent fifteen weeks at #1, across the summer of 1944. *The Green Years* followed at #1 later in 1944. In 1945, *The Green Years* held the #1 spot until the end of April. *Earth and High Heaven* was #1 on April 22, and Rosamond Lehmann's *The Ballad and the Source* was #1 on April 29 and on May 2, 1945. In nonfiction, in April 1945 Richard Wright's autobiography *Black Boy* achieved the #1 spot. He describes his experience from childhood in the South to his adult years in Chicago.

Samuel Shellabarger's *Captain from Castile*, #1 on May 13, 1945, is a historical romance set in Spain and in Mexico in the sixteenth century. It became #1 again on June 24 and remained there through July 1. *A Lion in the Streets* by Adria Locke Langley and *Wide House* by Taylor Caldwell both made a strong showing in the top five during June. *A Lion in the Streets* became #1 on July 8, and it held that position to September 23. *So Well Remembered* by James Hilton rose to the #1 position on September 23, followed by *The Black Rose* by Thomas Costain at #2. In September, Costain's historical novel was joined in the top five by James Ramsey Ullman's *The White Tower*, another historical novel. On October 7, #1 was *The Black Rose*; #2 was *So Well Remembered*; #3 was *The White Tower*. Sinclair Lewis's *Cass Timberlane*, on October 28, rose to #2 behind *The Black Rose*. It was *Publishers Weekly*'s #5 on their fiction list for the year. Throughout the rest of the year the top books on the fiction list were *The Black Rose*, *The White Tower*, and *Cass Timberlane*. *The Gauntlet* by James H. Street and *The River Road* by Frances Parkinson Keyes also entered the top five. The *Black Rose* was #3 on *Publishers Weekly*'s bestseller list. *The White Tower* was #4.

In 1945, Ernie Pyle's *The Brave Men* and Bill Mauldin's cartoons in *Up Front* told vignettes of wartime experience. Richard Wright's *Black Boy*, an autobiography, told a different story: one of racial tensions and struggle in America. It sold 195,000 in bookstores and 546,000 via book clubs, observes Alice Payne Hackett.[26] *Brave Men* was #1 in January. *Yankee from Olympus* by Catherine Drinker Bowen was #2. Will Durant's *Caesar and Christ* was #3. Conflict resolution was sought in *The Anatomy of Peace* by Emery Reves, which was on the list in January. The war in Europe drew to a close in May. On June 2, *Brave Men* was #1 on the nonfiction list and *Black Boy* was #2. On July 1 the order reversed. Readers could pick up *These Are the Russians* by Richard Lauterbach, the *New York Times* Moscow bureau chief, or *The Best Is Yet* by Morris Ernst, founder of the American Civil Liberties Union. On August 5, Mauldin's *Up Front* was #1, *Brave Men* #2, and *Black Boy* #3. The war in the Pacific ended in August. On September 2 *Up Front* at #1 was followed by Gertrude Lawrence's *A Star Danced* at #2 and Pyle's *Brave Men* at #3. In November, readers learned about atomic power through Henry Smyth's *Atomic Energy for Military Purposes*, which was #5 on November 18. General George Marshall's *Report* was #2 that Thanksgiving. *The Perennial Philosophy* by Aldous Huxley entered the list at #14 on November 25 and rose to #7 on December 2. On that day, *History of World War II* by Francis Trevelyan Miller was in its first week on the list. *The Age of Jackson* was #12, and Norman Cousins, at #14, insisted that *Modern Man Is Obsolete*.

Once the war was over, some servicemen went to college on the GI Bill. Bert Tryon commented: "Most of the people in my fraternity figured I was a little bit weird because I spent more time reading books then, not textbooks." John Berglund, who became a pharmaceutical salesman, recalled his school reading to an interviewer: "I read Hemingway, of course. I did a great big paper, which was probably on *For Whom the Bell Tolls*. And I read everything I could get my hands on."[27]

In *The Green Years* by A. J. Cronin, Robert Shannon is sent to Scotland to his grandparents; the story begins with his arrival in Scotland after his parents have died. His grandfather is an important figure in his life, and the boy loves nature. He has a somewhat foolish-looking green suit that his grandmother has made, and he is teased for it at school. During his adolescence his best friend dies. When the grandfather dies, he has left an inheritance for Robert Shannon, who can now pursue his dreams of exploring science.

1946

The historical novel made a strong showing on the list immediately after the Second World War. In January of 1946, *The Black Rose* by Thomas Costain remained at #1. The top five works of fiction on the bestseller list were *The Black Rose, The White Tower, River Road, Forever Amber*, and *Cass Timberlane*. From January 6 through January 20, *Up Front* by Bill Mauldin was joined by *The Egg and I* (#2), *Brave Men* (#3), *Soldier of Democracy* (#4), and Arthur Schlesinger's monumental *The Age of Jackson* (#5). *The Anatomy of Peace* stood at #5 on January 20, with *The Age of Jackson* at #6. In February, Daphne du Maurier's new novel *The King's General* swept past the other fiction bestsellers to #1. *The King's General* was #1 on *Publishers Weekly*'s 1946 fiction list. *The Black Rose* was #2 and briefly returned to #1 on January 27. Evelyn Waugh's *Brideshead Revisited* rose to #3. *The King's General* stayed at #1 throughout February; *Arch of Triumph* by Erich Maria Remarque appeared on the list and rose to #2 on February 24 and to #1 on March 10. It stayed at #1 through April. *Arch of Triumph* was #7 on *Publishers Weekly*'s end-of-year fiction bestseller list. Book sales for hardcover fiction increased overall in 1946.

In April, the story of *King David* joined *The King's General* and *The Black Rose* in the top five on the bestseller list. *This Side of Innocence* by Taylor Caldwell also made its first appearance in the top five. Taylor Caldwell (Janet Miriam Taylor Caldwell) was one of the most popular authors of the era. *This Side of Innocence* is a story that revolves around a family in upstate New York. *This Side of Innocence* rose to the #1 position on the list on May 19. It was #2 on *Publishers Weekly*'s 1946 fiction list. An intriguing new entry, *The Snake Pit*, Mary Jane Ward's fictionalized account of life at a mental institution, appeared on the list at #2. This novel was #1 on May 12, 1946, and remained at the #1 spot for nine weeks. It was #10 overall on *Publishers Weekly*'s 1946 fiction list. Ward drew upon her own experience in the Rockland State Hospital in Orangeburg, New York. She wrote the story of a woman who was treated for depression with electric shock therapy, drugs, hydrotherapy, and psychoanalysis. Ward also wrote *The Professor's Umbrella* (1948), *A Little Night Music* (1951), *It's Different for a Woman* (1952), *Counterclockwise* (1969), and *The Other Caroline* (1970). The final two novels are on psychiatric issues. Theodore Dreiser's *The Bulwark* registered at #5 on April 25. However, this final grand work by Dreiser was only on the list for a few weeks.

As summer arrived, so did Frederic Wakeman's *The Hucksters*. It went to #1 on June 23 and stayed there throughout July and August. The advertising business grew rapidly following the Second World War, and public interest kept *The Hucksters* on the bestseller list for half a year. It was #5 on *Publishers Weekly*'s 1946 nonfiction list. *This Side of Innocence* and *The Snake Pit* continued with strong showings on the bestseller list. On September 1, Howard Fast's *The American* was at #5 and Robert Penn Warren's *All the King's Men* was #6. Curiously, *Animal Farm* by George Orwell first appeared on the list in the category of nonfiction. It was moved to the fiction category and was #7 there on September 29. *The Hucksters* continued to dominate the list in October and remained at #1 through November 17. *East River* by Sholem Asch was #2. *The Miracle of the Bells* by Russell Janney rose to #3. The novel concluded the year at #4 on *Publishers Weekly*'s bestseller list. *East River* became #1 on November 24. This story, set in a Jewish immigrant neighborhood on the Lower East Side of Manhattan at the beginning of the twentieth century, focuses upon a shopkeeper and his two sons.

John P. Marquand returned to the bestseller list with *B. F.'s Daughter*. His novel quickly rose to the #1 spot on December 1. It is the story of a girl who is the daughter of a business industrialist. Kenneth Roberts's historical novel *Lydia Bailey* followed at #1 on the bestseller list. The story follows the fortunes of a lawyer from Maine who travels to Haiti during the early years of the nineteenth century and has dealings with Napoleon, Thomas Jefferson, and the war in Tripoli. Marquand's novel stayed at #1 through the end of the year. On Christmas 1946, the *New York Times* bestseller list recorded *B. F.'s Daughter* at #1, Sholem Asch's *East River* at #2, Russell Janney's *The Miracle of the Bells* at #3, and Mary O'Hara's *The Green Grass of Wyoming* at #4. Pearl S. Buck's

Pavilion of Women was #5. Among other novels on the list were *The Salem Frigate* by John Jennings, *The Fall of Valor* by Charles Jackson, Pat Frank's *Mr. Adam*, Thomas Heggen's *Mister Roberts*, and Arthur Koestler's *Thieves of Night*. The next #1 book was *Gentleman's Agreement* by Laura Z. Hobson. In this book a journalist pretends to be a Jew to explore problems of anti-Semitism.

The nonfiction list was led by *The Egg and I* at #1 nearly every week from January 6 to October 6. It was #1 overall on *Publishers Weekly*'s nonfiction list. On January 6 *The Egg and I* was followed by *Brave Men*, *Pleasant Valley*, and *Soldier of Democracy*. On March 10, *The Anatomy of Peace* by Emery Reves was #2. *The Ciano Diaries* by Galeazzo Ciano climbed to #3. *The Autobiography of William Allen White* was #3 two weeks later. On May 19, *Top Secret* by Ralph Ingersoll reached #2 behind *The Egg and I*. Simon and Schuster had three books in the top seven on June 9: Harry C. Butcher's *My Three Years with Eisenhower*, *I Chose Freedom* by the Russian Victor Kravchenko, and *Starling of the White House*. In July *Peace of Mind* by Joshua Lieberman entered the list. On July 21, Malcolm W. Bingay's *Detroit Is My Home Town* was #7. The historical account *Alexander of Macedon* appeared at #8. Reader interest in biography emerged with sales of Hesketh Pearson's *Oscar Wilde*, which was #5 on September 29, and *Brandeis: A Free Man's Life*, #4 on October 20. Americans' interest in sports brought Warren Brown's book *The Chicago Cubs* to #9 on October 9, during the time of the World Series. *The Detroit Tigers* by Frederick Lieb was on the list on October 20.

One of the biggest bestsellers of the time was titled *Peace of Mind*. That seems to be exactly what people needed immediately following the Second World War. Rabbi Joshua L. Lieberman's book was #2 for fourteen weeks and then at #1 for fifty-eight weeks. During much of the next year it remained among the top five bestsellers. It was #2 on *Publishers Weekly*'s 1946 nonfiction list. Lieberman wrote a self-help book filled with psychological and religious thought to provide insight and encouragement. Readers who purchased *Peace of Mind* made it the #1 book in November and December. On December 29 *Peace of Mind* was #1, followed by *The Egg and I* (#2), and John Roy Carlton's *The Plotters* (#3). *The Roosevelt I Knew*, an account of the life of Franklin Roosevelt by Francis Perkins, was #4. Elliott Roosevelt's *As He Saw It*, *Balzac* by Stephen Zweig, and Eric Sevareid's *Not So Wild a Dream* were among the top ten books. *Thunder in China* by Theodore H. White and Annalee Jacoby was #12. John Hersey's *Hiroshima* was #14. At the end of the year a book by Sumner Welles was asking *Where Are We Going?* Bob Hope's #10 bestseller looked more hopefully to the future and observed: *So This Is Peace.*

This Side of Innocence by Taylor Caldwell was six months on the bestseller list and spent nine of those weeks at #1. Caldwell was born in Manchester, England, and arrived in the United States at the age of seven. As a child, she wrote an essay on Charles Dickens. As a writer of fiction, she brought the background of historical events into her stories. Among her bestselling historical novels was *Great and Glorious Physician* and *The Earth Is the Lord's*, which focused on Genghis Kahn. In 1918–1919 she was in the United States Naval Reserve, and she was married in 1919. Taylor Caldwell then became a court reporter in the New York State Department of Labor in Buffalo. She served in the U.S. Department of Justice in 1924. Attending the University of Buffalo, she graduated in 1931, went through a divorce, and then married Marcus Reback. After this she was employed with U.S. Immigration. In 1934, *Dynasty of Death*, a family saga, was written with Reback. *The Eagles Gather* (1940) appeared as Britain entered the Second World War. *The Final Hour* (1944) was a novel of suspense and family issues. The American intellectual Left did not like *Devil's Advocate* (1952), a Cold War dystopian novel concerning Communist political gains within the United States. Caldwell's other novels of the period included *The Balance Wheel* (1951).

Arch of Triumph by Erich Maria Remarque, his postwar novel, tells the story of a doctor from Berlin who escaped from the Nazis. He has to work in a brothel. Remarque himself worked several curious jobs, as John Bear points out.[28] He was an organist in an insane asylum and a tombstone salesman. Either of those jobs might have provided material for some interesting stories. Remarque's *All Quiet on the Western Front* is one of the classics that preceded the bestseller list. His book was censored by the Nazis for being antiwar.

1947

The year 1947 brought the Truman Doctrine, the Marshall Plan, and the breaking of the sound barrier. Jackie Robinson signed with the Dodgers, breaking racial barriers in baseball as well. The Cold War had begun, and the House Un-American Activities Committee was formed. The International Monetary Fund was established. The air force became a separate branch of the military. Witnesses claimed a UFO sighting in Roswell, New Mexico.

The year began with *B. F.'s Daughter* by J. P. Marquand still at #1. Throughout January it was #1 on the bestseller list, followed by *East River*, *The Miracle of the Bells*, *Pavilion on Women*, and *Green Grass of Wyoming*. *Lydia Bailey* by Kenneth Roberts, #4 on January 26, rose to #1 on February 2 and remained there through March. *Gentlemen's Agreement* by Laura Z. Hobson rose to #1 on April 27. On May 25 it was still #1, followed by *The Vixens* by Frank Yerby and *Lydia Bailey*. John Steinbeck's *The Wayward Bus* entered the list at #4. These books were joined on the list by *There Was a Time* (#3) and *The Big Sky* (#4) on June 8. On June 29, *Gentleman's Agreement* at #1 was followed by *Kingsblood Royal* by Sinclair Lewis, which was #1 for two weeks in early July 1947.

On August 3, *The Moneyman* by Thomas B. Costain appeared on the list, and it surpassed Lewis's novel in the #1 spot on August 17, 1947. This was Costain's second historical novel to achieve that. *The Moneyman* was the story of Jacques Coeur, who was a merchant and moneyman for King Charles VII in fifteenth-century France. Samuel Shellabarger's *Prince of Foxes* was #2 on August 24. These novels remained #1 and #2, respectively, on the list into September. The historical novel continued to be a popular genre. *House Divided* by Ben Ames Williams, a lengthy and powerful Civil War novel, was #3 on October 5, and it became #1 on November 16 and remained in that spot throughout December. Marcia Davenport's *East Side, West Side* became #2. *Came a Cavalier* by Frances Parkinson Keyes was #3, and *The Moneyman* was #4. Much further down the list, at #11, was John Steinbeck's little gem *The Pearl*.

While readers were interested in history and in historical fiction, they were also interested in finding a sense of inner peace after years of war. *Peace of Mind* led the nonfiction list in January. It was followed by *The Roosevelt I Knew*, *The Egg and I*, and *The Plotters*. In March, *Peace of Mind*, at #1, was joined by the *Information Please Almanac* at #2. These books stayed in the top places on the list through March 30. Readers were also interested in *An Essay on Morals* by Philip Wylie and *Human Destiny* (#2 on May 18). George Edward Morgenstern's *Pearl Harbor* was on the list at #6, and *The Lincoln Reader* by Paul M. Angle was #7. *Pressure Cookery* by Leone Rutledge Carroll was #9. James Burnham's *The Struggle for the World* noted other pressures. *A Study of History* by Arnold Toynbee appeared at #6 on April 20 and rose to #3 on May 18. *Peace of Mind* was #1 and *A Study of History* was #2 on June 1 and through June 22. John Gunther's *Inside USA* replaced *Peace of Mind* at #1 on June 29 and July 6. *Inside USA* (1947) is one of three John Gunther books that reached the bestseller list. Gunther gives his readers facts about America, its people, and its leadership. His book appears to attempt to demonstrate what America's values and purposes are following the war.

The Common Book of Child and Baby Care* by Benjamin Spock, published in July 1946, became an influential guide for the baby boom era. In *Just Getting There: An Autobiography*, a physician, Lloyd Duncan, recalls reading Benjamin Spock's book on baby care: "I bought Dr. Spock's book, read it, and then threw it away."[29] Duncan certainly kept his Easton Press leather volume set of 100 Greatest Books, however. He recalls that when he was young his family had the One Volume Library that his mother brought home one day.[30] Besides this, the family had one reference book, as well as *The Adventures of Tom Sawyer* and a copy of *Hans Brinker and the Silver Skates* that he "read over and over."[31] In elementary school Duncan was drawn to history books: on the Alamo, or World War II aircraft.[32] As an adult this taste for history, biography, and the social sciences, rather than fiction, persisted.[33]

Some families sat side by side in their homes, reading. Anne Rotholz, interviewed years later, thought of her childhood at home: "One distinct memory I have is of sitting by the fire reading. My father would be reading; my mother would be reading, reading by the firelight." H. Boyd Woodruff said, "So, I always loved reading and in fact got into trouble lots of times with it, because, back in those days, we didn't have any electricity yet in our area." Marion Pinsdorf from Teaneck, New Jersey, recalled her family: "I mean, we were all readers and we would decide who would buy which book and then we'd circulate it around and we used the library a lot." Her comment reminds us that in families there were usually multiple readers for a single book. Frieda Finkelstein Feller commented: "We'd play cards, nothing exciting. We'd read a lot. I can remember spending summers reading at Osborne Street Library. I think we read everything there." Herbert Gross of New Jersey recalled his father: "He was always reading and reading." Mr. Gross was primarily reading on history and politics.[34]

Inside USA and *Peace of Mind* remained among the top books on the bestseller list through October. On November 2, William Shirer's *End of a Berlin Dairy* was #5. *Inside USA* was #1 on November 9 and James F. Byrnes's *Speaking Frankly* was #2. *Peace of Mind* was #3. On December 14, *Speaking Frankly* was #1, followed by *Inside USA, Peace of Mind,* and Roger Butterfield's *The American Past.* General George S. Patton had the #6 book on the bestseller list during the holiday season, and *The Fireside Book of Folksongs* by Margaret Bradford Boni was a valuable holiday gift for families that was #8 on the list. Christmas brought a blizzard in which 26.4 inches of snow fell on New York City.

Kingsblood Royal by Sinclair Lewis is a story that examines the difficulties of a man who believes he was born as a white man and then finds out that he also has some "Negro blood." In the spirit of *Elmer Gantry* and *It Can't Happen Here,* he again investigates one of the persistent problems in American society: racial prejudice. A reader from New Jersey, John Berglund, recalled: "Oh, I read Sinclair Lewis's *It Can't Happen Here.* I had to say 'This is a book. It's only a book.'"[35]

House Divided by Ben Ames Williams reveals that Abraham Lincoln's distant relatives and in-laws do not like his policies. The Civil War erupts around them. This story of Southern gentry entangled in the Civil War is perhaps one of the great "forgotten" books of the twentieth century. Williams also gathered and edited Mary Chesnut's *Diary from Dixie.* He wrote the popular bestseller *Leave Her to Heaven,* a mystery thriller, and he was among the most popular writers of the 1940s. The Mississippi-born Ben Ames Williams absorbed stories of the Civil War during his childhood. He was often read to by his mother, who was a niece of Confederate general James Longstreet.

1948

The Civil War historical epic *House Divided,* #7 on the *Publishers Weekly* list for 1947, began 1948 at #1 on the bestseller lists. In 1948 the Democratic Party divided, and the Dixiecrats decided to make a stand in the Truman-Dewey presidential election, fielding a candidate of their own: Strom Thurmond. On February 1, *House Divided,* at #1, was followed by Marcia Davenport's *East Side, West Side* (#2), *Came a Cavalier* (#3), and *Raintree Country* (#4) by Ross Lockridge. *East Side, West Side* reached #1 on February 8, 1948. It was #9 on *Publishers Weekly*'s 1947 list, and its strength in the market persisted into 1948. On February 22, the same books appeared in the top four. Mary Roberts Rinehart's mystery, *A Light in the Window*, was #5. Truman Capote's *Other Voices, Other Rooms* was #7 on the list.

From March 7 through March 21 *House Divided* continued to lead the bestseller list. *East Side, West Side* was #2 and *Raintree Country* was #3. *Eagle in the Sky* by Van Wyck Mason was #4. The historical novel rose to the #1 position on March 7, 1948. This story was set during the American Revolutionary War. The fourth volume of his tetralogy, 1780–1781, it featured the stories of four medical doctors. Mason produced nearly sixty books: novels, nonfiction, and biography. Yet, reputations fade. Books fall out of print. Quantity does not necessarily equal quality or guarantee that one's books will last the test of time. On the other hand, Thornton Wilder's *The Ides of March* and many of his other works have stood the test of time. Wilder, who won the Pulitzer Prize for both fiction and drama, may be considered one of America's significant men of letters. *The Ides of March* was his fifth novel: a historical novel that is set in the months before the assassination of Julius Caesar. It is partly an epistolary novel, since it makes use of the devices of letters, documents, journals, and reports to tell the story. *The Ides of March* by Thornton Wilder became #1 on April 4. *Raintree Country* was #2 on that day and became #1 on May 2.

Elizabeth Goudge's *Pilgrim's Inn* reached the top five during April. It reached the #1 spot on May 23, 1948. It was her second #1 bestseller of the 1940s. Goudge's novel stayed at #1 for three weeks, from May 23 through June 13, before being overtaken by the climb of Norman Mailer's *The Naked and the Dead*. Goudge's family story of the Eliots features the matriarch Lucilla, who oversees the family as they buy the Pilgrim's Inn. In England, her book was called *Herb of Grace*. In some respects, it seems like a distant precursor to *Downton Abbey*. Frank Yerby's *The Golden Hawk* was #2 on June 6, but it dropped lower on the list when the next blockbuster appeared.

Norman Mailer's *The Naked and the Dead* reached #2 on the list on June 13. Mailer's novel topped the bestseller list on June 20, 1948. It stayed there through August. *The Naked and the Dead* was a stirring novel about the Second World War, set in the region of the Pacific in and near the Philippines. It was as much a character study of men and human dignity, of power and military bureaucracy, as it was of the pressures of the war on the psychology and lives of his cast of characters. Roland Winter of Perth Amboy said bluntly, "*The Naked and the Dead* is bullshit. Norman Mailer was never over there." He added that he "had no taste for it . . . it's all a novelist's imagination." Robert L. Hoen of Maplewood had a different view: "I liked that book, Norman Mailer. . . . After a while I got sick of silly war movies."[36]

Meanwhile, readers were treated to books by Taylor Caldwell (*Melissa*, #3 on August 1), Evelyn Waugh (*The Loved One*, #2 on August 1), Graham Greene (*The Heart of the Matter*, #5 on August 15) and A. J. Cronin (*Shannon's Way*, #2 on August 29, rising to #1 in September). A. J. Cronin's *Shannon's Way* was his third #1 bestseller of the 1940s. It edged into the top spot on September 5, 1948, and remained on top of the list for three weeks before Mailer's novel again seized #1. *Shannon's Way* follows the story of a man who feels rather forlorn and like he has gotten off track in life. Meanwhile, the world slips into war. Mailer's novel was #1 on October 10, 17, and 31. On November 7 the #1 bestseller was *The Young Lions*, Irwin Shaw's energetic novel about three men involved in the Second World War. *The Naked and the Dead* was #2 and returned to #1 for one week on November 21. *Remembrance Rock* by Carl Sandburg was #3. (It did not appear as a top bestseller on the *Publishers Weekly* fiction list.) Shaw's novel was #1 on December 1. Then Lloyd Douglas's *The Big Fisherman*, his sequel to *The Robe*, became #1 on December 19. It remained in that position, followed by *The Young Lions* (#2), *Dinner at Antoine's* (#3), *The Naked and the Dead* (#4), and *Remembrance Rock* (#5) at the end of the year. *Publishers Weekly* listed *The Big Fisherman*, *The Naked and the Dead*, and *Dinner at Antoine's* as the top three bestselling fiction books of the year.

In nonfiction, James F. Byrnes's *Speaking Frankly* was #1 in January 1948. The former secretary of state provided his memoirs of the Second World War. (Byrnes served in many government roles: as congressman, senator, Supreme Court justice, and secretary of state.) *Inside USA* was #2. *Peace of Mind* returned to #1 on March 7 and March 14. The *Information Please Almanac* was #2, followed by #3. The famous Kinsey study, *Sexual Behavior in the Human Male*, entered the list at #4. On April 11 this was the #3 book on the list. It reached the top of the bestseller list on

May 23, 1948. A. C. Kinsey, Wardell Pomeroy, and Clyde E. Martin led a team of researchers based in Indiana who provided scientific findings. The study remained on the bestseller list for the entire year. Their subsequent study *The Human Female* also reached the bestseller list a few years later, in the early 1950s. Sales for *Peace of Mind* remained strong, and it returned to #1 on June 6. *The Kinsey Report* was #2 and Kenneth Clark's *Civilization* was #3. Also on the list appeared historian Charles Beard's *Roosevelt and the Coming of the War* (#6) and *The Goebbels Diary* by Louis Lochner (#8), *Peace of Mind* at #3, and *The Kinsey Report* at #4.

The United States recognized the new nation of Israel on May 14. Readers of self-help books in 1948 continued to be encouraged by Rabbi Joshua Lieberman's *Peace of Mind* and by Reverend Norman Vincent Peale's *A Guide to Confident Living*. Dale Carnegie advised on *How to Stop Worrying and Start Living*, which became a #1 bestseller. His earlier book *How to Win Friends and Influence People* was one of the most popular books of the period. It has proved to be a lasting classic and the source of what might be called self-development or human potential workshops. His sequel rose to #1 on August 2, 1948. The book held that spot for fourteen weeks and was high on the list for the next six months. The success of the Dale Carnegie, Joshua Liebman, and Norman Vincent Peale books, the top four on *Publishers Weekly*'s list, suggest that readers were seeking inner peace after years of global conflict.

Despite Dale Carnegie's advice against worry, a disturbing story underlined the nation's new anxieties about nuclear war. The *New Yorker*'s publication of Shirley Jackson's "The Lottery" in June 1948 led to the most mail from readers than had ever received by that magazine in response to one of its articles or stories. Jackson's biographer Ruth Franklin says that the author kept them in a scrapbook that is today in the Library of Congress. Among those letters is one from Caroline Green of New Milford, Connecticut, who wrote: "Gentlemen, I have read 'The Lottery' three times with increasing shock and horror. . . . Cannot decide whether [Jackson] is a genius or a female and more subtle version of Orson Welles." The reference is likely to Welles's 1939 radio broadcast of the *War of the Worlds*: an invasion scare that the public responded to with apprehension and uneasiness. Other letters were more critical.[37]

The Palomar telescope was completed in California on June 3. Women entered the air force on June 12. June 24 brought the blockade of

Berlin by the Soviets; this occurred during the same time as the Republican National Convention in Philadelphia. The city also hosted the Democratic National Convention from July 12 to 14. President Truman introduced a peacetime draft on July 20. Idlewild Field was dedicated in Queens, New York, on July 31. It would later be renamed as John Kennedy International Airport in the 1960s. In August, the House Un-American Activities Committee confronted Alger Hiss and Whitaker Chambers, leading to the indictment of Hiss on December 15. A pensive and melancholy figure appeared in Laurence Olivier's *Hamlet*, which opened in movie theaters in the United States on September 29. In baseball, the Cleveland Indians defeated the Milwaukee Braves in the World Series. Serious readers began to explore Thomas Merton's biography *The Seven Storey Mountain*, published on October 11. Harry S. Truman was re-elected as president on November 2.

George Orwell's *1984*, which critiqued totalitarian oppression, appeared high on the bestseller list. *All the King's Men* by Robert Penn Warren centers on the life of Jack Burden, who investigates the sources of his own life, family history, relationships, and the political world of his boss. These classic works by Orwell and Penn Warren rode high on the *Times* bestseller list but neither reached #1.

The Second World War was documented for readers in Winston Churchill's six-volume series that began with *The Gathering Storm* (1948). Every subsequent book in the series was on the bestseller list. Dwight Eisenhower wrote *Crusade in Europe*, his war memories, which jumped to the #1 spot on December 26, 1948, within one month after publication. The Eisenhower book appeared as #1 on *Publishers Weekly*'s nonfiction bestseller list. Book buyers also read playwright Robert Sherwood's *Roosevelt and Hopkins*. On December 19, 1948, Sherwood's history of the president and his chief advisor reached #1. Sherwood, who served the government with the Office of Information, worked from Hopkins's papers and documentary records. He also wrote the Academy Award–winning screenplay for the film *The Best Years of Our Lives*.

East Side, West Side by Marcia Davenport imagined the life of a woman who is both Irish and Jewish. Unfortunately, she is married to a well-off man from a notable family who likes to play around and engage in affairs. Davenport was a musician, the daughter of opera singer Alma Gluck and violinist Efrem Zimbalist. Her first book was a biography of Mozart.

The Young Lions by Irwin Shaw was a bestseller toward the end of the year. Born in the Bronx, Shaw attended Brooklyn College and became a playwright and screenwriter, as well as a novelist. Shaw's play *Bury the Dead* (1936) was about soldiers who had died but whose spirits insisted upon staying alive. His next play, *Quiet City* (1939), fell quiet after two performances. Shaw served in the military in Europe and wrote propaganda scripts. Following the war, he continued writing film scripts and fiction. *The Troubled Air* (1951) concerned McCarthyism and anti-Communism. Shaw was placed on the Hollywood blacklist, and he left the United States to live in Europe. While overseas, he adapted Eugene O'Neill's *Under the Elms*, and he wrote many short stories. Among his novels were *Lucy Crown* (1956) and *Two Weeks in Another Town* (1960). Shaw is best remembered for his bestseller *Rich Man, Poor Man* (1970), which became a television series in 1976.

Never Love a Stranger by Harold Robbins, his first bestseller, demonstrated that sex sells. His first novel was written because he believed that he could write something more compelling than the scripts that he was reading. The titillating seductions in his stories and his lifestyle would later become models of hedonism. He was born as Francis Kane and orphaned; he was renamed Harold Rubin and raised by a Jewish family. He worked as a shipping clerk for Universal Pictures in New York and then moved to Los Angeles. Like the Hollywood scripts he read, *Never Love a Stranger* (1948) is a melodrama. It was a rags-to-riches story with some traces of obscenity and a few X-rated scenes. Harold Robbins next wrote *The Dream Merchants* (1949), about the movie industry. *The Carpetbaggers*, one of Robbins's biggest bestsellers, is filled with feisty characters and ranges from New York to California. Robbins might be considered the first in a line of sex and glamour culture potboiler writers that include Danielle Steel, Jackie Collins, and Judith Krantz. Cynthia White and Michael Korda were his editors. In the *L.A. Times*, Elizabeth Venant refers to Robbins as "the icon of sleaze." She observes that in *Piranhas* he drew "violence and sheer meanness in human nature" with the sharp attention of "a cartoonist."[38]

1949

The bestselling novel of 1949, according to *Publishers Weekly*, was *The Egyptian* by Mika Waltari. *White Collar Zoo* by Clare Barnes was at the top of *Publishers Weekly*'s nonfiction list. Serious readers turned to George Orwell's *1984*, or to the monk Thomas Merton's *The Seven Storey Mountain* and *The Waters of Siloe*. *Publishers Weekly* listed *The Seven Storey Mountain* at #3 in nonfiction for the year, after *How to Win at Canasta*. The bestselling nonfiction book of 1949 on the *Times* list was *Cheaper by the Dozen*, an account of a family with twelve children. Frank and Ernestine Gilbreth's story charmed readers and made them laugh. It was also a story appropriate for the age of the baby boom, which arose in full force after the war. *Cheaper by the Dozen* remained at #1 for two consecutive months. Biblical stories were also popular; *The Greatest Story Ever Told* was written by Fulton Oursler, an editor at *Reader's Digest*. This story of the life of Jesus followed the success of Lloyd Douglas's *The Robe* and later became a motion picture. *The Big Fisherman* by Lloyd Douglas was #1 from January to June. *Publishers Weekly* and the *New York Times* also listed *Mary* by Scholem Asch, *Dinner at Antoine's* by Frances Parkinson Keyes, and *High Towers* by Thomas B. Costain.

In 1949, J. P. Marquand's *The Point of No Return* was at #1 for twenty-two consecutive weeks. The novel spent thirty-four weeks in the top fifteen. *Publishers Weekly* placed it in the fifth position on their end-of-year list. John O'Hara's *Rage to Live* became #1 for six weeks. It was *Publishers Weekly*'s #4. The #1 on that list, *The Egyptian* by Mika Waltari, was a historical novel that was originally published in the Finnish language in 1945. Naomi Walford's translation of the story appeared in Britain and the United States in 1949. Meanwhile, parents continued to purchase copies of Dr. Benjamin Spock's advice on baby care, making that book one of the top-selling books of the day. Other people sought books that would enhance their card game. As canasta became a popular trend, they bought copies of *How to Win at Canasta* and *Canasta: The Argentinian Rummy Game* (1949). The postwar years brought the rise of the paperback book and growth for the publishing industry. In the 1950s, the rise of television promoted celebrity. Historians can point to the paperback revolution and to the increase in textbook production with the GI Bill that followed the war. In his book on bestsellers, Michael Korda suggests that readers in the 1940s and 1950s "welcomed a challenge." They were able to look at America's flaws.[39]

The Egyptian by Mika Waltari is set in Egypt in the reign of Pharaoh Akhenaten in the Eighteenth Dynasty. The story dates back to the Twelfth Dynasty. Waltari's play on Akhenaten staged in Helsinki was a source for his novel. In his story Sinuhe is the pharaoh's physician, and critics have said that King Suppilulluma is much like Hitler. Nefertiti and King Tut also are memorable figures within the dynasty. Waltari wished to respect Egyptology and write history accurately. Of course, he also had to dramatize his story. The book was a bestseller in 1949 and the top "foreign" novel in the United States.

3

THE 1950s

Cold War Anxiety: From Holden Caulfield to James Bond

America created suburban culture in the 1950s. Towns grew in population with the construction of new homes, tree-lined streets, roads, and stores. In schools, children practiced air raid drills, huddling and squirming under desks in impossible poses for implausible safety from the atom bomb. In a Nevada desert the hydrogen bomb was tested. It detonated in a fireball and thrashed sand and disintegrated land for three miles in all directions. It was a new age of anxiety.

1950

On January 5, 1950, in his State of the Union address, President Harry S. Truman called for national health insurance and raising the minimum wage. He spoke on the federal budget at a press conference two days later. On January 31, he announced development of the hydrogen bomb. Across the nation people were reading Mika Waltari's *The Egyptian*, which remained at #1 throughout January and much of February. It was overtaken at #1 in February by Daphne du Maurier's *The Parasites*. Eleanor Roosevelt's *This I Remember*, at #1 on January 15, contributed to the tone of nostalgia with her post–White House recollections. On that same Sunday, television broadcast *Meet the Press* and *The Perry Como*

Show. While television had entered homes across America, so had the paperback book and the hardcover selections of the Book of the Month Club. The BOMC circulated more than seven million books, Alice Payne Hackett points out in the introduction to *70 Years of Bestsellers* (1967).[1] The Literary Guild distributed 8.8 million.

Books from the 1950s can be found today in libraries, tucked away and forgotten in the corners of older homes, or stacked in rows at garage sales. In his essay "Personal Matters," John Updike describes how, at the church book fair, he would sneak between the bestsellers of Anne Tyler and Leon Uris and his own books. Updike describes how he would wander from table to table amid the discarded bestsellers of yesteryear: those of John P. Marquand, Thomas B. Costain, A. J. Cronin, Mary Ellen Chase, Pearl Buck, Frank Yerby, John Gunther, and Hendrik Willem van Loon "and those innumerable others who, in the long middle of our finally terminating century, studded the best-seller lists and the sun porches, bedrooms and dens of the local bourgeoisie." He remarks that the book business has attempted to imitate the well-financed glamour of films, television, and the music business. However, in the book business the important factor is the books themselves: "the humble, durable husks or dregs of the reading experience."[2]

For fiction readers, the reading experience sometimes provided a diversion from the news of the day. However, those imaginative stories also carried the tone and mood of the era. By 1950, tensions between the United States and the Soviet Union had escalated. On January 21, 1950, Alger Hiss, who had been accused of spying for the Soviet Union, was sent to prison for perjury. Weeks later Britain jailed Klaus Fuchs, a physicist, for selling nuclear secrets. The Sino-Soviet Pact was signed in February, making China and the Soviet Union allies. Julius and Ethel Rosenberg were charged with passing atomic secrets to the Russians and sent to Sing Sing prison to await execution. In Wheeling, West Virginia, on February 9, 1950, Joseph McCarthy (R-Wisconsin) declared that there were Communists in the government. He held up a piece of paper that was purportedly a list of 205 Communist sympathizers who, he said, were known to the State Department. There was no such list. However, McCarthy's assertion contributed to an era of Cold War anxiety. Westerns, detective stories, spy novels, and science fiction bore traces of that anxiety and tension.

On March 5, 1950, people were reading Harry Overstreet's *The Mature Mind*, a pop psychology tour of the way in which socialization shapes people's thoughts and behavior. Overstreet asserted that there are specific characteristics of maturity. His book spent nine weeks at #1. On the fiction list, Samuel Shellabarger's historical novel *The King's Cavalier* held on to the third spot on the fiction list into March. *The Wall* by John Hersey then shot quickly up the bestseller list to #1 by the end of that month. *The Wall* is the fictional account of life and struggle in the Warsaw ghetto told by a quirky Jewish man who maintains a documentary record of the actions and conversations of the inhabitants. Henry Morton Robinson's *The Cardinal* became the next #1 fiction bestseller at this time. Robinson's book was published both in hard cover and paperback and remained high on the list into the summer months.

Developments in science fascinated many readers, and so did the unsubstantiated dreams of pseudoscience. Immanuel Velikovsky, in *Worlds in Collision*, claimed that a comet that hit the earth changed human history. The comet had traumatized the planet, paralyzing it and stopping its natural rotation. Velikovsky theorized that Jupiter experienced an explosion and Venus was projected across space past Earth. According to Velikovsky, several miracles could be explained away by this phenomenon. Many scientists found the view to be preposterous; an astronomer at Harvard, Harlow Shapley, read Velikovsky's essay "Cosmos without Gravitation" and dismissed it. Physicists asserted that they were unable to reconcile Velikovsky's ideas with Newtonian celestial mechanics. From the perspective of the religious community, his claims seemed both fantastic and improbable. The writer's given name was also curious, religiously minded critics said, since such the position he was taking would tend to disprove the coming of Emmanuel. Yet, this book spent eleven weeks on the bestseller list. The book was published on April 3, and by May 7 it was at #1. It remained at that position throughout the summer. Carl Sagan later remarked that Velikovsky's ideas were not original or correct. *Scientists Confront Velikovsky* appeared in 1977. Sagan expanded upon his position in his bestselling book *Broca's Brain* and later in his PBS series and book *Cosmos*.

While readers had their attention riveted upon outer space, *The Egyptian* by Mika Waltari continued to appear in the top five of the bestseller list with Gwen Bristow's *Jubilee Trail*. *The Horse's Mouth* by Joyce Cary began to enter the top ten on the list. In the top six, *The Wall* and *The*

Cardinal were joined by Kathleen Winsor's *Star Money*. Nelson Algren's *The Man with the Golden Arm* had just entered the top fifteen.

The Korean War began on June 25, 1950, when the North Koreans streamed across the thirty-eighth parallel into South Korea. The United Nations approved a resolution to protect South Korea. President Harry S. Truman sent American troops to halt the North Korean invasion. He did so without congressional authorization. When General Douglas MacArthur engaged his forces in a strategy to foil the North Korean advance, China attacked, decimating American troops and forcing them back south of the thirty-eighth parallel.

In summer 1950, sociologist David Reisman's book *The Lonely Crowd* was circulating its message that America's middle class was "other-directed" and alienated. Reisman asserted that people were living conforming lives rather than independent ones fostered by inner beliefs and values. Readers made this serious study a bestseller. Meanwhile, into middle-class homes, television brought Milton Berle, George Burns and Gracie Allen, *What's My Line?*, and a variety of other game shows. On the radio listeners heard Frank Sinatra singing and Nat King Cole singing "Mona Lisa."

John Gunther's *Roosevelt in Retrospect* attained the highest position on the bestseller list on July 9, 1950. *Courtroom*, a biography of Judge Samuel Liebowitz written by attorney Quentin Reynolds, also drew reader interest and earned the top spot August 27. In fiction, Robert Penn Warren's *World Enough and Time* rose to #2 the first week in September. Henry Morton Robinson's *The Cardinal* maintained its #1 position. Princess Elizabeth and Princess Margaret were featured by their governess Marion Crawford in *The Little Princesses*. While her book was far from the tell-all Princess Diana story in 1997–1998, some critics complained that Crawford was invading the privacy of the royal family and the princesses.

By October 8 American readers were turning their attention from outer space and princesses to the adventures of Thor Heyerdahl in *Kon-Tiki*. The Swede navigated across the ocean in a raft to support the claim that ancient people from South America could have sailed to Polynesia. This powerful adventure tale was one of the most popular nonfiction works of the era. It was #5 on *Publishers Weekly*'s yearly list, following a popular cookbook, a baby book, and a health book. On October 15, Ernest Hemingway's *Across the River and into the Trees* was #1 on the fiction list. It remained at #1 through November 26. Hemingway, by this time, was a celebrity. His *The Old Man and the Sea* entered the bestseller list September 14, 1952, at #13. (It rose as high as #3 on the list but did not surpass Thomas B. Costain's *The Silver Chalice* or Herman Wouk's *The Caine Mutiny*, the top fiction bestsellers of 1952.)

With an interest in health and fitness, readers were also turning to Nutritionist Gayelord Hauser's *Look Younger, Live Longer*. Of course, readers would have to stop reading the book long enough to exercise more. Hauser's health-conscious text advocated a diet that called for increasing vitamin B and reducing sugar and flour intake. Born in Germany, he had to contend with tuberculosis in childhood and learned that developing a positive attitude and a healthy regimen of exercise, mineral baths, and herbal remedies was crucial in the process of healing. He became a consultant to Hollywood celebrities and an active self-promoter and publicist for natural healing.

At the end of the year, Budd Schulberg's novel *The Disenchanted* rose to the top of the fiction list, where it remained throughout December. Schulberg wrote the screenplay for the 1954 film *On the Waterfront* with Marlon Brando. *The Disenchanted* sold 70,000 copies via bookstores and 225,000 when book club copies are included in the total. *Joy Street* by Frances Parkinson Keyes, published in December, was at #2 in December and rose to #1 on January 14, 1951. This story of a wealthy couple in Boston that welcomed people of different backgrounds into their house stayed at #1 for eight consecutive weeks. *Publishers Weekly* placed the book at #2 on the 1950 list. Sales for the year totaled 140,285, according to Alice Payne Hackett's records.[3] James Jones's World War II book *From Here to Eternity* took over the #1 spot on March 25 in 1951.

Publishers Weekly listed Henry Morton Robinson's *The Cardinal*, Frances Parkinson Keyes's *Joy Street*, Ernest Hemingway's *Across the River and into the Trees*, and John Hersey's *The Wall* as the top four novels of the year. *The Cardinal* sold 588,400 copies and *The Wall* sold 104,000 copies, according to Alice Payne Hackett's records. She points out that Hersey's novel was promoted by the Book of the Month Club, which sent out as many as 230,000 copies.[4] *Betty Crocker's Picture Book* with 300,000 in bookstore sales and *The Baby* were #1 and #2, respectively, on *Publishers Weekly*'s 1950 list.

1951

The Catcher in the Rye by J. D. Salinger was published in 1951. The story of Holden Caulfield addressed teenage angst and alienation in plainspoken, rough language and offered a sharp rejection of phoniness. Herman Wouk's *The Caine Mutiny* and James Jones's *From Here to Eternity* recalled scenes from military service in the Second World War. Onstage, Rodgers and Hammerstein's *The King and I* featured Yul Brunner. Lucille Ball appeared in *I Love Lucy* on television; the show attracted a large audience and suggested the aspirations of young women across the country. On April 11, 1951, President Truman relieved General MacArthur of his command. The general had set his sights on attacking China if North Korea and China did not sit down for talks to resolve the war. Rather than expanding the war, Truman focused upon containing the fighting and moving toward a settlement.

Recalling the Second World War, Herman Wouk's *The Caine Mutiny* took the #1 spot on August 12. Wouk's novel and Jones's novel alternated atop the list for the rest of the year. *From Here to Eternity* spent twenty weeks at #1, and *The Caine Mutiny* more than doubled that number, spending forty-eight weeks at #1, into 1952. J. D. Salinger's *The Catcher in the Rye*, Nicholas Monserrat's *The Cruel Sea*, and J. P. Marquand's *Melville Goodwin* all were popular bestsellers. *The Catcher in the Rye* appeared at #14 on July 29, quickly rose into the top ten, and held strong at the #4 spot for most of the autumn. It was not in the year's *Publishers Weekly* top ten. Of course, it became a classic novel, one more often read in later years than most of the other novels on the bestseller list in late 1951. *The Cruel Sea* was at #2 from September 30 through the end of the year. The novel sold about seventy thousand copies. James Michener's *Return to Paradise* was in the top five bestsellers at this time. William Faulkner's *Requiem for a Nun* entered the top ten. William Styron's *Lie Down in Darkness* was also in the top ten during the autumn. On October 3, sports fans in New York heard an ecstatic radio announcer react to Bobby Thomson's three-run home run in the ninth inning of a game against the Dodgers by repeating, "The Giants win the pennant!" Graham Greene's *The End of the Affair* appeared in the top five in December. Mika Waltari returned to the bestseller list with *The Wanderer*, and Scholem Asch also returned to the list with *Moses*. *From Here to Eternity* was *Publishers Weekly*'s #1, followed by the *Caine Mutiny* at #2.

The Catcher in the Rye (1951) by J. D. Salinger is a coming-of-age novel in the voice of an alienated teenager. In *The Catcher in the Rye*, Holden Caulfield, the first-person narrator, writes in crisp, flippant language from an institutional setting where he deals with his sense of alienation. We are brought back to Pencey Preparatory Academy, a boarding school. Holden's story unfolds in a stream of consciousness recollection of episodes in his life.

Salinger's last published story was "Hapworth 16, 1924," which appeared in the *New Yorker* in June 1965. In a documentary and book, David Shields and Shane Salerno assert that Salinger left instructions for publication of five different works he had written. In his daughter Margaret Salinger's memoir *Dream Catcher* (2001), she says that her father showed her a vault where he kept his manuscripts.[5] So far, nothing has emerged from the vault into publication. In 1986, J. D. Salinger filed a lawsuit to block Ian Hamilton's biography *J. D. Salinger: A Writing Life* and to prohibit any use of his letters in his biography. Hamilton wrote that the reclusive writer would walk each day to his concrete structure where he would write.

In *Letters to J. D. Salinger*, Chris Kubica and Will Hochman provide a path into helping us to understand how common readers responded to the author's fiction. Several readers remark that they related personally to Holden Caulfield. One reader concludes that *The Catcher in the Rye* didn't help him to grow up. "It mirrored my frustration," he says. At the age of fifty-five he picked up Salinger's stories again.[6] Another reader confides that his cousin David recommended the book. He writes with honesty about his loneliness and depression, listening to punk rock and reading Salinger.[7] "Lone wolves communicate at a distance," a reader wrote to Salinger, insisting that he respected the writer's privacy.[8] Perhaps this reader recognized what Elizabeth N. Kuria, in her doctoral dissertation, called "the plea for silence" in Salinger's fiction.[9]

1952

In 1952, Dwight D. Eisenhower ran for the presidency. Richard Nixon, the vice-presidential candidate, told the nation about his campaign finances. Appearing on television immediately after *The Milton Berle Show*, Nixon gave his "Checkers" speech in which he referred to his

black-and-white family dog. Checkers was the only campaign contribution that he had kept, he said. The Eisenhower-Nixon ticket was elected
into office that autumn, defeating their Democratic opponent Adlai Stevenson in a landslide vote. America evidently sought the security that a
celebrated general with a Republican agenda might provide; the public
placed their confidence in Eisenhower. Country star Hank Williams sang
"Your Cheatin' Heart." In American homes, *Ozzie and Harriet* and *Drag-
net* appeared on the television.

   U.S.A. Confidential by Jack Lait and Lee Mortimer was atop the nonfiction list in spring 1952. It sold two million copies. *Publishers Weekly*
placed it as #3 on their list of 1952 bestsellers. The book's fortunate rise
to #1 on April 27 rested upon the success of their previous book, *Washington Confidential*, which sold some 227,130 copies. Lait and Mortimer
were journalists, and their book might be best understood within the
context of the early 1950s. A contemporary reader is likely to find much
of it not only politically incorrect but insensitive. Their aim, obviously,
was to expose the nasty underbelly of Washington politics and affairs and
to sell a lot of copies of their book. They typecast "commies, clip joints,
easy women" with their own gutter brand of racism and misogyny. They
claimed to investigate philanderers, scheming lawyers, deceitful diplo-
mats, and moneymen. They mocked men in Washington whom they iden-
tified as gay. In their chapter "Garden of the Pansies," some of their
comments are homophobic: "With more than 6,000 fairies in government
office you may be concerned about the security of the country." Perhaps
one might be more concerned about the insecurities and prejudices of Lait
and Mortimer. The authors asserted that lobbyists aimed at committee
chairs and congressional leaders. The authors said that lobbyists made use
of local "hostesses," who set up parties for them so that they could gain
access to these key members of Congress. They quickly characterized
some of the power brokers, like Burton Wheeler and the IRS man Joe
Nunan. Abe Fortas and his legal partners were the men to go to for
business with the Department of the Interior. One might also work to
persuade Leon Henderson, who made things happen in Washington and
then could be seen "making a fool of himself with some young blonde"
on a dance floor in New York.[10] More recently, Jake Tapper's political
thriller *Hellfire Club* (2018) has provided a more nuanced view of Washington in the 1950s. There is scandal and intrigue in his novel. However,

Tapper's turn toward fiction, unlike *Washington Confidential*, portrays political egos without prejudice.

Daphne du Maurier's *My Cousin Rachel* spent eight weeks at #1 on the fiction list, beginning on March 30, 1952. The novel was #4 on *Publishers Weekly*'s 1952 bestseller list. Du Maurier was one of the best-selling authors of the era. *Rebecca*, published before the *New York Times* bestseller list was created, would clearly have been a #1 novel. It received an additional boost from the award-winning Alfred Hitchcock film. *My Cousin Rachel*, her historical mystery-romance, is set in Cornwall in England. This was her third #1 novel. In this story, Ambrose Ashley owns an estate in Cornwall and has a nephew Philip to whom he is the guardian. Ambrose travels to Florence, Italy, where he meets cousin Rachel and marries her. However, his letters home to Philip indicate that he has become ill. When Ambrose dies, Philip is heir to the estate. Rachel arrives on a ship at Plymouth, and she begins living at the estate. A letter by Ambrose is found by Philip that raises the question of whether Ambrose died in suspicious circumstances. He lives at the estate with Rachel and thinks that she may have poisoned her husband. Richard Burton and Olivia de Havilland acted in the film adaptation, which appeared later in 1952.

Through much of the first months of 1952, Herman Wouk's *The Caine Mutiny* and James Jones's *From Here to Eternity* continued to be widely read and distributed. Sales of 240,000 copies of Jones's novel and 236,000 of Wouk's novel are recorded by Alice Payne Hackett.[11] The sales of *The Caine Mutiny* pushed it to #2 on *Publishers Weekly*'s fiction bestseller list for the year. By the autumn, Thomas B. Costain returned to the bestseller list with *The Silver Chalice*. This historical novel tells the story of Basil, who created and shaped the chalice that would hold the cup that Jesus drank from at the Last Supper. *The Silver Chalice* was the #1 fiction book on *Publishers Weekly*'s 1952 bestseller list. It sold 221,000 copies. *The Caine Mutiny* was #2 with sales of 189,000 copies. John Steinbeck's *East of Eden* was #3, which sold 140,000. Ernest Hemingway's *The Old Man and the Sea* was #7 on *Publishers Weekly*'s list.

On June 22, 1952, the #1 nonfiction book was *Witness*, Whittaker Chambers's story of spying, secret documents, and the trial of Alger Hiss, the former undersecretary of state. Chambers's memoir became the nation's #1 bestseller on June 22 and stayed there for thirteen weeks. Attracted by Marxism, Chambers joined the Communist Party in 1925 and was recruited as a spy. He was disturbed by Stalin's purges and began to turn away from Communism. He joined *Time* magazine in 1939, writing his first article on James Joyce's *Finnegan's Wake*. Chambers later became fiercely anti-Communist and editor of the *National Review* from 1957 to 1959. *Witness* was #9 on the annual *Publishers Weekly* nonfiction list.

While political intrigue, the war story genre, and the mystery romance of du Maurier all attracted much reader interest, the trend of religious topics also remained strong with *The Cardinal*, *A Man Called Peter*, and Scholem Asch's *The Apostle*. The years 1948–1949 had brought *The Big Fisherman*, *The Seven Storey Mountain*, and *The Greatest Story Ever Told*. September 1952 brought *A Man Called Peter*, Catherine Marshall's recollection of her life with her husband, the chaplain of the United States Senate, who had died. This was a meditation from a Christian writer. The book gradually climbed to the #1 position on the nonfiction bestseller list, remained there for five weeks, and stayed on the list for quite a long time. Catherine Marshall's biography offered an appreciation of her husband Peter's dedication and commitment and an account that readers could share in their own quest for a meaningful life. This was a story of faith in which Catherine Marshall had to retrace some difficult memories and emotions, including recalling her husband's death. However, those recollections are among the most affecting parts of her book. The celebrity story of Tallulah Bankhead was the next nonfiction bestseller that autumn. It rose quickly to #1 on October 26 and remained there for sixteen weeks. *The Sea around Us* by Rachel Carson sold 167,181 in 1951 and 105,795 according to *Publishers Weekly* records consulted by Alice Payne Hackett. [12] It was #6 on its nonfiction list in 1951 and #4 on the list in 1952.

John Steinbeck's *East of Eden*, one of his most enduring novels, also made use of a biblical story—that of Cain and Abel—as a basis for his story. The Trask family is troubled, and the Hamilton family is more stable. Steinbeck weaves together their stories. *East of Eden* became the #1 book in the country on November 2, 1952. The novel spent eleven weeks as #1 and remained high on the bestseller list into 1953. *Publishers Weekly* listed *East of Eden* as the #3 fiction bestseller.

The Silver Chalice by Thomas Costain (1952) was one of Costain's top-selling historical novels. In his grail story, Costain includes biblical figures: the apostles Luke and Peter, Joseph of Arimathea, and Simon

Magus who flies above the crowd in the Acts of the Apostles. A discovery by archaeologists in Antioch of a chalice set this story in motion in Costain's mind. His protagonist, Basil, a silversmith, is asked to make a holder for the cup by Joseph and by Luke. The story begins after the death of Jesus. Basil, who has been adopted by a wealthy man, loses his stepfather, is cheated by his uncle, and becomes a slave. He learns the art of the silversmith and he becomes a freeman. He is then asked by Luke to create a cover for the chalice. Joseph of Arimathea hires Basil and encourages this making of the chalice cover. Basil travels to meet the apostles, who are now preaching at diverse locations across the ancient Mediterranean world. Costain's novel was in the top spot or second spot on the *New York Times* bestseller list from September 7, 1952, to March 1953. It remained on the list for sixty-four weeks.

Casino Royale by Ian Fleming (1952) introduced James Bond to readers of popular fiction. Fleming's James Bond stories were fantastic commercial successes in the United States and Britain during the Cold War. *Casino Royale* (1952) stirred reader interest in Bond: a dashing agent of M16 who became one of the bestselling fictional spies of all time.

Ian Fleming's father was a member of Parliament for Henley. His mother was Evelyn St. Croix Rose. He studied at Eton and anticipated service in the Foreign Office and studied in Europe. During World War II he was brought into Naval Intelligence as an assistant to the director John Godfrey. Fleming thought up schemes to use against the enemy. He served with the British Office of Strategic Services. He created a commando unit in 1942 and was involved with Operation Overlord. He started writing his James Bond novels after 1950; *Moonraker* is built upon his awareness of Target Force efforts to find engines to be used in the German V-2 rocket. Fleming managed a newspaper group after the war.

Bond stands for qualities that are different from those of his adversaries. Will the hero wrest free and achieve the objective or fall under the shadow of a dark power? Bond overcomes the monster and foils conspiracies that threaten Britain, the West, or the world. Bond saves the damsel in distress with her double-entendre name. The energetic bravado of the hero tends to obscure his treatment of women as fantasy objects that are as disposable as Bic razors. For Bond, in the classic novels of the 1950s, "M" tends to be a father figure. Bond is that surface figure who does not develop depth through the course of the novels or films.

Ian Fleming's last complete James Bond adventure was *You Only Live Twice*. Once married, Bond sees his wife murdered and the next day he falls apart. Blofeld is in charge of a vast terrorist organization called SPECTRE, and "M" calls upon Bond to confront them. In Japan, the collector of death in a poisonous garden is Blofeld. Bond travels to a dark and mysterious place and on to a fishing village, a Shinto priest, and Kissy Suzuki, who was once an actress in Hollywood. Bond travels to her Japanese village and then back to that sinister garden where death and destruction and the villainous Blofeld await. He is reported to be dead, but he is not, for Suzuki has rescued him for another day. Prone to amnesia, Bond sees the name Vladivostok and somehow knows that he must leave for Russia.

Bond is a hero on behalf of his country. He is "a type of policeman who essentially is forced on a quest against mythical beasts," says Clive Bloom. In the Cold War, with British prestige in decline "amid spy scandals and the debacle of Suez," James Bond provided imaginative relief. The only thing that seemed predictable about Bond was that he would win the day. While promiscuous, he was, says Bloom, a hero who was tied to an older, supposedly stable "Edwardian life of class snobbery" in a universe that was "deeply conservative and tied to a nostalgic vision of history as heroic myth."[13]

1953

World affairs were reported to Americans in newspapers and on television in 1953. The death of Soviet leader Josef Stalin, the appointment of Marshal Tito in Yugoslavia, and earthquakes in the Greek isles were all on the front page. The Soviets put down a strike and riot in East Germany by using tanks and military troops. The American CIA arranged to replace Mohammad Mossadegh with the Shah Reza Pahlavi in Iran. Edmund Hillary and Tenzing Norgay climbed the heights of Mount Everest. In the world of theater, Samuel Beckett created *Waiting for Godot* and Arthur Miller critiqued McCarthyite "witch hunts" with *The Crucible*. James Baldwin published *Go Tell It on the Mountain*. The first issue of *Playboy* appeared with a centerfold of Marilyn Monroe, from a photo taken of her in 1949. Film actor Marlon Brando starred in *The Wild One* and in *Julius Caesar*.

Maurice Herzog's *Annapurna* was at #1 on February 22, 1953. This was a nonfiction account of climbing one of the highest mountains in the world. *The Power of Positive Thinking*, filled with its own encouragement of human aspirations, took over the #1 spot. Norman Vincent Peale's encouragement to think positively would make his book a lasting bestseller. Polly Adler's *A House Is Not a Home* and works by philosopher George Santayana, monk Thomas Merton, and statesman Adlai Stevenson were all in the top five in February and March of that year.

Desiree by Annemarie Selinko was arguably the strongest fiction bestseller of 1953. Her story illustrates the life of an enchanting silk merchant's daughter who became engaged to Napoleon and later married one of his generals, Bernadotte. The novel became an international bestseller and a feature film. Desiree's allure is obvious, and her story, perhaps, caught the romantic aspirations and hopes of the novel's readers. This novel by a previously unknown author, a woman from Vienna who lived in Denmark, swept past Steinbeck's *East of Eden* and Thomas B. Costain's *The Silver Chalice* to spend thirty-two weeks atop the bestseller list. (*Publishers Weekly* recorded *Desiree* at #3 after *The Robe* and *The Silver Chalice* on its 1953 list.) Leon Uris's *Battle Cry*, Ernest Gann's *The High and the Mighty*, and the stories of J. D. Salinger also appeared in the top five during this period. (*Battle Cry* was #4 on *Publishers Weekly*'s fiction list overall.) The mystery of a man's discovery of his father whom he thought was dead appears in A. J. Cronin's *Beyond This Place*, which rose to #1 on October 11. The father is in prison, accused of murder. His son tries to exonerate him from the charges against him. With *Lord Vanity*, an adventure story, Samuel Shellabarger returned to the top of the bestseller list November 29. His historical fiction was set in the eighteenth century. Lord Vanity was the illegitimate child of a wealthy member of the nobility who had to find himself and make his own way. Postwar Americans were doing just that: finding their way amid the new opportunities of the fifties.

In 1953, the #1 nonfiction bestsellers included the Holy Bible, Revised Standard Edition (RSV), which was on the list for more than a year, and *The Power of Positive Thinking* by Norman Vincent Peale, one of the bestselling books #1 books of all time. Reverend Peale drew continually from the Christian scriptures and from Hebrew scripture in his encouraging self-help book. It was initially called "The Power of Faith" and was retitled by Peale's editor Myron Boardman. Reportedly, Dr. Peale did not have a lot of faith at first in the book, and his wife insisted that he get it published for the sake of his readers. *The Power of Positive Thinking* reached #1 on May 17, 1953. It stayed at #1 through 1953 and 1954 into 1955 for a total of ninety-eight weeks. *Publishers Weekly* placed it at #2 on its 1953 list, following sales of the Bible (RSV). Elmer Davis's *But We Were Born Free* dislodged *The Power of Positive Thinking* for two weeks, April 28 into early May, by asserting the power of positive freedom, liberty, and patriotism. Davis claimed that politicians opposing Communism in the McCarthy era were affecting American freedoms. *A Gift from the Sea* by Anne Morrow Lindbergh overtook Dr. Peale's book at the #1 spot on April 17, 1955, and spent forty-six weeks at #1. *Publishers Weekly* recorded *The Robe* and the Bible as the #1 books of the year.

1954

In *Brown v. Board of Education* in 1954, the Supreme Court ruled against the "separate but equal" policy of racial segregation. Chief Justice Earl Warren wrote the opinion: "We conclude that in the field of public opinion the doctrine of separate but equal has no place. Separate educational facilities are inherently unequal." This momentous decision occurred in the same year that British writer William Golding's *Lord of the Flies* cautioned about aggression, violence, and group behavior among children in his story set on an island.

Readers could turn to fantasy. J. R. R. Tolkien's *The Lord of the Rings* appeared with the publication of *The Fellowship of the Ring*. They could turn to television, which brought *Father Knows Best*. Or, they could turn to music. This was the year of Elvis Presley's first single, which was recorded in Memphis. Musicians played at the first Newport Jazz Festival.

The year 1954 brought Morton Thompson's *Not a Stranger*, another story of a young man's of growth and development. In his story, the protagonist becomes a doctor and then has to maintain his marriage. This novel intersected with a trend in medical interest in the media and with the strong emphasis upon marriage and family that developed in the 1950s. *Publishers Weekly* listed the novel as the #1 bestseller for the year. Daphne du Maurier again returned to the bestseller list. *Mary Anne* was her story of Mary Anne Clarke, who was a mistress to the son of George

III, Frederick, the Duke of York. This was both a coming-of-age story and a historical novel. It participated in both of these successful trends: the historical setting, as in Costain and Shellabarger, and the story of a strong female protagonist's growth to maturity and influence, as in Selinko's *Desiree*. Du Maurier's new novel was a fictionalized biography, and it made for intriguing summer reading. It was #2 on *Publishers Weekly*'s 1954 fiction bestseller list.

In the autumn, Irving Stone's *Love Is Eternal* ascended to #1. The story inquired into the relationship between Mary Todd Lincoln and Abraham Lincoln. Irving Stone's inclination toward fictionalized biography would later bring forth his #1 novel about Michelangelo, and his bestseller *Lust for Life*, the story of Vincent van Gogh. Stone's story of the at times unhappy marriage of the sixteenth president and his wife reached the #1 spot on October 17, 1954, and was at #1 for eleven weeks. *Love Is Eternal* became the #3 fiction bestseller on *Publishers Weekly*'s list for the year. Hamilton Basso's *The View from Pompey's Head* gave readers the story of a lawyer who goes home to the South to solve a case. One might consider the book a precursor to the legal thrillers of John Grisham, who was born the next year.

The mid-1950s, the Eisenhower years, were somehow caught in between the age of anxiety and the power of positive thinking. Concern about Communism and the atomic bomb met with the growth of the suburbs, advertising, and what Eisenhower would later call the military industrial complex. It was a time of the organization man, television, increasing specialization in research and development, and a continuing baby boom. The Bible and *The Power of Positive Thinking* were again the #1 and #2 nonfiction bestsellers on the *Publishers Weekly* list.

1955

In 1955, Rosa Parks courageously refused to move from her seat on a bus in Montgomery, Alabama. Her act was a powerful symbolic assertion of civil rights. Sloan Wilson published *The Man in the Flannel Suit*, casting an image of business conformity. (His book was #5 on *Publishers Weekly*'s nonfiction list for the year.) The AFL-CIO was formed as the two labor organizations merged. Jonas Salk's vaccine for polio went through an array of experimental trials. Bill Haley's "Rock around the Clock" initiated an era of rock and roll. The Gallup Poll asked Americans if they were reading books at the present time. In 1937, some 27 percent of respondents had said that they were. Gallup's 1955 poll indicated that 55 percent of the people surveyed had read a book in the past six months.

Novelist J. P. Marquand had recently written *Sincerely, Willis Wayde*, his fourth #1 bestseller. It was another novel that focused attention on the life and development of a self-made man: a millhand whose enterprising skill and effort transforms him into a business executive running a large corporation. Trading on the Horatio Alger story, *Sincerely, Willis Wayde* charted the rise of this Fortune 500 company CEO. It was a fictional version of a testament to business success like Lee Iacocca's bestselling autobiography or Donald Trump's *The Art of the Deal*. On April 10, 1955, the novel reached #1 and, selling briskly, it remained there for six weeks.

On May 22, Francoise Sagan's *Bonjour Tristesse* translated into English a young Frenchwoman's story. When she was eighteen, Francoise Quoirez was unable to get into the Sorbonne because she had not passed an entrance examination. She redirected her energy into creating this story in which a girl tries to keep her father from remarrying and damages his relationship with the woman he would marry. Published under the pen name Sagan when Francoise Quoirez was twenty, the novel became a smash bestseller in the United States and in England. It was atop the *New York Times* bestseller list for twelve weeks, from May 22, 1955, through the summer.

Something of Value by Robert Ruark took the #1 spot for two weeks, July 3 and July 10. America readers were looking outward to the world, this time toward Africa. The newspaper columnist had lived and worked on the African continent, and his novel brought his readers to Kenya. In this story an English boy and his African friend confront the Mau Mau uprisings and experience adventures. *Auntie Mame* was more domestic but perhaps even more feisty. Edward Everett Tanner chose the pen name Patrick Dennis and gave readers this well-drawn picture of a woman of ample personality. *Mame* would become a Broadway hit in years to come. It reached #1 on the fiction bestseller list on August 28, where it remained throughout September. The novel was #2 on *Publishers Weekly*'s bestseller list overall. On October 2, Herman Wouk's *Marjorie Morningstar* rose on the horizon. Wouk's other fiction bestsellers—*The Caine Mutiny, The Winds of War, War and Remembrance*—all had military characters and contexts. This novel is the story of a Jewish girl. It begins with her experiences as a teenager and brings us through her relationships and love affairs to her life in the suburbs. Wouk's devotion to his own Jewish roots later led to his development of a nonfiction bestseller on Jewish life and Judaism. *Publishers Weekly* listed Wouk's novel as #1 on its 1955 fiction bestseller list.

1956

On New Year's Day 1956, the disturbing tale of *Andersonville* by McKinley Kantor was #1 on the fiction bestseller list. This Civil War novel traced the story of the Georgian man who provided the land for one of the war's most notorious prisons. Kantor, who wrote for newspapers and magazines, researched and wrote at length about the prisoners of Andersonville. His novel was another big book about the Civil War, a topic that has had perennial interest among American readers. Along with numerous historical accounts, from Douglas Southall Freeman's *Lee's Lieutenants* to Bruce Catton's *A Stillness at Appomattox*, Civil War novels have been an enduring part of American literature, from those of Albion Tourgée and Stephen Crane to Margaret Mitchell's *Gone with the Wind*, Shelby Foote's *Shiloh*, John Jakes's *North and South*, Gore Vidal's *Lincoln*, and prize-winning novels by Michael Shaara and Charles Frazier. *Andersonville* was #3 on *Publishers Weekly*'s 1956 fiction bestseller list.

The most stirring book of the year for some readers was Edwin O'Connor's *The Last Hurrah*. It is a bit surprising that this story of American politics has faded from view. The environment of Irish American city politics was worth taking into account in 1956 when Senator John F. Kennedy first considered a bid for the White House and Adlai Stevenson became the Democratic candidate for the second time against Dwight Eisenhower. On March 25, 1956, this novel reached the #1 spot, and it spent twenty weeks atop the bestseller list. *The Last Hurrah* was #2 overall on *Publishers Weekly*'s 1956 bestseller list.

The Birth of Britain, Winston S. Churchill's first volume of his four-volume *History of the English-Speaking Peoples*, was the #1 bestseller on May 27, 1956. It was Memorial Day in America and Churchill's World War II series, beginning with the #1 bestseller *The Gathering Storm*, had been among the *New York Times* bestsellers since 1948. This series showed signs of becoming another huge success. Churchill was not only a well-known statesman, he was a fluent and compelling writer, as Jonathan Rose has shown in *The Literary Churchill*.

Of course, health remained a concern that supported a long shelf life for books on diet, exercise, and health care. Dale Alexander wrote *Arthritis and Common Sense*, and his nutrition and exercise plan reached the #1 spot on July 15. The book was widely distributed to health food stores as well as to bookstores. However, Robert J. Donovan's *Eisenhower: The Inside Story* soon arrived at the top of the nonfiction list. Eisenhower's war memoirs, *Crusade in Europe*, had already been a #1 bestseller in December 1948 and January 1949. Now Eisenhower, seeking a second term in office, cooperated with Donovan's "insider" collection of documents, and this new campaign biography topped the list.

On October 21 the nonfiction list saw the rise of Kathryn Hulme's *The Nun's Story*. This book told the story of her friend, a pre–Vatican II Catholic nun who found her lifestyle in a Belgian convent too rigid and decided to leave the convent after seventeen years as a devoted religious sister. Readership for religious topics and curiosity about this nun's experiences and decisions remained strong, and this book remained for fifteen weeks at #1.

Nuns do not seem to have a lot to do with *Peyton Place*, however, and that notorious bestseller of sex and adultery was the blockbuster of late 1956 and 1957. *Peyton Place* was twice at #1 for extended periods. Grace Metalious's steamy near-X-rated soap-opera drama revealed what lay behind surfaces of a New England town's life. Bawdy and racy enough to attract attention and hold interest, *Peyton Place* underscored the fact that sex and violence were ingredients in a spicy mix that could sell remarkably well and find its way to the screen. *Peyton Place* seized reader interest in 1956 with Grace Metalious's assertion of the independent woman and her suggestion of scandal. Some sixty thousand copies of the novel were sold in the first ten days after publication. *Peyton Place* was *Publishers Weekly*'s #3 in 1956 and #2 in 1957.

On the nonfiction bestseller list, *The Organization Man* by William Whyte told a story about American society and the business organization. Americans heard the news that actress Grace Kelly had married Prince Rainier of Monaco and had become a princess. On the movie screen, Charlton Heston became Moses and Yul Brunner became the Pharaoh in

The Ten Commandments. John F. Kennedy's *Profiles in Courage* was published. Americans saw Elvis Presley on *The Ed Sullivan Show*, and they listened to Harry Belafonte's calypso songs on their radios. Suburban homes welcomed Teflon cookware, Crest toothpaste, Pampers diapers, and blue-green Comet cleanser. Overseas in Europe there were crises in the Suez Canal that involved Egypt, France, Britain, and Israel. In Hungary, Soviet tanks crushed a rebellion. The soap operas *The Edge of Night* and *As the World Turns* began on television. Don Larsen pitched a perfect game for the New York Yankees in the World Series.

Peyton Place (1956) was Grace Metalious's blockbuster bestseller. After its fifty-nine weeks on the bestseller list it became a cultural catchphrase signaling the sexy and the scandalous. *Peyton Place* served as the basis for a film in 1957, a television series from 1964 to 1969, and a soap opera from 1970 to 1974. In the novel three women seek to rediscover their personal identities. The story critiques hypocrisy and class and privilege and tells a tale of lust, murder, adultery, and abortion. *Peyton Place* traces back to 1937 and proceeds across the years of the 1940s. Constance MacKenzie has an illegitimate daughter named Allison. Selena Cross, her employee, is a working-class woman whose life has been troubled by incest. (In earlier drafts of the novel she sought to kill the perpetrator: her stepfather. Kitty Messner, an editor, called for a change of this in the story.) Constance goes to New York City from her New England town and she meets Allison MacKenzie, a man with whom she has an affair. When their daughter, Allison's namesake, is born, she tries to make her appear legitimate by altering records. Nellie marries Lucas Cross when Selena Cross is born. Selena is not his child. He has a son named Paul who accuses Lucas of taking his money. Nellie and Lucas live with Selena in "the shacks": a poor part of town. When Selena is fourteen, Lucas abuses her, and she becomes pregnant. A doctor performs an abortion and urges Lucas to leave town. Nellie hangs herself. The novel suggests that the surfaces of life in the town hide its ills. In this respect the town is like that of Sherwood Anderson's *Winesberg, Ohio*, in which the young reporter George Willard interviews individuals with troubled and twisted lives. *Peyton Place* lifts those character quirks to a higher level of passion and intrigue.

The Last Hurrah (1956) by Edwin O'Connor is a political novel that focuses on city politics. A film adaptation starring Spencer Tracy returned it to the bestseller list. The story appears to have been suggested by the political activities of Boston mayor James M. Curley, an Irish American political boss who held strong sway of the city. Mayor Curley and the city of Boston are never mentioned in the novel. *The Last Hurrah* was a Book of the Month selection and a selection of *Reader's Digest*. This novel focuses effectively on city politics and political campaign strategy in the 1950s: a kind of politics and contact with the electorate that has changed since. Frank Skeffington is a machine politician. He was previously the state's governor, and he is again running for mayor. He is a seventy-two-year-old man of many personal flaws. While he has been politically successful in the past, some members of the party wonder if he should run for reelection. Kevin McCluskey is a new political candidate, and he will be Skeffington's opponent in the election. McCluskey, a handsome World War II veteran, is inexperienced in politics and without much of a political strategy. Adam Caulfield, a cartoonist for a local newspaper, is Skeffington's nephew. Maud Caulfield is his wife; Maud's father, Roger, is critical of Skeffington. A friend of Adam's says that the election is going to be "the last hurrah" for the style of politics that Skeffington represents. U.S. public life has changed, and now television ads have become important. So is media presence, something Skeffington lacks. Amos Force, a Protestant city newspaper owner, opposes Skeffington; so does the cardinal. Sam Weinberg, an aide to Skeffington, worries that the former governor may lose this election. Ditto Boland is a political hanger-on and lackey. He imitates everything that Skeffington does, including his voice and his manner.

1957

About 4.3 million Americans were born in 1957. They were among the twenty-nine million children of the baby boom. Dr. Seuss stimulated childhood reading beginning with *The Cat in the Hat* in 1957. Daphne du Maurier returned to #1 on March 24, 1957, with *The Scapegoat*. This romance-mystery was her fifth #1 bestselling novel. It unseated *Peyton Place* from the #1 spot for fourteen weeks. *Peyton Place* then surged back to #1. The success of du Maurier's novel may be attributed both to her talent and her notoriety. Perhaps as much as any other writer of the 1950s, Daphne du Maurier's name recognition meant brisk sales. Readers knew that they could expect interesting, well-rounded characters and an often mysterious or romantic plot. In this story, an Englishman meets with a man who is his double. He not only looks like the man, he is forced to adopt the man's life and to become him.

That September, James Gould Cozzens returned to the bestseller list with *By Love Possessed*, a novel that would be awarded the Pulitzer Prize. *Guard of Honor* had been a bestseller in 1948, and Cozzens had begun *By Love Possessed* in 1949. He set the novel aside while working on other projects and returned to it in the mid-1950s. His story focuses upon forty-nine hours in the life of a lawyer and, as the title suggests, deals with his love life. It reached #1 on September 22, 1957. Cozzens's *By Love Possessed* remained in the top five through April 20, 1958, slipping to #6 the next week. *Publishers Weekly* listed it as the #1 best-selling novel of the year. It sold 217,000 copies.

In nonfiction, in February 1957 Donald Whitehead's *The FBI Story* brought attention to the Federal Bureau of Investigation. The agency was then under the tight rule and oversight of J. Edgar Hoover, who approved of the book and wrote the foreword. (Hoover's own book, *Masters of Deceit*, was the #1 bestseller one year later in early May 1958.) After *The FBI Story*'s seventeen weeks on top of the nonfiction bestseller list, a book of recent history replaced it at the top spot. Walter Lord's *The Day of Infamy* looked back to Pearl Harbor. He attempted to trace the action by Americans and the Japanese that led to the invasion that precipitated America's entry into the Second World War. Meanwhile, Jim Bishop appealed to that strong readership for religious fiction with his dramatic narrative *The Day That Christ Died*. He would later write similarly on the Lincoln assassination. This book made use of biblical accounts to follow the course of the day upon which Jesus was crucified. The book reached #1 on June 23, 1957, and spent seven weeks at #1. The increase of advertising in American society was featured in Vance Packard's *The Hidden Persuaders*. Packard's research investigated this trend, explored the uses of psychology and sociological research by advertisers, and tapped considerable reader interest in this topic. Packard's third #1 best-seller reached the top of the list on August 4, 1957. Clearly, the American reading audience was attuned to the thought that more was going on than met one's eyes. From FBI investigation and McCarthy red-baiting and the notion of hidden spies, to the hidden lusts of *Peyton Place* and *The Hidden Persuaders* of advertising, readers were looking at the world undercover and the world under the covers.

So maybe it was also time for an autobiography from a great financier. *Baruch: My Own Story* was presidential advisor Bernard Baruch's popular account of his life and his work. The book appeared at #1 on September 22, 1957, and remained there for nineteen weeks. In volume 1, Baruch discusses his rise to success on Wall Street and his role in the Woodrow Wilson administration and as advisor to other presidents. Volume 2 of his autobiography followed. Baruch wrote these memoirs when he was in his eighties. He completed his account of his life when he was eighty-seven years old.

Something lighter soon sparked reader interest: *Please Don't Eat the Daisies*. Jean Kerr made people laugh with her stories of being a stay-at-home mom with four boys. Her book sold about 107,000 copies. As a playwright, Jean Kerr developed an ear for sharp and convincing dialogue. She was one of the first in a line of humorists, from Bob Hope in the 1940s to Erma Bombeck in the 1990s, who have cheered readers. In 1960, *Please Don't Eat the Daisies* became a film with Doris Day and David Niven. It became an NBC television sitcom from 1965 to 1967, featuring the Nash family in Ridgemont, New York. During that time Jean Kerr and her husband lived in Larchmont, New York.

In 1957, Ayn Rand would have been able to compose her novel *Atlas Shrugged* on a portable Smith Corona typewriter. Brooklyn Dodgers fans were heartbroken as their team announced a move to Los Angeles. The New York Giants would be moving too, to San Francisco. Teenagers danced to the music on *American Bandstand* with Dick Clark; Jerry Mathis was the central character on *Leave It to Beaver*; and Raymond Burr solved cases as Perry Mason. Significantly, the Russian Sputnik launched the space race on October 4, 1957.

By Love Possessed (1957) is James Gould Cozzens's Pulitzer Prize–winning novel, published in August 1957. Cozzens was always interested in professionals: in lawyers, judges, or military men. The story takes place across two days, with flashbacks into the past to fill in information for us about the protagonist and his relationships with the other characters. Arthur Winner, an attorney, married the daughter of his father's legal partner. Hope died in giving birth to their child. He is currently married to Clarissa, his daughter's tennis coach, but his attention wanders. Arthur tells his wife Clarissa that he simply does not know how to love. He has an affair with the wife of Julius Penrose, his legal business partner. Meanwhile, he insists that his son Warren become a lawyer. He is at work on the probate of the estate of Michael McCarthy and a case in the arrest of Ralph Detweiler for rape. McCarthy's investment in the trolley went bankrupt because of the wide availability of cars. Detweiler is in trouble. The pastor of an Episcopalian church has asked Arthur to help supervise the church.

1958

Explorer Edmund Hillary reached the South Pole on January 3. Sputnik, returning from space, dissolved in the atmosphere upon reentry on January 4. Cuban revolutionaries captured Havana on January 8. On January 13 nuclear scientists issued a petition for a ban on nuclear arms testing. The following week, Sam Cooke performed for five nights at Club Elegante in Brooklyn. In February, baseball star Ted Williams signed a contract for $135,000 with the Boston Red Sox, becoming the highest-paid player in the game. Photographer David Attie began photographing Truman Capote for a montage for his novel *Breakfast at Tiffany's*. In one photo we see Capote standing beside a winding spiral staircase. A white banister curves around behind him like the curve of a dress.

On the weekend of March 7–9, *Anatomy of a Murder* was #1 on the fiction bestseller list. This novel about a murder investigation was written by Michigan Supreme Court judge John Donaldson Voelker, who used the pen name Robert Traver. He set his story in northern Michigan. This was one of the first bestsellers for St. Martin's Press. It was a huge bestseller in its day and spent twenty-nine weeks at #1. *Publishers Weekly* listed it at #2 overall for the year. In mid-March a blizzard cast a cloak of white snow across the Northeast. At the Ninety-Second Street Y in Manhattan, the Alvin Ailey Dance Theater gave their first performance.

Published in the United States on August 18, 1958, after being banned elsewhere, Vladimir Nabokov's *Lolita* was controversial. The story of Humbert Humbert's obsession with a female who was only twelve met with resistance from censors from 1955 to 1959. Bookstores and libraries refused to carry it. France banned it. Yet, it found its way to the bestseller list. Nabokov was a fine writer, even if he puzzled some readers with this novel, or with unreliable narrators in some of his other novels. *Lolita* was #3 on *Publishers Weekly*'s 1958 fiction list.

Other books took readers' imaginations around the world. Thor Heyerdahl's *Aku-Aku* was a bestselling fiction book published by Rand McNally, better known for maps and geography. Following the success of *Kon-Tiki*, this story introduced readers to the exotic location of Easter Island. Heyerdahl later wrote another raft-travel adventure that depicted a journey from Egypt to the Caribbean Sea. *Inside Russia Today*, John Gunther's third #1 book in his "Inside" series, reached the top of the bestseller list on July 6, 1958. Readers were invited to travel with Gunther and to reflect on politics after Stalin. Herbert Hoover's study of Woodrow Wilson held the #2 spot. *Only in America* by Harry Golden moved up the list to #1 on September 21. Golden applauded American ingenuity in his essays. As a Jew in the American South, he edited the *Carolina Israelite*. His book drew a lot of attention, and it was discovered that he had previously been in jail for mail fraud. He served his term, and his reform was attested to by Adlai Stevenson and the poet Carl Sandburg.

The year 1958 concluded with the enduring bestseller *Dr. Zhivago* by Boris Pasternak. A physician-poet is married but has a romance with another woman. Set during the Russian Revolution and written in the Soviet Union, Pasternak's novel was first published in Italy and then translated into English and published in the United States. It rose to #1 on November 16, 1958, and stayed in that position into the next year. Boris Pasternak won the Nobel Prize. However, he was pressured to refuse the prize. *Dr. Zhivago* remained #1 through November. *Publishers Weekly* listed the novel as the #1 bestseller of the year. *Lolita* was #2, selling more than three million copies in paperback. Leon Uris's *Exodus*, his story of the Jews of Europe, was selling briskly.

Lolita by Vladimir Nabokov was published in the United States in summer 1958. It continued to be banned for obscenity in England and France until 1959. The novel explores Humbert Humbert's obsession with a twelve-year-old coquette, Dolores Haze. He becomes her stepfather, and their contact leads to a sexual affair. He uses the name Lolita when he recalls her in his memoir. The story emerges through Humbert's perspective. He has been focused upon young girls ever since the death of Annabel, his teenage girlfriend. Holding this peculiar obsession, he has a breakdown and is hospitalized. After this he moves to the United States. When a widow named Charlotte Haze rents a room to him, his attention turns to Charlotte's daughter, Lo, or Lolita. In his diary he begins to write about his fantasies about her.

1959

In 1959, Leonid Feldman walked into a park warily, under the cover of night. It was eleven o'clock. From the shadows came a man who handed him a briefcase. "Take a taxi and go home," the man said. Feldman sensed that there was danger. Now that he had a copy of Leon Uris's *Exodus*, a book about the Israeli struggle for independence, he felt a kind of pride mixed with unease. Feldman was told by the stranger that he should return the book, "finished or not," at a specific time. Ira Nadel tells this story in his biography on Uris, and it sounds like a scene out of a John le Carré novel. Uris's novel *Exodus* begins in British-occupied Cyprus with survivor refugees and proceeds to the 1948 formation of Israel. The fictional ship *Exodus* carries 4,500 Holocaust-displaced refugees to the Holy Land.

In January 1959, Alaska became the forty-ninth state. Hawaii followed on August 21. In Cuba, Fidel Castro's guerrillas forced Fulgencio Batista to resign. February 3 was the day the music died, as a plane carrying Buddy Holly, Richie Valens, and J. P. Richardson (the Big Bopper) went down in Iowa. Artist Alexander King's *Mine Enemy Grows Older* was #1 on April 12, 1959. King became a television personality, promoting his books on Jack Paar's *Tonight Show*. He had been a *Life* editor who nearly undid his own life as an addict. He wore a bow tie and regularly spoke about his past drug habit, ill health, marriages, and affairs. King's *May This House Be Safe from Tigers* became a #1 bestseller on March 13, 1960. King's bohemian antics may have suggested the emergence of a more significant trend. The bohemian critique of society emerged in the sociology of C. Wright Mills and in the work of the Beat poets. Among the most famous of these works were Ginsberg's *Howl* (1956), Jack Kerouac's *On the Road* (1957), and William Burroughs's *Naked Lunch* (1959). During the summer, Vance Packard's *The Status Seekers* was #1. Packard explored class structure in the United States. His book became #1 on June 14, 1959, and stayed at #1 for seventeen weeks. Harry Golden also returned to #1 on September 13 with *For 2 Cents Plain*. It contested for sales on the bestseller list with his book *Only in America* and with James Thurber's *The Years with Ross*. Moss Hart's *Act One*, his compelling and sometime hilarious autobiography, was #1 on November 11, 1959. It was #5 on *Publishers Weekly*'s nonfiction list.

On May 17, Leon Uris's novel *Exodus* became #1. *Publishers Weekly* placed it at #1 on its 1959 fiction bestseller list. Uris was a correspondent during Arab-Israeli conflict in 1956. He researched Israel extensively by traveling there often, reading numerous volumes, and interviewing people. Uris focused his story on Palestinian agent Ari Ben Canaan, whose father Barak heads the Jewish agency for Palestine, and an American nurse, Kitty Fremont. Ari Ben Canaan has planned to transport Jewish refugees to Palestine on the *Exodus*. The love of his life, Dafna, was raped and murdered by Arabs. Her name becomes the name of a youth village, which is important in the story. The novel was an international bestseller, and it attracted further sympathy and support for the state of Israel. Director Otto Preminger's film starred Paul Newman as Ari Ben Canaan.

Allen Drury's *Advise and Consent* was the great political novel of its time. The U.S. president has selected his nominee for secretary of state, who has to go through confirmation hearings. A senior senator opposes his confirmation. The novel reached #1 on October 4, 1959, and spent thirty weeks as #1 on the bestseller list. It maintained its position at #2 during 1960. *Advise and Consent* was #4 on *Publishers Weekly*'s 1959 fiction bestseller list.

Richard Nixon (in July) and Nikita Khrushchev (in September) exchanged state visits and engaged in a debate. As if that were not strange enough, this was the year that Rod Serling created *The Twilight Zone*, which had its debut on October 2. Larraine Hansberry's *A Raisin in the Sun* won the Drama Desk Award. Charlton Heston was back on the film screen in *Ben Hur*, and Rodgers and Hammerstein produced their hit musical *The Sound of Music*. The Guggenheim Museum opened in New York. American girls got their first Barbie dolls. *Dr. Zhivago* by Boris Pasternak was #2 on *Publishers Weekly*'s 1959 bestseller list. Hawaii became the fiftieth state, and James Michener's *Hawaii* was a huge bestseller. Michener's *Hawaii* held the #1 spot into 1960 for forty-eight of the fifty-two weeks of the year. It was #3 on *Publishers Weekly*'s 1959 bestseller list and #2 on its 1960 list, following *Advise and Consent*.

Advise and Consent (1959) concerns the Senate confirmation hearings of Robert Leffingwell for secretary of state. The Cold War context is clear. Concerns circulate that Leffingwell has been a Communist Party member and that such a past orientation may have an impact upon Robert Leffingwell's decision-making. In the United States Constitution, Article

II, Section 2, clause 2 states that the president will nominate his cabinet members and appoint ambassadors with the "Advice and Consent of the Senate." Drury offers his readers a novel about protecting American democracy against a perceived Communist threat. There is a warning that liberalism may contribute to a climate in which Communism insidiously sneaks into the fabric of American life.

Drury's characters may have been composites drawn from his imagination as well as reflection upon the public behavior of U.S. senators like Alben Barkley, Robert Taft, or Joseph McCarthy. Indeed, Senator Fred Van Ackerman reflects some of the characteristics of McCarthy and his goal to root out Communist influences. Franklin Roosevelt and Harry S. Truman appear to be models for Drury's president and vice president. In Drury's story, the president names his potential secretary of state in order to seek a friendly rapport with the USSR. However, Seabright (Seab) Cooley of South Carolina doubts Leffingwell, and the nomination process stalls. Cooley discovers Gelman, who says that twenty years earlier Leffingwell, while a professor at the University of Chicago, invited him to join a Communist organization. However, Gelman is found guilty of perjury and his testimony is disregarded by chairman Brig Anderson of Utah. At this point it appears that the nominee may be approved. Cooley investigates Gelman's testimony and tries to determine the identity and background of James Morton, a figure in this dilemma. The president is irritated by the investigation and pressures the Senate majority leader Robert Munson to encourage Brig Anderson and the party toward compliance. There is an issue of blackmail as a press photo suggests a homosexual relationship during the war. The president ignores Leffingwell's past and will use the photo to keep Brig Anderson quiet. Senator Fred Van Ackerman, a scoundrel, is given the photograph, and he uses it to discredit Anderson by revealing his secret to Anderson's wife and to the press. Anderson commits suicide. Still, Leffingwell's confirmation hangs in the balance.

That the revelation of a homosexual relationship would completely derail a politician's standing and prompt his suicide seems to date this novel a bit. The McCarthy-like suspicions and backroom politics in this novel are features of its time. However, investigations of issues concerning the Russians continue to be part of the politics of our own time. In August 1959, the *Saturday Review* observed the power of this political novel and wrote: "It may be a long time before a better one comes along."

Richard Newberry, in the August 1959 *New York Times*, wrote: "Rarely has a political tale been told with such vivid realism." *Advise and Consent* spent 102 weeks on the bestseller list.

Exodus by Leon Uris was published in 1958 and became a huge bestseller in 1959. Uris was the historical novelist who also wrote *Trinity* (1976), his story of Ireland, and suspense novels like *Topaz*. His father was a Polish immigrant from czarist Russia who was a paperhanger and a storekeeper. His mother was Russian American. The name Uris derives from the Hebrew Yerushalmi, or "man of Jerusalem." At the age of seventeen, Uris enlisted in the United States Marine Corps and went to the South Pacific in New Zealand; he caught malaria and developed asthma. He fictionalized the fight in the South Pacific in *Battle Cry*. While he was recovering in a hospital in San Francisco he met Betty Beck, who was also a Marine, and they married. Uris wrote for a newspaper, and he wrote an article for *Esquire* in 1950. He then wrote *The Angry Hills*, which is set in Greece. Uris's deep concern about Israel led to his novel *Exodus*; he visited Israel several times and was attentive to the problems in Sinai. Uris spoke with hundreds of people and dug into research on the Jewish people. His novel focused on their history from the nineteenth century to the rise of Zionism and the founding of the state of Israel in 1948. Uris wrote many other popular novels. *Topaz*, set during the Cuban missile crisis of October 1962, became a film. *Mila 18* was about the uprising in the Warsaw ghetto. *Trinity* was a history of the Irish nation and nationalism and became a huge bestseller. With *Redemption*, the sequel, he looked at the early years of the twentieth century in Ireland, including the Irish Rebellion, and developed his story up to the First World War. *The Haj* is set in Middle East history. *QBVII* is the story of a Polish doctor interned in a German concentration camp. The papers of Leon Uris, including drafts of his works, are in the Harry Ransom Archives at the University of Texas.

Alan Elsner recalls that he first read *Exodus* at the age of sixteen. He wrote on April 24, 2013, that he had recently reread the novel and "found it disturbing and unsettling in many ways." Whereas, he had once felt "swept away by the romance of the story," now as an adult reader he was concerned about the issues and that Uris does not point to "a path for the future."[14] In a review of Ira Nadel's *Leon Uris: Life of a Best Seller* (2010), Robert Cohen writes: "A world-wide phenomenon, Uris' *Exodus* galvanized worldwide Jewry and helped establish an international Jewish identity." Can a book alone do this? It can contribute to the conversation. Cohen asserts that Uris's novel takes to task those who are unwilling to accept the Jewish refugees.[15]

Hawaii by James Michener was published in 1959, as Hawaii became the fiftieth state. Michener wrote grand sagas filled with information. His novels often dominated the bestseller list in the 1960s and 1970s with stories of families and interesting characters living in specific geographies. *Tales of the South Pacific* (1947) brought together a series of stories drawn from his experiences in the Pacific during wartime. The book won the Pulitzer Prize in 1948, and portions of it were adapted to the stage in the musical theater of Rodgers and Hammerstein's *South Pacific*. James Michener's *Hawaii* is written in episodes. Michener narrates the story of the first Hawaiians exiled from Bora Bora, American missionaries, and immigrants from Japan and China. The chapters detail the arrival on the islands of groups of people. We meet Abner Hale and the Hale and Whipple families. The story moves "From the Farm of Bitterness" (chapter 3) to "From the Starving Village" (chapter 4), as Chinese immigrants arrive for sugar plantation work. The Kee family patriarch faces leprosy and is sent to Molokai. In "From the Inland Sea" (chapter 5), Japanese workers move to Pearl Harbor. "The Golden Mean" (chapter 6) views the changes in Hawaii's culture, intercultural contact, and intermarriage.

Michener was adopted as child and was raised by his mother, a Quaker, in Doylestown, Pennsylvania. His lengthy fiction seems to be, in part, a search for origins through family histories. Michener taught English and worked for Macmillan Publishing before being drawn into military service in the United States Navy in the Second World War. After the war, he worked as an editor of the *Reader's Guide to Periodical Literature*. Michener spent many hours each day writing his long novels. In his earliest books he trained his attention on the Pacific and on the Far East. In 1960, *Hawaii* was a huge seller, with its publication coinciding with the admission into the union of the fiftieth state. *Caravans* (1963) explored the Middle East and was followed by *The Source* (1965) and *The Drifters* (1971). Michener's expansive *Centennial* (1974) and *Chesapeake* (1978) each had a sustained run at the top of the *New York Times* bestseller list. Michener chose vast regions and a wide sweep of history as his topics for his fiction. *The Covenant* (1980) was followed by the broad vistas of *Space* (1982), *Poland* (1983), *Texas* (1985), *Legacy* (1987), and

Alaska (1988). From the icy cold of the North he went to *Caribbean* (1992). Seven more novels followed, including *Mexico* (1992). There were also about thirty nonfiction works by Michener, including studies of Asia, travelogues of Iberia and Cuba, studies of political elections, an inquiry into what had occurred at Kent State in May 1970, visits to Poland and Rome, and an appreciation of sports in America. Michener was also involved with the television adaptations of some of his novels: *Hawaii, Centennial, Space*, and *Texas* among them.

A reader posting online in 2012 wrote that "in high school my love of historical fiction blossomed after reading *Hawaii*." She wrote of her wish that all children could experience the adventure and education that comes from reading. Writing on his blog, Michael Sappir called James Michener's *The Source* "an amazing book about Israel and Jewish history written over twenty years before I was born." Betty Lytle, who had read *Hawaii* forty-eight years earlier, reread it. Lytle said that she first read the novel in 1960 when she lived in Maui for a year. She visited places that Michener referred to in the novel. More recently, she said that she liked seeing the harmony of all different races working together. [16]

4

THE 1960s

New Frontiers: From Harper Lee to Kurt Vonnegut

1960

Did 1960 mark the beginning of a new era? The Kennedy-Nixon debates involved the first extensive use of television in a presidential campaign. John F. Kennedy's presidency signaled a youthful hope for America. While *Exodus* and *Advise and Consent* dominated the fiction bestseller list in 1960, a variety of nonfiction books reached #1. In the autumn, *Born Free* by Joy Adamson was selling widely. People responded to the story of humans interacting with and nurturing young lions in the wild. A popular film followed, and "Born Free" became a hit song sung by Andy Williams. Vance Packard had another book on the list with *The Waste Makers*, a book about conspicuous consumption and the creation and elimination of waste. William Shirer's *The Rise and Fall of the Third Reich* drew a wide readership with one of the most incisive and dramatic accounts of the Nazi period. Shirer was a correspondent in Berlin for CBS News and he rendered an informative, "you are there" first-person account. His book became the #1 book in the nation in December 1960. There were "serious" books on the bestseller list. Jonathan Rose provides a list of bestsellers in the 1950s and 1960s that were decidedly not middlebrow and that engaged with social and political issues. He points out that "all of them ranked among the top ten on the *Publishers Weekly* annual ranking of non-fiction bestsellers."[1]

The year 1960 was a big year for Chubby Checker and the twist. Dave Brubeck recorded "Take Five." *Lady Chatterley's Lover* was set free in a famous censorship and obscenity trial. *A Separate Peace* by John Knowles became an instant classic bound for high school reading lists. The pilot Gary Powers was shot down on April 30 during a mission to observe Soviet military installations. Morocco felt the power of an earthquake. Belgium gave up the Congo. France tested an atom bomb in the desert in Algeria. Nazi hunters captured Adolph Eichmann. On a lighter note, 1960 brought the public the *Flintstones* cartoon and, on a creepier note, Alfred Hitchcock's *Psycho*.

In spring 1960, among the notable works of fiction on the bestseller list were Morris West's *The Devil's Advocate*, Taylor Caldwell's *Dear and Glorious Physician*, and John Knowles's *A Separate Peace*. Novels by Irwin Shaw, John O'Hara, Irving Wallace, Marcia Davenport, and Mary Stewart were among the top ten bestsellers. Paul Horgan's *A Distant Trumpet*, C. P. Snow's *The Affair*, and William Styron's *Set This House on Fire* joined the books in the top ten during the summer months. *The Chapman Report* by Irving Wallace finished the year at #4 on the *Publishers Weekly* list. *Ourselves to Know* by O'Hara was #5. *The Constant Image* by Davenport was #6.

Publishers that had been privately owned went public to raise capital. Random House sold 30 percent of its stock to the public in 1959. In 1960, Alfred and Blanche Knopf sold their company to Random House. (Pat Knopf had left the company to establish Atheneum.) Independent publishing endured. Pantheon sold to Random House, as their principal executives Kurt and Helen Wolff retired in 1961. In the 1960s, John Wiley Publishing stayed independent. Houghton Mifflin and Putnam made a public stock offering in 1967. Magazine publishers and newspaper publishers saw book publishers having similar interests to theirs. Publishers looked to movie studios for adaptations. There were mergers between publishing houses. Random House bought Ballantine. Holt, Rinehart and Winston bought Bantam and Popular Library. Doubleday bought Dell and made it a paperback imprint. Harper merged with Row, later Harper-Collins. Scribner's merged with Atheneum, raising capital for growth.

In August, *To Kill a Mockingbird* by Harper Lee entered the top ten of the list of bestselling books. It would become one of the most enduring classics of modern American literature. With its dramatic story of human dignity, justice, and injustice, *To Kill a Mockingbird* became a notable feature film and has been frequently introduced to readers in secondary education. The novel appeared in the bestseller list top fifteen in late August and rose into the top five by October, remaining there through the end of the year. On October 12, Nikita Khrushchev banged down his shoe on a desk at the United Nations General Assembly. John Fitzgerald Kennedy won the election for president of the United States by 118,574 votes. *To Kill a Mockingbird* was #2 in May, June, and July 1961 alongside the #1 novel, *The Agony and the Ecstasy*. It remained among the top three fiction bestsellers through the end of 1961. The novel sold more than five million copies by 1965, including paperback sales.

To Kill a Mockingbird by Harper Lee (1960) gives us a story told by Scout Finch about her father, Atticus Finch, a lawyer who struggles to prove that a black man accused of rape is innocent. Finch has become an iconic figure in popular culture representing the lawyer's quest for justice. Harper Lee brings the southern gothic into a story about racial injustice. The novel is frequently taught in high schools and college classes. Harper Lee's story won the Pulitzer Prize and became a notable film. Three book clubs picked up and marketed the novel. The novel sold about two hundred thousand copies across the first two years of publication, according to Alice Payne Hackett.[2] However, Harper Lee did not publish a novel again until *Go Set a Watchman*. In July 2015 that book rose to a top spot on the bestseller list.

Rabbit Run by John Updike (1960) was the first of the award-winning novels featuring Updike's character Rabbit Angstrom. Updike is on almost anyone's list as among the finest of American novelists. He was also an essayist, an art critic, a poet, and a short-story writer. Updike was a chronicler of America and a literary stylist. His brilliant use of language often drew attention to itself, even as he gave readers entertaining, well-crafted stories. Updike was clearly a dedicated artist and he also became a literary celebrity. The writer's work extended across critiques of modern life, narratives of verbal dexterity and poetic invention, experiments with interior monologue or with magical realism, portraits of suburban life, and inquiries into spirituality and mystery. Updike is perhaps best known for his bestselling novels featuring Harry "Rabbit" Angstrom, a former local basketball star who becomes a middle-class suburbanite, car dealer, and focal point for characterizations of American life. Updike's first bestseller was *Couples*, a lively, sex-filled story of relationships and tangled affairs. *The Witches of Eastwick* was also a bestseller and became a feature film.

In childhood, John Updike lived in Shillington, Pennsylvania. Much of his adult life was spent in Massachusetts. His mother sought to be a writer, and he followed her example. After graduating from Harvard in 1954, he went to the Ruskin School of Drawing and Fine Art at Oxford. Upon returning to the United States, he began writing stories as a contributor to the *New Yorker* and he became a staff member at the magazine. His short stories appeared in *The Carpentered Hen* (1958). Several stories explored issues of loss or of infidelity. Updike's fiction took his readers through an examination of the changes in American life. *Rabbit Run* (1960) introduced Rabbit Angstrom, a character whom Updike readers followed in *Rabbit Redux* (1971), *Rabbit Is Rich* (1980), and *Rabbit at Rest*. *Rabbit Is Rich* won the National Book Award. *Rabbit at Rest* won the Pulitzer Prize and the National Book Critics Circle Award. Updike's fiction ranges from *The Coup* (1978) to the comic short-story cycles of *Bech: A Book* (1970), *Bech Is Back* (1981), and *Bech at Bay* (1998). In novels like *Roger's Version* (1986) and *The Beauty of the Lilies* (1996), we can see that Updike's work is saturated by an intellectual religious quest that was supported by his reading of the theologian Karl Barth and the Danish philosopher Soren Kierkegaard. *Roger's Version* explores the question of God through a computer program and the tangled questions of a character who is drawn by sexual enticements. *The Beauty of the Lilies*, beginning in its Paterson, New Jersey, setting, explores religion through historical perspective, well-drawn characters, and colorful writing. In the early 1990s, Updike recalled *Memories of the Ford Administration* (1992) and wrote his novel *Brazil* (1994). *Terrorist* (2006) follows a Muslim extremist in New Jersey. Updike returned to an earlier setting and characters with *The Widows of Eastwick* (2008).

1961

Irving Stone's novel of the life of Michelangelo, *The Agony and the Ecstasy*, led the fiction list on the day John F. Kennedy became the president of the United States. "Ask not what your country can do for you; ask what you can do for your country," said Kennedy at his inauguration. He added: "All of this will not be finished in the first hundred days . . . but let us begin." Would Kennedy's new frontier resemble an artwork, a new edifice, something awesome like that ceiling of the Sistine Chapel? No one recognized that the youthful new administration would end a few years later in the sadness of a Pieta: the president assassinated, slumped in the back of an open limousine in Jacqueline Kennedy's arms.

The Agony and the Ecstasy (1961) was Irving Stone's bestselling fictionalized biography of Michelangelo. Stone drew some of his unique narrative from the artist's letters, translated by Charles Speroni. He asked sculptor Stanley Lewis about Michelangelo's methods. Stone also drew upon his own experience of living in Rome and Florence. This novel begins in the artist's studio where Brunelleschi critiques Donatello's crucifix and Donatello challenges him to do better. Michelangelo says that he likes the earthy austerity of Donatello's image. We see Michelangelo exploring his own work. *The Agony and the Ecstasy* was *Publishers Weekly*'s #1 fiction bestseller for the year.

The Last of the Just by Andre Schwarz-Burt topped the list on March 26. In his story the Levy family line represents the Jews of Europe who have faced anti-Judaism and anti-Semitism, from the attack upon them in 1185 England to the horrors of Auschwitz in the 1940s. The book interrupted James Michener's *Hawaii*'s place at #1 for one month. Henry Miller's *Tropic of Cancer* was also on the list at this time: freed from censorship, rich with expletives, filled with fondness for sex, and energized by creative writing. On April 15, the United Nations voted to censure South Africa for apartheid. From April 17 to 19 the Kennedy administration faced the problem of Cuba. The CIA-orchestrated invasion, the Bay of Pigs, was repelled.

Graham Greene's *A Burnt-Out Case* and John Dos Passos's *Midcentury* appeared in the top five at the end of May. The New English Bible from Oxford University Press was the #1 book on May 28, 1961. It followed the Revised Standard Version as another modern language approach to the Bible. *The Winter of Our Discontent* by John Steinbeck ironically became a summer bestseller. Steinbeck's story of a suburbanite going through a midlife crisis and a moral crisis was his last novel. The world lost Ernest Hemingway to suicide on July 2. The Berlin Wall commenced construction on August 13. It would extend thirty miles with concrete and barbed wire, separating Soviet-controlled East Berlin from the West. It became the most visible boundary between the West and the Soviet bloc. That autumn Roger Maris of the New York Yankees hit his sixty-first home run, topping Babe Ruth's sixty-home-run record for the most home runs in a baseball season.

Theodore H. White's study of the Kennedy-Nixon contest in the 1960 election became the #1 bestselling book on September 10, 1961. White focused his journalistic skills on both the Nixon and Kennedy campaigns. One reaches for this book with its blue dust jacket and opens to a stirring account of what occurred each week in the election campaign that made Kennedy the president. The book was #1 on the nonfiction list at the same time as J. D. Salinger's *Franny and Zooey*, a series of short stories about the Glass family who had appeared in his *Catcher in the Rye*. *Hawaii*, *To Kill a Mockingbird*, and *The Agony and the Ecstasy* remained in the top five. Harold Robbins's *The Carpetbaggers*, Leon Uris's *Mila 18*, *The Edge of Sadness* by Edwin O'Connor, and *Clock without Hands* by Carson McCullers were also on the bestseller list. Joseph Heller's *Catch 22* was published during the year. *Franny and Zooey* appeared at #2 on *Publishers Weekly*'s fiction list. *To Kill a Mockingbird* was #3. *Mila 18* was #4. In nonfiction, *The Rise and Fall of the Third Reich* by William Shirer cost ten dollars and sold about 112,000 copies. It was #2 on *Publishers Weekly*'s list, following the New English Bible, which was #1. *Better Homes and Gardens Sewing Book* and *Casserole Cook Book* were #3 and #4, respectively, on *Publishers Weekly*'s bestseller list.

1962

In 1962, one of the most influential books to appear was Rachel Carson's *Silent Spring*. Carson carefully researched DDT pesticide use and made a vigorous case against the spraying of these chemicals. *Silent Spring* launched a notable critique of the environmental impacts of human behavior. Whereas *The Sea around Us* had been a beautiful exposition of the mysteries of the oceans, *Silent Spring* was a scathing argument against the spraying of DDT by the agricultural industry. Rachel Carson's book took to task that industry for polluting and poisoning the environment. The book generated concern and has had continuing impact upon the environmental movement.[3]

Among the bestsellers of 1962 was the paperback issue of *Dr. No* by Ian Fleming, as Sean Connery portrayed James Bond on the screen. *The Spy Who Loved Me* sold 2.7 million copies. John Glenn took off for space on February 20. Johnny Carson was now the host of *The Tonight Show*. *West Side Story* became a film that won ten Academy Awards. Wilt Chamberlain scored one hundred points in a basketball game. The Beatles released their first single, "Love Me Do." In Rome, Pope John XXIII initiated Vatican II reforms in the Catholic Church. In the United States, Michael Harrington wrote *The Other America*, documenting a story of American poverty. Mickey Spillane's *I, The Jury* sold an extraordinary 5,390,195 copies, according to Alice Payne Hackett. Six other Spillane novels sold more than 4.6 million copies.[4]

A trial lawyer, Louis B. Nizer, started off 1962 at the top of the nonfiction bestseller list. After a long newspaper strike, on March 25 readers exchanged famous legal cases for counting calories. Herman Taller's *Calories Don't Count* asserted that—well, the title will tell you. Nizer could have issued a follow-up book that put Taller on trial for dubious claims. The Romanian-born doctor advocated a low carbohydrate diet. The FDA asserted that Taller was peddling safflower oil capsules and that claims that they could help in cases of obesity or cardiovascular problems were unfounded.

Katherine Anne Porter's #1 *Ship of Fools* was a heavily publicized novel from one of America's premier short-story writers. The story is set on board a ship making a journey from Mexico to Germany across a month in 1931. The novel held the #1 spot from April 29 for twenty-six weeks. *Publishers Weekly* placed the book at #1 on its 1962 fiction bestseller list. Readers also turned to an account of the banking family *The Rothschilds* by Frederic Morton in June. The Rothschilds became the #1 nonfiction bestseller on June 24. Focusing on the different personalities in the family, the book spent sixteen weeks at #1.

John Steinbeck's *Travels with Charley* was his account of a cross-America trip with his poodle. Steinbeck portrayed America with the eye of a skilled novelist and journalist in a text that was part travelogue and part commentary. The newspaper strike interrupted the record of the book's strong sales and distribution at #1. *Travels with Charley* ended the year at #10 on *Publishers Weekly*'s 1962 fiction list. The record of Allen Drury's #1 bestseller *A Shade of Difference* was also interrupted. This novel brings us inside the United Nations among American and African delegates in the UN General Assembly. The United Nations returned to readers' attention with the late Dag Hammarskjold's *Markings*, his jottings from his journal, The UN general secretary died in a plane crash in

Africa. Bearing a yellow dustcover, *Markings* reached #1 on the nonfiction list on December 20, 1964, and remained at #1 for thirty-one weeks, well into 1965. *Seven Days in May* by Fletcher Knebel was another book that brought attention to issues of government. In this suspense drama the president's approval rating is lagging and the Joint Chiefs of Staff attempt to take over the government. The book was high on the list at election time and reached #1 on November 18. *Publishers Weekly* recorded diet book *Calories Don't Count* at #1 in nonfiction for the year. The New English Bible was #2.

1963

J. D. Salinger's popularity continued with *Raise High the Roof Beam, Carpenters*, which reached #1 by St. Patrick's Day and stayed there in spring 1963. It was #3 on *Publishers Weekly*'s 1963 fiction bestseller list. Actress Hedda Hopper turned her syndicated column into a book, *The Whole Truth and Nothing But*, which reached #1 on May 19. It was a fun read for that summer. Daphne du Maurier returned to the top of the bestseller list with *The Glass Blowers*. She fictionalizes the life of her ancestor Robert du Maurier, who was a glassblower in France. Robert du Maurier escaped the violence of the French Revolution by going to England and settling in London. The author researched the life of her ancestor through family letters penned by Robert du Maurier's sister. The novel was #8 on *Publisher Weekly*'s 1963 fiction list.

As the weather was heating up, so too was the bestseller list of 1963. James Baldwin's *The Fire Next Time* collected his essays on matters of race, civil rights, and the future of America. Bob Hope lightened things up with *I Owe Russia $1200*. Morris West's *The Shoes of the Fisherman*, the story of a new pope who had spent time in Russia's prisons, offered a more serious approach to faith and issues of human dignity during the Cold War. The Australian novelist's story reached #1 on June 30 and stayed at #1 for fourteen weeks. *Publishers Weekly* recognized the novel as the #1 fiction bestseller of the year. Next at #1 was Mary McCarthy's *The Group*, her story about girls from Vassar and where their lives go afterward. *The Group* was #2 on *Publishers Weekly*'s fiction list. *Elizabeth Appleton* by John O'Hara was another top-selling novel. It was #5 on

Publishers Weekly's list. The *New York Times* listed these books in the top positions on its bestseller list.

The civil rights movement had one of its most memorable moments when two hundred thousand people gathered on the National Mall in Washington, D.C., on August 28 and heard Martin Luther King give his "I Have a Dream" speech. However, on September 15 a bomb blew up in a church Sunday school in Birmingham, Alabama, killing four black girls. The autumn brought other troubling events. The assassination of South Vietnamese leader Ngo Dinh Diem sparked unrest that led to further U.S. involvement in Vietnam and a commitment that was to soon pull the United States into war.

The nation was shocked by the assassination of John F. Kennedy in Dallas on November 22, 1963. The #1 nonfiction book at that time was a critical look at the president by Victor Lasky, *JFK: The Man and the Myth*. It dipped down lower on the list after Kennedy's death, and more glowing recollections of the man and his administration took its place across the next several years. The Warren Commission found that a lone gunman had fired shots from the Texas School Book Depository. Subsequently, dozens of books contested this view. They offered a variety of conspiracy theories about the assassination. *Publishers Weekly* listed *JFK: The Man and the Myth* as the #3 bestselling nonfiction book of the year. The reissue of Kennedy's *Profiles in Courage* was #4. His only competition for the top spots was Charlie Brown: Charles M. Schultz's *Peanuts* was #1 and #2 on the *Publishers Weekly* list.

The year 1963 was the year that Richard Burton and Elizabeth Taylor starred in *Cleopatra* and fell for each other, perhaps harder than Marc Antony and the Egyptian queen had fallen for each other. Betty Friedan's *The Feminine Mystique* asserted women's equality, dignity, and strengths. While some readers pondered Jessica Mitford's *The American Way of Death*, an account of the funeral industry, Kennedy's *Profiles in Courage* was reprinted and soared to #1 on December 29, 1963.

The Group by Mary McCarthy (#2 on *Publishers Weekly*'s list) and *The Shoes of the Fisherman* by Morris West (#1 on *Publishers Weekly*'s list) were joined as top sellers by *Caravans* by James Michener (#4), Helen MacInnes's *The Venetian Affair*, and *The Living Reed* by Pearl S. Buck. Moving up the list behind them was Cold War spy intrigue in Ian Fleming's James Bond, *On Her Majesty's Secret Service*. Alice Payne Hackett records sales of 3,142,184 by 1967. *Thunderball, Goldfinger,*

You Only Live Twice, and *From Russia with Love* each also sold more than three million copies.[5]

In *Shoes of the Fisherman* by Morris West, Kiril Pavlovich Lakota is selected as the papal successor. He seeks to defuse conflict and relieve global hunger. The world is on the verge of nuclear war, and trade sanctions have prompted famine in China. Kiril wanders out into the street with his assistant. He goes to the Soviet Union undercover to seek a resolution to the crisis. He is friendly with Father Telemond, who is perhaps based on Pierre Teilhard de Chardin, the Jesuit paleontologist who was censured by the Church for his views on evolution. This novel anticipates a Slavic pope who could intervene in concerns of the Cold War. Karol Wojtyla of Poland became the pope fifteen years later.

Morris West brought religious and humanitarian themes to his novels *The Devil's Advocate* and *The Clowns of God*. He gained insight into the working of the Vatican as a member of the Christian Brothers order. He left the religious order without taking vows and was married. West served in the Australian Royal Air Force and later worked for the prime minister and in radio broadcasting. West was widely traveled, and he wrote international espionage thrillers. In his novels he scrutinized modern organizations and issues of evil and corruption, highlighting moral accountability and virtue.

1964

The Beatles arrived in America in February 1964, prompting a kind of mass hysteria among fans that was called Beatlemania. This was the start of the "British Invasion": a wave of English bands from the Kinks and the Animals to Herman's Hermits, the Yardbirds, the Rolling Stones, and the Who, that were soon all over the American radio airwaves and launched a new phase of rock music. Meanwhile, Motown launched the Supremes. John Coltrane recorded *Love Supreme*. In sports, Cassius Clay (later Muhammad Ali) knocked out Sonny Liston in the heavyweight championship boxing match on February 25.

In early 1964, John le Carré's *The Spy Who Came in from the Cold* was a spy-novel sensation. The spy Alec Leamas, now at the age of fifty, is thinking of retiring from the spy business. He decides to go on one more mission. David Cornwall was a British Secret Service agent before he began writing fiction. As John le Carré, his extraordinary career as a writer of thrillers began with this novel. At #1 on February 23, 1964, it held that spot for thirty-four weeks. This was the #1 novel on *Publishers Weekly*'s 1964 bestseller list. By 1966 the novel had sold 260,000 copies in hardcover. It had sold 1.7 million paperback copies by 1966 and more than two million copies in paperback by 1967. Since then, copies have been produced by a variety of publishers.

American Heritage quickly put together a volume on Kennedy and the assassination: *Four Days*. It was assembled from newspaper articles, reached #1 on March 22, 1964, and was at #1 for three months. Bruce Catton provided an introduction for the book. *Four Days* was #1 on *Publishers Weekly*'s nonfiction list for 1964. Readers were in a memorializing mood with the passing of Kennedy. They were also interested in the memoirs of Douglas MacArthur and the journal notes left by Dag Hammarskjold. Both these notable men had died during the year.

President Lyndon Baines Johnson declared the hopeful agenda of "the Great Society." The goal of new legislation and government programs was to infuse new energy into America with economic opportunity, the creation of a jobs corps, and by initiating Medicare, Medicaid, food stamps, a volunteer corps (VISTA), and the Department of Housing and Urban Development. Significantly, President Johnson also signed the Civil Rights Act into law in July.

America was about to step deeply into one of the most controversial foreign conflicts that the nation had ever encountered. The Gulf of Tonkin Resolution followed attacks on the USS *Maddox* and the USS *Turner Joy*. President Johnson was given powers to respond. Without any congressional declaration of war, the United States entered the fight against the Vietcong and became mired in a long and drawn-out war. Johnson's administration was sharply criticized. Pressured by events and criticism, he decided not to seek reelection in 1968.

In New York, plans were made for the construction of the World Trade Center. The U.S. surgeon general asserted that smoking is hazardous to one's health. (At the time about 39 percent of Americans were smokers of tobacco. Tobacco was a big cash crop and cigarettes contributed to a large industry.) The year 1964 was rich with popular entertainment in film, in theater, and on television. *Mary Poppins* included songs and colorful animation. Sidney Poitier won an Oscar for Best Actor for *Lilies of the Field*. He was the first African American actor to win the award. On Broadway, Barbra Streisand starred in *Funny Girl* and Carol Channing was in *Hello Dolly*. On television, CBS featured *Gilligan's Island* and *The Munsters*. Peter Sellers starred in the film *The Pink Panther* as the bumbling Inspector Clouseau.

Herzog by Saul Bellow was a commercial success, a bestseller that appeared amid the distinguished career of one of America's finest writers. Throughout Bellow's well-crafted narratives there is a philosophical turn of mind, cultural exploration, and sustained characterization. There is a reflective texture to his probing of the lives of modern men and women. In *Herzog*, a middle-aged professor writes to friends and to deceased people.

From his home in Chicago in the 1940s, Bellow wrote *Dangling Man*. Notable works like *The Adventures of Augie March*, *Henderson the Rain King*, and *Seize the Day* followed. For Bellow, Chicago was a microcosm and representation of American city life and culture. When Bellow placed *Mr. Sammler's Planet* in New York City, he told the story of a man who had experienced the Holocaust. Readers are introduced to Sammler on a crosstown bus on which he wonders if he has been followed by someone. We are introduced to his daughter and begin to encounter his memories. In *Humboldt's Gift* (1975), Bellow made use of Rudolph Steiner's anthroposophy. His final novel was *Ravelstein*. Bellow was awarded the Nobel Prize in 1976. He was the recipient of three National Book Awards.

1965

In 1965, Saul Bellow's *Herzog* continued its run atop the bestseller list. Prentice Hall Publishing had its second #1 book on May 8 with *Up the Down Staircase* by Bel Kaufman, the granddaughter of playwright Sholem Aleichem. Bel Kaufman's protagonist is a teacher whose initial experience of teaching is recorded in notes and letters and student papers. Her title came from an administrator's disciplinary note: "Please admit bearer to class. Detained by me going up the Down staircase." The Prentice Hall building was in Englewood Cliffs, New Jersey, a few miles from the George Washington Bridge. Better known as a publisher of textbooks and books for lawyers, accountants, and other professionals, it was absorbed by Simon and Schuster in the 1980s. *Up the Down Staircase* was #2 on

Publishers Weekly's fiction bestseller list. *Herzog* was #3 for the year. These books followed James Michener's #1 bestseller *The Source.*

A newspaper strike interrupted the bestseller listings in 1965. James Michener's *The Source* attained the #1 position July 11 and remained there for thirty-six weeks. It was Michener's second big bestseller, following *Hawaii.* Like his subsequent books, this novel is encyclopedic. The story digs back into an archaeological site in Israel named Makor and ranges across twelve hundred years of history. It concludes with the creation of the state of Israel. *The Source* was #1 on *Publishers Weekly*'s 1965 fiction list.

In nonfiction, Theodore H. White returned atop the bestseller list with *The Making of the President, 1964* (#10 on *Publishers Weekly*'s 1965 list.) White's account of the Johnson-Goldwater election followed the same format as his previous book on Kennedy and Nixon. He would follow this with his commentary on the campaigns of Nixon and Humphrey in 1968 and Nixon and McGovern in 1972. His books remain among the best windows into the process of those presidential elections. Meanwhile, two associates of President John F. Kennedy, Ted Sorenson and Arthur Schlesinger Jr., wrote #1 bestselling accounts of the Kennedy administration. From 1964 into 1965, Sorenson, a friend and speechwriter for Kennedy, diligently produced his somewhat weighty volume of recollections. *Kennedy*, with its light blue dust jacket cover, topped the *Times* bestseller list on Halloween, a Sunday. It was #9 on *Publishers Weekly*'s nonfiction list. Schlesinger's book *A Thousand Days* (#7 on the *Publishers Weekly* list) drew upon the notes he had developed while associated with the Kennedy White House. Kennedy did not live to write his memoirs. Schlesinger's book gathers up some of the material that might have appeared in them. His book was #1 on January 9, 1966, and spent about a month at the #1 spot.

In 1965, America moved deeper into its commitment in Vietnam. There were 125,000 American soldiers in Vietnam, and the draft was increasing that number by about 35,000 more monthly. At home, President Johnson signed the Voting Rights Act on August 6. The Watts race riot broke out in Los Angeles on August 11. In popular music, the Who recorded "My Generation." Bob Dylan was criticized for plugging in electric guitars at the Newport Festival. The Rolling Stones released "(I Can't Get No) Satisfaction." The Beatles' Paul McCartney recorded "Yesterday." Sonny and Cher broke through the Beatles' hold on #1 on the Billboard charts with "I Got You Babe." On Broadway, Neil Simon introduced *The Odd Couple*.

1966

At the start of the year, Truman Capote's *In Cold Blood* was the sensational and graphic shocker that quickly rose to #1 on February 6, 1966. The author brought together the techniques of a novelist and a journalist to tell the story of the murder of a Kansas family. *Publishers Weekly*'s nonfiction bestseller list listed *In Cold Blood* at #3 for the year, after *The Human Sexual Response*. *Games People Play*, at #4, sold 465,000 copies across two years. *A Thousand Days* by Arthur Schlesinger Jr. at #5 was a Pulitzer Prize winner that told the story of John F. Kennedy's presidency. *The Last Battle* by Cornelius Ryan, the author of *The Longest Day*, topped the nonfiction list on May 8. Ryan investigated the final months of the Second World War in Europe, including the Allied march on Berlin. *How to Avoid Probate* by Norman Dacey showed readers how to do that—and how to avoid having to pay lawyers in the process. The lawyers were not happy with the book. Dacey did not have a license to practice law, and he was sued by the New York Bar Association. The New York Supreme Court ordered the book removed from bookstores, but the U.S. Court of Appeals overruled the decision. It sold more than 575,000 copies. *Publishers Weekly* listed the book as the #1 nonfiction book for the year. Another attorney produced a timely topical bestseller on the Kennedy assassination, which rapidly rose to #1. Mark Lane started the conspiracy theory ball rolling when he rejected the findings of the Warren Commission that Kennedy had been killed by a lone gunman. He repeated his interpretation of the events in a 1992 bestseller. An April 1967 #1 bestseller, William Manchester's *The Death of a President*, also dealt with the assassination. Manchester was a friend of the Kennedy family and with family approval gathered up accounts of the Kennedy administration. The fiction list at the end of the year featured Robert Crichton's *The Secret of Santa Vittoria*. It was the story of Italian townspeople who fooled the Nazis and hid one thousand bottles of their cherished wine. The novel spent eighteen weeks at #1, from November 20 into the next year. The novel sold 116,700 copies in its first four months of publication. It followed *Valley of the Dolls* and *The Adventurers* by Harold

Robbins on *Publishers Weekly*'s list of bestsellers for the year. The #4 book on *Publishers Weekly*'s list was Allen Drury's *Capable of Honor*.

In 1966, Thurgood Marshall was appointed to the United States Supreme Court, and he brought further attention to civil rights concerns. On television, *Star Trek* made its debut with William Shatner as Captain James Kirk and Leonard Nimoy as Spock. In popular music, the Beatles recorded "Eleanor Rigby." Their albums *Revolver* and *Rubber Soul* showed a growth and development in their musical art beyond their earlier rock-and-roll-based pop love songs. In sports, NBA star Bill Russell of the Boston Celtics became the first black player-coach.

The Valley of the Dolls by Jacqueline Susann features three young women who seek romance, fame, and new experiences. Anne Wells is from New England and envisions New York as her city of dreams. Neely O'Hara is a vaudeville actress. Jennifer North is a showgirl who is seeking love. They become dependent on barbiturates and amphetamines. Each of them is in "the valley of the dolls." They meet an array of interesting characters. Helen Lawson, a Broadway actress, comes into their lives. Lyon Burke is a theater attorney; Kevin Gilmore is a rich cosmetics business owner. Tony Polar is a pop singer, and Ted Casablanca is a fashion designer. Bernard Geiss Associates first published the novel on February 10, 1966. For a time, it was America's favorite dirty book. The reviewer for *Publishers Weekly* called the novel "big, brilliant, sensational" and "poorly written" and concluded: "It might more accurately be described as a highly effective sedative, a living doll." *Valley of the Dolls* spent sixty-five weeks on the *New York Times* bestseller list. It has since sold an estimated thirty-one million copies.

It is May, and the sun is shining in through the window where a young woman sits on the sofa, bare feet on the floor. She holds the new book that everyone is talking about, Jacqueline Susann's *The Valley of the Dolls*, and sips from the wineglass that she lifts from the table. It is one of those semiopaque long-stemmed glasses, and she holds it with her thin wrist raised, her pink fingernails extended. She thinks that maybe she should try doing something like the characters are doing in the chapter she has been reading. Could she be so bold to declare her independence, stir up some trouble, and turn her own life toward a new page?

On May 8, Jacqueline Susann's *The Valley of the Dolls* was #1. This was the story of a model, an actress, and a singer seeking glamour and success. Susann's story appeared exactly one decade after Grace Metalious's *Peyton Place*, and she began appearing frequently on television to promote her book. *Valley of the Dolls* was Jacqueline Susann's first novel. The novel was #1 overall on both national bestseller lists.

1967

Money and celebrity topped the bestseller list. Sam Levenson's *Everything but Money* made money as the #1 bestseller in January 1967. He had an appreciative television audience to support the book. Levenson mixed some comic relief with stories of his poor but happy childhood in New York. Readers appear to have been especially interested in autobiographies and biographies at this time. Cornelia Otis Skinner's biography of Sarah Bernhardt, *Madame Sarah*, was spiced up with romance and celebrity tidbits. The actress was presented in the glowing light of friends' favorable memories. Film director Elia Kazan wrote *The Arrangement* about a man in advertising who tries to break free from his work routine and struggles with near mental collapse. The paperback cover portrayed the images of his characters' faces set in small squares. The book was at #1 for twenty-three weeks from March 26, 1967. Kazan wrote five more novels.

John Kenneth Galbraith made economics available to a popular audience with clear and thoughtful writing. *The New Industrial State* was a study of American industry, commerce, and the American public. Galbraith projected that this was the prevailing trend that would emerge after the 1960s. The book was #1 for seven weeks, beginning on July 23, 1967. (Galbraith's other bestseller was *The Affluent Society*.) Steven Birmingham's *Our Crowd: The Great Jewish Families of New York* followed, reaching #1 on September 10. It appeared at #1 on the bestseller list for twenty-four weeks.

In 1967, Christiaan Barnard of South Africa became the first man to perform a successful heart transplant operation. The "Summer of Love" broke into new expression among the West Coast "hippie" culture. In popular music, the Beatles amazed many listeners with their multi-tracked, innovative album *Sergeant Pepper's Lonely Hearts Club Band*. Aretha Franklin sang "Respect." Simon and Garfunkel sang "Mrs. Robinson," and their song appeared in the Mike Nichols film *The Graduate*, featuring actor Dustin Hoffman. *The Carol Burnett Show* premiered on television. Television also welcomed PBS, the Public Broadcasting System. Elvis Presley married Priscilla Beaulieu on May 1; June 18 brought the Monterey Pop Festival. Twiggy appeared on magazine covers, evidently insisting that young women should attempt to appear skinny and emaciated.

In 1967, Gabriel Garcia Marquez's *One Hundred Years of Solitude* was among the literary novels of the year. The 1967 fiction market included #1 books like Thornton Wilder's *The Eighth Day*, Chaim Potok's *The Chosen*, and William Styron's *The Confessions of Nat Turner*, all of which have a sense of the historical saga about them. Wilder presents two families in Coaltown, Illinois, whose lives intersect with each other. Potok, a conservative rabbi, wrote the story of two teenage boys in Brooklyn. Styron's novel is the fictionalized story of Nat Turner's 1836 slave rebellion in Virginia told through the voice of the man investigating it.

Before Stephen King and before the movie *Damien*, there was *Rosemary's Baby*, Ira Levin's story of the appearance of the devil in a birth in New York City. The hardcover made the bestseller list, and the bloodred-covered paperback circulated widely. Rosemary Woodhouse has moved into a New York City apartment building and finds out that her neighbors have a witches' coven and that they may steal her child. She cannot get anyone to believe her. The baby to be born is to become the antichrist. In an inversion of the Virgin Birth, the father is Satan, not Rosemary's husband, Guy. This was one of the first horror novels to appear on the bestseller list. It was #7 on *Publishers Weekly*'s fiction bestseller list for the year. Other top bestsellers were Chaim Potok's *The Chosen* (#3), Leon Uris's *Topaz* (#4), Catherine Marshall's *Christy* (#5), and Thornton Wilder's *The Eighth Day* (#6). *The Arrangement* by Elia Kazan was #1 on *Publishers Weekly*'s 1967 fiction bestseller list. *The Confessions of Nat Turner* was #2.

The Confessions of Nat Turner by William Styron, his fictional memoir of Nat Turner, leader of a slave rebellion, won the Pulitzer Prize. Styron recalls this historical event through imaginative scenes. At a time of racial strife and countercultural protest in the United States, the novel seemed to strike a chord with the reading public. There was some criticism of a white author writing in the voice of a black slave. James Baldwin, who wrote *Another Country* (1962), had predicted that Styron would be criticized. Baldwin's novel has a female character who was involved in an interracial relationship with a black man. He had spent time with Styron shortly after he wrote that novel.

Styron was from Virginia, and southern history and culture found a way into some of his fiction. In this regard, William Faulkner and Thomas Wolfe were among his influences. *Lie Down in Darkness* (1952) was the story of a troubled family. Styron was called into service during the Korean War served as a first lieutenant in the U.S. Marine Corps. *Set This House on Fire* (1960) told the story of American expatriates on the Amalfi coast in Italy. In *Sophie's Choice* (1979), a southern writer tells the story of a Polish Catholic woman who has faced the terrors of Auschwitz and now lives in Brooklyn. Sophie is forced to choose which of her children shall live through the Holocaust. Styron had to make an artistic choice to develop his character as a non-Jewish victim of the Nazi "Final Solution." Sophie's Jewish lover struggles with paranoia and schizophrenia. A 1982 film adaptation of the story, featuring Meryl Streep as Sophie, was nominated for five Academy Awards. Styron's candid discussion of his bouts with depression in *Darkness Visible* (1990) later drew perhaps a stronger sympathetic response from readers than some of his novels. He wrote that this often-hidden pain that people suffer needed attention, treatment, and care.

1968

The year 1968 began with William Styron's *Confessions of Nat Turner* at #1. It was closely followed by Leon Uris's *Topaz*, a story of intrigue and romance that recalled Russian influence in Cuba. Catherine Marshall's *Christy*, Mary Stewart's *Gabriel Hounds*, and John O'Hara's *The Instrument* were also listed in the top five through the month of January. During the month of March, in fiction, Fletcher Knebel's *Vanished* was at #3 and Morris West's *Tower of Babel* and Gore Vidal's *Myra Breckinridge* had climbed onto the charts. The nonfiction bestseller *Between Parent and Child* by Dr. Haim Ginott encouraged healthy relationships between parents and their teenage children. From February 25, 1968, it held at #1 for eight weeks. *The Naked Ape* by Desmond Morris let people know how much they shared with primate behavior. (One might say it swung to the top of the list on March 3.) *The Money Game*, by the appropriately named

Adam Smith, was a summer bestseller on July 7 and held that position for forty-two weeks.

Meanwhile, terror struck with Arthur Hailey's *Airport*. This was a disaster suspense novel that reached #1 on April 7 and on spent thirty weeks at #1, a position that was occasionally interrupted. *Airport* was #1 on the *Publishers Weekly* fiction list for 1968. John Updike's *Couples*, filled with sex and infidelity, was #1 on June 30. Then *Airport* flew back to the #1 spot. Mystery and intrigue followed with Helen MacInnes's *The Salzburg Connection*. A list of the men who assisted Hitler is discovered buried in a lake in the mountains of Austria. The American CIA and the Russians seek the chest. There are threats that these men indicated on the list could reemerge, blackmailed into repeated nefarious deeds. On the 1968 *Publishers Weekly*'s bestseller appeared *Couples* (#2) and *The Salzburg Connection* (#3). *A Small Town in Germany* by John le Carré was #4.

The year 1968 is often cited as a turning point. The Vietnam War escalated with the Tet Offensive. The campaign for the American presidency was filled with energy and tensions, including protests at the Democratic National Convention in Chicago. In Czechoslovakia the Czech people challenged the Soviets and were suppressed. In April, Martin Luther King Jr. was assassinated in Memphis. Pierre Trudeau became Canada's prime minister. In May, French students staged their plan to overthrow the government and workers went on strike. On June 5, Robert Kennedy was assassinated in Los Angeles following a campaign event. President Johnson's advisors urged de-escalation of the war in Vietnam and Johnson rejected General Westmoreland's call for 206,000 troops. The My Lai massacre was a horror reported throughout the U.S. media. The Democratic Party nominated Hubert Humphrey of Minnesota to face Richard M. Nixon in the election; however, Nixon won the election and became the president-elect.

In popular culture, *60 Minutes* made its television debut; Arthur Ashe won the U.S. Open. Stanley Kubrick's *2001* brought Arthur C. Clarke's science fiction story to the screen, and the Beatles recorded "Hey Jude." Shirley Chisholm became a New York congresswoman.

Airport by Arthur Hailey was written by a master of the human-interest story. Hailey developed melodramatic plots that also informed readers about businesses like airport management, auto manufacturing, and banking. The action of his stories occurred in public settings like airports and airplanes and hotels. There are filmic and journalistic qualities to his stories. In *The Moneychangers* (1975), Hailey could take readers into the boardroom at banks and stir up concern about counterfeiters and scandal. In *Wheels* (1971), he contrasts the wealth of auto executives with the workers on the assembly line. Immediately we are introduced to an executive at a motor company who is at home with his wife. The story brings us into the world of Detroit car manufacturing. With Hailey's fiction we recognize that we are all in this public world, as John Sutherland observes in his reflections on Hailey's novels. We are entertained by a tale about the modern machinery of society. Hailey's first novel was *The Final Diagnosis* (1959). *In High Places* (1962) is set in Canada. *Hotel* (1965) and the bestselling *Airport* (1968) reflect places where people regularly congregate. Hailey uses these settings as scaffoldings for his stories. In *Hotel* we are brought to a hotel in New Orleans. In *Airport*, the airport setting is threatened by a fierce winter storm.

1969

The Salzburg Connection held the #1 spot in January 1969. *A Small Town in Germany* by John le Carré and *Preserve and Protect* by Allen Drury were at #2 and #3, respectively. They appeared as bestsellers on both major bestseller lists. *Portnoy's Complaint* by Philip Roth, one of America's finest writers, was #1 on March 16, 1969. Alexander Portnoy ponders his life and explores it with his analyst. He questions his relationships with women, particularly with his Jewish mother, and seeks meaning in his life. After fourteen weeks at #1 this novel by a great writer gave way to the sensationalized slush of a not so great one. Jacqueline Susann geared up *The Love Machine* as a sexy follow-up to her smash bestseller *The Valley of the Dolls*. Robin Stone is a broadcast media personality with a voracious sexual appetite. The story reached #1 on June 13 and titillated audiences at #1 for thirteen weeks. *Publishers Weekly* listed the novels by Roth and Susann as the #1 and #2 bestsellers, respectively, for 1969.

Airport remained in the top ten on the bestseller list into June 1969 and then dipped down. Other books that reached the top ten during this time included Kurt Vonnegut's *Slaughterhouse Five*, Mario Puzo's *The Godfather*, John Cheever's *Bullet Park*, Harry Kemelman's *Sunday the*

Rabbi Stayed Home, and Vladimir Nabokov's *Ada, or Ardor: A Family Chronicle*. Michael Crichton's *The Andromeda Strain* entered the top ten bestsellers list on June 29.

Readers were absorbed in Harrison Salisbury's *The 900 Days*. This journalist was the *New York Times* Moscow bureau chief in 1954–1955. He would become one of the newspaper's leading lights as creator of its op-ed page (1970) and assistant and associate managing editor (1970–1973). In *The 900 Days* he explored the Nazi attack upon Leningrad in the Second World War. Salisbury was in the city soon after the siege of the city. He went back to the city in 1954, following Stalin's censorship of war records, to find documentary evidence for *The 900 Days*. The book reached #1 on May 4, 1969. It was followed by *Jennie* by Ralph Martin, a biography of Winston Churchill's mother, who was born in America. *The Peter Principle* by Lawrence Peter and Raymond Hull, a summer bestseller in 1969, asserted that mediocrity rises to the top of many organizations. In their view, an ambitious individual gets promoted to the level at which he or she cannot do the job effectively. This tribute to incompetence and conformity was twenty-two weeks at #1. During this time, Neil Armstrong and Buzz Aldrin landed on the moon on July 20, 1969, while Michael Collins circled in the Apollo 11 spaceship above them. In August, thousands met in mud and rain at Yasgur's Farm in upstate New York for the Woodstock Festival.

Mario Puzo's *The Godfather* arrived at #1 on September 21, 1969. Puzo's stories of the Mafia were encouraged by an editor at Putnam who gave him an advance to write his book. It was a wise investment. *The Godfather* spent twenty-two weeks at #1 and became the basis for the *Godfather* films. Puzo followed his novel with *The Sicilian*: #1 on January 20, 1985. Crichton's *Andromeda Strain* had climbed to the #4 spot through much of August and September and was #3 in October. Joe McGinnis's *The Selling of the President,1968* reached the top of the nonfiction list on November 30, 1969, with an account of the advertising schemes that were utilized to support Richard Nixon's bid for the White House. *Publishers Weekly* listed *Portnoy's Complaint* atop the year's bestseller list. Immediately following it was *The Godfather* (#2) and *The Love Machine* (#3). *The Inheritors* by Harold Robbins was #4. *The Andromeda Strain* was #5.

The New York Mets won the World Series. Burt Bacharach and Hal David wrote "Raindrops Keep Falling on My Head"; Sly and the Family

Stone sang "Everyday People." Actors stripped down to their birthday suits for *O Calcutta* on Broadway. Robert Redford and Paul Newman starred in *Butch Cassidy and the Sundance Kid*. There were the troubles in North Ireland. There was also the horror of the Manson murders. The end of the year also saw the problems of the music festival at Altamont. Simon and Garfunkel sang "Bridge over Troubled Water" and then dissolved their partnership. The Beatles were also falling apart, even as they created their *Abbey Road* album. However, on a lighter note, *The Brady Bunch* came to TV. Joe Namath led the New York Jets to a 16–7 win over the Baltimore Colts in the Super Bowl.

The Godfather by Mario Puzo was autumn 1969's bestselling work of fiction. If one is reading, or rereading, Mario Puzo's *The Godfather*, it is difficult to forget about the movies. Puzo fostered public fascination with his story of Mafia families and underworld crime. *The Godfather* became a huge bestseller; it became a culture text and it fostered mob narratives and television fare like *The Sopranos*. Chris Messenger's *The Godfather and American Culture* examines Puzo's novel and Francis Ford Coppola's adaptation of it. The author decides not to apply critical strategies to critique Puzo's writing. He is more concerned with the story, its characters, issues of power, and the popular reception of the novel and film. He does, however, critique Puzo's writing: "His text seemed out of his control, both internally chaotic and contradictory." Even so, he recognizes that the novel, which sold thirty million copies in the 1970s, has its merits. It is "an American melodrama" that looks at "new world mobility and old-world identity." People loved these movies and repeated lines from them, he observes. Who was Puzo's reading audience? Messenger writes: "Surely it cuts and cross-cuts among critically trained readers and consumers who only read bestsellers."[6]

Portnoy's Complaint by Philip Roth topped the bestseller list on March 16, 1969. Modern Library placed the novel in the top one hundred novels of the twentieth century in the English language. Roth's novels have often been on the bestseller list, and he is among contemporary American literature's most honored writers. *Goodbye Columbus* (1959) was his first novel, and it won the National Book Award in 1960. The Library of America has published a series of books that collect his writings, placing Roth among America's pantheon of significant writers. *Goodbye Columbus* looks at Jewish culture in America with wit and jest. *Portnoy's Complaint* is Alexander Portnoy's no-holds-barred monologue to Dr. Spielvogel about the Jewish protagonist's twisted mother-love, personal dilemmas, and incessant libido. Among Roth's best-known characters is Nathan Zuckerman, who has appeared in four of Roth's novels, including the Pulitzer Prize–winning *American Pastoral* (1997). Among Roth's works are *The Breast* (1972), *Our Gang* (a satire about the Nixon White House), *I Married a Communist* (1998), *The Human Stain* (2000), and *Everyman* (2006), a novel about sickness and dying. Roth was born in Newark, New Jersey, the setting in which he begins his dystopian novel *The Plot against America* (2004). In this story, the anti-Semitic aviator Charles Lindbergh has won election to the presidency. Roth's fiction is often drawn from autobiography and imaginatively connects fiction and experience. His stories bring us into the world of his protagonists and are often rich with social commentary.

Slaughterhouse Five by Kurt Vonnegut is a fabulist fiction. It is a satire based upon his terrifying wartime experience of being a prisoner of war while the city of Dresden was being bombed. He survived by hiding away in a meat locker. Vonnegut's brother was a scientist and had encouraged him to study biochemistry at Cornell, and Vonnegut had been trained in the military as a mechanical engineer. He studied at the University of Chicago on the GI Bill after the war and worked for General Electric as a publicist. Later, Vonnegut lived on Cape Cod in Massachusetts, writing short stories and essays for magazines. Across the years, he also wrote seven plays. *Player Piano* (1952) was his first novel, and it reemerged in a paperback following the success of *Slaughterhouse Five*. *The Sirens of Titan* (1959), *Mother Night* (1961), *Cat's Cradle* (1963), and *God Bless You, Mr. Rosewater* (1964) followed, each book displaying striking creativity. In the imaginative romp of *Cat's Cradle*, the narrator, John, plans to write about the nuclear scientist Felix Hoenikker, who has created Ice 9. If a particle of this solid ice is placed into water, it will become deadly. John then goes off to investigate Bokononism on San Lorenzo, an island in the Caribbean.

Vonnegut's fiction became particularly popular during the mid- to late 1960s as he wrote wittily about contemporary anxieties, politics, and science. *Slaughterhouse Five* echoed in sympathy with antiwar protest during the Vietnam War and rose to #1 on the bestseller list. In his review of the novel in the *New Republic*, Michael Crichton declared: "He writes about the most excruciatingly painful things. His novels have attacked our deepest fears" (review of *Slaughterhouse Five*, by Kurt Vonnegut,

1969). *Breakfast of Champions* (1973) followed *Slaughterhouse Five* on the bestseller list with Vonnegut's creative sparkle and edgy social criticism. The novel contains the astute and hopeful observation: "New knowledge is the most valuable commodity on earth. The more truth we have to work with the richer we become." *Jailbird*, published in September 1969, rose high on the bestseller list. *Galapagos* appeared in October 1985 and *Bluebeard*, in October 1987, followed. *Hocus Pocus* (1990) and *Timequake* (1997) were among his final novels. Vonnegut continued to write short stories and articles.

Students from Xavier High School in Manhattan wrote to Kurt Vonnegut in 2006. Writing back to them, he told them that he could not visit them. He was now eighty-four. However, his note to them was filled with encouragement to express creativity in their lives and in their work. To Michael Perin, Eric Maurer, Cameron McFeely, Michael Batten, and young Mr. Conguista in Erin Lockwood's class he wrote: "Do art and do it for the rest your lives."

The Andromeda Strain by Michael Crichton was his first bestseller. Crichton was a doctor, a science fiction writer, and a sometime film director who received his M.D. from Harvard Medical School and studied at the Salk Institute for Biological Sciences. He researched some of his material for his novels at the Massachusetts Institute of Technology (MIT) in the 1980s. In the 1960s, he wrote *A Case of Need* under the pseudonym of Jeffery Hudson. Following his success with *The Andromeda Strain*, he wrote novels like *Sphere* and *The Great Train Robbery*. Crichton's *Jurassic Park* became a bestseller and continued on the list following the release of the Steven Spielberg film adaptation of the novel, which was a box office sensation. *The Lost World* was its pop novel sequel. *Disclosure*, concerning a Japanese business and a crafty technological dilemma, was also a bestseller. In *State of Fear*, Crichton argued that there was limited human impact on global warming. He explored computer modeling and addressed a variety of scientific-technological topics. Crichton was deeply interested in anthropology and in many areas of science. His nonfiction included *Five Patients*, concerning medicine. Crichton won an Emmy Award for his television drama series *ER*, which was based upon his experiences as a young doctor. An inquisitive and informative writer, Crichton explored the mysteries of science in his popular thrillers. His work is characterized by group protagonists and the integration of science, scientific ethics, and anthropology with theatrical plots.

5

THE 1970s

The Age of Narcissism

1970

The 1970s brought satellite transmission and television expanded across the globe, instantly bringing images of events into American living rooms. In 1970 the antiwar movement was vigorous with protests of the Nixon administration's expansion of the war into Cambodia. People gathered in Washington and in parks around the United States for the first Earth Day on April 22, 1970, to draw attention to their concern about the environment. The women's movement held a strike for equality on August 26, 1970, and an Equal Rights Amendment was proposed. However, this was also a time during which American optimism began to fade in the shadows of troubling events and Americans began to lose confidence in their national institutions. The idealistic social energy of the sixties began to fade. In May 1970 thirteen students were shot by National Guardsmen and four were killed during a student protest of the Vietnam War. Neil Young wrote a scathing song, "Ohio," that was immediately recorded by Crosby, Stills, Nash, and Young. The same day that protests erupted on campuses all across the United States, a freelance writer named Seymour Hersh won the Pulitzer Prize for Journalism for his reporting on the My Lai massacre the previous year.

John Fowles's *The French Lieutenant's Woman* became the #1 popular novel in America in February. Fowles's well-crafted story is set in

Dorset in the Victorian period. The story involves a love triangle between Charles Simpson who is engaged to Ernestina Freeman, the daughter of a wealthy businessman, and the French lieutenant's woman, Sarah Woodruff, who has a checkered past filled with romances and scandals. The novel is a postmodern tour de force. It participates in historiography and metafiction, and Fowles offers several possible endings to the story. On February 8, 1970, Fowles's novel rose to the #1 position on the *New York Times* bestseller list. It was #1 for twelve weeks. Fowles's other critically acclaimed novels included *The Magus* (1965), which emerged from his time on the Greek island of Spetses, and *Daniel Martin* (1977). *The French Lieutenant's Woman* spent its final week at #1 on May 3, 1970. Saul Bellow's *Mr. Sammler's Planet* was #6, and James Dickey's *Deliverance* and Mario Puzo's *The Godfather* were among the top five. Eudora Welty's *Losing Battles*, a well-crafted classic about the Renfro family, was soon on the bestseller list on May 10 but fought a losing battle to crack into the top position.

Love Story (1970) by Erich Segal reached #1 on May 10, 1970, with a sappy, sentimental tale about a pretty girl who dies. With forty-one weeks at #1, it swept away virtually all other competition for the #1 spot for the rest of the year. The story began as a screenplay and eventually became one for the film that followed the book. *Love Story* was widely talked about, including in elementary schools. It was a slight book and a quick read. Someone nominated it for the National Book Award, and the five judges were revolted. *Love Story* was #1 on *Publishers Weekly*'s 1970 fiction list. *The French Lieutenant's Woman* was #2. Ernest Hemingway's posthumous *Islands in the Stream* was #3.

On March 1, 1970, *Everything You Always Wanted to Know about Sex (but Were Afraid to Ask)* offered Dr. David Reuben's suggestions about sex. His book was a big bestseller with a long and seductive title that led the nonfiction bestseller list for twenty-five weeks. The title promised to tell the reader—"You"—everything you ever wanted to know, even if you were bashful about asking. For anyone who didn't think that sex sells, *The Sensuous Woman* by the anonymous "J" reached #1 on September 20 and was followed by former call girl Xaviera Hollander's *The Happy Hooker* in 1971. However, the women's movement also remained strong at this time. Germaine Greer's feminist book *The Female Eunuch*, at #1 on July 25, 1971, provided women's history and advice for liberation and equality. *Everything You Always Wanted to Know about Sex* was

#31 for the year on *Publishers Weekly*'s nonfiction list. *The Sensuous Woman* was #3. In between them on the list was one of the bestselling books of all time: the Bible.

A concern with business success has propelled several books to the top of the bestseller list across the years. On May 3, 1970, *Up the Organization* by Robert Townsend offered practical advice. Townsend may have "tried harder" like the slogan of his own organization said. He was the CEO of Avis rental cars and called upon his managerial experience to discuss approaches to achieving business success. At #5 on the list, it followed a *Better Homes and Gardens* cookbook (#4). *Ball Four* by baseball pitcher Jim Bouton was #5.

A contrary position appeared in *The Greening of America* by Charles Reich. Riding on the momentum of the sixties, Reich touted an alternative worldview of liberated lifestyle and awakened consciousness. Reich was an accomplished attorney who asserted that he had had seen the light. Enough people were fascinated by his book to make it America's #1 bestseller on December 27, 1970, and sustain it at #1 for twenty weeks.

Love Story by Erich Segal (1970) is a sentimental love story–tragedy that began as a screenplay. The film company, Paramount, sought a book to precede their release of the film. In 1970, *Love Story* was #1 and spent forty-one weeks on the *New York Times* bestseller list. The paperback, with its distinctive cover design, appeared to be everywhere. Oliver Barrett IV is the likely heir of a business fortune, and Jennifer Cavilleri is a music major at Radcliffe College who hopes to study in Paris. Oliver's father opposes their marriage. Refused support by his father, Oliver has to find money for his studies at Harvard. He gets a job assisting in a law firm. Jenny learns that she has an illness and goes through therapy, but the illness is fatal. Eventually, Mr. Barrett apologizes to his son. The phrase that entered popular culture from the novel was Oliver's response: "Love means never having to say you're sorry."

A sequel, *Oliver's Story*, reached #1 on April 10, 1977, and also kept possibly more deserving books out of the #1 spot on the list. (These books included *Trinity* by Leon Uris [#2], *Falconer* by John Cheever [#3], Clive Cussler's *Raise the Titanic* [#5], and John Gardner's *October Light* [#8].) Erich Segal himself was a curious phenomenon. He wrote heart-tugging popular fiction while he was a professor of classics at Yale University. He certainly knew something about the sources of literary tragedy when he wrote his two sad and sappy novels that caught the imagination of the reading public. He was born in the Midwood section of Brooklyn and attended Harvard. He wrote both an academic book, *The Comedy of Plautus*, on the Roman playwright, and the screenplay for the Beatles' *Yellow Submarine*. Segal was also an accomplished marathon runner. Although he was athletic, he later suffered from Parkinson's. *The Class*, based upon his experience at Harvard, and *Doctors* were also bestselling novels.

1971

Readers were interested in *Civilisation* by Kenneth Clark, his lectures on the history of Western Europe that became a BBC television series. (The book title retained its British spelling in its distribution to American readers and its television broadcast.) On January 10, 1971, his book reached #1 on the *New York Times* bestseller list. Clark was a well-studied individual with a doctorate from Oxford who chose to be a popularizer. Most often scholars are specialists who focus their intellectual efforts in a particular area of study. However, the traditional man of letters often took a broader and more general interdisciplinary approach to research and learning. Clark was like Will Durant in this respect: a thoughtful writer who could explain the history of civilization to people in a clear and colorful manner. This was followed on the nonfiction list by readers' encounter with Dee Brown's provocative story of the Native American's life in the American West. *Bury My Heart at Wounded Knee* told the brave and pitiable story of a determined and often oppressed people. The book was #1 for twenty-five weeks.

Leon Uris's *QBVII* became #1 on February 21, 1971. The problems of the Nazi regime and Nazi science are recalled in a courtroom drama set in Queen's Bench Seven. A novelist has written that Nazi doctors practiced experimental surgery on the Jewish inmates of a concentration camp. Uris's story was surpassed by Irving Stone's *Passions of the Mind* on April 25. Stone created a fictional biography of Sigmund Freud. Readers' interest in psychology turned that summer toward Father Karras and the contortions of a possessed girl in William Peter Blatty's *The Exorcist*. (Some books are "page-turners." This was a head turner.) Horror stories were seldom big bestsellers before Stephen King. *The Exorcist* in 1971 was on the list for twelve weeks. The suspense continued with *The Day of the Jackal* by Frederick Forsyth. The Jackal, a trained assassin, is on an assignment to kill Charles de Gaulle. The protagonist is the villain. He has to elude French security forces, and there is much drama in how he pursues his plan. Another well-researched novel, Arthur Hailey's *Wheels*, followed at #1 on November 7, where it spent seven weeks. The story opens with an automobile company executive at home with his wife, and it proceeds to unfold Hailey's investigations in a plot-driven narrative. *Wheels* can be profitably set alongside *The Reckoning* by David Halberstam and Lee Iacocca's autobiography, *Iacocca*, by anyone who would like some insights into the automobile manufacturing industry. (*Wheels* was *Publishers Weekly*'s #1 and *The Exorcist* was its #2. *The Passions of the Mind* by Irving Stone was #3. *The Day of the Jackal* was #4.)

The #1 nonfiction bestseller on November 28 was Gay Talese's *Honor Thy Father*. This book may have traded on the success of *The Godfather*. Talese provides a history of the Mafia in Sicily and in America with the Bonanno family at the center of his narrative. The #1 spot on the list was quickly taken the next week by *Eleanor and Franklin*, Joseph Lash's biography of the Roosevelts. Lash had become well acquainted with Eleanor Roosevelt and was privy to the Roosevelt papers.

The Exorcist by William Peter Blatty (1971) was his novel of demonic possession. In Georgetown, in Washington, D.C., twelve-year-old Regan has become possessed. Father Damien Karras, a priest-psychologist, arrives at the family home. He has his doubts about his faith, and he resists the idea that the girl is possessed by a demonic presence. The bishop assigns an exorcist, Father Lankester Merrin, to perform the rite of exorcism. We have seen Father Merrin as we began reading the story. In the first scenes he is supervising an archaeological dig for ancient relics and he has found a statue of a demon, Pazuzu. Now in contemporary Washington, he allows Father Karras to assist him in confronting this case of demonic possession.

The Day of the Jackal by Frederick Forsyth (1971) was written across thirty-five days. Forsyth has pointed out that he had "no great literary expectations." In his midtwenties Forsyth was a journalist in Paris. Charles de Gaulle had granted Algerian independence. It was said that the OAS, the *Organisation de l'armee secrete*, planned to assassinate him. Forsyth befriended Charles de Gaulle's bodyguards. His fictional assassin, Carlos the Jackal, is a kind of James Bond in reverse: a dashing and compelling figure. The film by director Fred Zimmerman catapulted *The*

Day of the Jackal further on the bestseller list. On the fortieth anniversary of the suspense novel, *The Day of the Jackal* a piece appeared in the *Guardian*: "It is no exaggeration to say *The Day of the Jackal* has influenced a generation of thriller writers."[1] *The Outsider* is Frederick Forsyth's memoir of his experiences as a journalist, with British intelligence, and as an author of popular fiction.

1972

Arthur Hailey's *Wheels* was the #1 bestseller on January 2. Other top bestsellers were Frederick Forsyth's *The Day of the Jackal* (#2) and *The Winds of War* (#3), Herman Wouk's big novel recalling the Second World War. This was followed by *Message from Malaga* by Helen MacInnes (#4). Rabbit Angstrom again caught readers' interest in John Updike's *Rabbit Redux* (#5). William Peter Blatty's *The Exorcist* (#6) brought horror to the bestseller list. These books were followed by Alisdair MacLean's *Bear Island* (#7) and Agatha Christie's *Nemesis* (#8). *Our Gang*, Philip Roth's satire on the Nixon administration, was #7 on January 23. Harold Robbins joined the top ten on the list with *The Betsy*. *The Winds of War*, *The Day of the Jackal*, and *The Exorcist* all remained high on the bestseller list during the next several months. On March 12, *The Winds of War* was #1. *Wheels*, *The Exorcist*, and *The Day of the Jackal* were in the top five. *Rabbit Redux* was #7. On May 14, *The Word* by Irving Wallace became the #1 fiction bestseller. Michael Crichton's *The Terminal Man* was #6 on July 9, 1972, following his earlier success with *The Andromeda Strain*. *Publishers Weekly* listed *Jonathan Livingston Seagull* by Richard Bach as the #1 bestseller of the year. Aleksandr Solzhenitsyn's *August 1914* was #2. Frederick Forsyth followed with *The Odessa File* (#3), and *The Day of the Jackal* was still selling strongly (#4).

History and the thriller appear to have interested readers. A secretive metal box in the United States National Archives contained microfilm about German intelligence during the Second World War. *The Game of the Foxes* by Ladislas Farago came out of the author's discovery of that container. After ten weeks at #1 the book was followed by *The Boys of Summer* by Roger Kahn, his story of the Brooklyn Dodgers. Kahn took a look back at Ebbets Field and Dodgers baseball in the 1940s.

In June 1972 five men were caught breaking into the Democratic National Campaign Headquarters at the Watergate Hotel to install secret listening devices; the break-in was immediately traced to the Nixon reelection campaign. Bob Woodward and Carl Bernstein investigated the case for the *Washington Post* and discovered a widespread cover-up. Television viewers heard reports of the murder of Israeli athletes at the Munich Olympics. Swimmer Mark Spitz won seven gold medals in those Olympic Games. North Ireland erupted into violence with its second "Bloody Sunday." Thirteen protesters in a rally of ten thousand marchers in Londonderry were killed by shots from British soldiers. Governor Wallace of Alabama was shot by a would-be assassin on May 15. June 17 brought the arrest of the five men involved in the Watergate break-in. On June 29, the Supreme Court declared the death penalty unconstitutional. Candidate Thomas Eagleton dropped out as George McGovern's running mate on July 31 because of the stigma of mental health issues. On September 3, Bobby Fischer defeated Boris Spassky in a decidedly Cold War exercise of the world chess championship. In October, in an eleven-day bombing raid, the U.S. military dropped some forty thousand tons of bombs on Hanoi and Haiphong in North Vietnam. Richard Nixon was reelected president in a landslide victory in November; he received 45.9 million votes to George McGovern's 28.4 million votes and carried most of the states, winning the election in the electoral college. The Paris Peace Accords followed on January 27, 1973, leaving the status of governance of South Vietnam unclear. President Nixon called it "peace with honor," although American forces had withdrawn from the region without any victory.

The self-help psychology book *I'm OK, You're OK* by Thomas Harris was first published in 1969. It rose to the bestseller list in 1972 and spent twenty-three weeks at #1. The book advocated transactional therapy. Harris asserted that people enter several positions in dynamic interchange with others such as I'm OK, You're Not OK or I'm Not OK, You're OK. People could arrive at balance in their lives—at OK—and learn to deal with their difficulties in personal relationships. The book was on the list for two years. The late summer nonfiction bestseller in 1972 was *O Jerusalem!* in which Larry Collins and Dominique Lapierre analyzed the 1948 warring between the Jews and the Arabs over the city of Jerusalem. *Jonathan Livingston Seagull*, a rather slight inspirational book by Richard Bach, was again a big bestseller, thanks to a film. The book had been circulated since 1970. Aleksandr Solzhenitsyn's *August 1914* was #2 from October through December.

Jonathan Livingston Seagull by Richard Bach (1972) is a fable that encourages readers to be self-reliant, independent, nonconformist, and to take risks in the pursuit of higher consciousness and achievement. The cover's white outline of the gull against a dark blue sky was attention catching. It underscored the theme of accepting one's uniqueness, reaching to fly, and seeking perfectibility. The paperback text can be read in the matter of a couple of hours. (Quicker, if you are a fast reader.) This book held the #1 position across thirty-eight weeks. *Jonathan Livingston Seagull* was #1 from July through December.

1973

In 1973 Americans watched the Watergate hearings. They experienced gas shortages at their gas stations: a result of the impact of an oil embargo by OPEC nations in retaliation for U.S. support of Israel. American POWs returned from Vietnam. In *Roe v. Wade* the Supreme Court recognized constitutional protections on abortion. Secretariat won the horse racing Triple Crown. On television, Telly Savalas was Kojak, the Partridge Family sang, and *All in the Family* continued its humorous social critique. Pink Floyd created *The Dark Side of the Moon*, and Paul McCartney released *Band on the Run* with Wings. Major League Baseball added the designated hitter. On the radio one could hear Deep Purple's "Smoke on the Water." Barbra Streisand was singing "The Way We Were," and Tony Orlando was singing "Tie a Yellow Ribbon round the Old Oak Tree."

On March 25, 1973, the suspense novel *The Odessa File* by Frederick Forsyth replaced *Jonathan Livingston Seagull* at #1 for one week. This follow-up to the 1971 bestseller *The Day of the Jackal* is the story of a journalist in Germany who attempts to investigate a secret organization that hid former Nazi officers. That organization launches a fierce opposition to the journalist's investigation. At this time, *August 1914* by Aleksandr Solzhenitsyn was #7 on the bestseller list.

Jacqueline Susann returned to the #1 position with *Once Is Not Enough*. This is the story of a young woman's quest for identity, pleasure, and fulfillment. January Wayne, the daughter of producer Mike Wayne, returns home to New York from Europe to find that her world has changed. She enters a world of money, drugs, sex, secrets, and late sixties social transition. This was Jacqueline Susann's third consecutive #1 bestseller and her last. She died the following year.

Kurt Vonnegut's *Breakfast of Champions* followed at #1 on July 1 with its protagonists: the Pontiac car dealer Dwayne Hoover and the oddly named science fiction writer Kilgore Trout. Vonnegut characteristically wrote stories drenched in irony and black humor that were energized by his quirky imagination. In this novel the experiences of Hoover and Trout are given to us in a nonchronological narrative. Vonnegut added to his text swirls of doodles in sketches on some pages. When Trout hitchhikes to an art convention in Midland City, Indiana, to deliver a keynote speech, he meets the mentally imbalanced car dealer who takes his science fiction as truth. Dwayne, who owns much of the city, assumes that he is the character in the story: the only man with free will in a world of robots. The idea that humans are merely biological machines raises questions about free will. Enough readers apparently had the ability to choose to purchase the novel to make it #1 for ten weeks. *Breakfast of Champions* was #3 on *Publishers Weekly*'s 1973 fiction list. *Jonathan Livingston Seagull* was again #1. Jacqueline Susann's *Once Is Not Enough* was #3, *The Odessa File* was #4, and Gore Vidal's *Burr* was #5,

Gore Vidal's *New York Review of Books* essay from May 17, 1973, on bestsellers has often been recalled. The *New Yorker* mentioned it in an essay on June 27, 1994. Stan Persky in the *L.A. Review of Books* also referred to Vidal's essay in which Vidal asserted that contemporary writers write the way they do because they have seen too many movies. Gore Vidal offered a claim that television watching was overcoming the practice of reading. He wrote: "Those brought up on the passive pleasures of film and television find the act of reading anything at all difficult and unrewarding."[2] Vidal pointed out that the 1970s had brought Watergate and the titillating appeals of scandal. He called the reveal-all biography or autobiography the "celebrity sinner book." "Watergate criminals are also in demand," he wrote. "Particularly popular is the first-person confession of a washed up or caught up with celebrity who has found God." Others wish to be "credited with having written a memoir composed by someone else."[3]

Perhaps wishing to escape from the dissolution of contemporary politics, some readers were interested in fantasy. Mary Stewart's tale of Merlin the magician and the young King Arthur, *The Hollow Hills*, emerged as a sequel to *The Crystal Cave*. Stewart's initial aim to create a historical novel transmuted into mythology, fantasy, and enchantment. Rising to #1 on September 9, 1973, the novel spent thirteen weeks at #1.

A taste for the international story of suspense and intrigue was in the air as Graham Greene's *The Honorary Consul* reached #1 November 25, 1973. This story of a British consul in Argentina who is kidnapped was one of many of Greene's thrillers, which he called "entertainments." John le Carré's spy thriller *Tinker, Tailor, Soldier, Spy* would be #1 on the bestseller list less than nine months later, on August 9, 1974. Forsyth's *The Odessa File*, which had reached #1 on March 25, remained in the top ten through September 30. Morris West's *The Salamander*, another international suspense story, was at #6 on the Sunday that *The Honorary Consul* reached #1. West's story remained at #6 through December.

As December came, Gore Vidal's *Burr* slipped past Greene's novel to #1. *Burr* remained at #1 for twenty-two weeks. Gore Vidal's novel gives us two narrators: the journalist Charles Schuyler and the memoir journals and conversations with Schuyler of the unreliable Aaron Burr. America's founding and the years of the Jefferson presidency are recalled from the 1830s and Andrew Jackson's presidency. Burr is seventy-two years old in 1836. He is regarded as a traitor and the man who shot Alexander Hamilton.

Vidal finds Burr fascinating. After all, he was there at the start of the United States. His tie with Jefferson in 1800's presidential campaign resulted in his becoming the vice president. The narrative structure of Burr allows Burr to speak, as an unreliable narrator, even as Vidal allows his own perspectives to seep into the text. Even while Burr connives, falsifies, fabricates, and casts aspersions, he provides a somewhat distorted lens through which we can look at Jefferson and the other founders.

Gore Vidal's *Burr* is not only concerned with the title character, Aaron Burr. The novel is also an inquiry into the Jeffersonian legacy. Jefferson's reputation and image has gone through a variety of shifts, as Merrill D. Peterson pointed out in the early 1960s. Since then Jefferson has been a central figure in gender and race studies. His approach to slavery has been exhaustively explored. His private life was first examined by Fawn Brodie in *The Intimate Jefferson*. His relationship with Sally Hemings has been studied by Annette Gordon-Reed. The character of this president has been interrogated by Joseph Ellis in *American Sphinx*. Historians have recognized Jefferson's influence, the ideals of his political philosophy, and the pragmatic features of his actions while in office. They have pondered whether there is a difference between Jeffersonian principles and the policies and programs enacted during his second term.

Vidal realizes that Aaron Burr was an ambitious, scheming, and cynical soul. He engineered Jefferson's electoral victory in the state of New York in 1800. He founded the political machine that later became Boss Tweed's Tammany Hall. Notoriously, he shot Alexander Hamilton in a duel on the Weehawken heights across the river from New York City. He was charged with assembling a plan between 1805 and 1807 to prompt the American Southwest to secede from the Union so he could be its sole executive; this is also recalled in Vidal's novel. In short, Burr is reputed to be a traitor.

Meanwhile, the reader is given Burr's cynical interpretation of Jefferson. Burr considers the Louisiana Purchase unconstitutional. We hear from Burr that Jefferson invested in the bank that he had publicly rejected. Jefferson's Republicanism was suspicious of Federalist central power. America would be a liberal democracy supported by a capitalist economy. The novel about the conspiratorial Burr was timely. On June 17, 1972, burglars were arrested in the Watergate Hotel. The Watergate case filled the news into 1974, as revelations of the Nixon administration's complicity in the cover-up of the break-in became increasingly clear. Later, in *Inventing a Nation* (2003), Vidal wrote: "In my youth I was fascinated by dramatic contradictions in character, in age; I am far more interested in those consistencies wherein lie greatness."[4]

The year 1973 also brought nonfiction that explored the Truman presidency and the Kennedy presidency, an Englishman's perspective on America, and expert advice on dieting, sex, and self-help. *Harry S. Truman*, Margaret Truman's study of her father's presidency, soared to #1 on January 14. She would write a series of murder mysteries, setting several of them in Washington, D.C. Public attention to Truman emerged following his death in 1972. Harry Truman appeared again at #1 in *Plain Speaking*, Merle Miller's oral biography that reached the #1 position on February 24, 1974, and held it for ten weeks. David Halberstam's *The Best and the Brightest* critiqued the Kennedy cabinet. The journalist was interested in uncovering the decisions and actions that got the United States involved in the Vietnam War. He probed diligently the backgrounds and character of the men who made the crucial decisions.

Dr. Atkins's Diet Revolution focused upon a high caloric intake and dieting advice. His book dominated the bestseller list for twenty-eight weeks. *The Joy of Sex* by Dr. Alex Comfort then became #1 for eleven weeks. On October 14 people were learning *How to Be Your Own Best Friend*. Mildred Newman, Bernard Berkowitz, and Jean Owen—the author and two psychologists—engage in conversations about relationships and taking responsibility for one's own lifestyle and actions. The book repeatedly returned to #1 in the first months of 1974.

Burr by Gore Vidal (1973) gives us two narrators: the journalist Charles Schuyler and the memoir journals and conversations of the unreliable Aaron Burr. America's founding and the years of the Jefferson presidency are recalled, from standpoint of the 1830s and Andrew Jackson's presidency. Burr is seventy-two years old in 1836. He is regarded as a traitor and the man who shot Alexander Hamilton. Vidal realizes that Aaron Burr was an ambitious, scheming, and cynical soul. He engineered Jefferson's electoral victory in the state of New York in 1800. He founded the political machine that later became Boss Tweed's Tammany Hall. Notoriously, he shot Alexander Hamilton in a duel on the Weehawken heights across the river from New York City. He was charged with assembling a plan between 1805 and 1807 to prompt the American Southwest to secede from the Union so he could be its sole executive. In short, Burr is reputed to be a traitor. The reader is given Burr's cynical interpretation of Jefferson. Burr considers the Louisiana Purchase unconstitutional. We hear from Burr that Jefferson invested in the bank that he had publicly rejected. Jefferson's Republicanism was suspicious of Federalist central power; America would be a liberal democracy supported by a capitalist economy. Jefferson held what we call Republican principles, as opposed to the Federalist positions associated with Alexander Hamilton—one learns about that in American history classes. However, the reality is a bit more complicated than any clear dichotomy between Jefferson's democratic ideals and the prized image of the self-sufficient agrarian yeoman farmer and Hamilton's assertion of centralized government and commercial concerns. Gore Vidal takes up the historian's puzzle, asking: To what extent did Jefferson's philosophy inform his political practice?

The narrative structure of *Burr* allows Aaron Burr to speak, as an unreliable narrator, even as Vidal allows his own perspectives to seep into the text. Even while Burr connives, falsifies, fabricates, and casts aspersions, he provides a somewhat distorted lens through which we can look at Jefferson and the other founders. Jefferson has left a long record of accomplishment and an extensive trail of documented writings. There are Jefferson journals, letters, and speeches; the official papers of his presidency; his diplomacy; and his scientific and artistic explorations. Burr left little more than letters filled with trivia, racy comments, and matter-of-fact accounts.

The importance of time in the narrative of Vidal's novel is emphasized by Anthony Hutchison in *Writing the Republic* (2007). The "gap between past and future" is crucial. Vidal places *Burr* in the 1830s. Aaron Burr is looking back upon his younger days from within the new era of Andrew Jackson's presidency. Vidal points out that the events leading to Martin Van Buren's election are central in this context. The story is narrated by Charles Schuyler, who is a journalist in New York. The sections that bring us Burr's voice come to us through his memoirs. Schuyler tells us that Burr has been branded as a traitor. The man he shot and killed, Alexander Hamilton, was the forerunner of this new era of burgeoning commercial development and centralized government. Jefferson could not prevent this trend of the modern economy, or stop the "treasuro-bankites." Hutchison points out that Jackson's democratic positions—his attack on the national bank, his assertion of states' rights, his antielitist populism—bear traces of "the Jefferson tradition."[5] The Jacksonians claimed that they were bringing power back to the people. Yet, Jefferson's resourceful yeoman farmer was less the future than the commercial man. The future would be built by democratizing the economy, annihilating monopoly privilege, canceling the national debt. All of this looked rather Jeffersonian. Jackson evoked nationalism and the image of democratic rule by the masses. Of course, toward the inevitable trend in America was the expansion of capitalist enterprise.

Vidal's history reflects upon the modern situation of the 1970s and can be likewise interpreted for our own time. What legacy have the Founding Fathers of America left to us? What did they intend? How might they have wished that we would interpret the Constitution, or the history and principles of the American Revolution? In our time the musical *Hamilton* is popular. It is the story of a man who sought centralized government. The play features diversity and a lively score.

The New York City of *Burr* is one in tumult. There is new media: in this case the penny newspapers. They "make a fortune by each day giving the public some atrocious novelty."[6] There are commercial buildings on the rise, immigrants surging into the ports, anti-Catholic sentiments, and abolitionist riots. Even as Alexis de Tocqueville visits America and writes *Democracy*, change is occurring; modernization is happening; the old agrarian society of Jefferson's dreams is transforming and bursting at the seams. Novels in the 1830s and 1840s attended to this transition. There were a variety of fearful city mysteries whose terrors matched concerns about the increased flow of strangers into America's cities. The world that Vidal's journalist Schuyler speaks to us from is already one quite different from that of 1776. Through Burr's memoirs, readers receive a view of Jefferson in which he is treated cynically. Burr sees Jefferson's dealings at variance with the popular glorious heralding of his reputation. He rejects the Louisiana Purchase as unconstitutional. Jefferson should be held to account for his own imperialism, for his attempt to "subvert the Constitution and shatter the court" in the Justice Samuel Chase matter.[7] Burr may be self-serving and corrupt, but his claims must be considered. We look back at Burr and Jefferson with hindsight. We have seen the shifts in American politics and economy, modernization and commercialism, political corruption, and expressions of nobility.

The Other Side of Midnight by Sidney Sheldon (1973) was one of the first of his many bestsellers. Sheldon was a television screenwriter and theater writer who wrote for comedy and drama. He wrote for popular culture shows like *I Dream of Jeannie* and *The Patty Duke Show*. His style reveals the links between television and popular fiction. In middle age he wrote some of the bestselling novels of the 1970s and 1980s: *Rage of Angels, If Tomorrow Comes, Master of the Game, Windmills of the Gods, The Sands of Time*. He also wrote scripts for more than twenty films. The *Los Angeles Times* called him "the prince of the potboilers" ("Mr. Blockbuster," September 25, 2004).

Gravity's Rainbow by Thomas Pynchon (1973) won the National Book Award and it reached the bestseller list. A background in physics contributed to *Gravity's Rainbow*. The novel is a self-reflexive work that expresses concern about the universe's entropy, ventures critiques of racism and of conspiracy, and possesses ecological awareness. There is physics and psychology, math and history, and a host of literary allusions in its pages. Some readers may find the novel too oblique. Others may be intrigued by Pynchon's novel. How he has connected disparate ideas and scientific background is one of its remarkable features. The narrators cannot see the future, and there is much that we can see about how history has unfolded that they cannot. Pynchon is a fascinating and complex postmodern writer. One does not see much of him, since he is rather reclusive and solitary.

Pynchon was born on Long Island. He served in the U.S. Navy and attended Cornell University; after graduation, he was a technical writer for Boeing in Seattle. Experiences of the West Coast counterculture followed. *V* appeared in 1963. Then came *The Crying of Lot 49* (1966), with a curious, winding, complicated plot. The *New York Times* published his account of the Watts race riots in 1966. His novels are complex, multilayered, and innovative and include *Vineland* (1990), *Mason and Dixon* (1997), *Against the Day* (2006), and *Bleeding Edge* (2013).

1974

Alistair Cooke's America emerged from a thirteen-part television series to which Cooke brought his personal reflections on America. The book sold more than two million copies. The *New York Times* called the illustrated book "a gold mine" and attributed its success to television ("'Alistair Cooke's America' Is a Gold Mine," December 21, 1973, 48). Toward the end of the book he writes, "The institutions of this country still have great vitality; the Republic can be kept but only if we care to keep it." While his background was British, Cooke studied at Yale University and became a U.S. citizen in 1941. His book is richly illustrated and might be considered a TV-generated tabletop book: one as much for display as for reading. Meanwhile, a recession produced a book of encouragement: *You Can Profit from a Monetary Crisis*. The reading audience for 1973–1974 appears to have been drawn toward practical how-to advice. Attention turned to diet, sex, self, money, and titles that spoke to "you."

In February 1974, millionaire heiress Patty Hearst disappeared, and the news media reported that she had been kidnapped. She became a Symbionese Liberation Army terrorist. The episode became a television news sensation. Nostalgia for the Kennedy years and the Kennedy family was evoked by Rose Kennedy's *Times to Remember*; her recollections written with care were the #1 book on May 10, 1974, and stayed #1 well into June. That is when Bob Woodward and Carl Bernstein's exposé *All the President's Men* shot to #1 with the story of their investigation of

Watergate. The book reached #1 upon the wave of media attention and public concern on June 30, 1974, about five weeks before Richard Nixon resigned from office. Reader interest in the investigative journalism of the *Washington Post* reporters persisted. Even so, *All the President's Men* was replaced at #1 by *All Things Bright and Beautiful* by James Herriot. This was veterinarian James Alfred Wight of Britain writing under a pseudonym. This first of his bestsellers published by St. Martin's Press ascended to #1 on November 17.

The fiction list had been headed late that past spring by a peculiar surprise. The novel *Watership Down* by Richard Adams was something like an animated animal film on paper about rabbits in search of a home. A seagull had reached #1 not long before, so why not rabbits too? The story was issued in two thousand copies by Collins and then reprinted as a juvenile book by Penguin. Macmillan brought it out as an adult book in the U.S., and it rose to #1 on May 5, 1974. The surprise bestseller spent eleven weeks at #1. It was then surpassed by John le Carré's espionage thriller *Tinker, Tailor, Soldier, Spy.*

On July 30 the Watergate special prosecutor ordered the release of the Watergate tapes; on August 8 President Richard Nixon resigned. Gerald Ford pardoned Nixon on September 16. His words spoken earlier echoed again: "Our long national nightmare is over."

That autumn, on October 13, James Michener returned to #1 on the list with *Centennial*. His story is set in Colorado in the town of Centennial. Michener's history of the American West, of course, expands in a time frame that goes back to prehistory. The title of his novel suggests the upcoming bicentennial of the United States in 1976. Like most of Michener's novels, *Centennial* is an overview of what the French historian Braudel would call the *longue durée*. It provides a broad narrative that ambles across a vast terrain of time and humanity. Michener wrote thick volumes. About eight to ten pudgy Michener books would probably take up a fair-sized bookcase shelf. His novels also were among the longest to last at the #1 spot on the bestseller list. This one held there for twenty-nine weeks. It was at last effectively replaced by Arthur Hailey's third #1 novel *The Moneychangers*, which followed *Airport* and *Wheels* and rose to #1 on May 4, 1975. This Hailey novel looks into the workings of a financial institution. The banking industry is at the center of another of his plot-driven novels. *Centennial* was the #1 fiction bestseller on *Publishers Weekly*'s 1974 list. *Watership Down* was #2. *Jaws* by Peter

Benchley was #3. *Tinker, Tailor, Soldier, Spy* by John le Carré was #4. *Something Happened* by Joseph Heller was #5.

1975

James Michener's *Centennial* remained the #1 fiction bestseller through the first months of 1975 until May 4 when *The Moneychangers* became #1. On March 16 *Centennial* was #1 and a new Sherlock Holmes story by Nicholas Meyers, *The 7 Percent Solution*, was #2. Joseph Heller's *Something Happened* was #3. *The Ebony Tower* by John Fowles and *Lady* by Thomas Tryon were in the top five on the list. *The Moneychangers* by Arthur Hailey was #2 on April 13. It became #1 on May 4 and remained #1 throughout May, June, and July. *Publishers Weekly* placed it at #2 overall on the 1975 fiction bestseller list. On July 2 *Looking for Mr. Goodbar* by Judith Rossner became a fiction bestseller. It was #1 on August 3. *Looking for Mr. Goodbar* was #3 on *Publishers Weekly*'s annual list following Agatha Christie's *Curtain*.

Suspense and mystery were central to the success of Charles Berlitz's account of the puzzle of *The Bermuda Triangle*. Imagine flying on a plane into a mysterious zone from which one would never return. The author managed to bring together theories and hearsay into a mix that appealed to readers' curiosity and anxiety much like the novels of Michener and Hailey did. Dan Rather of CBS's *60 Minutes* and Gary Paul Gates wrote *The Palace Guard* and saw it reach #1 on February 19. Theodore H. White's account of the unraveling of Richard Nixon's White House, *Breach of Faith*, was nonfiction summer reading. With the glaring yellow streak of its title against a black dust jacket, White's searing exposé led the other bestseller of the summer: the gruesome story of the Charles Manson murders, *Helter Skelter*, by Vincent Bugliosi. Meanwhile, Judith Rossner's *Looking for Mr. Goodbar* chilled readers with a tale of seduction, murder, and investigation and became #1 on August 3 for three weeks.

In August, E. L. Doctorow's playful novel *Ragtime* arrived on the bestseller list, intersecting fiction and nonfiction, historical figures and period elements, and seriousness and comedy. Doctorow's turn-of-the-century cast included Harry Houdini, Luther Burbank, Henry Ford, Emma Goldman, and J. P. Morgan among his fictional characters. On

August 25, *Ragtime* reached the #1 spot and held #1 for thirteen weeks. *Ragtime* was #1 on *Publishers Weekly*'s 1975 fiction bestseller list. In September and October, with *Ragtime* at #1, Saul Bellow's *Humboldt's Gift* was rising up the list. On November 9 and November 23 Bellow's novel was #2.

The bestselling author of mystery, Agatha Christie, had produced her final novels. Her mystery aptly titled *Curtain* rose to #1 on November 30 and stayed on top of the bestseller list for nineteen weeks. This was the last novel she saw published and sold during her lifetime. At the age of eighty-five when the novel was published, she was one of the oldest writers to reach #1 with a novel. Agatha Christie remains one of the bestselling mystery novelists of all time. She was the creator of detectives Miss Marple and Hercule Poirot. Her more than seventy mystery novels collectively have sold millions of copies. The novels, television shows, and collections of her stories have entertained readers for many years. *Sleeping Murder* followed at #1 on November 7, 1976. It was a Miss Marple story written in 1946 and was #1 for seven weeks, thirty years after it was written. Readers who enjoyed mystery or adventure thrillers also read Joseph Wambaugh's *The Choirboys* (#4 on *Publishers Weekly*'s 1975 fiction list) and Jack Higgins's *The Eagle Has Landed* (#5). Higgins's fast-paced thrillers with heroic male protagonists were something of a precursor to the popular Tom Clancy novels of the 1980s and 1990s.

Michael Korda's #1 bestseller *Power!* hit the top of the list on November 23, 1975. Korda not only demonstrated that a dynamic publishing executive can also be a fine writer, he caught the striving spirit of the time. He published the book with Random House rather than with his own firm Simon and Schuster. *Power!* offers ambitious readers advice on how to navigate and negotiate the corporate power structure of American business. Of course, the overstressed corporate ladder climber might also want to turn to *The Relaxation Response*, Herbert Benson's bestseller on how to slow down a bit and breathe and meditate and lower one's blood pressure. These books were high up on the bestseller list at the same time along with actor David Niven's *Bring On the Empty Horses*. Another celebrity bestseller was *Doris Day: Her Own Story* by A. E. Hotchner, which reached #1 on March 14, 1976.

The war in Vietnam wound down to a close. Saigon fell to the North Vietnamese, who struck an alliance with the Soviet Union. China responded by supporting Pol Pot's Cambodia in which genocidal terror began that killed more than one million people. The Helsinki Accords by thirty-five nations affirmed that they would support "freedom of thought, conscience, religion, and belief" within their countries. In popular culture in America, *Saturday Night Live* made its television debut. Jack Nicholson starred in *One Flew over the Cuckoo's Nest*. Bruce Springsteen recorded *Born to Run*. *A Chorus Line* was a phenomenon on Broadway. Muhammad Ali triumphed over Joe Frazier in fourteen rounds of the heavyweight boxing championship.

Ragtime by E.L. Doctorow (1975), his breakthrough bestseller, was a work of clever humor and deft characterization. Doctorow was a novelist whose historical fiction could be written with wry humor, imaginative verve, or serious attention to characterization. He combined these fictional characters with historical personages and varied his narrative style from novel to novel. *Billy Bathgate* (1989) was a well-rounded portrait of a young urchin of the street and his introduction to a criminal element of the city. The atmosphere of yesterday came alive in *World's Fair* (1985), there was a mystery north of Manhattan in *Waterworks* (1994), and *City of God* brought a rich swirl of innovative writing. Doctorow brought us along with William Tecumseh Sherman as his troops marched to the sea in his novel *The March* (2005). He then wrote *Homer and Langley* (2009). *Andrew's Brain* (2014) was published posthumously.

Doctorow was born in the Bronx, attended Kenyon College, and served in the United States Army as a corporal in Signal Corps. Doctorow worked as a book editor with New American Library and as an editor at Dial Press. In the 1960s he was involved with novels by James Baldwin, William Kennedy, Norman Mailer, and Ernest Gaines, among others. *Welcome to Hard Times* was his first novel. *The Book of Daniel* (1971) was written after he left work in the publishing field and became a visiting writer at the University of California, Irvine. In his novel he fictionalized the story of Julius and Ethel Rosenberg. He then moved to New Rochelle, New York.

Shogun by James Clavell (1975) was a historical novel set in Japan that intrigued readers and was made into a television miniseries. *Noble House* (1981) followed. Clavell's first novel, *King Rat*, was based on his experiences as a prisoner of war in Java and then Changi Prison in Singapore. Peter Marlowe is his character in that novel, and he also appears in *Noble House*. Unlike bestseller novels that appear and vanish quickly, Clavell's novels were deeply researched and took years to write. Among these novels were *Tai-Pan* (1966), set in Hong Kong, *Whirlwind* (1986), and *Gai-Jin* (1993). *Shogun* is set in seventeenth-century Japan and concerns an English naval investigator. James Clavell was the son of a British Royal Navy commander, Richard Charles Clavell, stationed in Australia. Clavell was a screenwriter for *The Great Escape* (1963). He also wrote the script for *The Fly* and for *To Sir with Love* (1967). Clavell also translated Sun Tzu's *The Art of War*.

1976

In fiction, 1976 was mostly about two big bestsellers. Gore Vidal's *1876* framed a story with America's centennial during this bicentennial year. Readers could look back one hundred years to the too often corrupt administration of Ulysses S. Grant and the Whiskey Ring scandal. Issues of the past could be set alongside concerns of the present. Watergate was still on many people's minds. The Rutherford B. Hayes versus Samuel Tilden election was one of the closest in history, and the contest between Gerald R. Ford and Jimmy Carter also promised to be a close one. Leon Uris's *Trinity* was a big novel about Ireland. It suggested the present time of the Troubles in Northern Ireland and centered upon the experiences of an Irish family. The novel spent three months at #2 and then rose to a nearly unrivaled thirty-six weeks at #1. *Trinity* was the #1 novel overall on the *Publishers Weekly* 1976 bestseller list. Agatha Christie's *Sleeping Murder* displaced it for two weeks, and then it returned to the #1 spot amid a bestseller field that included novels by Robert Ludlum, Irving Wallace, and Helen MacInnes.

On April 25, 1976, Woodward and Bernstein returned to #1 on the nonfiction list with *The Final Days*. This was their follow-up account of the last days of Richard Nixon's presidency. Theodore White's book *Breach of Faith* had traced the downfall of Nixon one year after their *All the President's Men*. Woodward and Bernstein now had something more to add. *The Final Days* was the #1 nonfiction book on the annual *Publishers Weekly* list. After twenty-one weeks at #1 it was passed on August 29 by Gail Sheehy's *Passages*, a self-help psychology book about the developmental stages of a life. There was a claim by a UCLA psychiatrist that he was supposed to have been a cowriter of the book. Evidently, he had been, for the case was settled with a cash figure and percentage of royalties from the book's sales, which Sheehy had to let go of. One theme of this book was facing letting go of things in life. Then came the outstanding nonfiction bestseller of the year, Alex Haley's *Roots*. It rose to the top of the list on November 21 and remained at #1 for twenty-two weeks. *Roots* was the #2 nonfiction bestseller on *Publishers Weekly*'s list. *Your Erroneous Zones* by Wayne Dyer was #3 and Gail Sheehy's *Passages* was #4.

Who would have expected in America's bicentennial year that a Georgia peanut farmer would have become the next president of the United States? Jimmy Carter had been a former governor and had served on a Rockefeller-funded commission for economic stability. Carter was a committed Christian who insisted that he would make government responsible, moral, and efficient. This was reassuring for voters in the wake of Watergate. During the year the world welcomed the videocassette recorder (VCR). Elton John sang "Philadelphia Freedom," and Sylvester Stallone became Rocky Balboa in the film *Rocky*. Peter Frampton was heard widely on his recording *Frampton Comes Alive*. Barbara Walters became an ABC News anchor.

Interview with the Vampire by Anne Rice (1976) launched a series of novels that introduced contemporary readers to vampires. Her *Vampire Chronicles*, with her character Lestat, are a development of gothic fiction from John Polidori's *Vampyre* to Bram Stoker's *Dracula*. While imagining the supernatural contexts of her characters, Rice has proceeded in her own beliefs from lapsed Catholic and agnostic on to a period of faith expression and then back to a more secular position. In the 1980s she found a strong readership for her vampire stories, and her form of gothic story drew some critical analysis. New Orleans, Louisiana, is a setting for many of her stories. (The Louisiana setting also appears in Charlaine Harris's stories that were the basis for the HBO television series *True Blood*.) Most of the Rice bestsellers are in the gothic mode. *Servant of the Bones* was not a vampire story. Katherine Ramsland has written a biography of Anne Rice: *Prism of Night*. Rice lived in the San Francisco–Berkeley area of California from 1959 off and on through the 1960s. She left the doctoral program at Berkeley. "I wanted to be a writer, not a literature student," she later commented to Anne Metcalfe of the *Financial Times* in London ("Small Talk," November 15, 2010). Her husband Stan Rice was a poet and a painter; she had to deal with his passing and with their daughter's experience with leukemia. Her son Christopher became a writer. Anne Rice has written nonfiction as well as her fiction bestsellers.

Raise the Titanic by Clive Cussler (1976) was among his first bestsellers. Cussler is the author of adventure stories, particularly deep-sea adventures featuring his series character Dirk Pitt. Cussler has dived to explore underwater shipwrecks. His more than twenty bestsellers, some of them cowritten, have taken readers into the mysteries of the world's oceans. Cussler was in the air force as a young man, and he was an aircraft mechanic. He worked in the advertising industry afterward. Taking his skill for producing commercials and combining it with his military, historical, and marine science interests, Cussler began writing about shipwrecks and buried treasure. He created nasty, self-centered villains and developed stories with adventuresome protagonists and maritime technology. The novels tend to emerge from an occurrence that happened long ago, like a broken ship that has been submerged and has been discovered and is filled with secrets in its hold. That he has been an explorer of the sea adds credibility to his fiction.

1977

Trinity stayed on the bestseller list into 1977. The comparable family saga of 1977 was *The Thorn Birds*, a love story by Colleen McCullough set in Australia. In Drogheda, Maggie Cleary has a relationship with a priest, Father Ralph de Bricassart. This is an epic family saga of the Cleary family, ranging from 1945 to 1969. In 1983, *The Thorn Birds* became a television miniseries from March 27 to March 30. It followed *Roots* as the most-watched television miniseries to date. [8] Erich Segal's *Love Story* and *Oliver's Story*, recent #1s, conveyed a sentimentalism that was echoed in McCullough's much broader tale of a romance between a woman and a Catholic priest who becomes a church cardinal. The story's scenes take us to a vividly imagined Australian setting, but McCullough wrote it while working at Yale University.

On March 6, *Trinity* by Leon Uris was #1 on the fiction bestseller list. *Raise the Titanic* by Clive Cussler was #2. On April 3, *Oliver's Story* by Erich Segal was #2. It rose to #1 on April 17. *Roots* was still high on the list on May 8 when Dr. Wayne Dyer's *Your Erroneous Zones* reached #1 on the nonfiction list. Dyer had performed one of the most determined quests for book sales imaginable. He got into his car and embarked upon a cross-county tour of bookstores, community centers, and other venues to speak about his book. The self-help book met self-marketing and do-it-yourself. The effort he made supported the steady climb of the book. It launched a career that included years of public speaking encouragement to audiences that made Dyer one of the most sought after human potential/new age pop gurus of recent times. *The Book of Lists* was America's next #1, and it was immediately followed by Robert Ringer's own act of self-promotion *Looking Out for #1*, which could be looked for at #1 in August 1977, around the same time that Christopher Lasch was calling the 1970s *The Age of Narcissism*. On October 2, 1977 the Tolkien fad brought *The Silmarillion*, his story of Middle-earth, to the top of the bestseller list where it lasted for twenty-three weeks. *The Lord of the Rings* trilogy would surge to the bestseller list when the feature films appeared after 2000.

Falcone* by John Cheever reached #1 on May 22. One of the finest short-story writers in America, Cheever appears to have struggled with his novels *The Wapshot Chronicle*, *The Wapshot Scandal*, and *Bullet Park*. *Falconer* is the story of a man who is convicted of his brother's murder and is sent to Falconer Prison. On June 5 *The Thorn Birds* became #1 and remained there throughout much of the year. Then came detective fiction writer Joseph Wambaugh's *The Black Marble* and Richard Bach's *Illusions*, his follow-up to enlightened seagulls. Other top five bestsellers included William Safire's *Full Disclosure* and Anais Nin's erotica in *Delta of Venus*. *The Silmarillion* by J. R. R. Tolkien was #1 on October 9. *Daniel Martin* by John Fowles appeared at #5. On November 6, Howard Fast's *The Immigrants* was #5. *The Second Deadly Sin* by Lawrence Sanders was #6. The year ended with Tolkien's *Silmarillion* at #1 on December 28.

Looking back, we can recall 1977 as the year that *Star Wars* appeared in movie theaters and *Roots* was a miniseries on television. Toni Morrison published *Song of Solomon*; Woody Allen created *Annie Hall*; Fleetwood Mac's album *Rumours* shot up the pop music charts. The Alaskan pipeline opened, bringing crude oil from northern fields to refineries in Valdez. The United States agreed to the transfer of the Panama Canal to local authorities in Central America. Anwar Sadat and Menachem Begin found a temporary peace between Egypt and Israel. The United States tested a space shuttle. While disco continued to play and people continued to dance, rebellious punk dug in amid clubs in London with the Sex Pistols and at CBGBs in New York with Patti Smith, Television, the Talking Heads, and the Ramones.

A trend of enthusiasm for Tolkien's fantasy brought *The Silmarillion* to #1 on *Publishers Weekly*'s fiction bestseller list for 1977. *The Thorn Birds* was #2. The earlier success of *Jonathan Livingston Seagull* brought Richard Bach's *Illusions* to #3. *Publishers Weekly* listed *Roots* as the top nonfiction seller of the year.

Coma (1977) by Robin Cook was his first bestseller. The medical thriller is Cook's specialty. Cook is a physician, and his stories are supported by a sure knowledge of medicine. He went from Queens to Wesleyan and from Leonia, New Jersey, he crossed the George Washington Bridge into New York City to attend medical school at the Columbia University College of Physicians. He also served on a submarine. Cook consciously studied bestsellers to determine what made them work effectively. *Coma* concerned the need for organs to transplant. *Sphinx* (1979) and *Brain* (1981) followed as Cook weaved together medical fact with dramatic fiction. Cook's stories are often set in Boston. They focus on medical technology, and his fiction tends to educate readers about the medical field and topics like genetic engineering, in vitro fertilization, or medical research.

1978

In 1978, Gore Vidal observed that "last year" $600 million in "Christian books" were sold in the United States.[9] John Barth's novels appeared to Vidal to be written more to be taught than read. Vladimir Nabokov continued to write "very much in the elitist art-novel tradition," Vidal said.[10]

The Catholic Church cardinals elected the first non-Italian pope in four centuries when they chose Karol Wojtyla of Poland. The new pope traveled frequently throughout the world. In America, disco was a phenomenon that crossed from music and dancing to fashion and film. *Saturday Night Fever* appeared with "Stayin' Alive" sung by the Bee Gees. California voted for Proposition 13, which was created to eliminate property taxes. The Peace Accords at Camp David brought together Egypt's Anwar Sadat with Israel's Menachem Begin to forge an agreement over Palestine.

In nonfiction, the irony of *The Complete Book of Running* by James Fixx was that the author died from running. The book was popular; it reached #1 in early February 1978, and sustained eleven weeks at #1. There was a newspaper strike that interrupted the publication of the bestseller list. *The World according to Garp* by John Irving was published, and James Michener was putting the finishing touches on *Chesapeake*, which would be published in the summer.

Bloodline by Sidney Sheldon was #1 on March 12, 1978. Sheldon brought his sense of melodrama and the television medium to bear upon the novel. This novel is a mystery thriller of international activity and financial finagling. The firm of Roffe and Sons is characterized by family disputes. Everybody wants and needs money. There are debts, divorce, jewelry stealing, and blackmail. While we're on the subject of the unethical, one may ask why a convicted criminal should have a #1 bestseller. H. R. Haldeman did, with *The Ends of Power*—he told the world what he thought had occurred in Watergate. He had a lot of time while sitting in prison to write his thoughts down. Joseph DiMona helped Haldeman put those thoughts together into a book (he had previously assisted a stripper with her book on burlesque). Now DiMona assisted Haldeman to try to replace the veil over the Watergate cover-up that Woodward and Bernstein had stripped away. The *Times* reviewer called the book "frustratingly vague and curiously defensive."[11] They were soon more interested in comedy than in the Watergate fiasco. Erma Bombeck's weekly columns for the Dayton-based *Kettering-Oakland Times* were collected into a humorous bestseller about family life in America: *If Life Is a Bowl of Cherries, What Am I Doing in the Pits?* It was at #1 on May 28, 1978, and appeared at #1 for twenty-eight weeks.

Judith Krantz's *Scruples*, a story about a woman in the fashion industry, followed at #1 on June 18. The *New York Times* newspaper strike created a pause in records for the bestseller list. Subsequently, Krantz became a particularly popular author, with her first four works of fiction reaching the #1 spot on the bestseller list. Robert Ludlum, also often on the bestseller list, saw *The Holcroft Covenant* reach #1 on July 9, 1978. Ludlum was an actor as well as a writer of suspense thrillers. While managing the Playhouse on the Mall in Paramus, New Jersey, he wrote *The Scarlatti Inheritance*. Many more novels followed—including novels that have been written after his death by associates of the author. *The Holcroft Covenant* revolved around a Nazi plot to create a Fourth Reich.

Ludlum's next novel, *The Matarese Circle*, also reached #1 on April 8, 1979, with a story about American and Soviet agents. James Michener's *Chesapeake* followed on July 23 and stayed at #1 for twenty-four weeks that were broken up by the newspaper strike. Like previous novels, this one makes use of setting and history in telling the stories of life in Maryland. *War and Remembrance* by Herman Wouk was his sequel to *The Winds of War*, a bestseller in 1972 that was #1 for twenty-one weeks. The family saga focuses attention on the family of Commander Henry, a naval officer. The novel reached the public further through the television miniseries based on the books.

Scruples by Judith Krantz (1978) shot to #1 on the bestseller list. *Princess Daisy* also went to the top of the bestseller list. Krantz was born Judith Tarcher in New York. She worked in the magazine publishing field for *Good Housekeeping* and then as a fashion editor. She wrote for *McCall's*, *Cosmopolitan*, and other publications. Her husband Steve Krantz was a television producer who was a friend of news anchor Barbara Walters.

The World according to Garp by John Irving (1978) was his breakthrough novel. He had previously written *Setting Free the Bears* (1968), *The Water Method Man* (1972), and *The 158 Pound Marriage* (1974). His novels showed sensitive characterization and a streak of playful humor. *The World according to Garp* was the winner of the National Book Award in 1979. *The Hotel New Hampshire* (1981) followed. *The Cider House Rules* (1985) is set in an orphanage in Maine. It focuses not only on children but also on abortion. In *A Prayer for Owen Meany* (1989), a character named John Wheelwright tells the story of his life and his best friend: a curious, sympathetic character named Owen Meany, whose mother is accidentally killed at a baseball game. The story brings us to a boarding school and also probes the draft into the Vietnam War and the Reagan era of the 1980s. *A Son of the Circus* (1995) takes us to a variety of locations around the world, including India. As *A Widow for One Year* (1998) begins, Ruth Cole, a four-year-old, walks in on her mother's sexual affair with a sixteen-year-old. *The Fourth Hand* (2001) begins with a lion tamer in India who loses his hand while working with the lions. Irving also wrote *Until I Find You* (2005), an account of his search for his natural father. *In One Person* (2012) offers a story in first-person narration. William is a sixty-year-old bisexual man who looks back on his life. *Avenue of Mysteries* (2015) tells the story of Juan Diego, who is of

Mexican birth, and his sister Lupe, who reads minds and sees into the future. "Darkness as a Bride" was the working title of his most recent novel, he told Mike Kilen of the *Des Moines Register* ("What Author John Irving Has Learned from Dan Gable and Why It Could Become a Movie," October 26, 2017). Several of John Irving's novels have reached #1 on the bestseller list: *The Hotel New Hampshire* for seven weeks in 1981, *The Cider House Rules* on June 16, 1985, *Widow for One Year* on June 14, 1998, and *The Fourth Hand* on July 29, 2001.

The Eye of the Needle (1978) by Ken Follett is a spy thriller. It is Follett's first bestseller and arguably one of his best novels. Like many Ken Follett novels, the story is set in the World War II period. He deviates from the historical record with the D-Day plan in Calais rather than in Normandy. The goal of the Allies' counterintelligence is to fool the German army; however, there is a flaw in the plan, and the plot could have failed. Henry Faber is a young German spy, known as the Needle, who uses a stiletto as a weapon. He works in London at a railway station. Well situated as a spy, he gains information on troop movements. He then radios this in to the German command in Berlin. One day his landlady comes into the room and sees the radio transmitter. Like Dostoevsky's Raskolnikov, Faber kills his landlady, using his stiletto. He returns to his radio to send his message. David, an RAF pilot, and his wife are in a car accident, and he loses the use of his legs. His wife has a relationship with Faber, who continues to be the elusive spy, the Needle.

Ken Follett's character the Needle was once as daring and methodical as Frederick Forsyth's Jackal. When evening brought shadows, a man leaning on metal crutches might tap up the stairs to an apartment room. The lights in a hundred windows would flicker on, attempting to pierce the darkness. The sniper's rifle, concealed in the crutches and the backpack slung over his shoulders, would be set carefully out on a window ledge. A reader would feel anticipation.

Ken Follett's books have become long, historically based fictions that trace family members and their adventures across time. A reader of Follett's *A Column of Fire* says that she "loved stretching this book out over the past month." A couple asserts that Follett's novels are "a manly read."[12] In Claire Croxton's novel *Ex-Ray* (2014), the narrator steps into the living room and finds Joe on the couch, wearing "thick black-rimmed glasses and reading a Ken Follett novel."[13] A young critic of Follett says that she is pretty sure that there were other girls in her tenth-grade class with Mrs. Roby "who could write a more graceful sentence then [*sic*] this." (Bridget needs to learn how to spell.)[14]

1979

Thousands of people were actively buying and reading books, and some of those books became "bestsellers." Michael Korda points out that since books get passed around like this, the figures for hardcover book reading "are in some ways misleading."[15] The novels of bestselling popular authors in the 1980s and 1990s were selling more than a million copies per book and sometimes more than two million. Brand authors carried the industry. Their books earned more than seven figures in sales.[16]

Meanwhile, the quality paperback book emerged in the 1970s and 1980s. The cover was sturdier, and the paper was more durable. The movement of bookstores into shopping malls in the 1970s was followed by a period in which they were gradually swept away in the 1980s and 1990s by the multistory superstores of Barnes & Noble. In the big stores these popular books were placed out in front on displays. The stores became social centers, albeit one of mostly strangers to each other, many of whom were seeking the same books. Bestsellers were marked down. Classics were discounted. Readers bought more hardcovers and did not have to wait for the less expensive paperback.

Wouk's *The Winds of War* stayed at #1 in the new year. On February 25, 1979, Arthur Hailey's *Overload* brought a story on the utility industry to the #1 spot for two weeks. Joseph Heller's *Good as Gold* was #1 on April 22, 1979. Gold has received an advance for his book on Jewish people in America. Heller is best known for *Catch 22*, a book that is more convincing and moving. William Styron's *Sophie's Choice* told the story of one woman's awful decision during the Holocaust. The story of the Polish woman, Sophie, and Nathan, a Jew in Nazi-occupied Poland, was #1 on July 22 and stayed in the top ten for the rest of the year. Summer reading brought *Shibumi* by Trevanian about the international activities of an assassin; Peter Benchley's *The Island*; and fictional speculations on *The Third World War* by British general John Hackett and other NATO generals.

The dilemma of the Iranian Revolution flashed out in January, and the shah fled the country on January 16. He was allowed into the United

States, and students in Tehran stormed the U.S. embassy and took sixty-six hostages. President Carter was unable to free them. Meanwhile, in Afghanistan the Soviet Union went to war. In Britain, Margaret Thatcher became the Conservative prime minister. The leaking of coolant from a reactor at Three Mile Island near Harrisburg, Pennsylvania, unnerved many people; the emergency occurred when the radioactive core at the facility was exposed by a nuclear malfunction. During the year, Mother Teresa of Calcutta was awarded the Nobel Peace Prize. People played Trivial Pursuit and put earphones into their ears to listen to music on their Walkmans.

Meanwhile, the public had a taste for celebrity biographies. There was the tell-all about actress Joan Crawford by Christina Crawford, *Mommie Dearest*, and Lauren Bacall's autobiography, *Lauren Bacall by Myself.* The Crawford book spent ten weeks at #1 on the list, beginning on November 26, 1978, and extending its run at #1 into 1979. The Bacall memoir, written longhand by the actress, was the top nonfiction book on February 11, 1979, and spent seven weeks at #1. The readers gobbled up *The Scarsdale Diet.* Herman Tarnower and Samm Sinclair Baker, an internist and a cardiologist, respectively, assured readers that they could achieve weight loss. The book was #1 on April 1 and spent thirty-two weeks at the top position on the bestseller list. Coping replaced cooking when Erma Bombeck followed with her advice in *Aunt Erma's Cope Book.* Bombeck's humor-tinged wisdom for housewives and working mothers all across America was again a big hit with American readers. Bombeck wrote about situations with which they could identify, or simply laugh about. After a year that showed publishing success of celebrity biography, a self-help diet, and Bombeck's humorous personal essays, readers turned to a serious study of the U.S. Supreme Court, *The Brethren*, by Bob Woodward and Scott Armstrong.

In fiction, Kurt Vonnegut's *Jailbird* and Stephen King's *The Dead Zone* vied for #1 through October. In *The Dead Zone* a man comes out of a coma with the ability to tell the future. King had previously written *Carrie* (1974), *Salem's Lot* (1974), and *The Shining* (1977). Mary Stewart's *The Last Enchantment* continued the story of King Arthur and Merlin. Howard Fast's novel *The Establishment* broadened the family story he had begun in *The Immigrants* and held the #1 fiction spot to the end of the year. Its persistence at #1 was only broken for two weeks by British suspense writer Ken Follett's *Triple* on December 9 and 16. Norman

Mailer's *The Executioner's Song* and John le Carré's *Smiley's People* were also among the nation's bestsellers at the end of the year. *The Matarese Circle, Sophie's Choice*, and Arthur Hailey's *Overlord* were the top three fiction books on *Publishers Weekly*'s fiction list for 1979, followed by *Memories of Another Day* by Harold Robbins, *Jailbird, The Dead Zone*, and *The Last Enchantment*.

6

THE 1980s

The Rise of the Superstar Author

With a sense of impending doom, an active character in a horror genre story is propelled into a nightmare. The story begins with a break in this character's routine. Something different is happening. The reader feels anticipation of what will happen next. In *On Writing* (2000), Stephen King reminds us that a story emerges from a strong situation. Dialogue defines characters whose speech may reveal more about them than they are aware of. The fast-paced page-turner has to be paced carefully. Each story has its own pace, its own momentum. Writers ought to take care with simile and metaphor and to not overdo the research. Even if Michener and Clancy stories are filled with facts, they are story driven. King does not overly plot his stories. Instead, he lets them rip. R.I.P. into real interesting prose, he would tell a writer. Nothing rests in peace in his stories. They are stories to stay awake by. Standing outside Stephen King's house, you may recall his characters. The house is surrounded by a black wrought iron fence. It is a fine Gothic mansion, with turrets and gables, high windows, and red-painted walls. The mystery and imaginative horror that lives there comes from another source: the creative mind of Stephen King. You half expect the earth to open, the clouds to descend in a fog, and some supernatural phenomenon to appear on the lawn. Again, you feel a chill up your spine. Carefully, you ease your car back onto the road.

In popular fiction, the first years of the new decade of the 1980s would be filled with Stephen King's frightening imagination. The decade also saw the meteoric rise of Danielle Steel's stories to #1; popular books by Robert Ludlum (five #1s), Sidney Sheldon (six #1s), and John le Carré (four #1s); and the breakthrough novels of John Irving. James Michener's novels held the #1 position for seventy weeks of the decade. That number was topped by Stephen King's novels, which were #1 for seventy-eight weeks. Danielle Steel led the list for forty-three weeks across eight different novels. The 1980s saw the rise of many pop novelists who became commercially recognizable names: Tom Clancy (four #1s), Dean Koontz, Mary Higgins Clark, Anne Rice, Jeffrey Archer, James Clavell, Jackie Collins, and Martin Cruz Smith among them. The 1980s brought consolidation of book publishers into corporate groups. There were mergers, and several well-known publishers—such as Scribner's, Putnam, Harper, Morrow, and Little, Brown—became imprints as part of larger conglomerates like Bertelsmann, AOL-Warner, and the Murdoch Corporation.

During these years Salman Rushdie became targeted with death threats by the regime in Iran for his literary novel *The Satanic Verses* and Tom Wolfe critiqued excess and greed in *The Bonfire of the Vanities*. John Updike's *Rabbit Is Rich*, his third novel featuring Harry "Rabbit" Angstrom, was published in 1981 and won the Pulitzer Prize and the National Book Award. There appears to be no necessary correlation between literary merit and the bestseller list, however. More often commercial mass-market novels do not receive literary prizes. *Rabbit Is Rich* rose as high as #6 on November 15 and November 22. More often the novel sold well enough to be recorded at the #10, #11 and #12 spots on the list. Updike's essays were collected in *Hugging the Shore* and more novels followed, including the comic *Witches of Eastwick* and the probing story *Roger's Version*.

Ronald Reagan was elected president of the United States by 50.7 percent of American voters. The conservative leader, a former movie actor, became one of the most popular of U.S. presidents. Reagan brought together right-wing conservative voters with middle-of-the-road independents and "Reagan Democrats." Reagan projected optimism while holding a supply-side theory of economics. The goal of his economic program was to lower taxes, cut government spending, and stimulate business growth. The Reagan administration asserted that business was overregulated and that welfare programs were wasteful. Critics argued that there was no "trickle-down" effect in the economy and that poor Americans were abandoned by these policies. The national debt increased to $2.7 trillion. A recession unfolded in 1981 that lasted until 1983. The poverty rate for children rose to about 20 percent. Wages for workers remained at the same level. President Reagan represented an America that was mostly white, Christian, middle class, and conservative or moderate. The Republican Party included corporate executives, people who believed strongly in family values, voters who practiced evangelical Christianity, and those who were incensed by liberal permissiveness. The Democrats gathered in a fragmented party with a more liberal agenda including feminists, African Americans, Latinos, environmentalists, gay rights advocates, supporters of women's right to choose, and their traditional union base.

In the 1980s, the Reagan administration took a strong stand against Communism, particularly in the Soviet Union. In the USSR, changes began to occur following the reforms encouraged by Mikhail Gorbachev, as the Soviets attempted to modernize and revive their economy. Gorbachev urged perestroika (openness) and glasnost (restructuring). Ronald Reagan called the USSR "the evil empire." In 1983, before the emergence of Gorbachev, the United States announced the Strategic Defense Initiative (SDI) to develop a defense system against missiles and nuclear attack. This was colloquially called the Star Wars defense system. The administration attempted to assist the contras in Nicaragua to overthrow the Sandinista government. Money was to be illegally obtained from arms sales to Iran, and this resulted in a scandal. The Soviet Union, experiencing greater internal changes, was dissolving. In 1987, President Reagan famously called upon the Soviet leader, saying, "Mr. Gorbachev, tear down this wall!"

1980

Kurt Vonnegut's *Jailbird* and Ken Follett's *Triple* led the fiction list in the first weeks of 1980. Norman Mailer's *The Executioner's Song* was #5. On January 20, 1980, John le Carré's *Smiley's People* became the #1 fiction book in America. The British spy George Smiley has decided again not to retire, and he attempts to get the Russian spy Kala to defect. Judith Krantz's *Princess Daisy* also tells the story of a woman who comes from St. Petersburg, Russia, to New York. Three weeks after the book was published it reached the #1 spot and paperback copies were plentiful. Frederick Forsyth's *The Devil's Alternative* held the second spot on the list. Robert Ludlum's *The Bourne Identity* was the story that started off what has become a series of films. The character has forgotten much and tries to figure out who he is and what he has been involved with. On March 23 *The Bourne Identity* was #1 on the bestseller list, a position at which it spent sixteen weeks. *The Bourne Identity* was #2 on *Publishers Weekly*'s annual list of top-selling books. Sidney Sheldon's *The Rage of Angels* followed at #1 on July 13, with a female protagonist. It held the #1 spot for thirteen weeks. April brought novels by Marilyn French (*The Bleeding Heart*) and William F. Buckley (*Who's on First*) to the top ten. Buckley's novel concerned the Cold War tensions between Americans and Russians and the issue of a satellite. Summer reading included *Random Winds*, Belva Plain's story of doctors and their families; Jeffrey Archer's *Kane and Abe;*, and Eric Van Lustbader's *The Ninja*, which featured an erotic samurai. In August, Walker Percy's *The Second Coming* was among the top ten, alongside Margaret Truman's novel *Murder in the White House*. Mary Higgins Clark's *The Cradle Will Fall* was also climbing up the charts. Stephen King's *Firestarter* was #2 through September and reached #1 on September 28. King's novel was #5 of the bestselling books of the year according to *Publishers Weekly*.

The nonfiction list for 1980 began with Woodward and Armstrong's study of the Supreme Court, *The Brethren*, atop the list. Talk show host Phil Donahue's TV celebrity book arrived at #1. It was compiled from stories told by his staff. *Free to Choose*, by economist Milton Friedman and his wife Rose Friedman, told America that it was best to let the market function with less government interference. Their study of the connections between the economy and the government was featured on public television. Friedman was a Nobel Prize winner, a prolific writer in his field, and one of America's most important economists. *Free to Choose* was #3 overall on *Publishers Weekly*'s list for nonfiction in 1980. *Men in Love*, Nancy Friday's speculations about men's fantasies about women, reached #1 next on May 18. It was edged out by Gay Talese's *Thy Neighbor's Wife*, which was also about sexuality and gathered people's stories. He describes a free-love culture before the harsh realities of AIDS emerged in the 1980s. *Thy Neighbor's Wife* was #5 on the *Publishers Weekly* annual list of nonfiction bestsellers. Summer brought to the top of the bestseller list actress Shelley Winters's life story and Douglas

R. Casey's *Crisis Investing*. The economy was faltering, with mortgage interest rates at 20 percent. Casey declared that he had good advice for seeking profits despite what he called "the coming Great Depression." There was indeed a recession in the early 1980s. The United States was able to get out of it earlier than some other nations did. By fall 1982 the American economy was showing promise of recovery. However, Canada struggled with a high inflation rate, and Britain faced high unemployment, which was at three million by winter 1982. Margaret Thatcher, the new Conservative prime minister of the UK, instituted monetarist polices, tightening the reins on failing factories, shipyards, and coal mines and introducing trade legislation. *Crisis Investing* reached the #1 spot overall on *Publishers Weekly*'s 1980 nonfiction list. Wayne Dyer's *The Sky's the Limit* and Alvin Toffler's *The Third Wave* were also among the top ten books recorded by *Publishers Weekly*.

Readers during these hard times escaped into wonder about the solar system and beyond by reading astronomer Carl Sagan's *Cosmos*. Sagan's richly illustrated book was launched to the bestseller list by a television series. *Cosmos* was #2 on *Publishers Weekly*'s annual nonfiction list. While television viewers were looking up at the night sky and at images of a vast universe on their TV screens, Ken Follett offered fiction readers *The Key to Rebecca*, about German espionage in the North African campaign in 1942. *The Key to Rebecca* reached #1 on the fiction list on October 19, and *Cosmos* topped the nonfiction list on November 9. Sagan's book remained at #1 for sixteen weeks. Follett's novel was #6 on *Publishers Weekly*'s 1980 countdown of bestsellers. Other books on the bestseller list at this time were: *The Rage of Angels* by Sidney Sheldon, *The Tenth Commandment* by Lawrence Sanders, and *The Fifth Horseman*, about Libyan terrorists who place a nuclear device in New York. *The Covenant* by James Michener took the #1 spot in the first weekend of November. *The Covenant*, crossing the wide span of the history of South Africa, was the fifth Michener book to reach #1. It was #1 on *Publishers Weekly*'s annual list of bestsellers. Sheldon's *Rage of Angels* was #3, following Ludlum's *The Bourne Identity*. Also rising on the list were *Loon Lake* by E. L. Doctorow and Cynthia Freeman's *Come Pour the Wine*. In December, J. R. R. Tolkien's *Unfinished Tales* rose to the top five alongside *Firestarter* and *The Key to Rebecca*. However, Michener dominated the list at #1 for twenty-five weeks.

In 1980, Ronald Reagan became the U.S. president. El Salvador was caught in a painful civil war, and Catholic archbishop Oscar Romero was brutally murdered while saying mass. Mount St. Helens erupted in the state of Washington, spewing volcanic ash across a wide area. CNN was launched by Ted Turner on June 1. The news station covered breaking news via satellite as it occurred. Turner's TBS (Turner Broadcasting System) began the cable television industry. During the year George Lucas directed *The Empire Strikes Back*, and Robert De Niro appeared in Martin Scorsese's *Raging Bull*. Pablo Picasso's paintings were on exhibition at the Museum of Modern Art. TV watchers of *Dallas* asked: "Who shot JR?" The Philadelphia Phillies won their first World Series in ninety-eight years.

The Cradle Will Fall by Mary Higgins Clark was the first of a string of 1980s stories that firmly established her reputation as one of the most popular mystery-suspense writers of that decade and after. Clark, born in 1927 and now ninety-one years old as of December 2018, is a woman of generous personality who continues to ask: "What if?" Her fiction continues to entertain readers worldwide. Her first book was on George Washington. Her first short story was published in 1956. Born in the Bronx, she attended St. Francis Xavier Elementary School and Villa Maria Academy. She worked as a secretary, a copyeditor, and a stewardess for Pan Am, and she married Warren Clark. In 1964 tragedy struck: her husband died, and she was left to raise her five children, Marilyn, Warren, David, Carol, and Patricia. After some time writing *Portrait of a Patriot* radio scripts, she set to work on her first novel, *Where Are the Children?* By that time, her stories had acquired some forty rejections. Yet, there was something special about this one.

Meanwhile, always ready to take on a challenge, she returned to school and was studying philosophy at Fordham University. Her book on George Washington and his relationship with Martha Custis Washington was now on the shelves in the Fordham Lincoln Center Library. Simon and Schuster began to publish her suspense novels: *A Stranger Is Watching* (1975), *The Cradle Will Fall* (1980), *A Cry in the Night* (1982), *Stillwatch* (1982), and *While My Pretty One Sleeps* (1989). The fascinating and mysterious "Anastasia Syndrome" followed, in *The Anastasia Syndrome and Other Stories* (1989). Patricia Schartle Myrer worked as her agent, and Michael Korda was among her editors. In 1996, she married John Conheeney. The early 1990s had brought her novels to the top of the bestseller list. The stories appeared annually, often at the beginning of May: *Loves Music, Loves to Dance* (1991) provided a twist on personal ads and dating. There was *All around the Town* (1992), *I'll Be Seeing You* (1993), and *Remember Me* (1994). In 1996, she had recently completed her Christmas story, *Silent Night*, and the first of her several classic-song-titled novels: *Let Me Call You Sweetheart*. *Moonlight Becomes You* and *Pretend You Don't See Her* soon followed. The stories kept coming: *You Belong to Me* (1998), *Before I Say Goodbye* (2000), and *On the Street Where You Live* (2001). Since the turn of the century, there have been many more. More recently, she has been writing a series with Alafair Burke, which began with *The Cinderella Murder*. *I've Got My Eyes on You* was #1 on the *New York Times* fiction list in April 2018.

The Bourne Identity by Robert Ludlum (1980) was the first novel in his Bourne trilogy series featuring his series character Jason Bourne. The Bourne series has become familiar to a larger audience through film adaptations. Readers in the 1970s became fascinated by Ludlum's novels of suspense, which included *The Scarlatti Inheritance* (1971), *The Oster-man Weekend* (1972), *The Matlock Paper* (1973), *The Rhinemann Ex-change* (1974), *The Chancellor Manuscript* (1977), *The Holcroft Cove-nant* (1978), and *The Matarese Circle* (1979). Ludlum was an actor and theater manager for the Grant Lee Theatre in Fort Lee, New Jersey, and Playhouse on the Mall in Paramus, New Jersey, before his novels became bestsellers. Ludlum was a dramatic arts major at Wesleyan University, a setting for *The Matlock Paper*. He was a member of the United States Marine Corps. His work as an actor and theater manager likely helped him to develop his strong sense of dramatic action. His fictional characters and the kind of plots he created were extended after his death by writers with whom Ludlum made an arrangement. His novels are all still in print. Ludlum focuses on the heroic individual: a protagonist who is caught in a web of intrigue. This protagonist confronts evil adversaries who are engaged in networks that include corporations, politics, the military, and organizations engaged in conspiracies, terrorism, or other socially disrupting nefarious activities.

1981

The #1 nonfiction bestsellers of 1981–1983 appear lightweight . . . or about trying to lighten one's weight: *Jane Fonda's Workout Book* and two diet books topped the list. There were two Andy Rooney books and some Shel Silverstein poems and sketches. James Herriot wrote about animals in *The Lord God Made Them All*. In *Megatrends*, John Naisbitt suggested the social trends of the future. *The Search for Excellence* considered the successful patterns of business and was followed the next year by its #1 sequel *The Passion for Excellence*. The American hostages in Iran were freed on January 31 after 444 days in captivity. In 1981, Solidarity in Poland was led by Lech Walesa and moved the Soviet-backed Polish government to recognize workers' rights. MTV was created to broadcast music videos. Sandra Day O'Connor became the first woman on the U.S. Supreme Court. Walter Cronkite retired from CBS. Pac-Man was a new video game. Intel and Microsoft provided microprocessors; a Microsoft operating system for the personal computer (PC) was introduced by IBM. The first PCs cost $2,665.

Toward the end of 1981, Updike's *Rabbit Is Rich* was on the bestseller list. (The novel was awarded the Pulitzer Prize in 1982.) John Irving's *The Hotel New Hampshire* reached #1. Colleen McCullough's novel *Indecent Obsession* was #1 on November 15. Other novels were about fierce dogs and sins: Stephen King's *Cujo* (#2), Andrew Greeley's *The Cardinal Sins* (#2), and Lawrence Sanders's *The Third Deadly Sin* (#3). Also on the list appeared *The Legacy* by Howard Fast, *Noble House* by James Clavell, and *Remembrance* by Danielle Steel.

The #1 fiction of 1981–1982 included *Gorky Park* by Martin Cruz Smith (April 26), James Clavell's *Noble House* (May 10 for fifteen weeks until August 23), Stephen King's *Cujo* (from August 23 to September 27), John Irving's *The Hotel New Hampshire* (from September 27 to November 15), and Colleen McCullough's *An Indecent Obsession* through the end of the year. *Noble House* was the *Publishers Weekly* #1 bestseller of the year, followed by *The Hotel New Hampshire* (#2), *Cujo* (#3), *An Indecent Obsession* (#4), and *Gorky Park* (#5).

Gorky Park (1981) by Martin Cruz Smith streaked up the bestseller list. Three people have been murdered in Gorky Park and the tips of their fingers have been sheared off. Arkady Renko investigates and has to track the killer. *New York Times* reviewer Peter Andrews wrote that the novel "reminds you just how satisfying a smoothly turned thriller can be" ("Murder in Moscow, Arkady Renko on the Case," April 5, 1981). Martin Cruz Smith's descriptive skill brings us into settings and atmospheres across Russia, to Cuba, and from Ukraine to the Aleutians. We follow Arkady Renko's investigations and hear his flippant humor and satirical edge. Melancholy but resilient, he is willing to be subversive and to remain inquisitive while others may dismiss his dogged persistence.

With *Polar Star* (1989), the sequel to *Gorky Park*, one feels the chill of the Bering Sea as a ship moves past the barren edges of the Aleutian Islands. Some of the characters are as thin as ice, but Arkady Renko is compelling. Renko, exiled from Moscow, has passed through Siberia to work as a deckhand. When a woman's body is drawn up in the nets with the day's catch, Arkady is pressed into service to investigate. The mysteriously deceased Zina is intriguing, with her secrets, hasty romantic rendezvous, Rolling Stones tapes, and recorded-over cassettes. The stock characters are less well rounded. It is difficult to know who Susan, the American, is and Renko's adversaries are cartoonish heavies. However, the spy Hess is an interesting figure, hidden with technical equipment in a ship that is tracking submarine movements. In this novel, as state Communism in Russia declined in the late 1980s, the author introduced the idea of a collaborative fishing expedition in the icy waters between Vladivostok and Alaska. However, the *Polar Star* is more than simply a fishing factory ship working in cooperation with an American trawler during the time of perestroika. On July 30, Martin Cruz Smith's *Polar Star* was #2 on the bestseller list right behind John le Carré's *Russia House*. It rose to #1 on August 6.

The novels by John le Carré and Martin Cruz Smith, tracing changes in espionage during glasnost, were timely. In Poland, on June 4, 1989, Solidarity won electoral victories generating a summer of civil resistance that led to changes in Hungary, East Germany, Bulgaria, Czechoslovakia, and Romania. The Berlin Wall fell in November, opening the way toward German reunification.

1982

In 1982, Alice Walker's *The Color Purple* was published. It would be awarded the Pulitzer Prize and would become a major motion picture.

Other books of 1982 included Isaac Asimov's *Foundation's Edge*, Jean Auel's *The Valley of the Horses*, Ken Follett's *The Man from St. Petersburg*, Thomas Keneally's *Schindler's Ark*, and James Michener's *Space*. *Jane Fonda's Workout Book* led nonfiction sales according to *Publishers Weekly*. Leo Buscaglia's *Living, Loving, and Learning* was #2 overall on its nonfiction list for 1982. Rabbi Harold S. Kushner provided counsel with *When Bad Things Happen to Good People*.

On January 13, a plane crashed into the Fourteenth Street Bridge in Washington, D.C., killing several people. On March 5, popular comedian John Belushi died from a drug overdose. Madonna released her first single, and Michael Jackson released his *Thriller* album. On television, *Cheers* was in its first season and David Letterman was now on late-night TV. Steven Spielberg's *E.T.* was in the movie theaters and so was Ben Kingsley, in the role of Gandhi. Britain fought over the Falklands with Argentina. The Vietnam Memorial was unveiled in Washington, D.C., on November 13.

The year 1982 brought the Civil War family saga *North and South* by John Jakes (February 28 to March 21, 1982), *The Parsifal Mosaic* by Robert Ludlum (March 21 to July 4), *The Prodigal Daughter* by Jeffrey Archer (July 4 to August 15), Stephen King's four stories in *Different Seasons* (August 15 to September 12), and *Masters of the Game* by Sidney Sheldon. (These novels were all in the top twelve on *Publishers Weekly*'s annual list.) Then, as if his past geographies had not been broad enough, James Michener now published *Space*. It spent twenty-two weeks at #1 on the bestseller list. Readers evidently had their eyes trained on space and on the movie screen. *E.T. the Extra-Terrestrial Storybook* was #1 on *Publishers Weekly*'s annual list. The top twelve on the *Publishers Weekly* list include *Space*, *2010: Odyssey Two*, and *Foundation's Edge*. *Return of the Jedi*, a companion book to the *Star Wars* film, was the #1 book of 1983 according to *Publishers Weekly*.

A Is for Alibi by Sue Grafton (1982) marked the beginning of a popular series that continued until Grafton's passing in December 2017. Clearly, Grafton liked the alphabet. All of her best-known books begin with a letter of the alphabet. Grafton's website early in 2018 declared: "The mystery novel offers a world in which justice is served" (www.suegrafton.com). Grafton's series detective Kinsey Millhone worked from the fictional Santa Teresa, California, with cleverness but without the saint's mystical powers. Sue Grafton was the daughter of a detective novel writer, C. W. Grafton. When she began writing novels, among her favorite detective novel writers was Ross MacDonald (Kenneth Millar). Her female investigator Kinsey Millhone made use of a photostat, as does Lew Archer in the Ross McDonald novels. Grafton was originally from Louisville. She worked as a television writer and wrote screenplays. Grafton adapted Agatha Christie novels and other works and developed a strong sense of dialogue and dramatic action. Two stories were published with her husband Stephen Humphrey. From *A Is for Alibi* through novel number twenty-four called "*X*" (2015) to *Y Is for Yesterday* (2017), Sue Grafton became one of the most popular detective mystery writers in America. Grafton's series continues to sell, and she was able, in her lifetime, to eventually point toward the letter "Z."

1983

Space by Michener was #1 into 1983. The book that brought things back to earth at #1 was Judith Krantz's *Mistral's Daughter*. Krantz's novel was about generations of women in the art world and the fashion industry. (This book preceded the 2006 film *The Devil Wears Prada*, based on Laura Weisberger's 2004 novel concerning the fashion industry.) With *The Little Drummer Girl*, spy novelist John le Carré turned toward the plight of an English girl, Charlie, who is caught up in a web of Israeli agents and PLO terrorists. Spymaster Martin Kurtz is out to eliminate the terrorist Khali. Charlie is torn between lovers and is sent on a dangerous mission. After twelve weeks on the bestseller list, the next of the *Star Wars* movies, *The Return of the Jedi*, came to claim the top spot on the fiction bestseller list. This book was a colorfully illustrated creation based upon the film that reached #1 on June 12, 1983, and spent nine weeks at #1. Reading audiences backtracked from the future to the Middle Ages when they turned to the intriguing mystery *The Name of the Rose* by Umberto Eco. This was a well-crafted and developed murder mystery by a serious literary critic who focused professionally on semiotics: how signs and symbols function. Next, readers traveled to East Europe with James Michener's *Poland*, another of his expansive studies. In his novel they could read about seven centuries of Polish history and dozens of characters who presumably lived among the well-known people who appear in the historical record. After a mere twelve weeks (short for the stay at #1 of a Michener novel) Michener's book was knocked out of the #1 spot by Stephen King's *Pet Sematary*. (Yes, the story is as disturbing as that spelling.) It spent thirteen weeks at #1 on the bestseller list. Erma Bombeck made readers laugh with her #1 book *Motherhood* from October 23, 1983, for twenty-one weeks at #1. *Poland* was the #2 book on *Publishers Weekly*'s annual fiction list. *The Little Drummer Girl* by John le Carre (#4) joined King's *Pet Sematary* (#3) and *Christine* (#5) in *Publishers Weekly*'s top five. *Changes* by Danielle Steel (#6) was followed by Umberto Eco's mystery *The Name of the Rose* (#7). Other bestselling novels in the *Publishers Weekly* top fifteen were Louis L'Amour's *The Lonesome Gods*, Judith Rossner's *August*, Isaac Asimov's *The Robots of Dawn*, and Norman Mailer's *Ancient Evenings*.

In 1983, the first compact disc (CD) was produced. Martin Luther King Day became a national holiday. The Strategic Defense Initiative (SDI) was introduced. Stanley Karnow wrote *Vietnam: A History*. Michael Jackson sang "Beat It," and the Police sang "Every Breath You Take." Vanessa Williams became Miss America. Nancy Reagan started her antidrug campaign. An Apple computer user could now make use of a mouse. Cell phones began to be produced.

Hollywood Wives by Jackie Collins (1983) was a sure #1 among her many sex and romance novels. Thirty-two of them reached the bestseller list. Her books have sold more than five hundred million copies. Like her sister Joan Collins, a noted actress and celebrity, Jackie Collins sought to be an actress. She dropped out of school, and she acted in several B movies. She titled her first novel *The World Is Full of Married Men* (1968). During the next several years she started novels, stopped writing them, and then returned to working on them. *Lovehead* (1974) became *The Love Killers* (1989). The *World Is Full of Divorced Women* (1975) played upon the title of her first novel but was not a sequel to it. In the 1980s she began to develop her character Lucky Santangelo, the daughter of a gangster, in *L.A. Chances* (1981). *Hollywood Wives* (1983) reached the #1 spot on the list. It was #9 on *Publishers Weekly*'s annual list. Advertisements for the novel called it an exposé of scandalous behavior in Hollywood. From the mid-1980s, a series of Lucky Santangelo novels appeared, beginning with *Lucky* (1985) and the later *Lucky Boss*. Glamour, sex, and relationships were central in *Hollywood Husbands* (1986) and *Rock Star* (1988). From *Kiss* (1999) into the new century, Jackie Collins remained a bestselling author with *Lovers and Players* (2006),

Drop Dead Beautiful (2007), and *Poor Little Bitch Girl* (2009). *Married Lovers* (2008) looked at the affairs of personal trainer Cameron Paradise. Lucky appeared in *The Goddess of Vengeance*. Collins's *The Power Trip* (2013) also reached the bestseller list.

1984

The next year brought George Orwell's *1984* back to the bestseller list. The year's bestseller list began with the grisly murder mystery *Who Killed the Robins Family?* Its gimmick was to offer readers a cash prize for solving the mystery. When Rupert Holmes's adaptation of Dickens's *The Mystery of Edwin Drood* had its debut at the New York Shakespeare Festival in 1985, it offered audiences the opportunity to pick their favorite ending of Dickens's unfinished story. The interactive play, like the audience participation book, may have been a sign of the times. Video games were emerging between 1982 and 1984. We were on the edge of the digital revolution and the availability of personal computers. Steve Jobs and Apple introduced the Macintosh computer to the public on a Super Bowl commercial. *Time* magazine introduced Bill Gates on its cover on April 14.

The Aquitaine Progression by Robert Ludlum was #1 on the fiction bestseller list in April. Joel Converse, an attorney and former Vietnam War pilot, is drawn in to stop a conspiracy of generals who aim at world domination. The novel reached #1 on March 11. Behind it on the list were Judy Blume's *Smart Women* and Susan Isaac's *Almost Paradise*. Andrew Greeley's *Lord of the Dance* also entered the top ten. On June 3, Danielle Steel's *Full Circle* reached #1. *The Walking Drum*, a Western by Louis L'Amour, was #2, and it exchanged places with Leon Uris's *The Haj*. Right behind that international thriller was Dr. Seuss, who sent forth an illustrated warning about the nuclear arms race. John Updike's *The Witches of Eastwick*, at #7 on June 3, followed one of Frank Herbert's sequels to *Dune*, to which he gave the title *Heretics of Dune*. Updike's novel rose up behind Uris's *The Haj* the next week. On the last Sunday in June, Danielle Steel's *Full Circle* at #1 was followed by the surprise bestseller *And Ladies of the Club* by Helen Hoover Santmyer. *The Aquitaine Progression*, *The Haj*, and *The Witches of Eastwick* were joined in the top ten by Gore Vidal's *Lincoln* at #7.

On July 8, 1984, Santmeyer's novel, set in Ohio from the 1860s to 1932, rose to #1. She was at that time, at the age of eighty-seven, the oldest writer to reach #1. (Agatha Christie, Mary Higgins Clark, and James Michener are among the authors who have reached that #1 mark past the age of eighty.) Santmeyer wrote her first novels in the 1920s. Her bestseller for the 1980s had a remarkable journey. It began its life at the Ohio State University Press. A woman in Cleveland read it and contacted her son who was a Hollywood producer, who then sent it to an agent who connected the story with Putnam in New York. Gore Vidal's *Lincoln* rose to #4 behind Steel's *Full Circle* and Ludlum's *Aquitaine Progression*.

Suspense novels by Jeffrey Archer and Frederick Forsyth came from England and quickly rose on the fiction list. In *First among Equals*, Archer tells the story of men vying to be prime minister. (Of course, Margaret Thatcher continued to have a firm grasp on that position.) In Forsyth's *The Fourth Protocol*, a jewelry heist led to international intrigue. Stephen King teamed up with horror writer Peter Straub to write *The Talisman*. Their novel about parallel worlds was #1 on October 28: a fine addition to Halloween reading. It spent twelve weeks at #1.

In 1984, readers swept up biographies of celebrities: New York mayor Ed Koch, comic actor John Belushi, and the Kennedy family. *Iacocca* was thirty-nine weeks at #1. *Yeager*, a Book of the Month selection, was #1 on July 25, 1985. Priscilla Presley's recollection of Elvis followed this at #1. Meanwhile, Leo Buscaglia became everyone's favorite self-help author, with *Loving Each Other* and *Bus 9 to Paradise* both arriving at #1 on the nonfiction list.

Bruce Springsteen sang "Born in the U.S.A.," a song that was misinterpreted by Ronald Reagan. The president heard it as a triumphant anthem to America pride. Springsteen wrote it in the voice of a down-and-out former Vietnam vet. During the year, Arnold Schwarzenegger became the Terminator. Bill Cosby's TV show was on the air. Bernie Goetz shot back at would-be muggers on the New York subway. The Iran-contra scandal caused consternation. Indira Gandhi was assassinated in India and replaced by her son Rajiv. Literary novels included *The Unbearable Lightness of Being* by Milan Kundera, Gore Vidal's *Lincoln*, John Updike's *The Witches of Eastwick*, and Sandra Cisneros's *The House on Mango Street*. Tom Wolfe's *The Bonfire of the Vanities* was serialized in *Rolling Stone*.

The Hunt for Red October (1984) by Tom Clancy, like a submarine, emerged from the depths of obscurity and rose to the top of the list as a suspenseful Cold War thriller. In his story, the Soviet Ramius wishes to defect to the West. He has grown to hate impersonal Soviet rule. He holds anger toward the officials who freed an incompetent doctor, the son of a Politburo member, who caused the death of his wife. Jack Ryan, a CIA analyst, brings a group of U.S. Navy officers onto a Soviet sub. Tom Clancy's focus on American patriotism, heroism, and suspense continued with *Clear and Present Danger*, *Patriot Games*, and other novels that all soared to the top of the bestseller list. In hardcover, the book felt substantial and weighty. They were commercial productions: each one an adventure, a military espionage thriller, a tribute to American ingenuity and determination. Clancy never aspired to literature, the critic David L. Ulin observed in the *L.A. Times* ("Tom Clancy and the Critical Divide," October 2, 2013). He noted Michael Hiltzik's term for Clancy's fiction, the "technobabble thriller," and raised the question of whether there was a divide between critics and readers with respect to the wide popularity of Clancy's novels. Elements of Clancy's action novels were recast as video games.

Would Tom Clancy have journalistic standing with the First Amendment? That question was asked by Kraig L. Baker in the *Washington Law Review*.[1] Clancy seized upon concerns about international politics, drug trafficking, terrorism, and military technology. There were inquiries into the U.S. Special Forces and the branches of the military. *Executive Orders*, *Rainbow Six*, *The Cardinal of the Kremlin*, *Debt of Honor*, and *The Sum of All Fears* were among his many bestsellers. It might be suggested that the Cold War produced Clancy's concerns and his military-technology focus. Clancy attended Loyola University in Baltimore and was in the Army Reserve Officers Training Corps. He had to wear eyeglasses for his nearsightedness, and he worked for a time in the insurance field in Hartford, Connecticut. *The Hunt for Red October* sold for $5,000 to the Naval Institute Press. *Red Storm Rising* (1986) was his first cowritten work. Clancy also wrote nonfiction on America's military branches and on military technology and Special Forces. *The Teeth of the Tiger* (2003) brought his character Jack Ryan's son and nephew into the story. Clancy became a brand-name author who was paid highly for his novels. He bought the Baltimore Orioles with other investors, and he was interested in private space flight. Clancy held conservative Republican views. His novel *Debt of Honor* (1994) had a scene in which a Japanese airline pilot crashes into the United States Capitol while the U.S. president is speaking to Congress. Clancy was interviewed about this after September 11, 2001, by Charlie Rose on PBS and by Judy Woodruff of CNN. Clancy lived by the Chesapeake Bay, and his wife got him a Sherman tank for one of his birthdays. He set it out proudly on the lawn.

1985

The Godfather returned to the top of the bestseller list in January 1985 in Mario Puzo's *The Sicilian*. The novel was #1 on January 20. Between January 20 and January 22, the polar vortex shifted south and froze North America. On January 20, the thermometer in Chicago showed a chilly minus twenty-five to minus twenty-seven degrees and the wind blew at twenty-five miles per hour. Cleveland and Pittsburgh were at minus eighteen degrees. It was so cold that Ronald Reagan was inaugurated for his second term in a ceremony at the White House. The public ceremony followed the next day. Behind *The Sicilian* and *The Talisman*, a novel by Douglas Adams with the peculiar title *So Long and Thanks for All the Fish* was #3, and John Jakes's *Love and War* was #4. Madonna's "Like a Virgin" and Foreigner's "I Want to Know What Love Is" were #1 and #2, respectively, on the pop music charts.

Sidney Sheldon's *If Tomorrow Comes* and Danielle Steel's *Family Album* moved up the bestseller list behind Puzo's novel *The Sicilian*. Sheldon's novel was about a woman who was in prison although she was innocent. She now planned to get back at the people who had framed her. Steel's novel was about a family: two parents and five children. Sheldon's story was #1 on February 3 and was replaced at #1 by Steel's story on March 31. Four weeks later people had discovered that the unfamiliar name of Richard Bachman was a pseudonym for Stephen King. *Thinner* soared to the top of the bestseller list and stayed at #1 for a month. The #1 books by Sheldon, Steel, and King prove rather conclusively that a market "brand-name" author attracts a popular reading audience. In Stephen King's story, a curse is cast upon a lawyer by a gypsy, and each day he is becoming "thinner." When King's authorship of *Thinner* was concealed behind the nom de plume Richard Bachman, the novel sold relatively well. However, it was not a bestseller. Once readers found out that *Thinner* was written by Stephen King, everything changed.

Barbara Taylor Bradford's *Hold the Dream* was a family story that continued the story she had begun with *A Woman of Substance*. *Hold the Dream* was the #1 fiction book on June 9, 1985. Families were featured prominently in Danielle Steel's *Family Album* and John Jakes's *Love and War*. The loyalties (or disloyalties) of the Mafia family were central to Mario Puzo's *The Sicilian*. John Irving's *Cider House Rules*, set in a Maine orphanage, was about children without families who had found a new home with each other and their caretakers. It rose to the #1 position on June 16. A week later, Stephen King returned to #1 with a collection of short stories, *Skeleton Key*. Short-story collections are seldom on the bestseller list, but this was Stephen King. The book spent ten weeks at the top of the fiction list. *Lucky* by Jackie Collins replaced it at #1 on September 1 with her story of a glamorous woman attached to a crime boss who confronts an heiress to a wealthy shipping company. *The Accidental Tourist* by Anne Tyler, published August 18, went on to win the National Book Critics Circle Award.

Readers found a folksy, conversational storytelling in Garrison Keillor's *Lake Wobegon Days*, which reached #1 on September 15. The book was filled with stories from Minnesota that Keillor presented on National Public Radio. The radio show and the book were both popular and much talked about. Stephen King's *Skeleton Key* and Jackie Collins's *Lucky* held on in the top three. *The Fourth Deadly Sin* by Lawrence Sanders was at #4 with a murder mystery about a psychiatrist. At #5, *The Two Mrs. Grenvilles* was Dominick Dunne's high-society murder mystery of scandal and betrayal. Tom Clancy's bestseller *The Hunt for Red October* and Larry McMurtry's *Lonesome Dove* were at #6 and #7, respectively, on September 15. *Dancing in the Light*, actress Shirley MacLaine's explorations of her past lives and new age mysteries, was a popular book on the nonfiction list. Priscilla Presley and Sandra Harmon's *Elvis and Me* was #1 on September 29. (The title *Elvis and I* might have offered better English usage, but no one seemed to care about the lapse in grammar.) *Texas*, another big James Michener book, was the #1 fiction bestseller on October 13. Michener gives readers stories of Texas history, from its time as a Mexican territory through settlement and the story of the Alamo. His books are not brisk, lively reads. They tend to bog down in the historical and geographical details that are woven amid the storytelling. Yet, they are serious and literate novels, and readers can learn a lot from them.

Readers seem to have wanted to go back further in time than the four hundred or so years of Michener's Texas history. Jean M. Auel's *Clan of the Cave Bear* prepared the way for the sequel *The Mammoth Hunters* that rose to #1 on November 24. This fantasy in a prehistoric setting about her character Ayla developed a strong following and remained at #1 for eleven weeks.

World events included the emergence of Mikhail Gorbachev as the Soviet Union's dynamic new leader. British scientists claimed to have detected a hole in the ozone layer over Antarctica. General Electric bought and absorbed RCA and NBC. *Les Miserables*, the musical derived from Victor Hugo's novel, was staged in London.

Full Circle by Danielle Steel (1985) was a #1 bestseller that established her as a fixture on the bestseller list. Since the 1980s her novels have repeatedly appeared on the list. Before becoming a full-time novelist, she worked in public relations and advertising. Steel writes more than one novel at a time, and each one seems destined to be a bestseller. More than twenty of those stories have been adapted for television. Even with her prodigious output, her stories tend to not be sequels of previous ones. The books are often called formula creations. Critics have contended that there is more "tell" than "show" in her stories. Several stories focus on romance, the rich, glamorous, and famous and concern love and loss, family, divorce, and mental health. Her later female characters seem to be stronger in spirit and action than her earlier ones. Steel may hold the record for the most novels on the bestseller list for the most consecutive weeks.

When the Bough Breaks by Jonathan Kellerman (1985) was the first of his many novels on the bestseller list. Kellerman is a child psychologist as well as one of the bestselling popular detective fiction novelists in the world. He was born in New York and his family moved to Los Angeles, where most of his works of fiction are set. He is married to Faye Kellerman, whose novels have also appeared on the bestseller list. He has created the series character Alex Delaware, a psychologist-detective who works with the rough-and-tumble LAPD detective Milo Sturgis, who is gay. He has also introduced a female detective character, Petra Conner. Kellerman's father was an aerospace engineer and inventor, and his mother was a dancer. A psychologist might say that, amid that creativity, he was a product of nature and nurture. He drew illustrations, played and taught guitar, and studied clinical psychology. He became involved with the Children's Hospital of Los Angeles and developed a research career, writing *Helping the Fearful Child* (1981). Faye and Jonathan Kellerman contribute to the Children's Hospital of Los Angeles Hematology-Oncology Center. *When The Bough Breaks* won the Edgar Award in 1986 for a mystery novel. Novels soon followed almost annually: *Blood Test* (1986), *Over the Edge* (1987), *Silent Partner* (1988), *Time Bomb* (1990), *Private Eyes* (1992), and *Devil's Waltz* (1993). Kellerman introduced his character Petra Conner in 1997. He began to weave point of view and narrative across the perspectives of Alex Delaware, Milo Sturgis, and Petra Conner. Novels like *Monster* (1999), *Flesh and Blood* (2000), *The Murder Book* (2002), and *A Cold Heart* (2003) all jumped onto the bestseller list with covers in bold, primary colors. He then gave single-word titles to his subsequent novels: *Therapy* (2004), *Rage* (2005), *Gone* (2006), *Obsession* (2007). Such single-word titles for his novels have continued through 2017.

White Noise by Don DeLillo (1985) begins with the life of a character who decides to make Hitler studies his calling in life. In DeLillo's bestseller *Libra* he explored the mind of a fictionalized Lee Harvey Oswald. *Mao II* (1992) was a Pulitzer Prize finalist. *Underworld* (1998), a big novel, was also a Pulitzer Prize finalist. It has been named as one of the most significant works of American fiction from the past several decades. DeLillo attended Fordham University in the Bronx, graduating in 1958. He worked for several years in the advertising business. His first published short story was in Cornell's literary magazine *Epoch* in 1960. His work on novels began in the mid-1960s. In the 1970s he published six of them, including *Americana* (1971) and *End Zone* (1972), which combined football and nuclear war and had the dark comedic feeling that DeLillo would later bring to *White Noise*. After 2000, DeLillo's work included *The Body Artist* (2001), *Cosmopolis* (2003), *Falling Man* (2007), and *Point Omega* (2010), which began with reference to Teilhard de Chardin's Omega Point idea.

1986

On January 28, the Challenger spacecraft exploded about a minute after takeoff, killing the seven astronauts on the shuttle mission. This included Christa McAuliffe, a New Hampshire teacher. The Russian war in Afghanistan prompted Ken Follett's *Lie Down with Lions*, a novel that reached #1 on February 16, 1986. That war was still raging when Follett wrote his story. In December 1979, on Christmas, paratroopers landed in Kabul. The mujahideen fought back ferociously. The Soviets increased forces in Afghanistan in the mid-1980s. The cost in lives was high, and in 1987 the government led by Mikhail Gorbachev announced that withdrawal of troops would begin in 1987. Follett's story is a romantic melodrama in which a woman from England is trapped amid America CIA operatives and Russian KGB agents. More recent events in Afghanistan and the American military involvement there will have changed the context of this story for some readers.

Readers of *The Bourne Supremacy* today might visualize the face of the actor Matt Damon as they turn the pages. The actor was ten years old when Robert Ludlum's *The Bourne Identity* was published. He was fifteen when *The Bourne Supremacy* hit #1. In this Ludlum novel, there is a plan afoot to seize Hong Kong and lure China into a major war with the Western powers. When readers in the northern and eastern regions of the United States were coming out of the cold, John le Carré was giving them another #1 bestseller: *A Perfect Spy*. His novel about a British spy who has a con man for a father was #1 on May 6, 1986. After six weeks, Judith Krantz's *I'll Take Manhattan* took over #1 with her story about a woman involved in magazine publishing in New York. Bill Cosby's book *Fatherhood* spent twenty-six weeks at #1 beginning on May 25, 1986. Louis L'Amour's adventure story *The Last of the Breed* is about an air force officer in Siberia. It was his second #1 novel of the year. The L'Amour catalog is extensive. He wrote some ninety books, including several that are collections of short stories. Danielle Steel's *Wanderlust* was her annual #1, following her #1 *Full Circle* in 1984 and #1 *Family Album* in 1985. *Fine Things* would follow as her next #1 in 1987.

Tom Clancy's *The Hunt for Red October* did not at first have the distribution that could be provided by a major trade publisher. It did make the bestseller list, however, and it later became a hit movie. Clancy's *Red Storm Rising*, his next novel, did a lot of rising. Up went readers' blood pressure and up went sales income as readers absorbed this story about the coming of World War III. The conflict is initiated without nuclear weapons, but such weapons linger as a fearful possibility in the background. From August 17, Clancy's story held the top spot. Then came that great doorstop of a book: Stephen King's *It*. You could lift weights with *It*. In Derry, Maine, seven children experience terror. Georgie Denbrough loses his paper boat and chases it to a storm drain. Looking down the drain for it, he meets a pair of glowing, evil eyes. Dark memories, fear, and trauma live beneath the street and beneath the surfaces of suburban and rural town life in America. Stephen King's narrative method is interesting in this novel. While told in the third-person omniscient, the story alternates between two time periods. *Publishers Weekly* called it the top bestselling novel of 1986.

James Clavell had once horrified audiences as a screenwriter with his script for *The Fly*. He turned his attention to writing lengthy novels. They were not quite as long as Stephen King's *It*, but in paperback form they are chunky. Clavell may be best known for *Shogun*, his story set in Japan that was adapted into a television miniseries. Clavell brought his readers to Iran with *Whirlwind*, the #1 bestseller on November 23, 1986. The book remained at #1 into December. His previous novel, *Noble House*, concerned the competition between British and Chinese businessmen over a Hong Kong trading house.

Meanwhile, a Frank Sinatra biography was the #1 nonfiction bestseller. When *His Way* was about to be published, the singer and his management tried to stop production. The book by Kitty Kelley was published by Bantam. Writers and editors argued for the freedom to publish and not let Sinatra exclusively control his public image his way. The book's title comes from the song "My Way," popularized by Sinatra. Paul Anka's lyrics for "My Way" were set to a French composer's melody. The song was recorded by Sinatra in 1969.

The #1 nonfiction books that preceded the Sinatra biography included Leo Buscaglia's *Bus 9 to Paradise*, Dr. Seuss's *You're Only Old Once*, David Stockman's *The Triumph of Politics*, and Bill Cosby's *Fatherhood*. The coffee-table book *A Day in the Life of America* became #1 on November 30, 1986. Produced by Collins, with no author and no text, it was a nicely illustrated tribute to America. *Fatherhood* by Bill Cosby was #1 on *Publishers Weekly*'s annual list for nonfiction. *His Way*, Kitty Kelley's book on Frank Sinatra, was #3, following Harvey and Marilyn

Diamond's *Fit for Life*. Dr. Seuss came in at #5 with *You're Only Old Once*. Readers appeared unable to decide whether to eat or to diet. In *Publishers Weekly*'s top twelve were *The Rotation Diet*, *The Frugal Gourmet*, and *The Frugal Gourmet Cooks with Wine*.

Robert Penn Warren was named the first poet laureate. Richard Ford wrote *The Sportswriter*, and Margaret Atwood's *The Handmaid's Tale* was published. Paul Simon released his Grammy Award–winning album *Graceland*. The Statue of Liberty got a face-lift, and Americans celebrated the country's one hundredth anniversary.

Strangers by Dean Koontz (1986) started off his long run of bestsellers. Koontz's fiction spans mystery, horror, science fiction, fantasy, and comic satire. Koontz has had fourteen #1 bestsellers. He began by writing science fiction novels under a variety of pen names. Eventually, he developed a steady stream of suspense-horror fiction. *Demon Seed* was his first novel to reach the bestseller list. *Strangers* also made the list. From that point on, more than a dozen Koontz novels shot to #1. His novels were on the fiction bestseller list frequently throughout the 1980s. With *Midnight*, he introduced a dog as a character in his fiction. He later began a light-hearted series with his sympathetic Odd Thomas character. More recently, Koontz has returned to the suspense genre. Koontz's *The Whispering Room* is part of his series with his character Jane Hawk, an FBI special agent. A reader posting in Goodreads expresses disappointment with Koontz's "silly Odd Thomas" stories and is happy that Koontz has returned to his suspense stories. Another reader calls the book his "best yet" and says, "I almost forgot what a Dean Koontz book did to me." The Luther Tillman character who assists Jane Hawk is appealing according to another reader who has posted his thoughts on Goodreads. Maybe the story has "less heart" than the first volume in that series, the reader suggests. A reader named Suzanne finds the protagonist to be a female hero who is "just as competent as Jason Bourne, Jack Reacher, Mitch Rapp." Of course, for the past decade, the presence of a strong female protagonist in stories has been an evident trend in popular fiction.

1987

Whether the American mind was closing in 1987, as University of Chicago professor Allan Bloom claimed, is anyone's guess. Bloom's *The Clos-*

ing of the American Mind was a summer nonfiction bestseller that assessed liberal arts education and what he considered the distractions of
rock music and popular culture. Novelist Saul Bellow instigated the book
when he encouraged his friend Bloom to expand a *National Review* article to a book-length manuscript. The year also brought the publication of
Toni Morrison's *Beloved.*

In nonfiction, John Feinstein's *A Season on the Brink* provided an in-
person report on Bobby Knight's Indiana University basketball team. It
was followed at #1 by the UFO and alien abduction claims of Whitley
Strieber in *Communion.* Readers were evidently looking for the unusual
success or the unusual happening. They next turned to Bernie Siegel's
Love, Medicine, and Miracles. The doctor asserted that a positive attitude
and healthy emotional life could help patients recover from serious ill-
nesses.

James Clavell's *Whirlwind* was at #1 but soon was swept away by
Stephen King's return to #1 with *Eyes of the Dragon.* King experimented
with a children's story, and it sneaked up to #1 on February 1. Just as
swiftly it was passed by Sidney Sheldon's *Windmills of the Gods.* When a
woman is named the ambassador to an Eastern European country, there
are unexpected consequences. The U.S. president will designate Mary
Ashley, a scholar from Kansas, the ambassador. However, she hesitates
because her husband, a physician, has an active medical practice. When
her husband, Edward Ashley, dies in a suspicious auto accident she decides that she will accept the ambassadorship after all. Once overseas, she
is caught up in intrigue and conspiracies. Her adversaries are concerned
by her obvious talent and have sent a trained assassin after her.

Spring time brought *Fine Things*, a novel by Danielle Steel. A story of
a young person's growth and development from childhood in the 1960s to
adulthood in the 1980s, it was #1 on March 29, 1987. Louis L'Amour's
The Haunted Mesa became the #1 fiction book. L'Amour returned to a
western setting for this story of Native American cave dwellers. His novel
has been classified as science fiction because the story raises the notion of
apparently unexplainable time portals. Michael Raglan, a specialist on the
paranormal, receives a frantic call from Eric Hokart, a scientist who has
made his fortune from electronics. When Raglan goes to assist, Hokart is
nowhere to be found. But a mysterious package is delivered to him by a
beautiful woman. Just as soon as the package has arrived, someone tries
to steal it from him but the intruder is chased away. In the package is

Hokart's journal and a blueprint of a structure on the mesa. The blueprint is an unusual artifact that contains glowing lines that suggest a path into another world.

"You dirty birdie," exclaims a novelist's "biggest fan." In Stephen King's *Misery*, Paul Sheldon is a mystery writer of Victorian novels featuring his character Misery Chastain. When his car topples into a ditch in a snowstorm in a rural mountain area, he is found and brought home by Annie Wilkes, an insanely obsessed former nurse. She proceeds to trap and restrain him in her home under the pretext that she is helping to cure him. Sheldon soon catches on to the dilemma he is in and discovers that his obsessed fan will literally hack away at him. She has learned that he intends to kill off her favorite fictional character, Misery Chastain, and orders him to write a different ending. King's story was a comic satire on pop fiction writers, their fans, and critics who called pop writers hacks and hacked away at them with negative criticism. *Misery* was #1 on June 7, 1987, and was #1 for seven weeks.

Scott Turow's legal thriller *Presumed Innocent* reached #1 on July 26, 1987. Several lawyers have commented that the story credibly portrays prosecution methods and procedures. *Patriot Games* by Tom Clancy followed at #1 with further suspense. Jack Ryan of the CIA has to face a perilous world of terrorists in England and Ireland. Readers avidly bought that drama and kept the book at #1 for five weeks. Danielle Steel's *Kaleidoscope* followed at #1 on October 25. It also spent five weeks at #1. Stephen King had another big, fat, scary book on the bestseller list at the same time. When *The Tommyknockers* went to #1 it was his third #1 bestseller of the year. A female writer is the protagonist; she finds some strange things in the woods, and her discovery disrupts a little Maine town. King's novel was #1 through the end of the year and into the first weeks of 1988. (*Publishers Weekly* recorded this novel at #1 for the year. Tom Clancy's *Patriot Games* was #2.) Tom Wolfe's *The Bonfire of the Vanities* then took over the #1 spot. *Bonfire of the Vanities* appeared on *Publishers Weekly*'s 1987 and 1988 top bestseller lists.

The Bonfire of the Vanities by Tom Wolfe was the story with which the fiction writer in Wolfe broke out. In *Bonfire of the Vanities* a wealthy bond trader takes a wrong turn in a shattered section of the Bronx and ends up accidentally hitting a pedestrian. He learns "how the other half lives" as he is pulled off to jail and has to face the justice system. Issues of social class and race clash in this investigation of power, money, and the nemesis that follows hubris. At #1 on January 24, 1988, *The Bonfire of the Vanities* was a critical success as well as a bestseller. The film that followed was less compelling than the novel.

Tom Wolfe is one of those clever writers who use words well and effectively uncovers the quirks of society. He has engaged in sharp social observation in creative nonfiction journalism. In his fiction, he displays a keen eye and a talent for creating sympathetic characters and launching forth incisive social satire. From his *Electric Kool-Aid Acid Test* to *The Right Stuff*, he influenced a movement called "the new journalism." This was a form of nonfiction with a stylish mix of fictional techniques. From Richmond, Virginia, Tom Wolfe appeared sparklingly creative and polished, like a knight of old in a dashing white suit—his trademark. He was a reporter for the *Springfield Union*, the *Washington Post*, and the *New York Herald Tribune* and he wrote art criticism. He wrote *The Electric Kool-Aid Acid Test*, playing with the idea of Ken Kesey's Merry Pranksters. He wrote on the NASA space program in *The Right Stuff*. In *I Am Charlotte Simmons*, Wolfe focuses on a bright young female character who appears to be in an environment that is unsuited for her. In telling her story, he criticizes materialism, anti-intellectualism, and a sense of moral disintegration in America. The local bullies are evidently lower on the evolutionary scale than the gifted young girl. The basketball players make dexterous and creative uses of the F-word as adjective, noun, verb, and adverb. Charlotte has to deal with the limitations presented by school, family, and society. Wolfe's next novel, the bulky *A Man in Full* (1998), is set in Atlanta and in North Carolina. Wolfe varies the narration through several point-of-view characters: Cap'm Charlie Croker, a real estate salesman; Martha Croker, his first wife who is trying to maintain her privilege in society; Ray Peepgass, who wants to illegally mess up Croker; and Conrad Hensley, who discovers Stoic philosophy while in prison. *A Man in Full* begins with a reported rape of a white woman, heiress to a fortune, by a black athletic star named Fareek Fanon. This incident and his arrest could create rioting and have an impact on the city's politics.

Presumed Innocent by Scott Turow begins when Carolyn Polhemus is found dead, apparently killed in a sexual bondage incident. Rusty Sabich, a colleague in the prosecutor's office, takes on the case and becomes the accused. Previously, he had an affair with Polhemus, which was unknown to others in their circle. That is, all except his wife Barbara. That affair caused a strain in their marriage. Now Rusty has another problem: his fingerprint has been found on a glass in the deceased woman's apartment. Turow, an attorney, created a convincing courtroom drama. In Turow's sequel *Burden of Proof*, a lawyer tries to investigate his wife's apparent suicide and to defend his brother-in-law. The novel reached #1 on June 17, 1990, and stayed at #1 for eleven weeks. He went on to write several other bestsellers, including *Pleading Guilty* (1993). Turow has twice been president of the Authors Guild.

1988

Robert Ludlum's titles form an obvious pattern: *The Aquitaine Progression*, *The Bourne Supremacy*, *The Chancellor Manuscript*, and his next #1, *The Icarus Agenda*. In this story, Evan Kendrick, a U.S. congressman from Colorado, travels to Oman and encounters terrorists. Manny Weingrass is his only friend who has survived an incident that killed seventy-eight people. A recent incident of an uprising and hostage taking reminds him of the past troubles, and things begin to get complicated. Danielle Steel breaks up the suspense drama at #1 with *Zoya*, the story of a woman who flees from St. Petersburg to Paris during the Russian Revolution and then goes on to New York. The novel was followed on the list by Ludlum's novel and by Gabriel Garcia Marquez's *Love in the Time of Cholera*. On July 3, James Michener's *Alaska* took the #1 position. His character's stories intersect with vast tracts of history. By 1987 Michener's novels did not stay at #1 on the list nearly as long as they once did. Part of the reason for that might have been the reading audience. However, another reason was the appearance of works by writers like Tom Clancy, Sidney Sheldon, and Anne Rice, the popular chronicler of vampire stories. After *Alaska* had spent five weeks at #1, each of these writers followed with their own #1s. In Clancy's *Cardinal of the Kremlin*, Jack Ryan comes to the rescue of a double agent who is a Russian military officer. *The Cardinal of the Kremlin* led *Publishers Weekly*'s bestseller list for 1988.

In paperback, *The Queen of the Damned* had a black cover upon which the title was etched. The story follows *Interview with the Vampire* and *The Vampire Lestat* and reached #1 August 7, 1988. (Bram Stoker started us off with *Dracula*, years after John Polidori's *The Vampyre*. Rice may have initiated the vampire craze in contemporary popular culture that grew later with television shows like *Buffy the Vampire Slayer*, *True Blood*, and the *Twilight* series.) Rice's vampire stalked the bookstore shelves in October and rose from the dead to #1, notably, the day before Halloween. From November 20, Sidney Sheldon's *The Sands of Time* counted out the rest of the days of 1987 at #1. In his story, four nuns are caught up in a battle in Spain between Basques and the Spanish military. *Publishers Weekly* recorded the novel as the #2 fiction bestseller of the year. *Zoya* by Danielle Steel was #3, *The Icarus Agenda* by Robert Ludlum was #4, and *Alaska* by James Michener was #5.

The first #1 book on the nonfiction list for 1988 is one that some people have read or reread during the past year. *Trump: The Art of the Deal* was written by Tony Schwartz with Donald Trump. The *New York Times* called this the businessman's "exercise in self-congratulations."[2] Trump asserted his unique style and business savvy and his accomplishments. Michael Jackson's *Moonwalk*, his autobiography, reached #1 on May 15, 1988. Jackson was burning up the pop music charts with his songs from *Thriller* (1982) and *Bad* (1987). Donald T. Regan was secretary of the Treasury in the Reagan administration and no relation to the Reagans. Like David Stockman, he urged the supply-side economic program colloquially known as "Reaganomics." He was dismissed from his position as chief of staff and wrote his tell-all. In *For the Record* he claimed that the president had gone to see an astrologer. Staying in office was not in the stars for Donald T. Regan. The book was four weeks on the bestseller list, beginning on May 29, and then slumped down like his White House career. The #1 position was taken by a book with greater scope: physicist Stephen Hawking's *A Brief History of Time*. Reflecting on the universe "from the big bang to the black holes," Hawking wrote a serious book for the layperson about science and the search for a clear understanding of space and time. It is a thoughtful book that rewards the reader with learning. Some critics have questioned how many people who purchased the book actually read through it rather than simply looking at a few pages and putting it on the shelf. Even so, Hawking's scientific/cosmological papers are much harder to read. One does not need to know calculus or physics to read *A Brief History of Time*. In 2018, following Hawking's death, the book returned to the bestseller list in paperback form.

A biography of John Lennon hovered near the top of the list in 1988 and had its own brief history in time there. *The Lives of John Lennon* by

Albert Goldman is based upon interviews with associates of Lennon. Critics of the book, including Yoko Ono and Paul McCartney, argued that the book was scurrilous, unsubstantiated, and unfair to the former Beatle. A deceased artist like Lennon is unable to respond to the claims made about him in this book. Meanwhile, high on the list was Lee Iacocca's second book at #1. *Talking Straight* was *Times* reporter Sonny Kleinfield's fashioning of the stories that the Chrysler corporate executive had to tell. After two weeks at #1 it gave way on November 20 to *The Last Lion* by William Manchester: his volume 2 of a biography of Winston Churchill concerning the years 1932–1940. *Gracie*, George Burns's recollections of his wife and onstage partner Gracie Allen, was December's #1 bestseller.

The final months of the year brought several newsworthy events. George H. W. Bush was elected president. Pan Am Flight 103 from Lockerbie was blown up by Libyan terrorists on December 21. The world of literature will recall this as the year that Gabriel Garcia Marquez published *Love in the Time of Cholera* and the year that Salman Rushdie was issued death threats by the ayatollah in Iran. The Iranian leader rejected Rushdie's novel *The Satanic Verses* as blasphemous. Rushdie went into hiding.

Misery by Stephen King (1987) was his clever reply to those critics who hacked away with criticisms of his work. His character Annie Wilkes begins to hack away at his protagonist Paul Sheldon. When author Paul Sheldon drives off the road and crashes in a Maine snowstorm, he is "rescued" by Annie Wilkes, who brings him home instead of to a hospital. There she insists upon taking care of him and nursing him back to health. Paul Sheldon writes romance novels, and Annie declares that she is his "number one fan." Sheldon's series character Misery Chastain is her beloved obsession. Annie feeds Sheldon codeine painkillers and threatens to break his legs by forcing them into splints. Annie has bought a copy of the writer's recent novel in which he kills off his character Misery Chastain in the last pages. When she reads this she is infuriated. She requires that he burn his manuscript of *Fast Cars*, which he is working on, and that he write a new novel that brings Misery back to life. Annie is inclined toward big mood swings. Paul tries to figure out how to escape.

The Satanic Verses by Salman Rushdie (1988) drew the ire of the Ayatollah Khomeini in Iran, who placed a death threat upon Rushdie in

February 1989. In 2017, Rushdie told interviewer Tavis Smiley that he hoped that readers of *The Golden Horse* would experience a sense of recognition of the present cultural moment and that future readers will be able to gain a sense of "that's how it was." Rushdie has often been a writer of myth and fantasy and fabulist fiction, or magical realism. He draws upon Indian resources as well as upon Anglo-American literature. His *Midnight's Children* (1981) was a bestseller and a Booker Prize winner.

Rushdie was born in Bombay (Mumbai) and educated in England. His wide fictional scope joins East and West, the fantastic and the real. *Grimus* (1975), his first novel, was partly fantasy and science fiction. *Midnight's Children* reflects upon how India became a nation. *Shame* (1983) explored the conflict that emerged in the region of Pakistan following Indian independence. *The Moor's Last Sigh* also considers Indian history. When the threat on his life was issued, Rushdie was provided with police protection in Britain and several prominent authors upheld his right to create his fiction. He was recognized and knighted in Britain for his contributions to literature. He is now a citizen of the United States and has taught at Emory University and at New York University. He has written *The Jaguar Smile* (1987), about Nicaragua, short stories (as in his collection *East West* [1994]), and essays on writers like Jorge Luis Borges, Italo Calvino, Thomas Pynchon, Mikhail Bulgakov, Lewis Carroll, and James Joyce, which are collected in *Step across this Line* (2002).

1989

The year 1989 began with the stroke of *Midnight*. Dean Koontz's horror bestseller of that title stayed behind Sheldon's *The Sands of Time* throughout January. On February 5 it reached #1. *Midnight* was #1 for three weeks. (The next year Morrow published Sidney Sheldon's #1 sequel *Memories of Midnight*. That book appeared at #1 at the same time that Stephen King's *Four Past Midnight* was about to rise on the list to pass it.) In February 1989 Danielle Steel made another of her regular appearances at #1 with *Star*. Her novels appeared on the bestseller list like a tag team in a relay race. As *Zoya* began to fall from the list, *Star* began to rise. On March 26 *The Satanic Verses* by Salman Rushdie reached #1. Rushdie's novel weaved the story of two people who traveled from India to London. The Ayatollah Khomeini condemned the book as blasphemous and proposed that he would provide a reward to anyone who had the author killed. Authors testified in America and England in support of Rushdie.

Mary Higgins Clark's *While My Pretty One Sleeps* was #1 on May 28. In her story, a New York City gossip writer is murdered and the fashion industry in the city goes into a tailspin. Readers continued to read James Michener's *Caribbean*, #5 on *Publishers Weekly*'s list for the year. John le Carré's *The Russia House* reached #1 as the Berlin Wall came down and the Cold War faded. In Martin Cruz Smith's *Polar Star*, American and Russian spies conducted surveillance of a boat in the north Pacific. Tom Clancy turned away from the Soviet conflict with the West that was at the center of *The Hunt for Red October* and *The Cardinal of the Kremlin*. *Clear and Present Danger* told the dramatic story of chasing down the drug traffickers of Latin America. Jack Ryan again comes to the rescue. Tom Clancy's novel was #1 on September 3, and his story stayed there for nine weeks. Stephen King's *The Dark Half* rose to #1 on November 5. Thad Beaumont is less successful with his real name than with his pseudonym, George Stark. He gets rid of his pseudonym, which then comes back to life and goes on a rampage. *Publishers Weekly* called Tom Clancy's novel the biggest book of the year, and Stephen King's *The Dark Half* was a close second. The year came to an end with *Daddy* by Danielle Steel in the #1 spot. With *Heartbeat* at #1 in February 1991, she had written twenty books in ten years and had begun an unprecedented string of #1 novels rivaled only by Stephen King. *Daddy* and *Star* were #3 and #4, respectively, on *Publishers Weekly*'s 1989 list.

The nonfiction bestseller list in 1989 began with a surprise: Robert Fulghum's *All I Really Need to Know I Learned in Kindergarten*. His essays and the book's title drew a lot of attention, and the book was #1 for thirty-four weeks. It remained on the bestseller list into 1990. It was #1 for the year on *Publishers Weekly*'s nonfiction list. Joe McGinnis's *Blind Faith*, a true crime story, broke the string of Fulghum's book at #1 for two weeks. So did *A Woman Named Jackie*, C. David Heymann's biography of Jacqueline Kennedy Onassis. On July 2 David Halberstam's baseball book *Summer of '49* became #1 with its story of the New York Yankees and Boston Red Sox rivalry. Comedienne Gilda Radner from *Saturday Night Live* left the world too soon; she died May 20, 1989, and her book, which had been recently published, rose to #1 on July 16.

Nancy Reagan's *My Turn*, written with the help of William Novak, offered commentary. Robert Fulghum followed with another #1 bestseller with another long title: *It Was on Fire When I Lay Down on It*. It was #2 on October 15, right behind his other book that was #1. It replaced Nancy Reagan's *My Turn* on January 7, 1990. (*Publishers Weekly* listed the Nancy Reagan book as the #10 bestseller in nonfiction for 1989.)

San Francisco experienced an earthquake on October 17. The Berlin Wall began to come down on November 9. During the year China put down a student rebellion with violence in Tiananmen Square in Beijing. Time Incorporated bought Warner Communications and became Time Warner. The *Exxon Valdez* spilled eleven million gallons of oil off the coast of Alaska. Children were excited by mutant ninja turtles and *The Little Mermaid*; the musical *Miss Saigon* opened in London. Cincinnati Reds star Pete Rose, caught gambling, was banned from baseball, and Leona Helmsley was convicted of fraud. Pharmaceutical companies expanded their distribution of Prozac. The United States created the Stealth bomber. Bobby McFerrin's song "Don't Worry, Be Happy" faded from radio airplay, and another decade came to a close.

7

THE 1990s

Means of Ascent: Publisher Consolidation, Superstores, and the Internet

If you had a crystal ball, might you be able to peer into the future? In January 1990, *Megatrends 2000* took the #1 spot on the nonfiction bestseller list. The book by John Naisbitt and his wife Patricia Aburdene projected the future and was a follow-up to Naisbitt's previous bestseller, *Megatrends*. This book speculated on trends that pointed toward the horizon of the year 2000 and beyond. What might happen beyond the turn of the century? Such predictions are a bit risky. The information age, digital technology, biotechnologies, environmental issues, and changing politics and global economy were all proceeding apace into a new era. The 1990s was a period of technological innovation and globalization. The variety, quantity, and rate of turnover of books on the bestseller list seemed to bear out what the authors of *Megatrends* suggested would be an era of "multiple option."

Soon at #1 was Robert Caro's *Means of Ascent*, which continued his well-written multivolume biography of Lyndon Baines Johnson. Caro's new volume was a study of LBJ's campaigns for the U.S. Senate, to which he was elected in 1948. Caro's book reached #1 on April 8, 1990. *The Path to Power* (1982) was the first volume and *Means of Ascent* (1990) was the second. In his next volume, *Master of the Senate* (2002), Caro charted Johnson's rise to his role as a power broker in that legislative body from 1949 to 1960. The book won the Pulitzer Prize for Biography. The fourth volume, *The Passage of Power* (2012), dealt with Johnson's vice presidency and the presidential years. It won the National Book Critics Circle Award and a series of other awards. Caro looks through Johnson's political career to consider political power, history, and American culture.

In the 1990s, the fiction bestseller lists showed little freshness or newness. What was most popular was more of the same. This appears true if one looks through the bestseller lists. The 1990s in the book publishing industry reflected caution. It was easier to bank on the proven name product than to venture the new. However, without that risk and creativity there is stagnation and potential decline.

In 1990 and 1991, John Grisham broke through in a big way and his books each soared to sales of nearly 2.4 million copies in hardcover sales. (*The Partner* sold 2.6 million copies.) However, it was difficult for a new author to break through. Michael Korda identifies "perhaps two dozen or fewer top writers" dominating the list. He points out that practically every spot on the bestseller list of 1992 was taken by "a familiar name." To take risks on the new, the untried, the original is "the lifeblood of publishing," he says. The publishing house that only "plays it safe" is one that "may be destined to collapse."[1] During that period there would always be a Danielle Steel novel, a Tom Clancy novel, a Stephen King novel, or a John Grisham novel. In May there would be a Mary Higgins Clark novel. In October we would see an occasional vampire from Anne Rice.

Some novels stood above others in literary quality. John Updike's *Rabbit at Rest* was published in 1990. In 1991, Martin Amis published *Time's Arrow*. Jane Smiley retold the story of King Lear's daughters in *A Thousand Acres*. Amy Tan published *The Kitchen God's Wife*. Toni Morrison's *Jazz* and Michael Ondaatje's *The English Patient* appeared in 1992. There were also novels from Paul Auster, A. S. Byatt, Thomas Berger, and Ian McEwen in 1992.

Meanwhile, the nonfiction list was filled with books about celebrities, or books that celebrities themselves developed in connection with professional writers. There were numerous self-help books. In 1997, some literary hope flickered forth in the appearance of Don DeLillo's *Underworld*, a finalist for the National Book Award, and Charles Frazier's *Cold Mountain*, which won the Pulitzer Prize. These books sold well. There was also the long-lasting phenomenon of John Berendt's *Midnight in the Garden of Good and Evil*, set amid the mysteries and curiosities of Savannah. The

1980s self-help book tended to stir ambitions for business success. In the 1990s, the public turned toward new age prescriptions for spiritual enlightenment. Deepak Chopra became a star of this type of book while James Redfield's *The Celestine Prophecy* stayed on the fiction list across an entire year. Books were also increasingly directed toward women readers, or specifically toward male readers, with fewer crossover volumes.[2]

The emergence of the e-book in the 1990s was a phenomenon that carried past 2000 with reading devices such as Kindle, Nook, and the iPad and cell phones. This has become a portable format. Amazon.com has come to dominate the market with online purchase and swift delivery of print books and e-books; however, readers can still peruse the wide variety of books on the shelves of Barnes & Noble stores and have a cup of coffee or attend an event there. There are hundreds of bookstores that attempt to prosper by applying their own personal touch. These stores sell hardcover books and paperbacks. After 2000, the paperback that once fit into a large pocket had expanded into a larger format and a higher price: the book was elongated and stood a bit taller on the shelf, and the cover price asked for closer to ten dollars from potential readers. With the American economy in an upswing, more popular books meant more dollars.

1990

Danielle Steel's novel *Daddy* continued to be #1 on the fiction bestseller list in January 1990. However, Dean Koontz and his publisher Putnam had by now begun their string of #1 Koontz mysteries. *The Bad Place* became #1 on January 16 on *Publishers Weekly*'s list and #1 on the *New York Times* list on February 4, 1990. Koontz tells the story of a sleepwalker who wants to understand why he is acting strangely. He hires a detective to find out. (Koontz's *Midnight* had been the #1 book the previous February; *Cold Fire* became #1 in February 1991; *Hideaway* was #1 on February 2, 1992; and in February 1993, *Dragon Tears* was at #2 just behind the #1 hit *Bridges of Madison County*. Remarkably, *Bridges of Madison County* was still #2 a year later in February 1994.) Mystery writer P. D. James's *Devices and Dragons* was #1 on February 18, 1990. The London police detective Adam Dalgliesh goes to the coast of Norfolk with his new book of poetry. He is soon engaged to solve the mysteries that begin unfolding as the administrator of a nuclear power station there is killed by a murderer called the Norfolk Whistler.

As the mystery genre novel held the #1 position through February, Dr. Seuss was on the loose right behind those stories with *Oh, the Places You'll Go*. It was primarily a children's book, but it entertained adults too. It reached #1 on March 4. James Michener's *Caribbean* was at #9, and Thomas Pynchon's *Vineland* was #10. On March 18, *The Bourne Ultimatum* by Robert Ludlum rose to #1 on both the *New York Times* and *Publishers Weekly* lists with the continuing suspense surrounding its familiar protagonist. Carlos the Jackal is out to kill him.[3] On April 29, George Will's *Men at Work* led the nonfiction list. George Will, the noted conservative columnist, was now writing about baseball. He focused on three players and a manager and asserted the game's virtue. His enthusiastic study, subtitled *The Craft of Baseball*, appeared well before disclosures of steroid use, doping scandals, or dollar signs became more prevalent in the national pastime.

September became #1 in April. Rosamunde Pilcher's novel came from Scotland to enchant readers with a romance. The novel's success suggests that the romance reading audience was quite strong. While some readers may have also read the adventures of Jason Bourne, the romance reading audience was composed primarily of women readers. Stephen King's *The Stand* followed at #1 on May 13 and May 18. The big book by its now big-name author had first appeared in 1978, when it was edited to a more manageable size by its publishers. Stephen King reworked his original manuscript from the 1970s and kept the original story's length. The book sailed to #1 and remained there for a month. Scott Turow's suspenseful *The Burden of Proof* was #1 beginning on June 17 and led the list for seventeen weeks. *Publishers Weekly* recognized *The Burden of Proof* as one of the top ten fiction books of the year. Danielle Steel's *Message from Nam* was *Publishers Weekly*'s #1 June 21. Clive Cussler's novel *Dragon* was also at the top of its list in June. John Bradshaw's self-help book *Homecoming* was #1 on *Publishers Weekly*'s nonfiction list on July 16. Then came two novels with "Midnight" in their titles: Sidney Sheldon's *Memories of Midnight* (#1 on September 2) and Stephen King's *Four Past Midnight* (four stories, #1 on September 16). King's book was #2 on *Publishers Weekly*'s annual list. Sheldon's book was #4.

Meanwhile, Donald Trump's book *Trump: Surviving at the Top* reached the top on September 9. It was there for two weeks and then took a nosedive off the bestseller list. The 1990 book's cover pictures Trump tossing an apple into the air. Charles Leerhsen wrote the book with the businessman, at a time when no one suspected that Donald Trump would one day become the president of the United States.

In fiction, *The Plains of Passage* by Jean M. Auel was #1 on October 17. *Lady Boss* by Jackie Collins was also high on the list. Anne Rice's *The Witching Hour* was #1 on November 14. In nonfiction, during September 1990 William Styron's account of his experiences of depression in *Darkness Visible* reached #1. This serious book was followed at #1 by the device of having the Bush family's dog talk about how life was like in the White House. The much-loved personality of Barbara Bush was the force behind *Millie's Book*. In contrast, *By Way of Deception* was an Israeli Mossad agent's stories of undercover work in the Middle East. Meanwhile, filmmakers Ken Burns and Ric Burns turned their remarkable television documentary *The Civil War* into a book filled with pictures and text. It was #1 for *Publishers Weekly* on October 12 and #1 on the *New York Times* list on November 11. In December, Charles Kuralt's *A Life on the Road* was a newsman's account of life in America seen through years of reporting. While this book was the nonfiction bestseller, Jean M. Auel's third story set in the Ice Age, *The Plains of Passage*, was heavily advertised in advance of its publication and took over the #1 fiction position on October 21. The story's horseback journey across prehistoric Europe returned to #1 in mid-November. It remained there through the end of the year and into January.

In 1990, Nelson Mandela was released from prison in Cape Town, South Africa; he had become the key symbol of resistance to apartheid. The Russian Supreme Soviet named Boris Yeltsin its chairman on May 29. On October 3, Germany was reunified, and lines separating East and West were overcome. American classical music lost composers Leonard Bernstein and Aaron Copland. *Seinfeld* premiered on television. Hollywood films included Patrick Swayze in *Ghost*, Mel Gibson in *Hamlet*, and Julia Roberts and Richard Gere in *Pretty Woman*. The Americans with Disabilities Act was signed, and the National Cathedral opened in Washington.

Postmortem by Patricia Cornwell began the fictional career of Kay Scarpetta, medical examiner and investigator of crimes. Cornwell was born in Miami. Her father was an appellate lawyer who had worked as a law clerk for Supreme Court Justice Hugo Black. The family moved to North Carolina. Patricia Cornwell was encouraged in her writing by Ruth Bell Graham, the wife of the evangelist Billy Graham, who was a family friend. After college, she was a reporter for the *Charlotte Observer*. Cornwell began writing a biography of Ruth Graham Bell around the same time that her husband Charles Cornwell became a student at the Union Theological Seminary. She later began to focus on writing mystery-suspense fiction. In 1985, she began working in the Office of the Medical Examiner for the State of Virginia. She worked there for six years. In 1990, after she had written three police procedurals, each of them rejected by publishers, her novel *Postmortem* was published. The story was drawn from a case of strangling that had occurred in Richmond. The novel won the Edgar Award and launched her career with her bestselling Kay Scarpetta series. Cornwell has claimed that artist Walter Sickert was the infamous Jack the Ripper and wrote a book to present the evidence for this view. Her bestsellers explore the secrets and manipulations of murder cases.

Female detectives in fiction cross stereotypical gender roles. Patricia Cornwell, Sue Grafton, Sara Paretsky, and other detective fiction writers "center mainstream fiction" written by women, as Bobbie Robinson pointed out in February 2006 in an article in the *Journal of Popular Culture*. She writes: "These heroines blatantly portray the disconnect between female gender and the historically masculine-constructed occupation of the private eye, forcing the female detective to perform as male to infiltrate this world."[4] Susan S. Lanser argues, "Patricia Cornwell is not a physician, as any reader of the book's blurb will see. . . . [Yet] here is Scarpetta authoritatively dispensing medical advice to ordinary people like those who read Cornwell's books."[5]

Cornwell engages in an "ethics of representation" as she presents the deceased body in her fiction, asserts Rose Lucas. Her novels "activate the reader's concerns" about death, says Lucas, who claims that "the repeated telling of the same kind of story . . . can be a way of adjusting to what is otherwise unbelievable."[6] "[It is] magical for me about Scarpetta's ability to handle these signs, her capacity to read them." writes Sue Turnbull, who recalled Cornwell's visit to Melbourne and Dymocks Bourke Street Bookstore, September 27, 1993. At the Swansea Bookstore, "Cornwell was clearly on a roll, and keen to tell her audience about it, and to reassure them that she had their interests at heart."[7]

The Gold Coast by Nelson DeMille was followed by the bestsellers *The General's Daughter* (1992) and *Plum Island* (1997). *Plum Island* introduced his character John Corey, who also appears in *The Lion's Game* (2000), *Night Fall* (2004), and *Wildfire* (2006). His John Sutter character from *The Gold Coast* returned in *The Gate House* (2008). DeMille writes longhand on legal pads. He makes use of Long Island settings with which he is familiar. He served in the First Cavalry Division in Vietnam and as an infantry platoon leader. Afterward, he completed his degree in political science and history at Hofstra University. His first novels were police procedurals focusing on the New York Police Department (NYPD). His *The Cuban Affair* reached #1 on the *New York Times* bestseller list in November 2017. Often DeMille's stories emerge as first-person narratives with chronological, linear plots. His heroes solve mysteries effectively, but they are incomplete in their personal lives. Usually they are forceful male characters who enter a web of intrigue and drama.

1991

In 1991, on January 20, John le Carré was back atop the bestseller list with *The Secret Pilgrim*. "Ned," a protégé of George Smiley, is the narrator who recalls the spy's time in the field of espionage. Smiley has recently spoken to an audience at Sarratt, where Ned runs a spy training center. Ned has stories to tell, and these are linked together to form the novel. *Cold Fire* by Dean Koontz, another early 1991 hit, tells the story of Holly Thorne, a reporter who investigates a man who has been saving people. Jim Ironheart has become notable for his apparent heroism and self-sacrifice. He has cold blue eyes and a rare gift: he anticipates the trouble that is on the way for people. He saves a boy from a drunk driver in Portland. In Boston he saves another boy from an underground explosion. In Houston he stops a man from shooting his wife. When Jim Ironheart gets another inspiration, a "message from God," he boards an American Airlines flight bound for Chicago. Holly Thorne follows him.

Danielle Steel, meanwhile, had another book rising to #1. *Heartbeat* brings together Bill Grant, a television producer, and Adrian, a television news writer, in an unexpected meeting. Adrian's husband, Steven, who was abused in childhood, insists upon never having a child. When Adrian conceives, Steven argues for an abortion. When he finds out that Adrian has rejected that idea, he decides to leave her. Bill Grant comes into her life. Bill, who is recently divorced, is planning on creating a soap opera, *A Life Worth Living*. His relationship with Adrian itself becomes something of a soap opera. On February 24, Danielle Steel's novel became #1 and it held that top position for the next two months. Danielle Steel also had a bestseller with *No Greater Love*. David Eddings's *The Seeress of Kell*, the fifth volume of his fantasy series, rose to #1 on April 21.

When *American Psycho* by Bret Easton Ellis reached the bestseller list, the *New York Times* said that it would remove it from the listing. Several readers declared in letters to *New York Magazine* in January of 1991 that *American Psycho* ought not to have been published. "Bravo to Simon and Schuster for withdrawing *American Psycho*," wrote Jeanne Rudmann from Floral Park, New York. "All that brouhaha over Bret Easton Ellis's book proves is that publishing bigwigs don't read many horror novels besides Stephen King," wrote William Scholl of New York. Marialuisa Finardi, from Mahwah, New Jersey, cited John Keats's poetic line that "a thing of beauty is a joy forever." Then she added: "A book of depravity is a sore forever. It will fester in a reader's mind: we would be better off without *American Psycho*."[8]

The nonfiction list in January saw a poet, Robert Bly, lead the pack with *Iron John*, his men's movement bestseller. Daniel Yergin talked about oil in *The Prize*, and his study of the history of the oil business enterprise sputtered up to #1 on February 10. Vincent Bugliosi followed his gruesome telling of the Charles Manson murders with another true crime murder story: *And the Sea Will Tell*. The book was #1 on March 17. Hollywood was the subject of the next #1 on April 7: *You'll Never Eat Lunch in This Town Again*, by Julia Philips. Then Kitty Kelley's unauthorized biography of Nancy Reagan stirred controversy, garnered publicity, and gained the #1 spot for five weeks.

Mary Higgins Clark returned to the top of the bestseller list with *Loves Music, Loves to Dance*. In the early days of the internet people are placing personal ads for dates. When Darcy Scott's friend is murdered while looking into the personal ads, she picks up the investigation and is drawn into a trap by the dancing shoe killer. Darcy Scott is convinced that one of the men she has dated might be the killer. The *Star Wars* films pulled this book off the #1 position on June 1, 1991, with *Heir to the Empire* by

Timothy Zahn. Amy Tan's *The Kitchen God's Wife* reached #1 on July 7, 1991. This story told by a Chinese grandmother followed her award-winning book *The Joy Luck Club*. Tom Clancy knocked it from #1 with his suspense story *The Sum of All Fears*. Alexandra Ripley's *Scarlett*, her sequel to *Gone with the Wind*, quickly shot up to #1. It stayed there for sixteen weeks. *Publishers Weekly* listed the novel as the top-selling novel of the year. It listed Tom Clancy's *The Sum of All Fears* at #2. Stephen King's *Needful Things* was listed at #3. Other bestsellers included John Grisham's *The Firm*, *The Doomsday Conspiracy* by Sidney Sheldon, and *Night over Water* by Ken Follett.

The nonfiction list of #1 bestsellers for summer 1991 extended from Bob Woodward's study of military leaders in *The Commanders* (#1 June 2 and for five weeks) and attorney Alan Dershowitz's reflections on the Jews, *Chutzpah* (#1 on July 21), to *Parliament of Whores* by P. J. O'Rourke, a lambast and lampoon of American political figures. Erma Bombeck brought humor with *When You Look Like Your Passport Photo, It's Time to Go Home*, which was #1 on September 1. Robert Fulghum kept readers laughing with *Uh-Oh*, at #1 on September 8. Katharine Hepburn's celebrity autobiography, simply called *Me*, held the #1 spot for the next twelve weeks. It was followed at #1 by the decidedly serious *Den of Thieves* by James B. Stewart on November 3. Stewart aims directly at the case against Michael Milken, Ivan Boesky, and other junk bond traders whose greed contaminated Wall Street. James B. Stewart is a lawyer and professor at the Columbia School of Journalism who has had a distinguished career as an editor of the *American Lawyer*, the *Wall Street Journal*, and *Smart Money* magazine. This was followed by a book on another serious topic: Oliver North's *Under Fire* commented on the Iran-contra scandal and alleged that Ronald Reagan knew about it. Author William Novak traveled to Washington regularly to meet with North, to gather his thoughts for this book. It was #1 on the first day of December 1991.

In retrospect, the year was notable for the United States' launch of Operation Desert Storm in February to free Kuwait from an invasion by Iraq. Clarence Thomas faced challenges to his nomination to the Supreme Court when Anita Hill charged him with harassment. He was confirmed by a vote of fifty-two to forty-eight in the Senate. Overseas, Serbia and Croatia were falling into a terrible genocidal war. Popular fiction and film included John Grisham's *The Firm*, Norman Mailer's *Harlot's Ghost*,

Oliver Stone's film *JFK*, and Jonathan Demme's film *Silence of the Lambs*.

The Firm by John Grisham was one of the biggest bestsellers of the year. A talented and unsuspecting young attorney is recruited by a law firm that is up to no good. Grisham began writing *A Time to Kill* based upon a legal case concerning a rape in Mississippi. What if the girl's father killed that rapist and was caught and tried in court? Grisham sent the story out, and more than twenty-five publishers rejected it. Eventually, Wynwood Press took the novel and paid an advance of about $15,000 for it. *A Time to Kill* initially had a five-thousand-copy print run. Grisham bought about one thousand of those copies. He was working as an attorney at the time. He had considered becoming a tax attorney during his studies at Mississippi State and the University of Mississippi, and he practiced criminal law and then civil law. Grisham had also been elected to the Mississippi state legislature. He spent the next two years writing *The Firm*. A movie scout at Paramount bought the rights to the story. Doubleday later bought the novel, bidding against other publishers for it. Grisham's fortune had changed overnight: *A Time to Kill* reappeared and sold briskly; *The Pelican Brief*, written across about four months, shot to the top of the bestseller list; *The Client*, released next, sold about one million copies each month; and *The Chamber*, while also a legal thriller, broke out of the whodunit mode. Readers already know the murderer and the attorney is the center of interest. Grisham's novels have risen quickly to the top of the bestseller list ever since. A Grisham story often hinges upon a matter of justice and moral or social concern.

A reader of John Grisham's fiction, Sheldon Nesdale, commented on his blog: "If you read his first book *The Firm* (1991) and then *Rogue Lawyer* (2015), the only things you'll notice is the technology that the characters use has changed. . . . You will barely notice a shift in writing style."[9] "I know that what I do is not literature," John Grisham told an interviewer from Britain's the *Telegraph*. "For me the essential feature is plot," he said. Of course, that is the central feature of most fiction bestsellers. He told the interviewer that he has books of literature "in the classic sense" at home and had to read them in school.[10]

John Grisham's *Camino Real* is "fun" and "it grabs a reader from the first paragraph," commented one reader in New Jersey at the Maplewood Library. There Sarah Lester and Barbara Laub have created "Readers Speak," which lets us know what some of their library patrons are reading. Readers comment on reading in bed, or in "an oversized easy chair . . . inherited from my mother."[11]

1992

Bill Clinton was elected as the American president in 1992. The Arkansas governor promised to transform Democratic politics and told audiences that he felt their pain. Los Angeles experienced the Watts riots following the forceful arrest of Rodney King in March. Delegates to the United Nations Conference on the Environment in Rio de Janeiro signed a treaty to reduce carbon emissions that are said to cause global warming. They established a treaty designed to protect endangered species with the Convention on Biodiversity.

The #1 run of Alexandra Ripley's *Scarlett* extended into January 1992. Dean Koontz had his fourth consecutive February bestseller with *Hideaway*. Michael Crichton's *Rising Sun* then burst onto the bestseller list and became #1 in March 1992. His suspense story featured a Japanese corporation and high-tech enterprise that reflected the emergence of a dot-com era. The American detective investigates and squares off against Japanese business executives who control the business, the press, and government resources.

Gloria Steinem wrote her self-help feminist book *Revolution from Within*, and it rose to #1 on the bestseller list February 9, 1992. The book contained a message that self-esteem was what the book's readers needed to claim—that self-esteem would propel the women's movement to new heights and move women toward accomplishment and fulfillment. Gail Sheehy's *The Silent Passage* was her second #1 bestseller. It followed Steinem's book at #1. This book was also directed toward female readers and concerned menopause and various issues that women have to deal with. As the title indicates, this was a phase of life that she might have discussed in her first bestseller, *Passages*.

John Grisham's first #1 bestseller, *The Pelican Brief*, reached the top of the list on March 15, 1992. There have been many #1 Grisham novels since. In the novel, a law student, Darby Shaw, uncovers the mystery swirling around the deaths of two Supreme Court justices. Cormac McCarthy's *All the Pretty Horses*, published in May by Alfred A. Knopf, appeared on the bestseller list at #13 in mid-June. It occasionally rose to

#13 during July. *All the Pretty Horses* was the National Book Award winner in 1992. Appreciated by critics, its place at #13 suggests a difference between critical regard and commercial bestseller sales.

Danielle Steel's *Jewels* took over the #1 spot on May 17, 1992. Her protagonist, Sarah, has become a wealthy woman. She looks back at her life, and we learn about her relationships, the duke she married, and the German seizure of their chateau in France during the Second World War. The duke loses his legs in battle. After the war, he and Sarah start a successful jewelry store in Paris. After one month at #1 on the bestseller list, Steel's book was passed by Stephen King's *Gerald's Game*. This was the sixteenth Stephen King book to reach #1. Gerald Burlingame plays sex games and handcuffs his wife to the bed in their bedroom. She accidentally kills him. The novel was at #1 on July 19, 1992, and was gruesome but compelling summer reading at the beach. Other readers picked up *Diana: Her True Story*, Andrew Morton's biography of the princess that he developed from his discussions with her friends and family. With its bright gold cover and sad and thoughtful stories, it rose to #1 on July 5 and remained at #1 throughout most of the summer. *Waiting to Exhale* by Terry McMillan was #3 on the fiction bestseller list. Judith Krantz and Alice Walker had novels in the top ten. At #8, Robert Harris's alternative history *Fatherland* asked what if the Nazis had won the Second World War. Clive Cussler's *Sahara* and Mary Higgins Clark's *All around the Town* were also moving up the bestseller list. Then Jimmy Buffett broke out of Margaritaville with *Where Is Joe Merchant*, #1 on September 20. Can a dead rock star who has now been reported to be still alive in the Caribbean be found?

On October 4, 1992, the top of the fiction bestseller list included Jimmy Buffett's story, *The Pelican Brief*, *Gerald's Game*, and *Waiting to Exhale*. Behind them, Donna Tartt's *The Secret History*, a story of a mystery on a college campus, was #5. Right behind that book was the rising title that would soon dominate the bestseller list for a year: *The Bridges of Madison County*. On October 18, Sidney Sheldon's *The Stars Shine Down* led the list and Tartt's book, *The Secret History*, had moved to #3. However, Anne Rice's *Tale of the Body Thief* just had to be #1 on Halloween.

On November 15, the stories by Anne Rice and Sidney Sheldon were followed on the list by stories by Douglas Adams, Dick Francis, Nick Bantock's *Sabine's Notebook*, and James Michener's *Mexico*. Suddenly, the next week, Danielle Steel's *Mixed Blessings* was #1. Stephen King's *Dolores Claiborne* shot past it to #1 two weeks later on December 1. Michener's *Mexico* climbed to #3 by December 20. Rush Limbaugh and General Norm Schwarzkopf held the #1 and #2 positions, respectively, on the nonfiction list at the beginning of December. Madonna's book *Sex* was #4. David McCullough's biography *Truman* was #4 during the last week of the year. *Truman* had been in the top five frequently since August. The book won the Pulitzer Prize for Biography. Al Gore's *Earth in the Balance* was also high on the bestseller list in the summer. It remained in the top ten until the first week of December.

The Bridges of Madison County by Robert James Waller tells the story of a lonely woman's affair with a photographer she meets while her husband and children are at the state fair in Illinois. The photographer has arrived to take photographs of covered bridges. Waller's lyrical writing and his story appealed to many readers, and the novel rose to #1 on the bestseller list. The book remained on the list for three years.

French Silk by Sandra Brown was set in New Orleans and concerned a televangelist and a curious mail-order company known as French Silk. Brown writes romance-suspense, blending those genres. She is originally from Texas and went to Texas Christian University (TCU). She married news anchor–documentary creator Michael Brown and reported on the weather for WFAA-TV. Her husband encouraged her to write; the result has been more than seventy novels, including several series. Her romance-suspense thrillers began in 1988 and brought her work to the bestseller list in the early 1990s.

1993

Throughout the year "brand-name" authors were represented by novels that sold widely and appeared in the top positions on the *New York Times* bestseller list and in *Publishers Weekly* listings. Stephen King and Danielle Steel both continued to dominate the fiction bestseller list. *Dolores Claiborne* by King was #1 on January 3, 1993. Steel's *Mixed Blessings* was now rivaled by John Grisham's *Pelican Brief*. Those books were followed by James Michener's *Mexico* (#8 on *Publishers Weekly*'s 1992 annual list). On January 24, Dean Koontz's *Dragon Tears* gained the #1 position on the list. Robert James Waller's *The Bridges of Madison*

County was about to overtake all of them. It would become the top best-selling book of the year. Waller's *Slow Waltz in Cedar Bend* would also rise to the #1 spot in the autumn.

Mystery, romance, adventure: readers found the spice of life in genre fiction. *The Bridges of Madison County* was the #1 fiction bestseller on January 31, 1993. The books by Koontz, King, and Grisham followed it on the list. Richard North Patterson and James Patterson stories vied for positions #4 and #5. Except for the appearance of John Grisham's *The Client* at #1 on March 21, Waller's novel would hold the #1 position until August 29. *Publishers Weekly* listed it as #1 with *The Client* behind it, at #2, on its end of the year bestseller list. Koontz's novel *Dragon Tears* was #2 throughout February: the month when his novels would often claim the #1 spot. The #1 *The Bridges of Madison County* also held off Grisham's *The Client*, which was #2 throughout April and May. Mary Higgins Clark's *I'll Be Seeing You* was the #3 book from May 23 through June 6. Scott Turow's *Pleading Guilty* rose to #2 on June 13 and held that position through June 27. During those weeks Robert Ludlum's *The Scorpio Illusion* was #3. Dr. Seuss made a daring appearance at #4 with *Oh, The Places You'll Go*. On July 18, John le Carré's *The Night Manager* took over the #3 spot behind *The Bridges of Madison County* and *The Client*. These books remained the top three books on the fiction bestseller list through August 8. On August 15, Danielle Steel's *Vanished* rose to #2. On August 29, Tom Clancy's *Without Remorse* broke *The Bridges of Madison County*'s long term at #1. *Without Remorse* remained at #2 behind *The Bridges* through the month of September, and Steel's *Vanished* held the #3 spot. On *Publishers Weekly*'s annual bestseller list, *Without Remorse* was #4, King's *Nightmares and Dreamscapes* was #5, and *Vanished* was #6.

Toni Morrison was awarded the Nobel Prize for Literature on October 8. *Paradise* had followed her novel *Jazz*. October brought Anne Rice and Stephen King books to the top five. On October 3 and October 17 *Lasher* by Anne Rice was #2. Stephen King's *Nightmares and Dreamscapes*, a collection of short stories, was #3. In nonfiction, Howard Stern's *Private Parts* was #1 on Halloween. *Private Parts* was the first #1 bestseller of the new *USA Today* bestseller list. Stern's book was battling it out with conservative radio commentator Rush Limbaugh's *See, I Told You So* and *The Hidden Life of Dogs*. None of this was exactly the deepest intellectual content ever to hit the bestseller list, but it was fun. TV show comic Jerry

Seinfeld's autobiography moved up to #3. Limbaugh, Stern, Seinfeld, and the dogs persisted and barked until the end of the year. In November, Margaret Thatcher's *The Downing Street Years* and William Shatner's *Star Trek Memories* were in the top ten.

On November 7, Robert James Waller's newly published *Slow Waltz in Cedar Bend* went to #2 behind *The Bridges of Madison County*. He was the first author since Stephen King to have books in the #1 and #2 positions. Stephen King's *Nightmares and Dreamscapes* was now selling briskly at #3. Robert Jordan's *The Fires of Heaven*, *Decider* by Dick Francis, and Ken Follett's *A Dangerous Fortune* were in the top ten. *Slow Waltz in Cedar Bend* rose to #1 on November 14 and remained there through the end of the year. *Nightmares and Dreamscapes* remained in the top three bestsellers, alongside the books by Waller. Herman Wouk's *The Hope* reached #5, with his story that extended from the founding of Israel in 1948 to the war in 1967.

In 1993, the Brady Bill was signed to strengthen gun legislation. Steven Spielberg's adaptation of Michael Crichton's *Jurassic Park* made $81.7 million in its first week in movie theaters. Denzel Washington and Tom Hanks starred in *Philadelphia*, directed by Jonathan Demme, and Bruce Springsteen received a Grammy for the title song. John le Carré wrote *The Night Manager*. Clint Eastwood won best director for *The Unforgiven*.

Along Came a Spider by James Patterson was the first of his novels to feature the detective Alex Cross. There have been at least nineteen sequels since. The prolific author of dozens of mystery-suspense novels was born in Newburgh, New York, and lives in Florida. He continues to write in collaboration with a variety of other writers who produce several bestsellers every year. In terms of productivity alone, the collective output of these writers might be called James Patterson Inc. It is a bestseller machine. Patterson's first novel, *The Thomas Berryman Number*, appeared in 1976 and won a major mystery writing award. It is a haunting novel set in Nashville in which the narrator visits an inmate in a prison. Before writing it, Patterson had been an advertising writer. In some respects, he continues to be a writer of a kind of fiction that resembles catchy advertising copy. He is a witty, creative writer who swiftly invents plots. He has sought to emphasize reading and to make reading something that people across America value. Patterson's Alex Cross series and his Women's Murder Club series have been notable. By now Patterson surely holds the record for the most #1 popular novels (followed by pop notables such as Danielle Steel and John Grisham). His coauthors include Maxine Paetro, Michael Ledwidge, Peter de Jonge, Andrew Gross, Mark Sullivan, Ashwin Sanghi, and Candice Fox. He has been writing a crime fiction novel with former U.S. president Bill Clinton. The James Patterson novel is today a highly marketable brand. It is a quick, snappy read, in which entertainment rather than language is evidently the focus. It does not seem likely that Patterson, a creative writing machine, will take a few years in his old age someday to write a deeper novel—although he may be quite capable of doing so. He continues to entertain thousands of readers with easily readable dramatic suspense fiction. Patterson has set up the "Page Turner Awards" to encourage reading. He has established a social networking site, "Read Kiddo Read," and teacher education programs at Appalachian State University, Florida Atlantic University, Michigan State University, and the University of Florida.

The Black Echo by Michael Connelly, which was published by Little, Brown, introduced the character Harry Bosch to readers. Connelly left another couple of novels in his drawer. The Black Ice (1993) followed, and The Concrete Blonde (1994) rose onto the bestseller list. Connelly is the creator of both the characters Harry Bosch and Mickey Haller. The LAPD detective Hieronymus Bosch is named after the painter. Mickey Haller is known as the Lincoln Lawyer and is played in film by Matthew McConaughey. Connelly is a writer who can be appreciated for his craft, his crisp dialogue, and his well-paced stories that bring his readers into sympathy with his protagonists and their investigations. Connelly attended St. Augustine High School in Fort Lauderdale, Florida. His mother was a reader of crime novels and his father worked in construction. Connelly worked for the Los Angeles Times, but he was particularly drawn to the detective novels of Raymond Chandler. Lost Coyote (1995) and The Poet (1996) appeared in the mid-1990s. There was no Harry Bosch in The Poet. Instead, the novel featured reporter Jack McEvoy. Then came Connelly's novels Chasing the Dime, Lost Light, Echo Park, The Scarecrow, and The Lincoln Lawyer. Connelly's novels began to bring together Bosch and Haller, as in The Burning Room (2014) and The Crossing (2015). The Wrong Side of Goodbye appeared in 2016, and Connelly's novel Two Kinds of Truth was #2 on the bestseller list on November 19 and remained on the bestseller list through December 2017.

1994

Slow Waltz in Cedar Bend and *The Bridges of Madison County* focused on rural areas of America. Waller's novels remained the top two books in fiction sales through the first half of January 1994. Tom Clancy's *Without Remorse*, Stephen King's *Nightmares and Dreamscapes*, and John Grisham's *The Client* followed. On January 23, the recently released Michael Crichton novel *Disclosure* leaped to #1. It stayed there through February. *Disclosure* was also in the top ten books chosen by *Publishers Weekly* as 1994's fiction bestsellers. Robin Cook's *Fatal Cure* was briefly #4 behind *The Bridges of Madison County*. Danielle Steel returned to #1 on February 27. Next appeared *The Celestine Prophecy*, James Redfield's story of insight and new age spirituality. The book reached #3 on March 20 and rose to #1 on April 3. It was a thin story, one open to mysteries and human potential, and it caught the public's interest and remained on the bestseller list for the rest of the year. It was #1 until May 22, when Mary Higgins Clark's *Remember Me* moved past it to #1. On April 24 Sue Grafton's *K Is for Killer* was #2 behind it. Alan Folsom's *The Day after Tomorrow* was #3.

Richard Nixon died on April 22, and services for him in California were broadcast on national television. On May 15, Clive Cussler's *Inca Gold* was #3 behind the James Redfield book and Mary Higgins Clark's *Remember Me*. On May 29 *The Celestine Prophecy* regained its place as the #1 selling book in America. However, John Grisham and his publisher had released *The Chamber*. Readers were evidently hungry for more Grisham legal thrillers, and *The Chamber* swiftly went to #1 on June 12. (*Publishers Weekly* placed sales of *The Chamber* at the top of its year-end list.) *Remember Me*, the Mary Higgins Clark novel, also rivaled Redfield's green-covered new age appeal to possibility.

That spring and summer, Betty Eadie's *Embraced by the Light* intrigued readers with reflections on near-death experience. William Bennett offered *The Book of Virtues*. Counselor Thomas Moore discussed relationships in *Soul Mates*, his follow-up to *Care of the Soul*, in which he had turned to myths to encourage reflection and self-help. Country singer Reba McIntyre's memoir, *Reba*, was #2 on the nonfiction list on May 8. Dan Quayle recalled times in the White House in *Standing Firm*. It was #2 behind *Embraced by the Light*. Richard Nixon's *Beyond Peace*, the former president's thoughts on international relations and world order, was #6. Stephen Ambrose's study of *D-Day* was out in time for the anniversary of that momentous day in 1944 on June 6. Meanwhile, television cameras were following O. J. Simpson's white Ford Bronco on June 17, as he attempted to elude police. He was charged with murder, and his trial was extensively publicized. On June 19 the Ambrose book was #2 and Nixon's book was #4. Bob Woodward's *The Agenda*, on the Clinton White House, was the #1 nonfiction on June 26. Books new to the fiction bestseller list included Cormac McCarthy's *The Crossing* (#3 on June 26) and Caleb Carr's *The Alienist* (#5 on July 3). Carr, a historian, set his detective mystery novel in the final decades of the nineteenth century. More recently, the novel was transformed into a television series on TNT.

In midsummer, America celebrated July 4 with fireworks and parades. People went to the beach with copies of *The Chamber*, *The Gift*, *Inca Gold*, *Remember Me*, Barbara Taylor Bradford's *Everything to Gain*, and *The Celestine Prophecy*. Grisham's *The Client* held the top spot on the bestseller list through July. Pat Conroy's *Beach Music* returned as popular summer reading at #4. In nonfiction, *Embraced by the Light* and *The Agenda* were joined in the top five by *Moonshot*, by former astronaut Alan Shepard on July 31. On August 7, Danielle Steel's *The Gift* was #1. It was her second #1 book of the year. Steel's *The Gift*, and Grisham's *The Client* held the #1 and #2 positions, respectively, until August 28 when *The Celestine Prophecy* was listed as #2. *Publishers Weekly* listed each of these books among its top bestsellers of the year. Disney's *The Lion King* was #8 on August 21 on the *New York Times* list. Detective fiction writer James Lee Burke's *Dixie City Jam* was #11. Tom Clancy's *Debt of Honor* peaked at #1 on September 4 and remained #1 into October on both major national bestseller lists. Mystery genre novels by Patricia Cornwell (*The Body Farm*) and Sidney Sheldon (*Nothing Lasts Forever*) entered the top five during this time.

Maybe there is something about October that brings out the ghosts and ghouls. Or maybe it is simply a writer and publisher's timetable. In October Anne Rice and Stephen King could be expected to have a frightening story on the bestseller list. In October 1994 both did. Anne Rice's *Taltos* was #1 on October 16. Stephen King's *Insomnia* was #1 on October 23. On the edge of Halloween, on October 30, they stood as the #1 and #2 fiction books in the nation. Stephen King's "The Man in the Black Suit," published in the *New Yorker* October 31, became the O. Henry Prize short story of the year. Novelist and television show writer Peter Blauner, in

Newsday, asked: "Has anyone noticed that Stephen King is becoming one of the most interesting writers around?"[12] *Insomnia*, set in Derry, Maine, probed abortion issues. Its glaring red-and-white cover was like a reversible jacket. Printings of the cover reversed the red-and-white title lettering and background.

Of course, not all was Stephen King scary. On the nonfiction list, *Barbara Bush: A Memoir* brought that personable First Lady's recollections to #1. James Herriot's reflection on cats was #2. Dolly Parton's memoir was #4. Filmmaker Ken Burns and Geoffrey C. Ward's *Baseball* was #4, supported by their television documentary. In fiction, John Irving's *Son of the Circus* was #13. On November 6, the life story of Nicole Brown Simpson rose to #1 as one of the many bestselling books that would be written about the murder trials of former football star O. J. Simpson. *Crossing the Threshold of Hope* by Pope John Paul II was second on the nonfiction bestseller list. At #3, the scary returned: *The Hot Zone* by Richard Preston worried readers with a disturbing account of potentially lethal viruses.

The midterm election in November shifted the balance of power in Washington. Led by Newt Gingrich, the Republicans achieved victories that would give them control of the 104th Congress. *The Celestine Prophecy* returned to #1 on November 13, with Stephen King's story at #2. The books held those positions on the list throughout November. On the nonfiction list, Pope John Paul II's *Crossing the Threshold of Hope* was #1 and the controversial *The Bell Curve* by Richard Herrnstein and Charles Murray was #2. Tim Allen of the *Home Improvement* series on television cautioned readers: *Don't Stand Too Close to a Naked Man*. His book reached #1 on December 18. It was #8 on *Publishers Weekly*'s end-of-year list. In fiction, *Politically Correct Bedtime Stories* rose to the top spot on December 11. The book was followed by Danielle Steel's *Wings* at #2 and Stephen King's *Insomnia* at #3. *The Celestine Prophecy* was in its forty-third week on the bestseller list. That holiday season readers were reading about baseball, cats, and Warren Buffett. Doris Kearns Goodwin's *No Ordinary Time*, concerning Eleanor and Franklin Roosevelt, was #15 on the list behind the naked man, Dolly Parton's memoirs, and *Cats and Virtues*.

In 1994, the existence of black holes was confirmed by the Hubble telescope. About fifteen million people logged on to the internet, which would revolutionize communications worldwide. The IRA reached an accord between Catholics and Protestant Unionists in Northern Ireland. A Rwandan civil war devolved into genocide. In America, the anniversary of Woodstock was celebrated that summer. Popular films included *Forrest Gump* and *Pulp Fiction*.

1995

Politically Correct Bedtime Stories, a satire by James Finn Garner, was the #1 bestseller on January 1, 1995. Tom Clancy's *Debt of Honor* was #2. On January 8 through January 15, Pope John Paul II's book *Threshold of Hope* appeared at #1 on the nonfiction list. Next on that list was pure fear. *The Hot Zone* by Preston soon rose to #1 with its distressful recognition of lethal viruses. Garner's bedtime stories contrasted with Clancy's suspense novel at #1 throughout the month. James Patterson's *Kiss the Girls* rose to #3. *The Hot Zone* was #1 in February's chill on February 5. O. J. Simpson chilled some other readers with *I Want to Tell You*, #1 on February 15. In fiction, P. D. James's *Original Sin* came up behind *The Celestine Prophecy* (#1). Dr. Seuss was at #5. *Border Music*, another book by Robert James Waller, was #3 on February 26. *Breaking the Surface* was swimmer Greg Louganis's #1 written with Eric Marcus. (This is one of many celebrity books told to coauthors.) March also brought to the bestseller list an argument against government regulations: *The Death of Common Sense*. On March 30, John le Carré's *Our Game* rose to #4 on the list. The novel went to #2 on April 2.

The Oklahoma City bombing on April 19 destroyed the Murrah Building and took the lives of 168 people, including children in the day care center. At the end of April 1995, John Grisham's *The Rainmaker* was #1. Robert McNamara's *In Retrospect* was #1 on the nonfiction list. On May 14, Mary Higgins Clark's *Let Me Call You Sweetheart* was #2 behind the Grisham title. In early June those titles remained the top two books on the list. Robert Ludlum's *Apocalypse Watch* was #3. *The Hot Zone* returned to #1 on the nonfiction list. On June 18 *The Bridges of Madison County* was at #2 behind Grisham's #1 novel. Those books alternated between #1 and #2 between June 18 and July 2. On June 25, *The Bridges of Madison County* was #1. On July 2 *The Rainmaker* was #1. *The Rainmaker* was #1 on *Publishers Weekly*'s end-of-year list. In nonfiction, *Spontaneous Healing* by Dr. Andrew Weil was #2 behind *The Hot Zone*. Robert Fulghum returned to the list at #10 with *From Beginning to End*. The nonfiction list included at #3 Dave Barry's *The Complete Guide to Guys*.

On July 11 the United States resumed diplomatic relations with Vietnam. In the heat of the summer months *Beach Music* by Pat Conroy reached #1 on July 16; Stephen King's *Rose Madder* was #2. The #1 nonfiction book on June 23 and June 30 was Newt Gingrich's *To Renew America*. Gail Sheehy's *New Passages* was one of its competitors. Gingrich's book was #1 again from August 6 through the 13th and on August 27. As the tide moved out on *Beach Music*, in came *Memnoch the Devil* by Anne Rice. She entertained readers with the story of the vampire Lestat who is taken from the world by the demon Memnoch. *Beach Music* flowed back to #1 on August 13 and then was overtaken at that spot by Patricia Cornwell's *From Potter's Field* on August 27. Following it was *Beach Music*, *Memnoch the Devil*, *Lightning* by Danielle Steel, and *The Celestine Prophecy*. These books remained in the top five on September 10. Readers also read about *Belgarath the Sorcerer* (at #13) and *The Return of Merlin* by Deepak Chopra (at #15).

On September 10, television personality and host Ellen DeGeneres replaced the Newt Gingrich book at #1 with *My Point . . . and I Do Have One*. Climbing to #1 on September 17, 1995, on the fiction list was Sue Grafton's *L Is for Lawless*. *Coming Home* by Rosamunde Pilcher was #2. On the nonfiction list, John Feinstein's book on the PGA Golf Tour, *A Good Walk Spoiled*, was #2 behind Ellen's book. Challenging the fiction by Grafton and Pilcher were Sidney Sheldon's *Morning, Noon and Night* and Nicholas Evans's *The Horse Whisperer*. On October 1 that book went to #1. It was followed by the novels by Sheldon, Pilcher, and Grafton. However, Michael Crichton's *The Lost World*, his sequel to *Jurassic Park*, jumped to #1. The nonfiction list was led by *My American Journey* by Colin Powell for the next several weeks. The former *Washington Post* editor Ben Bradlee's *A Good Life* was #3. Daniel Goleman's book on *Emotional Intelligence* was #5.

On October 3, O. J. Simpson was acquitted. On October 16, the Million Man March brought thousands of black men to Washington to affirm their human rights and dignity. On October 29, the bestseller list was still topped by *The Lost World* by Crichton. It was followed by novels by Mary Higgins Clark, Nicholas Evans, and Sidney Sheldon. On November 5 *Charles Kuralt's America* rose to #3 on the bestseller list with his record of his journeys across America as a journalist. November 19 the

Crichton and Clark novels were at #1 and #2, respectively. Amy Tan's *The Hundred Secret Senses* was #3. On the nonfiction list, Kuralt's book was joined in the top five by the memoirs of newscaster and journalist David Brinkley. David Herbert Donald's *Lincoln* was #6.

Suddenly, Howard Stern was #1 with *Miss America* on November 26. The radio personality's book stayed at #1 into December, with Colin Powell's book at #2 and *Emotional Intelligence* at #3. Howard Stern's book was #3 for the year on the *Publishers Weekly* list. On December 3, Americans were meeting at the Ritz in Danielle Steel's #1 *Five Days in Paris*. This novel and Steel's *Lightning* were both in the top five of *Publishers Weekly*'s list for 1995. Michael Crichton's *Lost World* was #2. Mary Higgins Clark's *Silent Night* was #4. William Bennett's *The Children's Book of Virtues* followed his previous volume: the top-selling *Book of Virtues*. Publishers targeted the holiday season: on December 7, *The Christmas Box* by Richard Paul Evans was #1. *Politically Correct Holiday Stories* by James Finn Garner followed Danielle Steel's *Five Days in Paris*, Michael Crichton's *The Lost World*, and Mary Higgins Clark's *Silent Night*. *The Lost World*, a sequel to *Jurassic Park*, was the #2 book on the annual *Publishers Weekly* list. On December 17, the nonfiction list was led by Bill Gates's *The Road Ahead*. His book, as you might expect, looked at innovation and technology in the information age. This book joined the books by Howard Stern, Charles Kuralt, Colin Powell, and David Brinkley and one about Mother Teresa that was at #7. The Lincoln biography was #9. Danielle Steel's *Five Days in Paris*, Michael Crichton's *The Lost World*, Mary Higgins Clark's *Silent Night*, Richard Paul Evans's *The Christmas Box*, and *Politically Correct Holiday Stories* led the bestseller list through the end of the year.

1996

In upstate New York, a snowy day turns tragic when horses collide and a truck skids into them. A girl is killed and another is badly injured. As Grace MacLean heals from her injuries, her mother seeks out Tom Booker, the horse whisperer in Montana, who nurses Pilgrim, a skittish horse, back to health. On January 23, *The Horse Whisperer* by Nicholas Evans was at #1, Danielle Steel's novel was #2, and Clive Cussler's adventure story *Shock Wave* rose to #3. On January 28, Dean Koontz's *Intensity* was

#1, followed the books by Steel and Cussler. W. E. B. Griffin's *Behind the Lines* and Robin Cook's *Contagion* reached #4 and #5, respectively.

On February 4, Hillary Rodham Clinton's *It Takes a Village* reached #1 on the nonfiction list. Clinton's serious and conversational tone was in contrast with Al Franken's *Rush Limbaugh Is a Big Fat Idiot*, a satirical attack on the political right and its notorious radio talk show star. *Emotional Intelligence* by Daniel Goleman was #2 and Bill Gates's book was #3. Behind Hillary Clinton's book, Senator Bill Bradley's *Time Present, Time Past* was #5 on February 18. *Primary Colors*, the anonymous political fiction bestseller, rose to #1 that week. On its red-and-white cover was drawn a Democratic donkey. A band of blue ran across the top. Joe Klein, its author, remained anonymous for a time. His novel fictionalized Bill Clinton's run for president, and it remained at #1 for the next month. Al Franken's book then became #1 on the nonfiction list. The politically minded public, it seems, was focused more on present events than the past, on current news more than history. Lincoln was at #13.

March brought LaVyrle Spencer's *That Camden Summer* to #2 behind *Primary Colors*. In her story a divorcée in Maine returns home. Koontz's *Intensity* and David Baldacci's *Absolute Power* were also showing strong sales and were in the top five. By March 31, *Blood Sport* by James B. Stewart had caught on with his report on the Whitewater case and the Clinton presidency. *Undaunted Courage*, Stephen Ambrose's account of the Lewis and Clark expedition, was a Book of the Month Club selection. It rose to #3, ahead of a chatty book by the actor-comedian and octogenarian George Burns. In April 1996, Elizabeth George's *In the Presence of the Enemy* told the story of British celebrities who face kidnappers. The novel rose to #2 behind *Primary Colors*. Nora Roberts's *Montana Sky* was #3. Judith Krantz's *Spring Collection* was #4 and Tami Hoag's *Guilty as Sin* was #5. In nonfiction, a seemingly endless array of books on the O. J. Simpson trial began to emerge.

Springtime brought flowers, sunshine, and *Moonlight Becomes You* by Mary Higgins Clark, which rose to #1 on the fiction list on April 28. *Primary Colors* dropped to #2 and William Shatner, of *Star Trek* fame, arrived where few men had gone before with a science fiction bestseller at #4. Shatner's *The Return* was cowritten with Garfield Reeves Stevens. *The Celestine Prophecy* was #5 on the list. *In Contempt*, an O. J. Simpson trial book, was #1 on April 28, and on May 5 *In Search of Justice* by Robert Shapiro with Larkin Warren arrived at #3 with more O. J. *Mid-*

night in the Garden of Good and Evil, John Berendt's story of Savannah at #6, was beginning its long stay on the bestseller list. *Moonlight Becomes You* remained at #1.

How Stella Got Her Groove Back by Terry McMillan reached #1 on May 19. A forty-year-old single mother heads for Jamaica to get her groove back, and readers went on the journey to new life with her. *The Tenth Insight*, James Redfield's sequel to *The Celestine Prophecy*, explored new age possibilities at #2. Basketball's Dennis Rodman's book with writer Tim Keown, *Bad as I Wanna Be*, scored and went to #1 on the nonfiction list. It was followed by a series of cartoons satirizing business, *The Dilbert Principle*. On June, John Grisham's *The Runaway Jury* shot up to #1, followed by *Stella, The Tenth Insight, Moonlight Becomes You*, and John Sandford's *Sudden Prey*.

At the time few readers expected that George R. R. Martin's *A Game of Thrones*, published that year, would become a smash HBO television phenomenon. Important books lurking in the shadows included Samuel P. Huntington's *The Clash of Civilizations*. Novels by Margaret Atwood (*Alias Grace*), William Golding (*The Double Tongue*), David Foster Wallace (*Infinite Jest*), and Joyce Carol Oates (*We Were the Mulvaneys*) had strong sales, but these literary novels did not rise to the stratosphere of bestsellerdom.

John Grisham's *Runaway Jury* remained at #1 through the first half of summer 1996. It was followed by *A Crown of Swords* at #2 and *How Stella Got Her Groove Back* at #3. Shel Silverstein's poems and sketches were #4. On the nonfiction list, attorney Vincent Bugliosi expressed *Outrage*, with more O. J. Simpson. Bob Woodward offered *The Choice*, a study of Bill Clinton and Robert Dole. *Undaunted Courage* by Stephen Ambrose was #5.

In midsummer, on July 21, Patricia Cornwell's series character Kay Scarpetta returned to #1 with *Cause of Death*. John Grisham's *The Runaway Jury* fell behind it. *Exclusive* by Sandra Brown was #3. The Clintons remained a popular subject, and FBI agent Gary Aldrich provided *Unlimited Access* to the Clinton White House. His book was #1 on July 28 and August 4. Roger Morris's *Partners in Power* kicked up some dirt in another discussion of President Bill Clinton and Hillary Clinton. The Clintons were in the news and on the book list on the eve of the Democratic National Convention. The novels by Patricia Cornwell and John Grisham were now joined by Mario Puzo's *The Last Don*, which was at

#3 in its first week on the list. On August 18, the vampires returned with Anne Rice's *Servant of the Bones* at #3. Her novel reached #1 the next week, on August 25. *The Dilbert Principle* by Douglas Adams, his cartoon satire on business, led the nonfiction list. That long-running bestseller *Midnight in the Garden of Good and Evil* was #5. On August 29, Bill Clinton won the Democratic nomination.

September 1 brought *Executive Orders* from Tom Clancy to #1. On the nonfiction list, political analyst Ed Rollins discussed his thirty years in politics in *Bare Knuckles and Back Rooms*. *Between Hope and History* by Bill Clinton was #3 on September 15. *All Too Human* by Ed Klein dug up dirt on John Kennedy and Jacqueline Kennedy. Clancy, Rice, Grisham, and Puzo were the top four sellers in fiction on September 8 and 15. James Patterson's novel *Jack and Jill* rose to #2 on September 29. On that day, another of the ongoing examinations of the O. J. Simpson case arrived at the top of the list. Readers were apparently hungry for more, and Jeffery Toobin delivered with *The Run of His Life*. At #5 was Rabbi Harold Kushner's *How Good Do We Have to Be?*

October brought *The Deep End of the Ocean* by Jacqueline Mitchard to #1. It was the story about the disappearance of a three-year-old boy. *Executive Orders* by Tom Clancy fell to #2 behind that novel. Both encountered *Desperation* by Stephen King, which leaped to #1 on October 13. Suddenly, Stephen King held both the #1 and #2 spots on the bestseller list. He wrote *Desperation* as Stephen King. *The Regulators*, his #2, was signed Richard Bachman. *The Notebook* by Nicholas Sparks (1996) raced up the bestseller list the week after it was published in October 1996. Sparks was selling pharmaceuticals before his novel *The Notebook* (1996) became a bestseller. Theresa Park, a lawyer-agent, took on Sparks and secured a contract from Time Warner that launched his career. About a dozen Nicholas Sparks novels have since been adapted to film. On the nonfiction list, Judge Robert Bork's *Slouching towards Gomorrah* critiqued American culture from a conservative perspective. It rose to #2 on October 27. The Taliban rebels now controlled Afghanistan and seized the city of Kabul.

On Tuesday, November 5, Bill Clinton was reelected, along with his running mate Al Gore. On November 10, 1996, *The Deep End of the Ocean* returned to #1. Scott Turow's *The Law of Our Fathers* was #2. In Turow's novel a probation officer is tried for his mother's murder. Stephen King's *Desperation* was #3, and sales of Mary Higgins Clark's *My*

Gal Sunday helped its climb to #4. David Baldacci appeared on the best-seller list for the first time with *Absolute Power*. His character Luther Whitney plans a robbery and breaks into a billionaire's house and discovers that the billionaire's wife is having sex with the president of the United States. There were also tragic stories in the nonfiction category. *American Tragedy* brought another perspective on the O. J. Simpson case and was yet another #1 that considered that subject. *M Is for Malice* by Sue Grafton rose to #2 on November 17. *The Soul's Code* by James Hillman, a Jungian psychologist, was #1 on the nonfiction list on that day.

Danielle Steel's *Silent Honor* was #1 on December 1 with a story recalling the attack on Pearl Harbor and American and Japanese families. Frank McCourt's *Angela's Ashes*, his recollections of life in Limerick, rose to #1 on the nonfiction list on December 15. The next Sunday, in its first week on the list, *Airframe* by Michael Crichton was #2. It quickly became the #1 bestseller on December 29. Readers of *Jurassic Park*, *The Lost World*, and *Disclosure* knew they were getting another suspenseful page-turner. By this time, Crichton was drawing upon information he gathered at the Massachusetts Institute of Technology (MIT) on the cutting edge of technology. *The Christmas Box* made an expected rise to #2 and was followed by *Silent Honor* at #3 and the return of *Executive Orders* by Tom Clancy at #4. *The Notebook* by Nicholas Sparks was making its climb up the list and was at #5. On the nonfiction list, Walter Cronkite's *A Reporter's Life* appeared at #2 in its first week. His memoirs rose to #1 on December 29.

THE OPRAH IMPACT

Oprah Winfrey, beginning in October 1996, presented forty-eight books on her television program. Inevitably, those books became bestsellers. In *Reading Oprah*, Cecilia Konchar Farr evaluates the cultural phenomenon of Oprah's Book Club and its social and economic impact. She sees Oprah as something like a librarian and teacher who advocates reading. Oprah's daytime audience was a broad audience that included both voracious readers and the occasional reader. It included college graduates who had continued to read books and those who had not picked up a novel since high school. Oprah sought empathy and reader identification. She emphasized social justice themes and recognized that formulaic reading is not enough to ensure one's social engagement. Her view, Farr contends, is that the novel can be "transformational, even inspirational." Her advocacy expressed reading as a "democratic encounter." [13] In her introduction to Farr's book, Elizabeth Long points out that Farr "finds issues in Oprah's penchant for sentimental novels." [14] Even so, Oprah's Book Club served in "broadening the audience for fiction." By April 2002, when Oprah Winfrey announced that she was discontinuing the book club, it was clear that she had enabled readers to "embrace serious novels." Each of Oprah's book selections sold an average of 1.4 million copies, and each of the books spent about seventeen weeks on the bestseller list. [15]

October 1996 to June 2002 was the first long run of Oprah's Book Club. During that time there was always at least one Oprah book on the bestseller list. Of the books on Oprah's list, including the more complex, multilayered novels, like John Steinbeck's *East of Eden*, or William Faulkner's fiction, Farr writes: "If a million buy the book suppose half read it." [16] Yes, and suppose that people will continue to read—that individuals will exercise their curiosity and desire self-improvement or for entertainment. Suppose that college students will actually purchase and read assigned texts and that people will buy and read books that delight them. If people continue to read, the encouragements of "teachers" like Oprah will not have been wasted. The lively minds of readers will benefit and those readers will bring to life their energy and an awareness broadened by books.

Absolute Power by David Baldacci was his breakthrough novel. A fictional U.S. president is having an affair, and Secret Service agents have to cover up the accidental death of the woman the president was having an affair with. Baldacci is from Richmond, Virginia. He went to University of Virginia Law School and practiced law for nine years. He has been writing stories since childhood. In 1996, *Absolute Power* became a bestseller, and more than thirty novels have followed it. He and his wife created the Wish You Well Foundation for literacy in the United States. Baldacci's fiction series includes the Camel Club series.

1997

The 1997 fiction bestseller list began with *Airframe*, *Executive Orders*, *The Christmas Box*, and *Silent Honor*. Perhaps the surprise bestseller was

Diana Gabaldon's *Drums of Autumn*, in which a Scottish couple experiences the coming of the American Revolution. Walter Cronkite's *A Reporter's Life* and Frank McCourt's *Angela's Ashes*, both memoirs, remained #1 and #2, respectively, on the nonfiction list. On January 26, Jonathan Kellerman's *The Clinic*, at #2, brought psychologist-detective Alex Delaware to solve another case. *The Unlikely Spy* by Daniel Silva appeared at #14. Silva had begun a successful series of bestsellers featuring Gabriel Allon, an Israeli Mossad agent who is an art restorer. In the top five nonfiction bestsellers were President Jimmy Carter's *Living Faith* and Neale Donald Walsch's *Conversations with God*. On February 2, Patricia Cornwell returned to #1 in fiction with *Hornet's Nest*. Crichton's *Airframe* was #2. David Baldacci's *Total Control* rose to #3 by February 9. *The Millionaire Next Door* by Thomas J. Stanley and William D. Danko explored what wealthy people have in common. Cardinal Bernardin offered *The Gift of Peace*, a book that rose to #2 on February 16.

Sole Survivor by Dean Koontz shot to #1 on March 2. Behind it was *Hornet's Nest* (#2), Baldacci's *Total Control* (#3), and Crichton's *Airframe* (#4). The nonfiction #1, *Personal History*, was the memoir of Katherine Graham, publisher of the *Washington Post*. On March 15, John Grisham's *The Partner* was the #1 fiction book. In *The Partner*, $90 million is stolen from a Mississippi lawyer: a man who is not dead but is in hiding. In *Murder in Brentwood,* Mark Fuhrman, star witness in the Simpson trial, provides his view for an audience still hungry for details about the case. On April 6 Grisham's novel was still #1, but *3001: The Final Odyssey* claimed #2 with Arthur C. Clarke's sequel to *2001: A Space Odyssey*. On the list at #3 was *Sanctuary* by Nora Roberts. *Chromosome* by Robin Cook was #4. *Angela's Ashes* reached #1 on the nonfiction list on that day. Danielle Steel's *The Ranch* joined those books at #2 on April 20. Mary Higgins Clark's *Pretend You Don't See Her* was #3 on April 27.

From May 4 to June 8, 1997, Mary Higgins Clark's novel was #1. John Grisham's *The Partner* followed at #2 and Danielle Steel at #3. (*The Partner* was #1 on *Publishers Weekly*'s annual bestseller list. *Cold Mountain*, Charles Frazier's Pulitzer-winning novel, was #2. Danielle Steel novels held the #3, #4, and #5 spots on its 1997 list.) *Underboss*, Peter Maas's Mafia novel, went to #1 on May 11. *Mason and Dixon* by Thomas Pynchon was a literary novel that rose as high as #4. Jon Krakauer's *Into*

Thin Air fascinated readers with an account of climbing Mount Everest. It reached #1 on the nonfiction list on June 8. *Without a Doubt* brought another account of O. J. Simpson's trial from prosecutor Marcia Clark. Billy Graham's memoirs *Just as I Am* soon rose to #1 on June 29. Nelson DeMille's adventurous *Plum Island* was #1 beginning on June 15. Jack Higgins's *The President's Daughter* went to #3 on June 29. Tom Clancy's *Into the Storm*, written with General Fred Franks about the Iraq battles of the Gulf War, was #3 on the nonfiction list. Obviously, there was an audience for dramatic and heroic adventures.

On July 6 Nelson DeMille's *Plum Island* was #1. Sandra Brown's *Fat Tuesday*, at #2, was set during Mardi Gras in New Orleans. In her story a policeman has gone rogue with the wife of an attorney. On July 13, Danielle Steel went directly to #1 with *Special Delivery*. On the nonfiction list, McCourt's *Angela's Ashes* was #1. *The Perfect Storm* by Sebastian Junger was #3. On August 10, John Berendt's *Midnight in the Garden of Good and Evil*, at #5, was in its 160th week on the bestseller list. *Unnatural Exposure* by Patricia Cornwell was #1 with the story of Kay Scarpetta facing the dilemma of a smallpox virus. Following Danielle Steel's *Special Delivery* was Charles Frazier's *Cold Mountain* at #3. His Pulitzer Prize–winning novel about a Confederate soldier returning home was written while Frazier lived in solitude in the North Carolina mountains. On August 31, Frazier's novel reached #1. *London* by Edward Rutherford and Arundhati Roy's *The God of Small Things* were now in the top ten on the bestseller list.

Princess Diana died in an accident on August 31. There would be several books about her the next year. Tony Blair had become the first Labour prime minister of England in twenty-three years. In America, the Dow Jones Industrial Average plummeted 554.26 points on October 27 and then rebounded in the following days.

On October 12, Sidney Sheldon's *The Best Laid Plans* was #2 and Clive Cussler's *Flood Tide* rose high on the list. Caleb Carr's *Angel of Darkness* was #4. *The Royals* was Kitty Kelley's scuttlebutt about the royal House of Windsor. *Diana: Her Own Story* returned to #2 and *Diana Princess of Wales* was #5. (*Diana: Her Own Story* was #6 on *Publishers Weekly*'s end-of-year list. The #5 nonfiction book was *The Joy of Cooking*.) Marty Roberts's *The Man Who Listens to Horses* was #3 on October 26. On November 3, Anne Rice's *Violin* was #3 with the story of a demonic violinist from Vienna who goes to New Orleans. In Robert

Ludlum's *The Matarese Countdown*, at #3, a CIA officer seeks an international group of power brokers. *The Ghost* by Danielle Steel was #1 on November 30; it was her second #1 bestseller of the year.

On December 7, 1997, *Cold Mountain*, *Ghost*, and James Patterson's *Cat and Mouse* led the list. In Patterson's novel, serial killers are out to get Alex Cross. Dominick Dunne turned the O. J. Simpson case into fiction, and his novel reached #4. Seymour Hersch's *The Dark Side of Camelot* dug up the dirt on John F. Kennedy. *Citizen Soldiers* by Stephen Ambrose followed the fighting in the Second World War from the Battle of the Bulge to the German surrender. It was #4 on the nonfiction list. On December 21, *Cat and Mouse* was at #2 behind *Cold Mountain*. A week later, on December 28, Danielle Steel's was the #2 book. *The Letter* by Richard Paul Evans extended *The Christmas Box* with this third book of his trilogy. David Baldacci's *The Winner* appeared at #6 and would rise to #2 in January 1998. Also in the top ten readers could find historian Doris Kearns Goodwin's recollections of life in Long Island as a fan of the Brooklyn Dodgers. *Angela's Ashes* by Frank McCourt was listed at #1 for the year by *Publishers Weekly*. The film *Titanic*, released in December, became the bestselling film of all time to that date.

Paradise by Toni Morrison landed on the bestseller list principally because Oprah Winfrey drew attention to it on her daytime television show. Morrison had recently won the Nobel Prize. Morrison's literary craft, imagination, and critical acumen are evident in her vivid characterization and engaging storytelling. *Paradise* was preceded by the poignant story of *Beloved* and the sharp dialogue and well-drawn characters of *Jazz*. Morrison's *Beloved* was selected as one of the top contemporary novels by a group of critics and authors enlisted by the *New York Times*. *Paradise* (1997) reveals the difficulties of Ruby, Oklahoma, and the women who live together in a former convent outside the town. Morrison layers their stories through flashbacks about their lives and the town's history. The men of the town interact with the women, looking for answers. *Paradise* is the third book of the trilogy that began with *Beloved* and included *Jazz*. The novel was Oprah's selection for her television book club in January 1998.

Morrison was born in Lorain, Ohio, to parents who shared with their daughter their love of African American folk songs. She attended Howard University and Cornell University, where she wrote on Virginia Woolf and William Faulkner for a master's thesis. These authors often investigate the interiority of their characters and make use of stream-of-consciousness techniques. Morrison taught English at Texas Southern and at Howard University. She then worked as an editor for L. W. Singer, a textbook publisher in Syracuse, and at Random House in New York City. As an editor, she brought African American literature into view by editing the volume *Contemporary African American Literature* (1972). *The Bluest Eye* was published in 1970. The book came to the attention of Robert Gottlieb at Random House, who subsequently edited several of her novels. *Sula* (1973) tells the story of the friendship of two black women. *Song of Solomon* (1977) was a Book of the Month selection. *Tar Baby* (1981) followed. In 1983, Morrison lived in a converted boathouse on the Hudson River. She taught at Rutgers and at the State University of New York. After *Beloved* (1987), *Jazz* (1990) explored a love triangle during the Harlem Renaissance. Morrison's literary criticism was collected in *Playing in the Park: Whiteness and the Literary Imagination* (1992). The Presidential Medal of Freedom was awarded to Morrison by President Barack Obama in 2012. Toni Morrison's *God Help the Child* (2013) features Bride, a fashion executive who has been affected by her mother's treatment of her for being dark skinned.

Harry Potter and the Philosopher's Stone by J. K. Rowling caused a sensation. The Harry Potter series fascinated young readers and became the dominant young adult fiction in the market. While Rowling carried her ideas about this character around with her for years, the idea for the first novel evidently came to her while she was riding on a bus. Her own apparently magical transformation from humble beginnings has become a popular rags-to-riches story. Today she is not only J. K. Rowling but also the mystery writer Robert Galbraith: a pseudonym for her adult bestsellers. Harry Potter became among the most well-known fictional characters of the 1990s, with Rowling's unprecedented string of #1 bestsellers. The constant appearance of Harry Potter on the *New York Times* bestseller list pushed popular adult novels further down the list. This generated concern for adult fiction. The *New York Times* responded by creating a separate children's bestseller list. Rowling's work as Robert Galbraith includes *The Casual Vacancy* (2012), *The Cuckoo's Calling* (2013), *The Silkworm* (2014), and *Career of Evil* (2015).

The Unlikely Spy by Daniel Silva was published in 1996, and it reached the bestseller list on January 26, 1997, at #13. About twenty more suspense novels have followed. Silva had to learn about art restoration.

His spy suspense novels focus on the activities of Gabriel Allon, an art restorer and Mossad agent. Born in 1960 in Detroit to parents who were teachers, Silva moved with his family to Merced, California, as a child. He became a journalist with United Press International (UPI) and was assigned to cover the Democratic National Convention. Silva was a Middle East correspondent in Cairo, a position that likely began to suggest a context for his stories. He returned to work for CNN in Washington, D.C., on the show *Crossfire*. There he met Jamie Gangel, who became his wife. In his novels he has included scenes of conflict with Russian agents, or with Islamic terror.

The Bone Collector by Jeffery Deaver was adapted into a film. Deaver is a mystery genre novelist and short-story writer. Some of his stories have featured the quadriplegic investigator Lincoln Rhyme. Deaver attended Fordham Law School. He writes brisk, entertaining stories that often end with a twist. His novels include *The Coffin Dance* (1998), *The Empty Chair* (2000), *The Stone Monkey* (2002), *The Vanished Man* (2003), *The Twelfth Card* (2005), and *The Cold Moon* (2006), in which he introduced his character Katherine Dance. Six more novels have emerged, from *The Burning Wire* (2010) to *The Cutting Edge* (2018). Deaver edited *The Best Mystery Stories* of 2009. He was authorized by the Ian Fleming estate to write a James Bond sequel, *Carte Blanche* (2011). Deaver is a master of the clever trick ending, and his short stories are a great deal of fun.

Tuesdays with Morrie by Mitch Albom rose to the top of the bestseller list. Morrie Schwartz spoke about living with ALS, a debilitating neuromuscular disorder sometimes known as Lou Gehrig's disease. The October 1997 bestseller paid for Morrie's medical bills. The book spent 205 weeks on the bestseller list. Albom's *The Five People You Meet in Heaven* (2003) also rose up the bestseller list. Albom's *For One More Day* (2006) appeared a few years later. Mitch Albom, who was born in Passaic, New Jersey, was a sportswriter. He also worked in the music business. Albom wrote a column in Detroit on popular sports, and he was a radio sports commentator on WLLZ-Detroit. In the 1990s, he began developing inspirational stories.

1998

Cold Mountain persisted at #1 in January. The novel's pace is fairly slow moving, compared with many other contemporary popular novels. It takes some patience and deliberate focus to read Charles Frazier's novel about a Civil War veteran journeying home. *The Winner* by Dave Baldacci, at #2, moved more swiftly than that soldier. However, *Cold Mountain* remained high on the list for a longer period of time. In P. D. James's *A Certain Justice* the detective Adam Dalgliesh pursues the murderer of a lawyer that people hated. On February 1, Toni Morrison's *Paradise* was propelled to #1 by Oprah Winfrey's Book Club. Many people discovered a great writer. Immediately behind the Morrison novel on the bestseller list was *Cold Mountain*, followed by Dean Koontz's *Fear Nothing*. Koontz's character only comes out at night to see the mysteries that he can find solutions to. These books remained in the top three until February 22, when John Grisham's *The Street Lawyer* jumped to #1. While Grisham's character was learning his firm's dark secrets, psychic James Van Praagh was at #1 on the nonfiction list with *Talking to Heaven*. *The Millionaire Next Door* was #2, followed by a book by Maya Angelou at #3. *Tuesdays with Morrie* by Mitch Albom was #4.

On March 1, 1998, with John Grisham's *Street Lawyer* holding the top position, Toni Morrison's *Paradise* and Charles Frazier's *Cold Mountain* were #2 and #3, respectively. Anna Quindlen's *Black and Blue* climbed to #4. In her story, a woman flees from her husband's domestic abuse to Florida with her son. Further down the list was *Birthday Letters*, which gathered poet Ted Hughes's letters to Sylvia Plath. Anne Rice's *Pandora* rose to #3 on March 29. In nonfiction, *Spin Cycle* by Howard Kurtz, at #1, analyzed the Clinton White House's spin of news and scandals reported by the press.

The Street Lawyer held the top position into April, with Rice's *Pandora*, Toni Morrison's *Paradise*, and Charles Frazier's *Cold Mountain* right behind it. Nora Roberts's *Homeport* was #5 and *Memoirs of a Geisha* by Arthur Golden was #6. *The Long Road Home* by Danielle Steel entered the list and swiftly rose to #3 on April 19 and then to #1 by May 3. In her novel, a woman with a broken past tries to come to terms with it. *Message in a Bottle* by Nicholas Sparks appeared and rose up on the list to #5 on April 26. Steel's bestseller was immediately in competition with Mary Higgins Clark's *You Belong to Me* for the #1 position. Simon and Schuster had begun making a practice of publishing her suspenseful mystery novels early each May, often on Mother's Day. In *You Belong to Me*, a radio show host is in danger when she tries to seek a killer who pursues women on cruise ships. The novel became the #1 fiction book in America on May 17. Immediately behind it on the list at #2 was Sue Grafton's *N Is for Noose*. Those stories were #1 and #2 the next weekend, and then Grafton's novel became #1. John Irving's *A Widow for One Year* entered the list at #11 on May 24. Irving's novel shot up to #2 on June 7 and then to #1 on June 14. This story offered a perspective by a fictional narrator, a writer, toward his mother. Further down on the list at #15 was Cormac McCarthy's *Cities of the Plain*.

John Irving's novel at #1 on June 28 was followed by the strong sales of Judy Blume's *Summer Sisters* at #2. In Blume's book these "sisters" are two very different women who join in new experiences on Martha's Vineyard. *Bridget Jones's Diary* by Helen Fielding was #3. Dr. Seuss returned to the list at #4. The top position on the bestseller list turned over again with Wally Lamb's *I Know This Much Is True*. A man has to care for his twin brother and face family dysfunction. *The Klone and I* by Danielle Steel climbed to #2. In this story a woman meets the man of her dreams, a high-tech specialist. Then she meets the man's clone. *Unspeakable* by Sandra Brown at #3 tells the story of a killer who goes back to Texas to cause trouble. Jeffrey Archer's *The Eleventh Commandment* and *Low Country* by Anne Rivers Siddons were also listed high on the list. *Point of Origin* by Patricia Cornwell, new to the list, rose quickly to #1 on July 28. This book alternated at #1 with the book by Wally Lamb throughout August. On the last days of that month, Tom Clancy's *Rainbow Six* moved to #1. In this story John Clark investigates terrorists in Switzerland, Germany, and Spain. Lamb's book slipped to #2 and Tony Hillerman's *The First Eagle* was #3. *Rainbow Six* held strong to the #1 spot through September and to October 4. This would become a video game and a media enterprise. It was also *Publishers Weekly*'s #2 book for the year. Sidney Sheldon's *Tell Me Your Dreams* reached #2 on September 13 and 20.

Stephen King often returns each fall to entertain his wide and enthusiastic audience with something new. On October 11 and October 18, *Bag of Bones* went to #1. It was still there at #1 on November 1 when Anne Rice's *The Vampire Armand* brought another echo of horror to #2. *Bag of Bones* was #3 on *Publishers Weekly*'s annual list. Nicholas Evans's *The*

Loop and Sidney Sheldon's *Tell Me Your Dreams* remained in the top five, along with *The Reef* by Nora Roberts. On November 8, Robert Jordan's *The Path of Daggers* from his Wheel of Time series went to #1. The books by Anne Rice and Stephen King were followed at #4 by *All through the Night* by Mary Higgins Clark, who now was also writing Christmas stories. *All through the Night* features a missing chalice and a missing child and a mystery that has to be solved by Christmas Day.

The top places on the bestseller list shifted when Tom Wolfe's big novel *A Man in Full* appeared. It went to #1 on November 22 and was immediately trailed by a rapid-fire mystery by James Patterson, *When the Wind Blows*, at #2. Tom Wolfe's novel remained at #1 even as another novel by Danielle Steel, *Mirror Image*, rose to #2. The Patterson book was #3 and Stephen King's book was #4. *Bag of Bones* was #3 and *A Man in Full* was #4 on *Publishers Weekly*'s end-of-year list. It was a prolific year for Danielle Steel, who had *The Long Road Home* and *Klone and I* in #5 and #6, respectively, on the *Publishers Weekly* list. Wolfe's novel at #1 was followed by David Baldacci's *A Simple Truth* at #2 for one week. Then Stephen King returned to the #2 spot. At the end of the year, on December 27, the top-selling books were by name writers: Wolfe, King, Steel, and Clancy. Barbara Kingsolver's remarkable novel *The Poisonwood Bible* was #6, with the books by Patterson (#7) and Clark (#8) following.

Tuesdays with Morrie led the nonfiction list in the spring of 1998. It would return to that spot from August 30 into October. On June 21 *A Pirate Looks at Fifty*, by songwriter-performer Jimmy Buffett, reached #2. It was *Publishers Weekly*'s #7 book on its annual list. Malachy McCourt's *A Monk Swimming* went to #1 on July 12. These were the three top books into August. *The Day Diana Died* by Christopher Anderson reached #2 with the story of the last day of Princess Diana. The former secretary of education's look at the Clinton presidency went to #2 on September 27 and became #1 on October 4. Books by radio host Laura Schlessinger and political brawler Ann Coulter both reached the top five. Mark McGwire and Sammy Sosa broke home run records.

An October surprise was Danielle Steel's #1 nonfiction recollections about her son who suffered from bipolar disorder. A. Scott Lindbergh's *Lindbergh* was #5. At this time John Glenn made a different kind of flight, returning to space to test the responses of aging adults. On October 25 comedian Steve Martin brought out *Pure Drivel* (#5). The Chicago

Bulls won their sixth basketball championship in 1998. In November, basketball star Michael Jordan scored with *For the Love of the Game* (#2). James Carville's *And the Horse He Rode in On* addressed the investigation by Kenneth Starr of President Bill Clinton. On December 19 the House of Representatives voted 228–206 to impeach Bill Clinton for "perjurious, false, and misleading" comments about his extramarital affairs. The Senate would spare his presidency.

The nonfiction list in December was led by *The Century*, written by news anchor Peter Jennings and Todd Brewster. This retrospective of the twentieth century was rivaled later in the month by a notable book by another news anchor, Tom Brokaw of NBC. Brokaw interviewed people who came to adulthood in the period of the Second World War. Many had grown up in the 1930s, the years of the Great Depression, and many had served in the armed forces during the war. They were a self-sacrificing generation with a strong sense of patriotism, and Brokaw called them and his book *The Greatest Generation*. This was a book that paid tribute to their efforts and brought us their personal stories. *The Greatest Generation* remained #1 into the new year of 1999. It was the #2 *Publishers Weekly* nonfiction book of the year.

1999

The final year of the century began with *A Man in Full* by Tom Wolfe at #1 and Stephen King's *Bag of Bones* on the fiction bestseller list. In hardcover these were two bulky books that each promised readers a good story. At #3 was Tom Clancy's *Rainbow Six*, which was followed at #4 by Danielle Steel's *Mirror Image*. *Publishers Weekly* listed *Mirror Image* at #5 on its 1998 list. The sales of that novel persisted into 1999. January 17 brought *The Poisonwood Bible* by Barbara Kingsolver to #2 and the new entries of David Baldacci's *A Simple Faith* (#3) and James Patterson's *When the Wind Blows*. The next decade would be filled with bestselling novels by Patterson and Baldacci.

In mid-January Dean Koontz's mystery *Seize the Night* was getting a strong start on the list at #5. It rose to #2 on January 24, with Jonathan Kellerman's *Billy Straight* at #3. Patricia Cornwell's *Southern Cross* passed by Wolfe and Koontz and reached #1 on January 31. Koontz's novel remained at #2 as February began. Bill Clinton was acquitted of perjury by the U.S. Senate on February 12, Abraham Lincoln's birthday. That week *Danger's Path* by W. E. B. Griffin went to #2. Suddenly, John Grisham's *The Testament* appeared, and it jumped to #1 in its first week on the list. Cornwell's novel was followed by Julie Garwood's *Ransom*, a brisk historical novel about a devious baron set in thirteenth-century Scotland. It is set in the same period as the film *Braveheart*, which was popular in 1995. March 7, 1999, showed the Garwood novel at #3 behind those by Grisham and Cornwell. Sandra Brown's *Send No Flowers* was #4.

In March, Grisham's *The Testament* was joined on the list by Nora Roberts's *River's End* in which a Hollywood couple has to come to terms with their past. *The Testament* would be the #1 novel on *Publishers Weekly*'s bestseller list for 1999. Nora Roberts novels would increasingly enter the bestseller lists. In Maeve Binchy's *Tara Road* (#3), two women exchange a house and learn about each other. Poland, the Czech Republic, and Hungary all joined NATO that month. The Dow Jones Industrial Average soared to 10,000 on March 29. On April 4 came Anne Rice's *Vittorio*, a vampire story, at #2. Danielle Steel's *Bittersweet* rose to #2 on April 18 with a story about a woman's midlife crisis and career choices.

In contrast with Anne Rice's dark tales of vampires, *Apollyon* by Tim LaHaye and Jerry Jenkins began the apocalyptic evangelical Left Behind series about Christian believers and the end times. The villain was the antichrist, and the authors held forth the prospects of rapture for the saved. Detective writer Elmore Leonard simply said, *Be Cool*. His novel brought readers into the mob world of Chili Palmer and his efforts to create a film. Barbara Taylor Bradford, in *A Sudden Change of Heart*, involved her protagonist in seeking the assistance of a friend who is an art dealer. On April 20 the horrible Columbine school shooting occurred, an incident that echoes along with the more recent Parkland High School shooting. While some readers were contemplating the end times, along came the first appearance of J. K. Rowling's Harry Potter, which would shake up the world of publishing almost as much as a fearful apocalypse. *Harry Potter and the Sorcerer's Stone* began on the list at the ominous spot of #13. By May 5 it had risen to #3, and it went to #1 on June 20, 1999. Tornados had hit Oklahoma and neighboring states on May 3. Ralph Ellison's novel *Juneteenth* was published posthumously on May 29.

Simon and Schuster was busy producing and distributing Mary Higgins Clark's annual April/May bestseller. In *We'll Meet Again*, a woman tries to get away from being a suspect in her husband's murder. *A New Song* by Jan Karon tells the story of a clergyman and his wife who have to move to create new beginnings. In *The Girl Who Loved Tom Gordon* by Stephen King, a girl is relieved by a Red Sox pitcher who saves her life in the woods. *East of the Mountains* by David Guterson tells the bleak story of a man with cancer who returns home to the state of Washington to die. Memorial Day brought the rise of a new *Star Wars* book. *The Phantom Menace* by Terry Brooks was #1 on May 30. The book had been released in connection with the movie, a "prequel," on May 19, 1999. It follows the Jedi knights Qui-Gon Jinn and Obi-Wan Kenobi on a mission to protect Queen Amidala. They are joined by Anakin Skywalker. *White Oleander* by Janet Fitch at #2 told the story of Astrid Magnusson, a twelve-year-old girl who is placed in foster care because her mother, Ingrid, has killed her cheating boyfriend. The novel was an Oprah Book Club selection in May 1999. Mary Higgins Clark's *We'll Meet Again* was at #3 as June began and John Sandford's *Certain Prey* was #4. *Hannibal* by Thomas Harris was loose and haunting readers. The novel about the deranged Hannibal Lecter rose to #1 by August. It remained a top book on the *Publishers Weekly* bestseller list. *Publishers Weekly* listed Grisham's *The Testament*, *Hannibal* by Thomas Harris, and *Assassins* by Jenkins and LaHaye as the top three novels on its bestseller list for 1999. *Tuesdays with Morrie* and *The Greatest Generation* were #1 and #2, respectively, on *Publishers Weekly*'s annual bestseller list for nonfiction. It listed the *Guinness Book of World Records* at #3.

On July 16, John Kennedy Jr., his fiancée, and his sister-in-law were lost in the fog over Martha's Vineyard and crashed into the ocean. In August, Danielle Steel's *Granny Dan* rose to #2 behind *Hannibal*. The Harry Potter novels *Chamber of Secrets* and *Sorcerer's Stone* followed at #3 and #4, respectively. Some interesting books were a bit further down the list. Ernest Hemingway's *At First Light* was a revised and condensed version of previously unpublished earlier writings about a safari. Melinda Haynes's *Mother of Pearl* (#6 on the list) was about a twenty-eight-year-old black man and a fifteen-year-old girl who meet in Petal, Mississippi, in the 1950s. On August 22, Patricia Cornwell's new novel climbed the list to #1. Her story again featured her series character coroner Kay Scarpetta, who probed a ship's cargo where a secret was revealed. Tim La-

Haye and Jerry Jenkins's *Assassins* offered another installment of the Left Behind series, in which Christians face off against the antichrist. This reached #2 on August 29. *Harry Potter and the Sorcerer's Stone* rose to #1 in September. On September 19 *The Alibi* by Sandra Brown rose to #1 in fiction with a story set in Charleston, South Carolina, about an attorney. The lawyer faces criminal charges while seeking elected office. On September 26, the magic of Harry Potter continued. On that Sunday, Harry Potter held the top three spots on the *New York Times* bestseller list. It was an achievement like that of the Beatles in 1964. Even Stephen King, a perennial bestselling author, could not break through. *Hearts in Atlantis*, his book with five interrelated stories, was #4.

It was not until late October 1999 that Scott Turow's novel *Personal Injuries* rose to #1. In his story, a lawyer and an FBI agent have some tantalizing secrets. Turow's *Personal Injuries* remained in the top positions on all national lists. Sue Grafton's *O Is for Outlaw* and Nicholas Sparks's *A Walk to Remember* joined the Turow novel in the top six behind the two Harry Potter novels, which were at #3 and #4, respectively. Harry Potter was so popular that it held off all competition from the #1 position on the list. *Pop Goes the Weasel* by James Patterson followed the Harry Potter books in November. In November, Exxon and Mobil completed a merger. On November 28, *Irresistible Forces* by Danielle Steel reached #4. On December 3, Harry Potter was again secure in the top three spots on the list; *Timeline* by Michael Crichton would surely have otherwise been the #1 book in December. In Crichton's story, computer techies assist historians who take a trip back in time to fourteenth-century France. *Timeline* was listed just behind the Harry Potter on the *Times* list. It was followed by Steel's *Irresistible* and *Saving Faith* by David Baldacci. It was #5 fiction book of the year on *Publishers Weekly*'s bestseller list. On December 26, *Timeline* fell behind *Atlantis Found*, a Clive Cussler novel in which Dirk Pitt dives into a shipwreck under the sea. *Timeline*, with its advanced technology hearkening back to the Middle Ages, presented a curious topic for the end of the twentieth century.

8

THE 2000s

E-books and the New Millennium

2000

Future historians of the book may look back at the dawn of the twenty-first century and see a book called *Timeline* amid the top books on the bestseller list. They may look back upon J. K. Rowling's Harry Potter and wonder how a little guy wearing eyeglasses was able to enchant readers so much that three books featuring him were the top three bestsellers in January 2000. Others might marvel that a completely unknown author, J. K. Rowling, was able to publish the Harry Potter novels and surpass the sales of name authors like Danielle Steel, Stephen King, and John Grisham.

The Harry Potter phenomenon appeared across America, including on most regional newspapers bestseller lists. It caused the *New York Times* bestseller list to call for an adjustment. Adult books had been pushed lower on the list by the sales success of the Harry Potter novels. [1] *Publishers Weekly* does not list the Harry Potter books on its list of annual bestsellers. The *New York Times* determined that a distinction should be made between the adult bestseller and the children's bestseller. So, there was a restructuring of the *New York Times* list. The "young adult" novel would be separated out from the list so that popular works for adult readers would not be pushed back behind the likes of a Harry Potter. (That, of course, is not to say that adults didn't also enjoy the J. K.

Rowling books and the subsequent films.) The newly revamped list established new categories. A children's book list would appear separately. There would continue to be a fiction and a nonfiction list and now there would also be an "advice/how-to" books list. There would be another separate list in each area for paperbacks. Once the new structure was implemented, the *New York Times* listed Danielle Steel's *The House on Hope Street* as #1. There was hope in the house again for adult novels.

Publishers Weekly would record a #1 bestseller position for *The Brethren* by John Grisham for 2000. *The Bear and the Dragon* by Tom Clancy and *The Last Precinct* by Patricia Cornwell would also be in the top five fiction bestsellers. Two books by Jerry B. Jenkins and Tim La-Haye sold well and were also listed in *Publishers Weekly*'s top five on its annual list. In the top ten of *Publishers Weekly*'s annual list, Danielle Steel had three novels, James Patterson had two, and Mary Higgins Clark had two. The *Congressional Quarterly* declared that the publishing industry was "abuzz" about e-books.[2]

At $26.95 in hardcover, Dean Koontz's *False Memory* reached #1 on January 26. *Timeline*, at #5, was priced similarly. So was *Lion's Game* by Nelson DeMille, which appeared at #6 on January 23 and went to #3 on January 30. The list was still open to variety. Koontz's novel was a psychological mystery with curious characters. DeMille's fiction was that of an aggressive thriller. Robert Morgan's *Gap Creek* told the story of an Appalachian couple in the early nineteenth century.

John Grisham returned to the top of the bestseller list on February 20 and February 27 with *The Brethren*. However, throughout March the Harry Potter books were selling briskly and each of them was listed in contention with Grisham's bestseller. On March 26, Danielle Steel's *Carolina Moon* was #2 behind Grisham's #1 novel. These books held the top spots into April. Danielle Steel published yet another novel, *The Wedding*, which went to #1 on April 23 and April 30 despite Harry Potter. *Harry Potter and the Prisoner of Azkaban* was #3. Grisham's *The Brethren* was #4.

Mary Higgins Clark's *Before I Say Goodbye* was her May bestseller that year. When a woman's husband dies when a boat explodes in New York harbor, somebody has to investigate, of course. That mystery went right to the #1 spot, followed by Danielle Steel's *The Wedding*. Tawni O'Dell's *Back Roads*, as an Oprah book selection, pushed Harry Potter down the charts a little. On May 28 *Before I Say Goodbye* remained at #1.

John Sandford's *Easy Prey* had reached #2. Toni Morrison's literary novel *The Bluest Eye* reached #4. On June 4, John Sandford's novel reached #1. On June 11, Tim LaHaye and Jerry Jenkins were back at #1 with *The Indwelling*. *Cradle and All* by James Patterson was #2. These books held strong on the top of the list into early July. Jeffery Deaver's *The Empty Chair* was at #9, and *Star Wars Rogue Planet* was about to enter the top ten.

With *The House on Hope Street*, Danielle Steel again was #1 on July 16. This followed hard on the heels of *The Wedding*. *Hope Street* remained #1 on July 23 and July 30. Mario Puzo's *Omerta* was #2. In Puzo's novel a FBI agent pursues a Mafia don who does not want his three children to be involved with the Mafia. Steel's novel continued at #1 through August 13. At #2, E. Lynn Harris's *Not a Day Goes By* features a romance between a woman and an ex–football player. It was replaced by *Riptide* by Catherine Coulter at #2. In this novel in Coulter's FBI Thriller series, Becca Matlock encounters a stalker who shoots the governor of New York. She hides out in Riptide, Maine, but once she is there more of a mystery develops. Rosamunde Pilcher's *Winter Solstice* was #1 on August 20 and 27 and Tami Hoag's *Dust to Dust* was #2.

With October came Tom Clancy's *The Bear and the Dragon*: #1 on October 8. *Publishers Weekly* and the *New York Times* recorded strong sales for the Clancy novel. *The Rescue* by Nicholas Sparks reached #1 the next week, on October 15. Sidney Sheldon's *The Sky Is Falling* was #3 during those weeks. Ruth Christina Schwartz's surprise bestseller *Drowning* went to #1 on October 29 with a story set in 1919 Wisconsin. When the protagonist's sister dies, she has to run the farm and take care of her niece.

November 12, 2000, brought Patricia Cornwell's *The Last Precinct* to #1 and Anne Rice's *Merrick*, about a near-mortal vampire, to #2. On November 19, Danielle Steel's *Journey* was #2. *Deck the Halls*, a Christmas season offering from Mary Higgins Clark and her daughter Carol, was #3. On November 26, *Winter's Heart* by Robert Jordan was #1. The novels by Steel and Cornwell were #2 and #3, respectively. On December 3 and on December 10 *The Monk* by Tim LaHaye and Jerry Jenkins was #1. *Journey* by Danielle Steel was #2. The next week *Roses Are Red* by James Patterson was #2. On December 17 and 24 *The Monk* and *Roses Are Red* were followed by Ken Follett's *Code to Zero*. His story is set in

1958. Four students at Harvard are confronted with the Cold War and *Explorer I* takes on the space race challenge begun by Sputnik.

Hot Six by Janet Evanovich (2000) *was* hot. Her sixth novel in the Stephanie Plum bounty hunter series went to #1. Her series has frequently been on the bestseller list and has included several #1 bestselling novels. More recently, in 2017, *Turbo Twenty Three* was another bestselling Stephanie Plum novel. This time Stephanie Plum is investigating a crime at an ice cream factory. *Hardcore Twenty Four* was her second novel on the bestseller list in 2017. On December 3 it reached the #2 spot on the list. The novel slipped down to #12 by the end of the year. Bright primary colors sometimes burst from the book covers of Evanovich's popular novels. Evanovich began writing romance novels as Steffie Hall, while working for a lingerie business in Trenton, New Jersey. As she turned to suspense novels, Stephanie Plum became her series character, and her stories have repeatedly climbed to the top of the *New York Times* list ever since. Evanovich lives in South River, New Jersey, and sets most of her novels in or nearby Trenton. Her character Stephanie Plum reminds us that the strong female protagonist is now a familiar figure in much contemporary popular fiction.

The Amazing Adventures of Kavalier and Klay (2000) by Michael Chabon integrates diverse styles and genres and offers us endearing characters and a fascinating world. Chabon's connections between of comics and myths, immigrant family history and the shadows of the Holocaust, superheroes and American dreams make for lively reading. *Kavalier and Klay* won the Pulitzer Prize. Chabon's work began with the appearance of *Mysteries of Pittsburgh* (1989). *Wonder Boys* secured his reputation as remarkable storyteller. Chabon works in the genre of detective fiction with his Lost World stories. His novel *Telegraph Avenue* was followed by *Moonglow*, which appeared in 2017.

2001

Tom Clancy's *The Bear and the Dragon* was #1 as the year began. Dean Koontz's *From the Corner of His Eye* took over that spot on January 28. A man with an enemy named Bartholomew stalks "Barty" who has been blinded and who starts to see again. *A Day Late and a Dollar Short* by Terry McMillan went to #1 on February 4 and 11. Immediately behind these books on were *Roses Are Red* by James Patterson and *The Monk* by Tim LaHaye and Jerry B. Jenkins. On February 11, Michael Connelly's *A Darkness More Than Night* was #2. In the story detective Harry Bosch investigates a film actress and becomes a murder suspect in the case. Dean Koontz's novel was #3. At #4 was Brad Metzger's *The First Counsel*, in which a White House lawyer dates the president's daughter and is drawn into a murder scheme. On February 25, John Grisham's recently published *A Painted House* immediately went to #1. The book remained there throughout the month of March. *The Bonesetter's Daughter* by Amy Tan was #2 on March 4. Terry McMillan's novel was #3. Jack Higgins's *Edge of Danger*, one of his many thrillers, was #4. (Fortunately, Harry Patterson writes his dramatic potboilers as Jack Higgins. That helps us to not be confused between Higgins and bestselling authors James Patterson and Richard North Patterson.) James Patterson was at #1 on April 1 with *1st to Die*, a search for a killer who stalks newlyweds. In the story, an assistant district attorney, a medical examiner, and a journalist join forces as a detective team.

Deep in the Maine woods, four hunters meet a stranger and a very peculiar creature in Stephen King's *Dreamcatcher*, which went to #1 on April 8. Nora Roberts's *The Villa* pitted rivals: a woman and a winegrower she is attracted to. King's novel stayed at #1 through April 22. *A Common Life* by Jan Karon rose to #1 with the story of a former priest Tim Cavanaugh and his marriage to a woman named Cynthia. This was the sixth book of Karon's the Mitford Years saga. Danielle Steel's *Lone Eagle* meanwhile sailed to the #2 spot.

Mary Higgins Clark's wonderful novel *On the Street Where You Live* created suspense. The well-crafted mystery concludes with Detective Phil Reap gazing in a window and helping to prevent an unfolding crime. In the novel a defense lawyer explores murders that occurred ten years apart. Clark's novels were often appearing around Mother's Day. This one was deservedly #1 for the entire month of May. On June 3, John Sandford's *Chosen Prey* reached #1. Lucas Davenport chases an art history professor who kills women. Amid the suspense, Anne Tyler's *Back When We Were Grownups* caught reader interest and rose to #3 on the bestseller list. On June 24, Sue Grafton's *P Is for Peril* was #1. In her story detective Kinsey Millhone, her series character, seeks a missing geriatric specialist. Janet Evanovich's series character Stephanie Plum brought another strong female sleuth to #1 in *Seven Up*. Stephanie Plum is a bounty hunter who seeks a mobster in the wilds of New Jersey. Danielle Steel's *Leap of Faith* leaped to #1 the next week on July 15. In Steel's novel a woman ventures to a French chateau where she finds love and danger. Grafton's *P Is for Peril* was #2.

John Irving is one of those writers who writes across the lines between the popular and the literary. On July 22, Irving's *The Fourth Hand* brought readers a story with a somewhat odd premise. He begins with a reporter whose left hand has been eaten by a circus lion in India. By July 29, *The Fourth Hand* was #1 on the bestseller list. However, on August 5 James Patterson's *Suzanne's Diary for Nicholas* became #1. In *Cane River* by Lalita Tademy, at #2, four generations of African American women hold the interest of the novel's readers. The novel remained high on the list through August. In Catherine Coulter's *Hemlock Bay*, an FBI agent investigates the disappearance of a teenage boy. The novel was #2 at the end of August.

On the fateful day of September 11, 2001, Clive Cussler's *Valhalla Rising* was atop the fiction bestseller list. His character Dirk Pitt was exploring the sinking of a luxury liner. The collaboration of Stephen King and Peter Straub brought forth *Black House*, which went to #1. A retired homicide detective in Wisconsin helps the police in solving a murder and finds himself in a parallel universe. Sandra Brown's novel *Envy* was #3 and Julie Garwood's novel *Mercy* was #4. On October 7, *Black House* by Stephen King and Peter Straub reached #1. *A Bend in the Road* by Nicholas Sparks was #2. The United States was experiencing the disturbing bend in the road caused by the 9/11 tragedy. The country witnessed the rise of an extraordinary unity and resolve among its citizens.

Two days before the cataclysmic events of September 11, 2001, the *New York Times Book Review* printed an article by contributing culture critic Judith Shulevitz on literary fiction and the American novel. On September 9, David Gates reviewed Jonathan Franzen's *The Corrections* in "Jonathan Franzen's American Gothic." Richard Eder reviewed Salman Rushdie's *Fury*. The Franzen novel was a tour de force that centered on a dysfunctional family. Rushdie's novel focused on New York City as a center of globalization: a process he depicted as having many flaws and limitations. Malik Solanka of Bombay (Mumbai), the creator of "Little Brain," a miniaturized puppet, attempts to renew his life by traveling to live in New York. Despite such creative works, Shulevitz sounded the lament of the decline of the novel and noted its ups and downs. She noted

that August was a month in which "few serious books were published."
Shulevitz was, in part, responding to an article in the *Atlantic* by B. R.
Myers, "A Reader's Manifesto: An Attack on the Growing Pretentiousness of American Literary Prose." Myers had written that Paul Auster,
Don DeLillo, Cormac McCarthy, and Annie Proulx create "artsy prose"
that is "too self-consciously literary." Some readers may wonder why the
view of Myers, whose expertise is in the area of North Korea studies,
would matter so much. Perhaps it was because the article appeared in the
Atlantic.

Myers critiqued Proulx as prolix and called the novels of David Guterson works of "sonorous tautologies." Even if some readers might agree
with that assessment, it is clear that he is way off the mark with Don
DeLillo and with Cormac McCarthy, who are writers who care about
sentences and ideas, as well as about fictional characters. With DeLillo's
White Noise, Myers appears to have missed the irony. The novel is en-
riched by satire about consumerism and about Hitler studies. DeLillo's
fictional craft is evident. Shulevitz concluded that Myers was missing the
point. In her essay, she referred to Dwight Macdonald's review of James
Gould Cozzens's *By Love Possessed*. Macdonald applauded Cozzens but
criticized his pretentiousness. Shulevitz also recalls Macdonald's essay
"Masscult and Midcult." She concludes: "We can roll our eyes at our
writers, we can laugh at their moments of baroqueness and vulgarity, but
we also get to love them."[3] We do get to love our writers: our literary
ones, as well as our creators of popular page-turner suspense.

Amid this newly aroused patriotism, Jonathan Franzen's *The Corrections* was a curiosity. Franzen's novel was a highly touted work of fiction,
the story of a dysfunctional family's homecoming at Christmas. The novel reached #1 on October 14, where it led *Black House* and a selection of
poems by Jackie Kennedy. On October 28, Patricia Cornwell's *Isle of
Dogs* went to #1. It was a rather different book for her, a story in which
the governor of Virginia puts speed traps on the streets and an island in
the Chesapeake Bay declares war.

The events of 9/11 had a ripple effect across America, including
among book readers. Even amid cultural disruption, Danielle Steel novels
were resilient. On November 11 Danielle Steel's *The Kiss* was #1. It is
the story of the wife of a Parisian banker who has an affair with a powerful man in Washington who is also married. Nora Roberts's *Midnight
Bayou* was #1 on November #4. In her story a Boston lawyer leaves his

law practice and moves outside of New Orleans into a house of secrets. Tim LaHaye and Jerry B. Jenkins were back to dispel secrets with *Desecration*, the newest installment of their Left Behind series. Make no mistake about it: there are thousands of Christian readers across the United States. Each of the LaHaye-Jenkins books rose to a position high on the bestseller list—often to #1. In Robert Ludlum's *The Sigma Protocol*, an investment banker and a Justice Department agent are caught in a political swirl. Ludlum had left his work to trusted associates, like suspense thriller writer Eric Van Lustbader. Those writers kept his characters and style of story alive after Ludlum himself was gone.

John Grisham was well prepared for December. *Skipping Christmas* was his next novel, and it was #2 on the bestseller list by November 25. It soon became #1. *Publishers Weekly* listed it as #2 for the year, with Grisham's *A Painted House* at #3. *The Fiery Cross* from Diana Gabaldon's Outlander series, at #3 in November, brought a time traveler to eighteenth-century Scotland. David Baldacci's *The Last Man Standing* presented an FBI rescue team. James Patterson's *Violets Are Blue* rose to #2. From December 9 through December 30, Grisham's *Skipping Christmas* was #1 and Patterson's *Violets Are Blue* was #2.

On the nonfiction annual list for *Publishers Weekly*, Bruce Wilkinson and Darlene Wilkinson had books in the top five. American history and principles were revisited in historian David McCullough's biography *John Adams*. McCullough's work on the life of the second president brought his second Pulitzer Prize for Biography.

Jonathan Franzen's *The Corrections* (2001) is a story about a dysfunctional family. It was a Pulitzer Prize finalist and a National Book Award winner. *Freedom* (2010) also earned literary awards. Franzen's novels are built carefully and emerge from a literary sensibility. His essay "Perchance to Dream" (1996) in *Harper's* sounded a lament for contemporary fiction. When *The Corrections* was featured by Oprah Winfrey, Franzen rejected the attention that the show brought to his novel. Regarding the selection of *The Corrections* as one of Oprah's picks, Franzen said that much reading is sustained by women who read while men are out golfing or watching football on television. With *The Twenty-Seventh City* (1988), a story set in St. Louis, it was clear that Franzen was intently focused upon postmodern fiction. *Strong Motion* (1992) concerns the dysfunctional Holland family.

2002

On January 20, 2002, Dean Koontz's *One Door Away from Heaven* was listed as #1. In that story, a woman tries to protect a boy whose stepfather thinks that UFOs are coming. Grisham's *Skipping Christmas* and Franzen's *The Corrections* were at #2 and #3, respectively. Mattie Stepanek's poems drew reader sympathy. Also high on the list, as part of Stephen King's Rose Red series, *The Diary of Ellen Rimbauer* was the fictional journal of a Seattle housewife. W. E. B. Griffin's *Under Fire* told the story of Marines in the Korean War. *Up Country* by Nelson DeMille arrived with the adventures of his character Paul Brenner. It was at #2 for a week in mid-February. John Grisham published another novel, *The Summons*, in which a law professor discovers three million dollars in a dying judge's study. On February 24 the book reached #1.

Winter passed with the legal drama of Grisham and the imaginative twists of Koontz and King. *The Summons* and *Up Country* held the top two spots on the bestseller list into March. *The Summons* by Grisham was the #1 bestseller on *Publishers Weekly*'s list for the year. Danielle Steel's *The Cottage* was #2 on March 17. Then James Patterson's collaboration with Andrew Gross, *2nd Chance*, reached #1 with a tale of the Women's Murder Club. Someone at Little, Brown Publishing had tipped off Patterson that Andrew Gross wrote female characters well. Patterson would subsequently team up with Michael Ledwidge, Maxine Paetro, and other writers to produce an amazing string of cowritten bestsellers that traded upon his talent and his famous, marketable name.

In April, Stephen King returned to #1 with *Everything's Eventual*, a collection of fourteen stories. That book was #9 on the *Publishers Weekly* 2002 annual list. King's *From a Buick 8* was listed at #11. Nora Roberts's *Three Fates* took the #1 spot on the *Times* list April 21. A survivor of the *Lusitania* was a thief and his grandson tries to find a statue that his ancestor stole. *The Nanny Diaries* by Emma McLaughlin and Nicola Kraus followed at #1 on April 28. Mary Higgins Clark replaced that book at #1 with her novel *Daddy's Little Girl*. Clark's novel remained at #1 on May 12, when it was faced with competition from a new *Star Wars* novel, *Attack of the Clones*. While *Star Wars* projected forward into the future, Jean M. Auel's *Shelters of Stone*, #1 on May 19, looked back to the Ice Age. Her novel was listed at #1 ahead of John Sandford's *Mortal Prey* through the rest of May. *Shelters of Stone* was #7 on the *Publishers Weekly* 2002 bestseller list.

The fiction of 2002 comprised a variety of romance, mystery, adventure, and detective stories. Summer 2002 brought readers the cowritten novel. This second week in June marked the rise of cowritten fiction by bestselling authors James Patterson and Clive Cussler, increasing their already considerable productivity. Jan Karon's *In This Mountain*'s place at #1 on June 16 was overtaken by *The Beach House* by James Patterson with Peter de Jonge. That book was #12 on the year-end list of *Publishers Weekly*. Patterson's *Four Blind Mice* was #8. *Fire Ice* by Clive Cussler with Paul Kemprecos became the #2 bestseller. In July, Janet Evanovich's *Hard Eight*, with her series character bounty hunter Stephanie Plum, took the #1 spot. Stephanie Plum is seeking the whereabouts of an abducted seven-year-old girl in New Jersey. On July 21 *The Remnant* by Tim LaHaye and Jerry B. Jenkins rose to the #1 position. Along with the summer mystery of *Beach House* emerged Danielle Steel's *Sunset in San Tropez*. Further down on the list was attorney Stephen L. Carter's *The Emperor of Ocean Park*. Carter was already well established as a thoughtful commentator on social issues in his nonfiction books. James Lee Burke's *Jolie Blow's Bounce* brought his lyrical writing and his detective Dave Robicheaux character back into the top ten on the list. Alice Sebold's *The Lovely Bones*, began its rise to #1 on August 18. The novel was well regarded critically along with its sustained presence on the bestseller list.

In *Red Rabbit* by Tom Clancy, his series character Jack Ryan attempts to prevent a plot against Pope John Paul II. On August 25 it was #1 in its first week on the list. *The Lovely Bones* and *Red Rabbit* exchanged places at #1 during the next few weeks. On September 29, *Dark Horse* by Tami Hoag was #1. On October 6 Nicholas Sparks's *Nights in Rodanthe* was #1. It is a typical Sparks romance, a story in which a woman's husband has an affair. She endures and finds romance. The Sparks novel was followed by *The Lovely Bones* (#2), Anna Quindlen's *Blessings* (#3), Clancy's *Red Rabbit* (#4), and Julie Garwood's mystery *Killjoy* (#5). *Mission Compromised* by Oliver North with Joe Musser, at #4, on September 29 had slipped further down the list. Stephen King's *From a Buick 6* became #1 on October 12. In King's new story an old Buick provides access to another dimension. *The Lovely Bones, From a Buick 6, Nights in Rodanthe, Red Rabbit*, and Jonathan Kellerman's *The Murder Book* held the top five spots on October 20. *Red Rabbit* was #2 on *Publishers Weekly*'s end-of-year list. *The Lovely Bones* was #4, following the Jenkins and LaHaye book *Remnant*. Sue Grafton's *Q Is for Quarry* was #1 on November 3 and 10. Kinsey Millhone joins two homicide detectives to investigate a cold case dating back to 1969. *Answered Prayers* by Danielle Steel surpassed it on the list and became #1 on November 17. Anne Rice's *Blackwood Fair* brought back vampires. On November 24, Nora Roberts's *Chesapeake Blue* was #1, Steel's *Answered Prayers* was #2, and *Visions of Sugar Plums* by Janet Evanovich was #3. *Skipping Christmas* by John Grisham returned to the list at #5. Scott Turow's *Reversible Errors*, in which a lawyer represents a man on death row, reached #6. The top five books at this point were written by women. Seven of the top ten books were by female writers and nine of the top twelve.

John Grisham's *Skipping Christmas* started off the year and also ended the year as one of the top three books on the bestseller list. December began with James Patterson's *Four Blind Mice* at #1 on December 8 in its first week on the list, followed by the Grisham novel. When Michael Crichton's *Prey* was released, it immediately jumped to #1 on December 15. In a Nevada desert, a science team confronts the failures and problems of an experiment gone awry. There are molecularized robots and nanoparticles this time rather than dinosaurs. Crichton began his career as a popular novelist with stories like *The Andromeda Strain* and *Sphere*, in which scientific teams face dilemmas. *Prey* builds the suspense and drama as Crichton probes human interaction with modern technology. *Prey* remained at #1 through the rest of the year and into January 2003. It appeared at #5 on the *Publishers Weekly* annual list.

Chesapeake Blue by Nora Roberts went to #1 in 2002, and *Birthright* peaked at #1 in 2003. Earlier books, *Carolina Moon* (2000) and *Midnight Bayou* (2001), were both bestsellers. Nora Roberts has written more than two hundred romance novels. She has also become the bestselling mystery writer J. D. Robb. Her fiction as J. D. Robb made the bestseller list in 2003. She was born Eleanor Marie Robertson from parents of an Irish background. From around 1979, when she set pen to page as a snow blizzard fell around the family-owned Boone Hotel in Maryland, she has been writing romance fiction diligently. She met her second husband, Bruce Wilder, a carpenter, when he was called upon to build bookcases for her. At the rate at which she produces fiction, she may need another set of bookcases every few years just to hold her own novels. Between

1982 and 1984 she produced twenty-three novels for Silhouette and more by 1987 for Bantam, under different pseudonyms. Literary agent Amy Berkower encouraged Nora Roberts to take on the pseudonym J. D. Robb as a suspense genre novelist. Her science fiction–oriented novels often feature detective Eve Dallas and her husband Roarke.

2003

During the first two weeks of 2003 the high-tech drama *Prey* remained #1. *The Lovely Bones* returned to #1 on January 19 and again on February 9. Dean Koontz's character in *By the Light of the Moon* (#2 in mid-January) anticipates crimes and gets to crime scenes before the crime is committed. *Crossroads of Twilight*, #1 on January 26, extended Robert Jordan's Wheel of Time series. John Grisham returned to #1 with *The King of Torts* on February 23. *The Lovely Bones* was #2. The science fiction novel *Pattern Recognition* by William Gibson rose to #3. In March, James Patterson and Andrew Gross hit the #1 position with *Jester*. *King of Torts* by John Grisham was #2. Danielle Steel's *Dating Game* was among the top three books. Also in 2003, a high-tech military campaign was about to begin in Iraq. American military forces were called to assemble for action. On March 20, the invasion of Iraq began.

The Da Vinci Code by Dan Brown reached #1 on April 6. It would repeat its standing in the #1 spot several times and would remain on the bestseller list throughout the year. By April 20 Nora Roberts's *Birthright* had swept to #1 with the story of an archaeologist who digs down to face her own troubled past. Laurell K. Hamilton's *Cerulean Sins*, at #2, brought readers a vampire hunter. In *Last Light*, Michael Connelly tells the story of Los Angeles–area detective Harry Bosch's search for the strangler of a young woman. *The Guardian* by Nicholas Sparks tells the tale of a young window with two men in her life.

May began with Mary Higgins Clark's *The Second Time Around* at #2 behind Tim LaHaye and Jerry Jenkins's *Armageddon*. It was more than the second time around for Clark on the bestseller list. She seemed to have a book every May destined for #1. In this new story the head of a medical research company is missing and a magazine columnist finds herself at the center of a scheming group. Sales of *The Da Vinci Code* also remained strong and kept Dan Brown's book in the top five.

The Da Vinci Code was #1 on June 8 and held that position through June 20. While Dan Brown's character Robert Langdon was seeking symbols and following clues, people were seeing the signs of a world that was changing. Increasing global interconnectedness was a feature of this world. Popular culture, business ties, and communications were increasingly global. The fiction bestseller list in America continued to indicate that books by name authors were the products that sold most. On June 29, The Lake House by James Patterson reached #1. The Da Vinci Code was #2. The Face by Dean Koontz at #4 was new to the list. In Johnny Angel, rising to #1 on July 20 and 27, Danielle Steel's character sees visions of her son who died in a car accident. Steel had experienced her own loss of her son previously. Clive Cussler and Paul Kemprecos teamed up for the novel White Death, which was at #3 behind The Da Vinci Code. The Devil Wears Prada by Lauren Weisberger, perhaps better known as a film with Meryl Streep, was #4. On August 3, To the Nines by Janet Evanovich went to #1.

The Da Vinci Code was the unmistakable bestseller of that year. Again, it returned to #1 on August 17. Publishers Weekly and the New York Times both listed Brown's book as the top fiction bestseller of the year. Brown's Angels and Demons was #5 on the year-end Publishers Weekly list. At #2 on the list was Catherine Coulter's Blindside; Janet Evanovich's To the Nines was at #3. The #4 book on the list was Naked Empire, a sword and sorcery fantasy by Terry Goodkind. Sweet Dreams by Faye Kellerman was #4 on August 24. Tom Clancy's The Teeth of the Tiger, which joins his series character Jack Ryan, now president, with his son, a counterintelligence agent, went to #1 the next week. Clancy's novel and Brown's The Da Vinci Code exchanged places in the top two spots on the list in September.

Our culture is "being dumbed down," cried literary critic Harold Bloom in an op-ed that appeared in the Boston Globe on September 24, 2003. Stephen King had been given the National Book Foundation's award for "distinguished contribution," and Bloom was appalled. This was "extraordinary, another low in the shocking process of dumbing down our cultural life," Bloom wrote. He called Stephen King "an immensely inadequate writer" and compared his popularity with that of J. K. Rowling, whose "prosy style, heavy on cliché, makes no demand on her readers." Indeed, he cringed at Rowling's clichés. To call Stephen King "a writer of penny dreadful" was "too kind." This award was merely a recognition of the commercial value of King's book, Bloom insisted. Bloom is also on record as saying that he cannot stomach reading the stories of John Grisham. [4]

However, readers of mass-market paperbacks tend to seek diversion and entertainment, not literary craft and psychological depth. America likes baseball and hot dogs and popcorn, and John Grisham's *Bleachers* was #1 on September 28. On October 5, *Bleachers* and *The Da Vinci Code* were the #1 and #2 books on the list, respectively. Harold Bloom's *How to Read and Why* could emphasize the merits of irony and narrative style in fiction, but the public simply enjoyed a good story. They were busy enjoying Nicholas Sparks's *The Wedding*, which was #3 on the bestseller list. Nora Roberts, writing as J. D. Robb, had brought together a romance with a police procedural in *Remember When*, which was listed at #4.

The Five People You Meet in Heaven was Mitch Albom's title for a story that caught readers' attention and went to #1 on October 12. David Baldacci's *Split Second* was #2 behind it on October 19 and #3 behind *The Da Vinci Code* on October 28. Patricia Cornwell's *Blow Fix* broke through to #1 with a story in which her series character Kay Scarpetta faces the Wolfman, a killer she previously helped to capture and get incarcerated. *The Da Vinci Code* returned to #1 through the rest of the month of November. Stephen King's *The Dark Tower* (Books 1–5) was at #2. The novels by Brown and King remained in the top positions on the list through December. They were joined by *Big Bad Wolf* by James Patterson, which passed by the Wolfman of Cornwell's book to #3. Clive Cussler's *Trojan Odyssey*, meanwhile, has his series character Dirk Pitt diving and exploring the Nicaragua coast with his two sons.

2004

The Da Vinci Code remained the bestselling book in America throughout January 2004. It was again the #1 novel on the *Publishers Weekly* list by the end of the year. In March, Brown's *Angels and Demons* joined *The Da Vinci Code* the bestseller list at #4. *The 3rd Degree* by James Patterson was the #1 bestseller on March 21. Danielle Steel's *Ransom* had entered the top five on the list. In April, the Left Behind series by Tim LaHaye and Jerry B. Jenkins continued with another big bestseller. *Glori-*

ous Appearing, in its first week on the list, overtook *The Da Vinci Code*. It would be #4 on *Publishers Weekly*'s annual list. Mary Higgins Clark's *Nighttime Is My Time* was #3 on April 25 and throughout the month of May.

The Rule of Four by Ian Caldwell and Dustin Thomason is something like *The Da Vinci Code*, in the sense that young scholars are seeking through a mystery. *The Rule of Four* also has about it the youthfulness and sophomoric elite college antics that are reminiscent of Scott Fitzgerald's *This Side of Paradise*. The story about the search for a Renaissance text went to #2 on June 13 and June 20. It was #9 on the *Publishers Weekly* end-of-year list. Stephen King's *Song of Susannah* went to #1 on June 27. Next at 31 was Janet Evanovich *Ten Big Ones*, in which her series character Stephanie Plum is challenged by a Trenton man. James Patterson was ready with a summer book, *Sam's Letters to Jennifer*. So was Danielle Steel, with *Second Chance*. *The Da Vinci Code* continued its reign at #1. On August 1 Sue Grafton's *R Is for Ricochet* was #1. *The Da Vinci Code* was #2. *Skinny Dip* by Carl Hiaasen rose to #3.

What fascinated people about *The Da Vinci Code*? Was it the mystery of symbols and codes? Were readers drawn to the dramatic figure of Robert Langdon, long before Tom Hanks took on the role? Was it the intrigue of mysterious secret societies or the theological arguments about Jesus and Mary Magdalene and the female role in Christianity? Or was it Da Vinci himself and the curiosities of the Italian Renaissance? *The Da Vinci Code* repeatedly returned to number #1. On September 5 it was followed by *White Hot* by Sandra Brown. On September 19, Julie Garwood's *Murder List* was #2. In Patricia Cornwell's *Trace*, her character Kay Scarpetta seeks to explain the death of a fourteen-year-old girl. Cornwell's novel was #1 October 3. On October 10 Stephen King's *The Dark Tower* took the #1 spot. *Trace* was #2 and *The Da Vinci Code* was #3. *Nights of Rain and Stars* by Maeve Binchy appeared at #4. *The Dark Tower* remained at $1 on October 17, followed by *Incubus Dreams*, a vampire hunter story from Laurell K. Hamilton.

On October 24, Philip Roth's *The Plot against America* reached #2. The narrator begins the story by recalling his youth and the emergence of an anti-Semitic presidential contender—Charles Lindbergh, the aviator. Stephen King's *The Dark Tower* remained #1 that week and was replaced at #1 by Nora Roberts's *Lunacy*, the story of an Alaskan chief of police discovering romance. Roth's entertaining novel slipped to #4. It rose to

#3 by the next weekend behind *Lunacy* and *The Da Vinci Code. Hour Game* by David Baldacci was #1 on November 21 and Janet Evanovich's fiction was #1 on November 21. *London Bridges* by James Patterson reached 31 on November 28. It was #7 on *Publishers Weekly* end of the year list. *The Da Vinci Code* was #2. In the #3 spot was Tom Wolfe's *I Am Charlotte Simmons*.

In December *The Da Vinci Code* was at #1 during the first week. Nelson DeMille's *Night Fall* became the #1 book on December 12. *Publishers Weekly* placed it at #12 on its list for the year. Mitch Albom was back with *The Five People You Meet in Heaven* on December 19. Following *The Da Vinci Code*, which was #2, was the songwriter-performer Jimmy Buffett's fiction: *A Salty Piece of Land*, at #3. Buffett portrays a 101-year-old woman who is a lighthouse keeper in the Bahamas. Michael Crichton's *State of Fear* jumped onto the list and was #2 in the last days of the year. In his story, people create evidence to attempt to prove that global warming is a reality. The novel was listed by *Publishers Weekly* at #6 on its list for 2004. Mitch Albom's *The Five People You Meet in Heaven* was #2. At #3 was John Grisham's *The Last Juror*. Brown's *Da Vinci Code*, Albom's *The Five People*, and Grisham's *The Last Juror* were the top three books on *Publishers Weekly*'s end-of-year list.

In nonfiction, Bill Clinton's autobiography, *My Life*, was #3 on *Publishers Weekly*'s bestseller. *The Purpose Driven Life* by Rick Warren stood at #1 at the end of the year, followed by Arthur Agatston's *South Beach Diet* (#2) and *South Beach Diet Cookbook* (#5). Jon Stewart and *The Daily Show* writers (*America*, #4) and Dr. Phil McGraw (*Family First*, #5) demonstrated that television sells books.

2005

Mitch Albom's *The Five People You Meet in Heaven* had been sixty-five weeks on the bestseller list when it again rose to #1 on January 2, 2005. *The Da Vinci Code* and *State of Fear* followed on the list. They became the top two books the next week. Then John Grisham's *The Broker* went to #1 on January 30. (*Publishers Weekly*, tallying up the year's bestsellers, listed Grisham's novel at #1 in sales for 2005.) The same books remained at the top of the list into February, with *Survivor in Death* by J. D. Robb (Nora Roberts) at #4. *Honeymoon* by James Patterson and Howard Roughan was the #1 book as March began. *The Rising* by Tim LaHaye and Jerry B. Jenkins was in the top three during the last two weeks of the month along with Danielle Steel's *Impossible*. *The Rising* rose to #1 in the first week of April. On April 17, *Da Vinci Code*'s #1 spot was challenged by the book for the *Star Wars* movie *Revenge of the Sith*. Mary Higgins Clark, whose books had faced *Star Wars* before, arrived at #1 with *No Place Like Home* on April 24. Clark's protagonist is attempting to hide her past and she is pursued by a killer. *The Mermaid* by Sue Monk Kidd, set in Charleston, South Carolina, was #2. She uses her name well. In that story, a woman has a relationship with a monk who is about to take his vows.

In *True Believer* by Nicholas Sparks, #1 on May 1, a man from New York writes for *Scientific American*. He finds romance with a librarian in a North Carolina town. *Publishers Weekly* placed the novel at #6 on its end-of-the-year bestseller list. In *4th of July* by James Patterson and Maxine Paetro, their character Detective Lindsay Boxer turns for help to the Women's Murder Club. This would become a very popular series from these authors. The detective is on trial but wants to investigate. (James Patterson, with various collaborators, had four novels in the top ten on *Publishers Weekly*'s 2005 bestseller list.) In *The Closers* by Michael Connelly, his character, L.A. detective Harry Bosch (Hieronymus Bosch, like the painter), pursues an unsolved case involving the death of a sixteen-year-old in 1988. These books continued to alternate in the top spots on the list through June.

On July 3 *The Historian* by Elizabeth Kostova became the #1 book in America, according to the *New York Times* bestseller list. The novel was listed by *Publishers Weekly* at #8 on its 2005 list. Janet Evanovich's *Eleven on Top* gained the #1 position the next week, and *The Historian* was at #2. *Until I Find You* by John Irving was #3. On August 7, *Lifeguard*, James Patterson's summer mystery, was #1. *The Interruption of Everything* by Terry McMillen held the #2 position, followed by *The Historian* and *Until I Find You*. However, by the last week of the month *The Da Vinci Code* was back at #1.

In September, readers could allow themselves to feel the drama and angst of Sandra Brown's *Chill Factor*, which went to #1 on September 5. The story features a magazine editor who is trapped in a cabin by a serial killer. In *Point Blank* by Catherine Coulter, #1 on September 11, Dillon Savich and Lucy Sherlock are married and investigating another couple.

The list went into *Polar Shift* by Clive Cussler and Paul Kemprecos, in which Kurt Austin is facing a group that is bent upon using a new technology blowing up the world. *The Historian* was #2 and Julie Garwood's *Slow Burn* was #3.

The Da Vinci Code and *The Historian* held the top two positions on the list on October 2. The Outlander series of Diana Gabaldon brought *A Breath of Snow and Ashes* to the top of the list on October 16. Gabaldon's novel features a time-traveling woman. In 1772, the British governor of North Carolina asks her character Jamie to support the king. In L. Frank Baum's *The Wizard of Oz*, Dorothy traveled to Oz and then returned to Kansas. The fiction complement to the play *Wicked* by Gregory Maguire, *Son of a Witch*, based upon Baum's story, traveled to #2 on October 16. Michael Connelly's defense attorney Mickey Haller in *The Lincoln Lawyer* was involved in a complicated case and reaching #1 while Nora Roberts's *Blue Smoke* was rising to #2. *Knife of Dreams* by Robert Jordan was #1 on October 30, as his eleventh book in his Wheel of Time series. Vince Flynn appeared on the bestseller list at #4 with a spy terrorism novel, *Consent to Kill*. *At First Sight* by Nicholas Sparks, his sequel to *True Believer*, went to #1. Readers no doubt wanted to see how the story was continued. *Predator* by Patricia Cornwell was #1 on November 13. Her coroner-detective Kay Scarpetta turns to a psychopath in prison as she investigates a case. (This aspect of the story is a bit like Thomas Harris's story of Clarice and Hannibal Lecter in *Silence of the Lambs*.) *Predator* was #5 on *Publishers Weekly*'s 2005 end-of-year bestseller list.

Then came *A Feast of Crows* by George R. R. Martin, the writer who imagined a world far from Bayonne, New Jersey: the remarkable fictional world of the popular HBO television series *The Game of Thrones*. Outlaws are seeking to gain the Seven Kingdoms. The goal of the Hollywood killer of *Mary Mary*, James Patterson's novel at #1 the next week, was not as titanic. However, Alex Cross's adventure in catching the killer was also dramatic. *Mary Mary* was #1 on the bestseller list until another sleuth foiled a sinister crime in Sue Grafton's #1 *S Is for Silence*.

2006

The year began with *Mary Mary*, *S Is for Silence*, and *The Da Vinci Code* each appearing in turn at the #1 spot. *Mary Mary* was #1 on January 1 and

8. *S Is for Silence* was #1 on January 15, and *The Hostage* by W. E. B. Griffin was #1 on January 22. *The Da Vinci Code*, #1 on January 29, had been on the bestseller list for 147 weeks. Stephen King's *The Cell* was #1 on February 12. In the *5th Horseman* by James Patterson and Maxine Paetro, the Woman's Murder Club is engaged in solving a dilemma in San Francisco. (Four Patterson books were on *Publishers Weekly*'s 2006 bestseller list.) *The Cell* was #2. (King's *Lisey's Story* and *The Cell* were #6 and #8, respectively, on the *Publishers Weekly* 2006 list.) Danielle's Steel *The House* went to #1 on March 19. *The 5th Horseman* was followed by Jodi Picoult's *The Tenth Circle*. *The Da Vinci Code* generated imitations, including Raymond Khoury's *The Last Templar*. On April 16, Jonathan Kellerman's *Gone* reached #1, with the investigation of his series character Alex Delaware.

In Mary Higgins Clark's *Two Little Girls in Blue*, a girl communicates telepathically with her twin who has been kidnapped. This became the #1 novel on April 23 and remained #1 through May 14. In Stuart Woods's #2 novel, his character Stone Barrington, a New York policeman turned lawyer, has now turned detective. He investigates the death of his cousin, who was with the CIA. James Patterson was back at #1 on June 4. *Dead Watch* by John Sandford was #2. *The Hard Way* by Lee Child was a Jack Reacher novel that went to #1 on June 11. Kidnapping remained a popular plot device; on June 18, *The Husband* by Dean Koontz was #1. In his story the wife of a kidnapped man seeks to gather the ransom. At the center of *The Book of the Dead* by Douglas Preston and Lincoln Child, at #4, was their quirky and unlikely detective Aloysius Pendergast. This was the final volume of a popular trilogy of novels in which we learn that Pendergast's brother is a criminal who has to be stopped. On June 25 and July 1, Judith Krantz's novel hit #1. *The Rapture* by LaHaye and Jenkins was #2. In Janet Evanovich's *Twelve Sharp* Stephanie Plum has to rescue a kidnapped child. At #2 Laurell K. Hamilton's Anita Blake returns and this time the vampire hunter is pregnant. *Coming Out* by Danielle Steel was #3 on July 16 and rose to #2 on July 23, behind the Janet Evanovich book. In *Angel's Fall* by Nora Roberts, #1 on July 30, a female chef from Boston is in Wyoming and locals there do not believe that she has witnessed a murder. On August 6 at #1 Terry Goodkind's *Phantom* was his latest installment in his Sword of Truth fantasy series. *The Message* by Daniel Silva was #3. *Pegasus Descending* by James Lee Burke was #4 that week. On August 20 *Judge and Jury* by James Patterson and Andrew

Gross was #1. An actress wannabe and an FBI agent chase the perpetrator of a crime. In the top five on August 30, Robin Cook's *Crisis* involves a medical malpractice trial. *Judge and Jury* stayed at #1 in early September, with *Ricochet* by Sandra Brown at #2.

In Diane Setterfield's *The Thirteenth Tale*, #1 on October 8, a biographer seeks to know about an elderly writer and his past. *The Book of Fate* by Brad Meltzer at #2 tells a story in which a presidential aide appears to have been murdered. There are Masonic secrets in Washington, D.C., and a code that was invented by Thomas Jefferson. With *For One Day* Mitch Albom returned to #1 with a story about a man's restoring his relationship with his deceased mother. Dick Francis's *Under Orders* and *The Mission Song* by John le Carré each reached #3 during these weeks. Anna Quindlen's *Rise and Shine* was #4. *The Friday Night Knitting Club* by Kate Jacobs scored high on several bestseller lists. On October 22, Albom's story was #1. *Thirteen Moons* by the recent Pulitzer Prize–winning novelist Charles Frazier was #2. Frazier's literary novels came more slowly than those of Grisham or Steel, and this was the first to rise high on the list since *Cold Mountain*. In this story a man raised in North Carolina travels across America. He is adopted by Native American people and meets an elusive woman. *For One Day* remained #1 on October 31. Michael Connelly's *Echo Park* gave us another Los Angeles crime story with Harry Bosch investigating. The *Los Angeles Times* awarded *Echo Park* fiction book of the year for 2006.

On November 5 Mitch Albom's story was #1 and *Echo Park* was #2. In David Baldacci's *The Collectors*, Camel Club members attempt to solve a murder at the Library of Congress. (*The Camel Club* was #15 on *Publishers Weekly*'s 2005 list.) *Lisey's Story* by Stephen King was #1 on November 12. *Dear John* by Nicholas Sparks, in which a soldier has a romance after 9/11, became #1 on November 19. The next week, following Sparks's novel was *Wildfire* by Nelson DeMille. *Wildfire* would become #13 on *Publishers Weekly*'s end-of-year list. *Cross* by James Patterson was #1 on December 3 and 17. Alex Cross, now retired from the FBI, pursues a rapist. Michael Crichton's *Next* rose to #2 with the story of genetic engineering gone haywire. (*Next* was #4 on *Publishers Weekly*'s end-of-year tally of bestsellers.) Albom's story returned to #1 during the holidays and stayed there in the first weeks of January.

The Road by Cormac McCarthy told a story of survival after nuclear destruction. McCarthy is generally regarded as one of America's literary craftsmen. *No Country for Old Men* became a bestseller, and its sales were supported by a successful film. *All the Pretty Horses* (1992) won the National Book Award and the National Book Critics Award. *Blood Meridian* (1985) is highly regarded. McCarthy was awarded the Pulitzer Prize in 2007, the year after he published *The Road*. *The Orchard Keeper* (1965) was his first novel. In Tennessee he sat in a barn writing *Child of God* (1973), which is set in Appalachia. *Suttree* (1979) appeared next. A MacArthur Fellowship afforded him the time to write *Blood Meridian* (1985). *All the Pretty Horses* was followed by *The Crossing* (1994) and *Cities of the Plains* (1998): his Border Trilogy. *No Country for Old Men* began as a screenplay and eventually became a film that won four Academy Awards. He also wrote a screenplay for *Sunset Limited* (2006) and *The Counselor* (2012). McCarthy's novels come fairly slowly compared with popular bestseller fare. He has been at work on several stories. (Texas State University in San Marcos has ninety-six boxes of his papers, with more to come.)

2007

For One Day remained at #1 through January 21. *Cross* at #2 and *Next* at #3 were followed by *The Hunters* by W. E. B. Griffin, which became #2 on January 21. On January 28, *Plum Lovin'* by Janet Evanovich, featuring her character Stephanie Plum, went to #1 and stayed there for two more weeks. *White Lies* by Jayne Anne Krentz also entered the top five on the list. On February 18 these books were joined by *The Alexandria Link* by Steve Berry in which a bookseller finds secret connections to the Alexandria Library and an international crime ring.

In March, *Step on a Crack* by James Patterson and Michael Ledwidge went to #1 with the story of a detective who is raising ten children and has to rescue hostages. *Sisters* by Danielle Steel took the #2 spot on the list. Her story is about four sisters living in a Manhattan apartment. J. D. Robb's *Innocent in Death* was #1 on March 11, with Detective Eve Dallas investigating the murder of a private school history teacher. Sophie Kinsella offered something different from the crime murder mystery in *Shopaholic Baby*. In Jodi Picoult's *Nineteen Minutes*, set in New Hampshire, a school shooting leads to questions about what is going on in an otherwise seemingly peaceful town. The story went to #1 on March 25.

On April 1 Jodi Picoult's novel was still #1. *Daddy's Girl* by Lisa Scottoline and *Whitethorn Woods* by Maeve Binchy were in the top five. One may wonder if the readers of these books were mostly female readers. James Patterson and Michael Ledwidge's *Step on a Crack* was #5. Did that book also appeal to many female readers? On April 15 Picoult's *Nineteen Minutes* was #1. Jonathan Kellerman's *Obsession* was #2. *I Heard That Song Before* by Mary Higgins Clark was #1 on April 22 and on April 30, Picoult's novel was #2, and *Kingdom Come* from Tim La-Haye and Jerry B. Jenkins was #3. *Simple Genius* by David Baldacci followed at #1 on May 20. New to the list was the witty Michael Chabon's novel *The Yiddish Policeman's Union* in which a detective investigates a neighbor's murder in a Jewish settlement in Alaska. On May 27, *The 6th Target* by James Patterson and Maxine Paetro focuses on a story in which Lindsay Boxer and the Women's Murder Club investigate a labyrinthine mystery. On June 3, behind that book at #2 was Lee Child's *Bad Luck and Trouble*, featuring his Jack Reacher series character.

A Thousand Splendid Suns by Khaled Hosseini, a sequel to *The Kite Runner*, rose to #1 on June 10. As it touched those heights, Michael Connelly's *The Overlook*, at #2, referred to a view from the hills across the greater L.A. area. Harry Bosch was back. However, Dean Koontz was claiming that his character was *The Good Guy*. In his story an ordinary man is drawn into a murder plot in a case of mistaken identity. Koontz's book was #3. Those novels remained among the top books through the end of June. Laurell K. Hamilton's *The Harlequin* joined them in the top four. *Splendid Suns* remained at #1 but was soon joined at #2 by *Blaze*, a story by author Richard Bachman, who was initially unknown but recently been revealed to be Stephen King.

On July 8 Janet Evanovich's *Lean Mean Thirteen* was #1. In her novel Stephanie Plum's ex-husband disappears and she becomes a suspect. After remaining high on the bestseller list, Evanovich's book was replaced at #1 by *The Quickie* by James Patterson and Michael Ledwidge. *High Noon* by Nora Roberts was #2. *The Judas Strain* by James Rollins was also in the top five on the list. *A Thousand Splendid Suns* returned to the top of the bestseller list on August 12. Daniel Silva's *The Secret Servant* was #2. Silva's story involves his protagonist Gabriel in a search for the kidnapped daughter of an American ambassador. *Splendid Suns* remained at #1 throughout most of September. On September 16, *The Wheel of Darkness* by Douglas Preston and Lincoln Child was #2. In the story Agent Pendergast seeks a stolen relic and faces evil. On September 30 James Patterson had yet another book, *You've Been Warned*, which he wrote with Howard Roughan. This book continued at #1 into October. John Grisham's *Playing for Pizza*, a different sort of book for him, sold quickly and landed at #1 on October 14. Nicholas Sparks's *The Choice* was #2.

World without End by Ken Follett was a large book. Follett was writing a historical novel and a family saga across several generations. This novel followed his big novel *Pillars of Earth*. Books like Grisham's *Playing for Pizza* seem trivial in comparison. Yet, *Pizza* was back at #1 on November 4. In Patricia Cornwell's *Book of the Dead*, her chief character Kay Scarpetta opens a practice in forensic pathology in Charleston, South Carolina. There is room on the list for a variety of books: Laurell K. Hamilton could write fantasies about fairies in *A Lick of Frost* (#2), and Vince Flynn, in *Protect and Defend*, could write about counterterrorism and operations against a nuclear Iran. At Thanksgiving, *Stone Cold* by David Baldacci was the #1 bestseller. In the story the members of the Camel Club are being killed to prevent their discovery of secrets in Washington, D.C. *Double Cross* by James Patterson rose to #1 on December 2. It was his third book to rise to that position within a few months. The novel remained #1 the next weekend, and *The Choice* by Nicholas Sparks was #2. Dean Koontz's *The Darkest Evening of the Year* was #2 the next week. On December 23 Sue Grafton's *T Is for Trespass* went to #1. In nonfiction, books by television personalities Stephen Colbert, Tom Brokaw, and Glenn Beck were the top three bestsellers. Caroline Kennedy's thoughts and poems were next on the list followed by books by comedian Steve Martin and rock musician Eric Clapton.

Nineteen Minutes by Jodi Picoult was #1 in 2007. Picoult was born in Nesconset, Long Island. Her family moved to New Hampshire, where her mother and father worked as teachers. She studied creative writing at Princeton, edited textbooks, and completed a master's in education at Harvard. *Nineteen Minutes* (2007) was followed by the #1 *Change of Heart* (2008). *Handle with Care* (2009) and *House Rules* (2010) also went to #1.

2008

Double Cross by James Patterson began the year at #1, along with *A Thousand Splendid Suns* at #2. These novels reversed places on January 20. Janet Evanovich's *Plum Lucky*, with her character Stephanie Plum, rose to #1 on January 27. In this story Stephanie's grandmother finds a bag of money and decides to go to Atlantic City with it to do some gambling. The problem is that she is now gambling with her life because the money will be pursued by its previous owner who lost it. The plot resembles a *Honeymooners* television episode in which Ralph Cramden finds a bag of money, begins spending the money lavishly, and is pursued by criminals. In New Jersey several organizations offer senior citizens the opportunity to take bus rides to Atlantic City on day trips. Put that into the plot with a popular series character like Stephanie Plum and out comes a bestseller. *Double Cross* remained at #2. In Geraldine Brooks's *People of the Book* (#3) a book expert finds secrets in a medieval manuscript. At #4 was a novel by Douglas Preston, who once worked at the Museum of Natural History in New York. With a supercollider, a CIA operative traces scientists who are planning to do some scary things to discover the secret of creation.

Stephen King and John Grisham were back with new novels in February. *Duma Key* by King was #1 on February 10. *The Appeal* by Grisham was #1 on February 17 and February 24. In Grisham's novel a court rules against a chemical company's dumping of harmful waste material. The novel held the top spot for several weeks. At #2 was another story by James Patterson and Maxine Paetro. On March 23, Jodi Picoult's *Change of Heart* was #1. In *Change of Heart* a death row prisoner has developed a unique ability to perform miracles. Sophie Kinsella's *Remember Me* was also in the top three on March 30.

April 2008 brought Jonathan Kellerman's *Compulsion*, in which detective-psychologist Alex Delaware investigates the murder of a woman in Los Angeles. *Unaccustomed Earth* by Jhumpa Lahiri was a surprise bestseller that reached #1 the next week. Published by Knopf, this is a well-crafted story about Bengali parents and their American children. *Small Favor* by Jim Butcher was #2. Simon and Schuster was right on target with its production of Mary Higgins Clark's *Where Are You Now?* The pattern to the release of novels by Clark continued. They invariably went to #1 in late April or early May. This story about a woman seeking the truth about her lost brother was #1 on April 20 and April 27. Mary Higgins Clark's New Jersey neighbor Harlan Coben reached the #1 position the next week with *Hold Tight*. On May 11 *The Whole Truth* by David Baldacci rose to #1. In his story an intelligence agent and a journalist chase a defense contractor. On May 18, *Sundays at Tiffany's* by James Patterson and Gabrielle Charbonnet went to #1. Debbie Macomber's *Twenty Wishes*, which told the story of a widow with a bookstore on Blossom Street, was #3.

Stephenie Meyer followed the phenomenon of her *Twilight* novels with *The Host*, the #1 bestselling novel on May 25 that was targeted more for an adult audience than for a young adult one. Dean Koontz's *Odd Hours* shot to #1 on June 8, featuring his character Odd Thomas. *Blood Noir* by Laurell K. Hamilton, one of her vampire hunter stories, was #2. In Lee Child's *Nothing to Lose*, a Colorado man's secrets are revealed by Jack Reacher. The book was #1 on June 22.

In August, readers were interested in spies. *Moscow Rules* by Daniel Silva went to #1. This was another of his thrillers about Gabriel Allon, the Mossad agent who is also a gifted art restorer. The public's taste for suspense stories with international intrigue sustained *The Bourne Sanction*, Eric Van Lustbader's story of the pursuit of an Islamic terrorist leader written in the manner of Robert Ludlum. The story carried Ludlum's name on the cover. On August 24, *Acheron* from the Dark Hunter series was #1. The #3 book had the quirky title *The Guernsey Literary and Potato Peel Society*, written by Mary Ann Eck and Annie Barrows about a postwar journalist who meets with Nazi occupation resisters. *Smoke Screen* by Sandra Brown, a murder mystery set in Charleston, South Carolina, was #1 on August 31.

September began with *Star Wars: The Force Unleashed* by Sean Williams accompanied the continuation of the *Star Wars* "prequel" on the screen and was #1 on September 7. It was soon replaced by *Devil Bones* by Kathy Reichs, in which her character Temperance investigates the victims of a voodoo cult. *Dark Curse* by Christine Feehan followed at #1 on September 21. Her characters Laura Calladine and Nicolas De la Cruz look for the truth of their pasts. *The Book of Life* by Brad Metzger was #2 on September 21.

In October, sales catapulted *The Story of Edgar Sawtelle* to the top of the list for two weeks, on October 5 and October 12. It had been #2 on August 10. In *The Lucky One*, Superman creator Jerry Siegel appeared. In mid-October, books by Nicholas Sparks and John Sandford were in the top five. *A Most Wanted Man* by John le Carré reached #4 on October 26. The character Mickey Haller—the "Lincoln Lawyer"—and Detective Harry Bosch are back investigating in Los Angeles in Michael Connelly's *The Brass Verdict*. Vince Flynn's *Extreme Measures* was #1 on November 9; on November 16, *The Gate House* by Nelson DeMille became #1. *Divine Justice* by David Baldacci took over that spot the next weekend on November 23. Glenn Beck, the television and radio host, produced *The Christmas Sweater*, an early holiday bestseller at #1 on November 30. *Cross Country* by James Patterson dominated the bestseller list in December. Glenn Beck's book was #2 and Clive Cussler's *Arctic Drift* was #3. The year ended with Patricia Cornwell's *Scarpetta* at #1, a title that makes use of her chief character's name, Kay Scarpetta. The pathologist is on assignment to New York.

Hold Tight by Harlan Coben made its debut at the top of the list in April 2008. Coben knows well the suspense that comes to families in a "typical" suburban community. He is married to pediatrician Anne Armstrong Coben, and they have four children in their New Jersey home. Coben is the author of *Home*, *Fool Me Once*, *The Stranger*, *Missing You*, *Six Years*, *Stay Close*, *Live Wire*, *Caught*, *Long Lost*, and *Hold Tight*: all #1 bestsellers. Coben played basketball in college at Amherst. He began writing a series about a sports agent, Myron Bolitar, and moved on to write the suspense thrillers for which he is best known.

2009

Following the Patricia Cornwell novel in the #1 spot was *Black Ops* by W. E. B. Griffin on January 18. The bright primary colors of a Janet Evanovich book cover again jumped out at potential book buyers. Stephanie Plum was back in *Plum Spooky*. *The Host* by Stephanie Meyer was #2. The success of *Black Ops* suggests a male audience, and the Evanovich and Meyer books appear to be targeted toward a young female reading audience. Of course, the readership doesn't in all cases fall along gender lines. John Grisham's novels cross over between both male and female readers. In *The Associate*, #1 on February 15 and February 22, a law school graduate goes into a large and brutal law firm. *Run for Your Life*, fiction by James Patterson and Michael Ledwidge, held the #2 spot on the list. *Handle with Care* by Jodi Picoult rose to #1 the next week. In her story a woman's daughter has a birth defect. Will she sue the obstetrician, who is a friend? The *Los Angeles Times* listed Clive Cussler and Jack Du Brul's *Corsair* at #1 on March 29, followed by Grisham's *The Associate* (#2) and Jodi Picoult's *Handle with Care* (#4). Readers also turned to *True Detectives* by Jonathan Kellerman, which was #1 on the *New York Times* list on April 12. (This is not the same as the television series of that title.) Picoult's *Handle with Care* was #2; Harlan Coben's *Long Lost* was #3. *Turn Coat* by Jim Butcher featured Chicago wizard detective as an installment in the Dresden Files series. In Mary Higgins Clark's *Just Take My Heart* at #2, a detective has had a heart transplant and risks her life on a new case. When the Mary Higgins Clark novel rose to #1 the next week, *Look Again* by Lisa Scottoline was #2. In *Look Again*, a reporter learns that her adopted son may have been abducted from his birth mother. In April, the Pulitzer Prize for Biography for 2009 was awarded to Jon Meacham for his biography on Andrew Jackson.

As May began, there was Mary Higgins Clark again with a novel at the #1 position. *First Family* by David Baldacci was #1 on May 10. James Patterson and Maxine Paetro had another #1 bestseller on May 17 with *The 8th Confession*. It was clear by now that Patterson liked numbers in his titles. Lindsey Boxer was working again with the Women's Murder Club. Even so, vampires continued to haunt the top of the list in J. R. Ward's *Love Avenged* (#2 on May 17) and Charlaine Harris's *Dead and Gone*, lifted to #1 by the *True Blood* television series. Sookie Stackhouse searches for the killer of a "werepanther." On May 31 John Sandford's *Wicked Prey* was #1 and Chuck Palahniuk's *Pygmy* appeared at #3. The *New York Times* bestseller list describes his story as one in which terrorists from a totalitarian country enter the Midwest disguised as exchange students. *Cemetery Dance* by Douglas Preston and Lincoln Child was also in the top five, featuring their quirky detective Agent Pendergast.

In June, in Lee Child's *Gone Tomorrow*, Jack Reacher faces a problem that goes back to the Soviet war in Afghanistan. In Michael Connelly's *The Scarecrow*, an *L.A. Times* reporter follows the path of a killer. *Gone Tomorrow* was #1 on June 7; *The Scarecrow* was #1 on June 14. *Skin Trade* by Laurell K. Hamilton brought back a vampire hunter, Anita Blake, to #1 the next week in a story set in Las Vegas. *Relentless* by Dean Koontz followed at #1 on June 28. The #2 book was *The Psychic Book of*

Deliverance by Katherine Howe, in which a graduate student investigates reports of a healer who is accused of witchcraft. *Knockout* by Catherine Coulter was #2. *The Bourne Deception*, another pseudo-Ludlum title about a struggle to avoid a world war, was next on the list.

The bright sunshine of July 2009 was reflected by the colorful cover of Janet Evanovich's *Finger Lickin' Fifteen*. *The Doomsday Key* was #2 behind it on July 15. *Swimsuit* was James Patterson's summer book, written with Maxine Paetro. It went to #1 on July 19, followed by Brad Thor's *The Apostle* at #2, in which his series character Scot Harvath, a Homeland Security agent, has to free a terrorist from a prison in Pakistan because of a ransom deal. *Black Hills* by Nora Roberts was #1 on July 26 with a story of a South Dakota wildlife biologist and an ex–police officer chasing a serial killer. *Best Friends Forever* by Jennifer Weiner went to #1 on August 2. Then Daniel Silva's *The Defector* (#1 on August 9) brought his series character Gabriel Allon back into action to try to find a missing Russian defector who had once saved his life.

One of the brightest summer sensations was probably the conclusion of the trilogy by Stieg Larsson: *The Girl Who Played with Fire*. His novel, featuring his character Lisbeth Salander, rose to #1 on August 16. Richard Russo's *That Old Cape Magic* reached #2 the next week, on August 23. It was followed at #3 by Kathryn Stockett's *The Help*, a novel about African American housemaids and domestic help in the South, which would stay on the bestseller list for more than a year. *South of Broad* by Pat Conroy was another substantial novel that became #1 on September 6. Pat Conroy remained best known as the author of *The Prince of Tides*.

The list went pop again with *Alex Cross's Trial* by James Patterson and Richard DiLallo, #1 on September 13. *Dark Slayer*, a *True Blood*–like vampire story by Christine Feehan, was #1 on September 20. *The Lost Symbol*, Dan Brown's follow-up to *The Da Vinci Code*, went to #1 on October 4. *The Lost Symbol* remained #1 for most weeks into November. Charlaine Harris brought another *True Blood* episode to #2 on the list with *A Touch of Dead*. *The Help* remained high on the list. At #2 behind *The Lost Symbol* on November 1 was Vince Flynn's *Pursuit of Honor* with his character Mitch Rapp asserting the cause of national security against al-Qaeda. *The Scarpetta Factor* by Patricia Cornwell was #2 behind *The Lost Symbol* on November 8 and November 15.

Familiar names characterized the top of the fiction bestseller list in November and December 2009. John Grisham's *Ford County* was #1 on November 22. Dan Brown's *The Lost Symbol* was #2. Nora Roberts writing as J. D. Robb had *Kindred in Death* at #3. *Under the Dome* by Stephen King, later a television miniseries, was #1 on November 29. In the story, a town is isolated, surrounded by an immense invisible dome of uncertain origin. On December 6, *I, Alex Cross* by James Patterson topped the bestseller list. It was followed by *Under the Dome*, *The Lost Symbol*, and *Ford County*. On December 20 *U Is for Undertow* by Sue Grafton became the #1 fiction book in the United States. *Pirate Latitudes*, a manuscript left by Michael Crichton who had died, was the #2 book. In this adventure story a pirate attacks a Spanish galleon. The year concluded with *The Lost Symbol* returning to the #1 position on the list. The next books on the list were *U Is for Undertow*, *I, Alex Cross*, and *Under the Dome*. They were followed by *The Help* and *Pirate Latitudes*.

9

THE 2010s

James Patterson Inc. and the Soul of America

What is a book in the digital age? Is it a self-contained unit bound between covers, or something else? Books mix with other media. In recent years hardcover book sales and paperback book sales have been supported by social media campaigns. Books are sold in bookstores, and they are also sold and distributed online by Amazon.com and dozens of other electronic online distributors. Hardcover popular novels sometimes appear on display in your local pharmacy, where only paperbacks once prevailed. Familiar name authors' books are featured in bookstore displays. Even with the now ubiquitous presence of the digital e-book, many readers like to hold a book in their hands. Potential readers roam through Barnes & Noble superstores in quest of the latest bestseller and see a wide variety of other options. We might ask if we can detect any trends among the books of the past few years. Might the commercial success of one novel have prompted the appearance of another? Has electronic media quickened our pace? Do the bestsellers suggest any trends of our time?

2010

Readers still reach for mystery, romance, suspense. The year 2010 began with *The Lost Symbol* by Dan Brown at #1 on the *Wall Street Journal* bestseller list and the *New York Times* list. James Patterson's *I, Alex*

Cross was a suspenseful mystery at #2. Stephen King's *Under the Dome* was #3. *The Help* by Kathryn Stockett, a story of African American domestic workers, rose to #1 on January 24. It stayed there throughout much of the next month. On January 24, *The Help* was followed on the *New York Times* list by *The Lost Symbol* (#2) and Anne Tyler's *Noah's Compass*, in which a retired teacher is recovering from an injury. On January 31, *The Help*, at #1, was followed by Robert Crais's *First Rule* at #2. Elizabeth Kostova, the writer of *The Historian*, had published *The Swan Thieves*, which was now #3 on the bestseller list. In this story a psychiatrist is treating a man who cut up a work of art in the National Gallery. The novel provides an educational benefit: readers can learn all about French impressionism. The *Los Angeles Times* listed *The Help* at #1 followed by *First Rule* by Crais at #2. Stieg Larsson's *The Girl Who Played with Fire* was making its rise on its list at #3, and Elizabeth Kostova's *The Swan Thieves* was its #4. *The Road* by Cormac McCarthy hovered around #8 on the *Los Angeles Times* list throughout January.

The *Wall Street Journal* was tracking bestsellers via Nielsen Scan. *Publishers Weekly* developed lists with attention to the publishing industry. The *New York Times* published several lists with its inscrutable method of tallying bookstore sales and online sales. The *USA Today* bestsellers tended to correspond to these other national lists. From February 21 into early March, *Worst Case* by James Patterson and Michael Ledwidge was the bestselling book. *Poor Little Bitch Girl* by Jackie Collins moved up to #4 on March 7. J. D. Robb, Nora Roberts's alter ego, produced *Fantasy in Death* about a Hollywood murder. It went to #1 on March 14. *The Help* returned to #2 on March 21 and March 28. *House Rules* by Jodi Picoult reached #1 at the end of the month. In April, in Harlan Coben's #1 novel *Caught*, a girl disappears in the suburbs. *Silver Borne* by Patricia Briggs replaced it at #1 on April 18. Jim Butcher's *Changes*, one of his Dresden Files novels with his Chicago-based magician-detective, became #1 on April 25. Of course, it was then time for another May bestseller from Mary Higgins Clark. One could almost gauge the arrival of the season by Simon and Schuster's annual publications of her stories of mystery and suspense. This one was *The Shadow of Your Smile*, an indication that the author was turning toward the titles of songs for her mystery stories, often ones that also indicated a touch of romance.

The *Los Angeles Times* reported that Stieg Larsson's novels were #1 and #2 on April 11. In David Baldacci's *Deliver Us from Evil*, #1 on May

9, agents chase after a human trafficker. *The Help* was #2. At #3 on the list was the Ladies' Detective Agency in *The Double Comfort Safari Club* by Alexander McCall Smith, which seems to reflect the popularity of the James Patterson novels, or perhaps that of novels read mostly by female mystery readers. On May 16, *The 9th Judgment* by James Patterson and Maxine Paetro went to #1 with a story of Lindsey Boxer's pursuit of a killer of women and children. On May 23, this slipped to #2 behind *Dead in the Family*, a *True Blood* vampire story. At the #3 spot on the list was Scott Turow's *Innocent*, a sequel to his bestseller *Presumed Innocent*. Charlaine Harris's *Dead in the Family* stayed at #1 on May 30. Emily Giffin's *Heart of the Matter* was #2 with a female lawyer who saves a man in an accident and joins forces with a pediatric plastic surgeon. The novel shows two highly competent professional women, strong female characters, pursuing a case. If one looks across the books of the mid- to late 1990s and 2000s, one sees the clear emergence of this strong female protagonist in popular fiction.

Of course, there was also the adventurous male hero. Such a character embodied great resolve, ingenuity, and near-superhuman tenacity. Jack Reacher, a former military man, was Lee Child's chief protagonist. In *61 Hours* (#1 on June 6), Jack Reacher is in South Dakota protecting a witness in a drug trial. This book was followed by John Sandford's *Stolen Prey* at #2. This was Sandford's twentieth novel in a series featuring his character Lucas Davenport. Series characters like Lee Child's Jack Reacher, Sandford's Lucas Davenport, or Charlaine Harris's Sookie Stackhouse were staples of the bestseller list. Once readers became acquainted with them, these figures were everywhere on the bestseller list. Readers encountered Robert Ludlum's Jason Bourne, Janet Evanovich's Stephanie Plum, Patricia Cornwell's Kay Scarpetta, Jonathan Kellerman's Alex Delaware, and Daniel Silva's Gabriel Allon.

A new star was Lisbeth Salander, the sharp-witted, rough-and-tumble survivor of abuse in *The Girl Who Kicked the Hornet's Nest*. This was volume 3 of Stieg Larsson's popular trilogy. Sadly, Larsson died of a heart attack. His estate, now wealthy from sales of the novels, was soon to be contested by a former live-in significant other and various family members. *The Girl Who Kicked the Hornet's Nest* was the bestselling book of the early part of the summer. It was #1 on June 20 and on June 30 on the *New York Times* list. *Hornet's Nest* was #1 on the *L.A. Times* list in July. *Publishers Weekly* also listed *Hornet's Nest* at the top of its list. The novel was the #1 bestseller of the year on *Publishers Weekly*'s 2010 end-of-year list. On July 11, *Mindfulness* by Buddhist monk Thich Nhat Hanh rose up on the *L.A. Times* bestseller list. A trend in psychology and meditation supported sales of that book.

In *Bullet*, Laurell K. Hamilton tells another story about her character Anita Blake, the vampire hunter. In *Spy*, Clive Cussler with Justin Scott tells the story of a 1908 murder that led to the uncovering of international spies who were trying to prevent the United States from developing battleships. In *The Overton Window*, by radio-TV personality and political pundit Glenn Beck (#1 on July 4), a public relations executive has a romance with an intriguing woman. *Sizzling Sixteen* by Janet Evanovich was another summer bestseller that took over the #1 spot the next week. It was #4 on the *Los Angeles Times* list on July 11. The *New York Times* listed *Private* by James Patterson and Maxine Paetro at #1 on July 18, another of the books emerging from Patterson like cars off an assembly line. In August, *Hornet's Nest* returned to #1 for the entire month of August, except for August 8 when Daniel Silva's *The Rembrandt Affair* was #1. The historical novel made an unexpected return with *The Red Queen* by Philippa Gregory. This is a story set during the War of the Roses that is focused upon the experiences of Margaret Beaufort, the mother of Henry VII. It was #2 on the bestseller list on August 22.

One can see considerable turnover in the top spot on the bestseller list in 2010. On September 5 *The Postcard Killers* by James Patterson and Liza Marklund was #1, featuring an NYPD detective and a Swedish reporter. (Given Patterson's youth in Newburgh, New York, and Marklund's rather Scandinavian last name, might they have been imagining their best selves?) On September 19, Jonathan Franzen's novel *Freedom* marked his return to the #1 position on the *New York Times* bestseller list. His story tells of the experiences of a midwestern family during the time of the George W. Bush presidency. The book held the #1 position on the list through the end of September. On October 3, Nicholas Sparks's *Safe Haven* was #1, but Franzen's novel returned to #1 the next week. On October 17, Ken Follett, who was now writing lengthy historical family sagas, had the #1 bestseller with *Fall of Giants*. Follett was writing about five families from five different countries and their encounters with events of the twentieth century. On October 24, Michael Connelly's *The Reversal* provided a reversal of the standings. Mickey Haller the Lincoln Lawyer and Harry Bosch the L.A. detective are back together investigating a child murderer. Also competing for those top spots on the list was James Patterson's *Don't Blink*, a book he created with Howard Roughan. *American Assassin* by Vince Flynn drew on reminders of the Lockerbie bombing and featured his counterterrorist protagonist Mitch Rapp. Another tough-guy novel, *Worth Dying For* by Lee Child, followed at #1 on November 7 with the character Jack Reacher investigating a cold case involving a missing child.

On November 14, John Grisham returned to #1 with *The Confession*. Hiding some dark crimes allows one man to stay free while another man is charged with the crimes and sent to death row in his place. Here is another Grisham novel that reflects upon justice. The man who has hidden his crimes wants now to confess, but he has to convince the authorities that he is telling the truth. On November 21, *Towers of Midnight* by Robert Jordan was listed at #1. *Hell's Corner* by David Baldacci was #1 on November 26. Baldacci's protagonist Oliver Stone (not the director) seeks to foil bombers who are near the White House. *Full Dark, No Stars*, four stories by Stephen King, was #2.

On December 5, *Crossfire* by James Patterson was his seventh #1 bestseller of the year. It held the #1 spot on December 12, followed by John Grisham's *The Confession*. On December 19, Patricia Cornwell's *Port Mortuary* became #1, with the story of pathologist Kay Scarpetta in her new role at a forensics center in Cambridge, Massachusetts. Scarpetta investigates the mysterious death of a young man at an air force base. *Dead or Alive* by Tom Clancy with Grant Blackwood was #1 on December 26. Characters from previous Tom Clancy novels reappear in that story to track down the terrorists of Emir. This was one of the final books by Clancy.

The year concluded with George W. Bush's *Decision Points*, a nonfiction bestseller in which he discusses his life and the decisions of his presidency. (President Bush had a reading contest with Karl Rove to see who could read one hundred books during the year. This activity extended to the rest of the Bush family.) *Decision Points* was the #1 *Publishers Weekly* nonfiction bestseller of the year. Autobiography was also in the air with *Autobiography of Mark Twain* at #3, officially released after one hundred years. Celebrity autobiographies also appeared: Keith Richards of the Rolling Stones with James Fox had the #4 book on the nonfiction list. In *Unbroken* by Laura Hillenbrand, an Olympic runner recalls survival among the Japanese in World War II. *Earth,* a largely pictorial volume from *Daily Show* host Jon Stewart, was #5. A biography of *Cleopatra* by Stacey Schiff was #6. Like Jon Stewart, Glenn Beck, in a book written with Kevin Balfe, could trade upon the large public platform that television provided. *Broke*, by Beck and Balfe, signaled that, while the country might be broke, they surely were not. *Decoded* by rapper Jay-Z was another celebrity book on the list. Bill O'Reilly pontificated about *Patriots and Pinheads* at #12. At #13 was *Colonel Roosevelt*, Edmund Morris's third and final volume of his magisterial biography of Theodore Roosevelt. In 2001 the *Los Angeles Times* gave the first volume of the Roosevelt biography its award for biography.

2011

The year 2011 began with Tom Clancy and Grant Blackwood's book *Dead or Alive* at #1. This was followed by John Grisham's *The Confession*, Stieg Larsson's *Hornet's Nest*, and James Patterson's *Crossfire*. On January 16, Dean Koontz's *What the Night Knows* reached #1, shifting the order. A killer of families must be stopped. The murders reflect crimes that occurred twenty years earlier. Brad Meltzer's *The Inner Circle* was #1 the following week with the story of an archivist who discovers a book that once belonged to George Washington that bears a secret. *Shadow Fever* by Karen Marie Moning was a #1 bestseller from a "new" author in which her protagonist seeks her sister's murderer. *Tick Tock* by James Patterson and Michael Ledwidge was #1 on February 13. Detective Michael Bennett calls upon assistance from a former colleague to prevent criminal activity. *Tick Tock*, *The Help*, and *The Inner Circle* were #1, #2, and #3, respectively, on February 20. At #2 on February 27, *A Discovery of Witches* by Deborah Harkness tells the story of the discovery of a lost manuscript in an Oxford library and how this produces ripples and waves of response in the criminal underworld.

The *Wall Street Journal* announced that it would begin tracking e-book sales via Nielsen Book Scan. Data would be collected from some twelve thousand locations. *USA Today* had begun tracking e-book sales in 2009. Individuals commenting on the *Wall Street Journal*'s initial launch of its e-book listing were optimistic that it would provide greater accuracy than other bestseller lists.

On March 13 at #1, J. D. Robb's characters Eve Dallas and Peabody investigate the murder of a grocer. *Pale Demon* by Kim Harrison was in the #2 position. *Gideon's Sword* by Douglas Preston and Lincoln Child was #3. *The Wise Man's Fear* by Patrick Rothfuss brought another new author and book to #1 on March 20. A magician, Kvothe, is the narrator of this story. *The Jungle* by Clive Cussler and Jack Du Brul, another cowrite, was the March 27 #1 bestseller featuring a story of rescue operations. *Sing You Home* by Jodi Picoult was #2. James Patterson was back again with another coauthor Neil McMahon. Their novel *Toys* appeared high on the list in early April. *Live Wire* by Harlan Coben was next at #1 on April 10. In Coben's story, Myron Bolitar seeks a missing rock star and raises questions about his own brother's absence. Readers went back in time into prehistory with Jean M. Auel's *The Land of Painted Caves*, which was #1 April 17. Other readers were brought to contemporary Los Angeles in *The Fifth Witness* by Michael Connelly, at #1 on April 24. In this story the lawyer Mickey Haller represents a woman who is accused of killing a banker who would have foreclosed on her home. It reflects some of the difficulties with the housing market during that year. Meanwhile, Danielle Steel was back with *44 Charles Street* at #4. Mary Higgins Clark's late April bestseller *I'll Walk Alone* tells the story of identity theft and the protagonist tracing her son's disappearance. Ron Chernow's biography of George Washington was awarded the Pulitzer Prize. His biography of Alexander Hamilton would have even greater cultural impact through Lin-Manuel Miranda's musical *Hamilton*.

Chasing Fire by Nora Roberts, a story set in Montana, became the #1 novel on May 1. In May 2011 there were several dramatic stories that chased *Chasing Fire* at #1. In *The Sixth Man* by David Baldacci, the lawyer for an alleged serial killer is murdered. In this whodunit a Secret Service agent seeks the killer. In *Dead Reckoning* by Charlaine Harris, the stories of vampires in Louisiana returned to #1. Another James Patterson and Maxine Paetro novel, *10th Anniversary*, was #2. John Sandford's *Buried Prey* was #2 the next week, and *10th Anniversary* dropped to the #3 spot. On June 5 that order of bestsellers was the same. *The Jefferson Key* by Steve Berry was #4. Another *Star Wars* story then appeared in the top three on the list. *Dreams of Joy* by Lisa See arrived at #1 with the story of a woman who is angry at her mother and escapes to Shanghai. *Hit List* by Laurell K. Hamilton followed the next week and went to #1. *Hit List* continued the escapades of vampire hunter Anita Blake who is pursued by "the Mother of All Darkness." *The Kingdom* by Clive Cussler and Grant Blackwood was #2. In *State of Wonder* (#3) by Ann Patchett, an American medical researcher seeks her former mentor: a mad scientist creating a fertility drug.

Tom Clancy's name lived on. In *Against All Enemies* by Tom Clancy with Peter Telep, Maxwell Moore pursues the terrorists who killed his brother in Pakistan. Janet Evanovich's *Smokin' Seventeen*, a completely different kind of novel, was #1 the next week. *The Devil's Colony* by James Rollins was #3 with the story of the investigation of a lost colony. *Now You See Her* by James Patterson and Michael Ledwidge was the third James Patterson novel to reach #1 that year. The James Patterson industry was in full gear, and the prolific storyteller and his writing partners showed no sign of stopping. In *Now You See Her*, Nina Bloom has changed her identity to be safe but now has to face her own past and a killer.

On July 31, *The Game of Thrones* made its first impact on the bestseller list. George R. R. Martin's *A Dance with Dragons* was #1 and his fantasy series on HBO was a smash hit. *A Dance with Dragons*, book five of *A Song of Ice and Fire*, was secure at #1 on August 7 as well. Jim Butcher's *Ghost Story* took over the #1 spot on August 16. However, it raised a problem: How is a novelist to continue a popular series when he kills off his principal series character? In this case Butcher kills off Harry Dresden, the wizard detective of Chicago, and Harry becomes a ghost to help a friend who is in danger. In Brad Thor's *Full Black* (#3), a counter-terrorist attempts to survive against the odds. Meanwhile, Agent Pendergast, the quirky creation of Douglas Preston and Lincoln Child, entertained readers in the twisting plot of *Cold Vengeance*, which was #1 on August 21. *Dances with Dragons* was back at #1 on August 28. A novel by Terry Goodkind replaced George R. R. Martin's novel at #1 on September, but with the budding fan base for *The Game of Thrones*, Martin's story remained at #2. *Flash and Bones* by Kathy Reichs was #1 on September 11. Her protagonist Temperance Brennan is a forensic pathologist. There is a direct connection with the television series *Bones*.

On October 29, 2011, the *Wall Street Journal* expanded its listing of bestsellers to include e-books. The books of autumn 2011 appeared in lively variety. In the #1 *New York to Dallas* by J. D. Robb, a child molester has escaped from custody and is pursuing Eve Dallas. *The Night Circus* by Erin Morgenstern, at #2, tells the story of a magical circus. In

Abuse of Power by Michael Savage (#4), a war correspondent exposes a terrorist group. *Heat Rises* by Richard Castle, #1 on October 9, gives us the story of an NYPD homicide detective who becomes aware of a conspiracy in the department. *Lethal* by Sandra Brown was #2. October 16 was the day that Lee Child's Jack Reacher was the character people were reading about in *The Affair*. Debbie Macomber's latest book in her Cedar Cove series was #2. *Feast Day of Fools* by James Lee Burke was #3. For some time Burke had been alternating southern Louisiana settings with stories that reached up into Montana. Rather than featuring his more well-known New Orleans Dave Robicheaux character, in this novel Hackberry Holland investigates a case in the desert. On October 23, John Sandford's *Shock Wave* was #1, with Virgil Flowers investigating the case. In *The Best of Me* Nicholas Sparks returned to #1. *The Marriage Plot* by Jeffrey Eugenides was #2. It was followed at #2 by another James Patterson novel penned with Rick DiLallo: *Christmas Wedding*. Iris Johansen had the #3 novel with *Bonnie*. When Eve Duncan's daughter is kidnapped, suspicion falls upon the father of the girl.

One can see that genre fiction almost invariably was at the top and the center of the nation's bestseller list. John Grisham's *The Litigators* made its expected appearance at #1 on November 13. The plot was simple and, after so many Grisham novels, repetitious: a partner in a small law firm faces a big case. Even so, the plot-driven story carried readers forward to a satisfying conclusion despite the rather limited characterization. *1Q84* by Haruki Murakami was, perhaps, a more fascinating novel. In 1980s Tokyo the protagonist ponders those who caused domestic violence. On November 20 *Zero Day* by David Baldacci was #1. The military must get an aspiring novelist who takes on a ghostwriting project that has to do with a conspiracy.

Stephen King's *11/22/63* recalls the fateful assassination of John F. Kennedy. In King's story an English teacher goes back in time by a portal in a diner in Maine. The *Los Angeles Times* named King's novel its Mystery/Thriller Award winner of 2011. *Kill Alex Cross* by James Patterson was #1 on December 4. King's story was #2. *V Is for Vengeance* by Sue Grafton was #3. *Explosive Eighteen* by Janet Evanovich was #1 on December 11. *The Drop* by Michael Connelly brought readers to the Los Angeles area for another well-written mystery and case to be solved. Stephen King's novel returned to #1 on Christmas Day. *Red Mist* by Patricia Cornwell was #2. John Grisham's *The Litigators* had risen up the list again to #3. *Death Comes to Pemberley* by P. D. James offered another mystery, with a British twist. The *New York Times* bestseller list described the novel as a story in which a nineteenth-century tycoon's mansion becomes a luxury apartment amid "evil forces." *Micro* by Michael Crichton appeared on the list toward the end of the year. Crichton's manuscript was reworked by Richard Preston, who was chosen to complete it. In *Micro*, graduate students are made miniature by an evil man in Hawaii's rain forest.

Leading the nonfiction bestseller list at the end of the year was Walter Isaacson's biography of Steve Jobs. The other bestselling books focused on American icons. *Killing Lincoln* by Bill O'Reilly and Martin Dugard, *Being George Washington* by Glenn Beck and Kevin Balfe, and *Jack Kennedy* by Chris Matthews brought the political news commentators to the bestseller list to comment on American presidents. *Killing Lincoln* was exploratory; *Being George Washington* was thoughtful; *Jack Kennedy* by Chris Matthews was laudatory and admiring. *Back to Work* by President Bill Clinton was further down the list at #14, seven places below Robert K. Massie's biography of Catherine the Great.

2012

Popular fiction is often more celebration than cerebration. George Orwell suggested as much in his essay "Good Bad Books" in 1945. Orwell, who examined popular story paper publications for boys in "Boy's Weeklies," wrote in the *Tribune*, November 2, 1945, of "the kind of book that has no literary pretention but which remains readable when more serious productions have perished." If art was the same thing as criticism, Orwell mused, "every intelligent critic would be capable of writing a readable novel." In "Boy's Weeklies" he pointed out that the popular fiction in *The Magnet* and *The Gem* were intentionally formulaic. They supported the reader's hope that "everything will be the same."

An essay titled "Easy Writers" in the *New Yorker* on May 28, 2012, recognized the merits of popular fiction. With its title recalling the popular film *Easy Rider*, this essay looked back upon Edmund Wilson's criticisms in "Who Cares Who Killed Roger Ackroyd?" and Harold Bloom's rejection of Stephen King's National Book Foundation Award. Popular fiction is predictable. However, plotting, inventing, and creating character quirks require a unique talent. To prefer Ken Follett's *On the Wings of Eagles* to Henry James's *Wings of the Dove* "is not a negligible bias," the author concluded. However, "we shouldn't sell short the likes of Follett, or for that matter, Ross Thomas . . . John Grisham, James Lee Burke, Sue Grafton, Janet Evanovich, Robert Crais or George Pelecanos, all of whom consistently deliver entertaining works in serviceable prose."[1]

Dean Koontz's *77 Shadow Street* was #1 January 15, 2012. *Private #1 Suspect* by James Patterson and Maxine Paetro was the next #1, and Janet Evanovich's *Love in a Nutshell* was #2. *Believing the Lie* by Elizabeth George was #1 the next week. *Private #1 Suspect* was #2. *Gideon's Corpse* by Douglas Preston was #3. On February 5 *Private #1 Suspect* was the top bestseller. In *Death of Kings* by Bernard Cornwell, King Alfred is near death. The Saxon warrior Uhtred has choose either to unite England or only his kingdom in the North. In *Taken* by Robert Crais, his protagonist Joe Pike goes to the rescue when Elvis Cole is taken. In *Home Front* by Kristin Hannah, a woman is sent in the military to Iraq. In *Kill Shot* by Vince Flynn, the character Mitch Rapp, a CIA agent, again investigates the Lockerbie incident.

In March, James Patterson was back with another book, *Private Games*, written with Mark Sullivan. It was #1 on March 4. With *The Wolf Gift* Anne Rice exchanged her usual fiction on vampires for a werewolf novel. On March 18 at #1 was another "wolf." In *Lone Wolf*, Jodi Picoult tells the story of a man who studies wolves and is injured in an accident. In *The Thief*, #1 on March 25, Clive Cussler and Justin Scott tell the story of Isaac Bell's attempt to save scientists from German spies. When *Lone Wolf* returned to the #1 spot on the list on April #1 its closest competition was a *Star Wars* novel, *Fate of the Jedi* by Troy Denning. In *Victims*, Jonathan Kellerman sets Alex Delaware back to work investigating a case with his sidekick Milo Sturgis. *Stay Close* by Harlan Coben, a story in which someone vanishes in Atlantic City, was #1 on April 8. *Love Reborn* by J. R. Ward was #1 on April 15. *Guilty Wives* by James Patterson and David Ellis, another collaborator, was #2. *Betrayal* by Danielle Steel was #3.

Mary Higgins Clark's late April bestseller in 2012 was *The Lost Years*. This was a story in which a biblical scholar has discovered the lost years of Jesus. Unfortunately, the scholar is then murdered. His daughter seeks his killer. John Grisham's new novel was climbing up the list, meanwhile. With *Calico Joe*, Grisham wrote a story that was a bit of a departure from his lawyer suspense novels. A baseball pitcher throws a pitch that hits a rookie batter in the head. The pitcher's son works toward reconciliation between them. Grisham's novel reached #1 on April 29.

The Innocent by David Baldacci started off the month of May at #1. In Baldacci's story, a hit man becomes the target of a government investigation. He rescues a girl whose parents have been murdered and finds himself in the middle of a conspiracy. *The Witness* by Nora Roberts was #2. On May 13, Stephen King's *The Wind through the Keyhole* was #1. The story was part of his Dark Tower series. Charlaine Harris's *Deadlocked* was #1 on May 28. As the twelfth vampire novel in the Sookie Stackhouse series, it joined *Definitely Dead*, *Dead and Gone*, and *Dead Reckoning*. James Patterson and Maxine Paetro produced *11th Hour*, another novel with a number in the title—and another #1 bestseller for Patterson on May 27. *Bring Up the Bodies* by Hilary Mantel was #2. This was a historical novel in which Thomas Cromwell is against Anne Boleyn. King Henry VIII now wishes to marry Jane Seymour. In Richard Paul Evans's *The Road to Grace* (#4 on May 27) an ad executive loses everything and begins a long walk from Seattle to Key West. *One Person* by John Irving appeared at #5.

We can see a great deal of turnover in the top positions on the list in summer 2012. John Sandford's *Stolen Prey* became #1 on June 12. Sandford was born John Roswell Camp in Cedar Rapids, Iowa. He became a journalist and was a features reporter. His turn toward fiction led to the Prey series with his memorable character Lucas Davenport's investigations. He has also developed the Virgil Flowers character in *Storm Prey* and other novels. On June 17, *The Storm* by Clive Cussler and Graham Brown was #1. On June 24, *Kiss the Dead* by Laurell K. Hamilton brought back Anita Blake the vampire hunter to #1. *Calico Joe* by John Grisham was at #1 on July 1. *Mission to Paris* by Alan Furst, set in 1938, was #2 on the list.

Fifty Shades of Grey and *Hunger Games* were featured as *USA Today*'s bestsellers of the year. The novels, *USA Today* suggested, signaled a trend of erotic dystopian novels. *Hunger Games* was first published in 2008 and became a top-selling feature film in 2012. *Catching Fire* and *Mockingjay* followed. The film for *Fifty Shades* appeared in 2015. In summer 2012, the novel *Gone Girl* by Gillian Flynn began a trend of successful domestic thrillers. Nick Dunne and his wife, Amy, have very different perspectives on their marriage. We learn about their views of each other from Nick and from Amy's diary. Both characters lose their jobs. The story spins off into intrigue when Amy disappears. *Gone Girl* was #1 on July 15 and July 22, and sales began to establish the novel as one of the top popular novels of the year.

Shadow of Night by Deborah Harkness was another vampire novel, and it climbed to #1 on July 29. *I, Michael Bennett* by James Patterson and Michael Ledwidge was #2 on that day. Daniel Silva's *The Fallen Angel* went to #1 on August 5. Behind a murder in Rome is a global criminal organization and Gabriel Allon is called upon to face it. *Gone Girl* had a strong resurgence in sales in August. At #2 on August 5, it shot back up to #1 where it stayed into September. *Odd Apocalypse* by Dean Koontz, with his character Odd Thomas, was #2 on August 9. *Sweet Talk* by Julie Garwood was #2 the next week. Debbie Macomber's *The Inn at Rose Harbor* was #2 on September 2. *The Beautiful Mystery* by Louise Penny rose up to #2 on September 16. *The Time Keeper* by Mitch Albom brought the inventor of the world's first clock to #1 on September 23. *Zoo* by James Patterson and Michael Ledwidge, later a television series, was #2. Lee Child's *A Wanted Man*, #1 on September 30, had his character Jack Reacher hitchhiking and encountering a conspiracy.

The autumn of 2012 saw the further development of Ken Follett's family saga and historical series with *Winter of the World*. His story, set between 1939 and 1949, includes the drama of the war years. This was book two of a trilogy and followed his novel *Fall of Giants*. J. K. Rowling produced *Casual Vacancy*, a book not at all about Harry Potter. In her story, a parish councilman has died suddenly and an English town reacts. In James Patterson and Marshall Karp's *NYPD Red*, #2 on October 28, the protagonists, Zack Jordan and his partner, chase a Bonnie-and-Clyde-like duo. *The Panther* by Nelson DeMille was #1 on November 4. The story's plot allows the reader's imagination to play across troublesome contemporary issues: in this case, tensions with terrorists in the Middle East. In DeMille's novel, John Carey takes on an assignment in Yemen. His wife is an FBI agent. Carey attempts to chase down an al-Qaeda operative who wants to avenge the death of a Libyan terrorist.

John Grisham returned to #1 on the bestseller list on November 11 with *The Racketeer*. Malcolm Bannister, an ex-lawyer, is now in prison, clearly on the wrong side of the law. He claims that he knows who killed a federal judge. He wants to gain his freedom and he has a plan. The Grisham novel remained #1 on November 18 and November 25. Danielle

Steel's *The Sins of the Mother* was #2 on November 18 with the story of a businesswoman who tries to heal her family's past and her relationships with her children. *Poseidon's Arrow* by Clive Cussler and Dirk Cussler takes us to the sea. *Flight Behavior* by Barbara Kingsolver, at #3, concerns butterflies in flight and a woman's attempt to save the monarch butterflies.

December was a month for the adventure novel. *The Last Man* by Vince Flynn, #1 on December 2, features his series character Mitch Rapp in Afghanistan seeking a missing CIA operative. *Merry Christmas, Alex Cross* was James Patterson's story at #2, all set for the season. Janet Evanovich offered something different with *Notorious Nineteen*, #1 on December 9. *The Forgotten* by David Baldacci ramped up the drama at #2. *The Agenda* by Glenn Beck and Harriet Parke was #3. Jim Butcher resurrected his character Harry Dresden for *Cold Days*, #1 in the cold days of mid-December. *The Black Box* by Michael Connelly added intrigue as Detective Harry Bosch connected a bullet found at a recent crime scene with a past crime. Back in 1992 a woman was killed during race riots in Los Angeles, and Bosch seeks clues to the mystery of her death. December 22 continued the public's fascination with suspense and adventure with Tom Clancy and Mark Greaney's *Threat Vector*. When China invades Taiwan, Jack Ryan, the president, responds.

The end of the year in nonfiction was particularly attentive to American presidential history. It was also filled with pop/rock music icons. *Killing Kennedy* by Bill O'Reilly with Martin Dugard was #1. The success of that book brought O'Reilly's *Killing Lincoln* back to the list at #3. Jon Meacham's biography of Thomas Jefferson was #2. *America Again* by Stephen Colbert and others, at #4, focused on how to bring America back to high standing in the world. Colbert has continued to pursue his interest in this theme through his late-night satirical critiques of the Trump administration. The testimony of former Navy SEALs was #5 at the end of 2012. This was followed by *Bruce*, a biography of Bruce Springsteen by Peter A. Carlin, *Roll Me Up and Smoke Me When I Die* by country music star Willie Nelson, and *Waging Heavy Peace*, a memoir from rocker Neil Young. *The Last Lion* by William Manchester and Paul Reid completed Manchester's biography of Winston Churchill. *The Patriarch* by David Nasaw tells the story of the life of Joseph Kennedy.

2013

The year 2013 began with John Grisham's *The Racketeer* at #1. This was followed by the Tom Clancy and Mark Greaney story *Threat Vector*. *Gone Girl* was back at #1 on January 13. Robert Jordan's *A Memory of Light* was #1 on January 27. George Saunders's *Tenth of December*, at #3, was the first collection of short stories to enter the top three since the collections of Stephen King's stories. Saunders is a fine writer, whose novel *Lincoln in the Bardo* would appear on the bestseller list in March 2017. *Kinsey and Me* by Sue Grafton also rose to a place among the top of the list. *Private Berlin* by James Patterson and Mark Sullivan went to #1 on February 10. Danielle Steel's *Until the End of Time* features two relationships that intersect and come together. *Gone Girl* was #2 and then returned to #1 on February 24. Patterson was back at #1 with *Alex Cross, Run* on March 10. *A Week in Winter* by Maeve Binchy was #2. It was a posthumous publication: Binchy had died in 2012. *Calculated in Death* by J. D. Robb was the next #1 bestseller; *The Striker* by Clive Cussler and Justin Scott was #2. *The Storyteller* by Jodi Picoult was #3. Set in New Hampshire, this novel refers to Holocaust stories. *Gone Girl*, still strong on the list, was #4. *Frost Burned* by Patricia Briggs was #1 on March 24. In Briggs's story shape-shifter Mercy Thompson is featured.

April began with Harlan Coben's *Six Years* at #1 on April 7. *Six Years* tells the story of a man who loved a woman who married someone else. *Lover at Last* by J. R. Ward followed at #1 on April 14. In Debbie Macomber's *Starting New*, topping the list on April 21, a Seattle lawyer loses a job and changes her life, supporting a knitting store. On April 28, *Daddy's Gone A'Hunting* by Mary Higgins Clark was her story about two sisters and a threat that returns from their family's past. It was another of Mary Higgins Clark's April/early May #1 bestsellers. *Don't Go* by Lisa Scottoline was #2 on the bestseller list.

With May came *Whiskey Beach* by Nora Roberts, rising to #1 on May 5. Readers went back in time in Paulo Coelho's *Manuscript Found in Accra*, which tells the story of a wise man in a Copt sect in Jerusalem before the influx of the Crusaders in 1099. *The Hit* by David Baldacci was #1 on May 12. Will Robie is a government hit man, and he uncovers a threat. On May 26 *Dead Ever After* by Charlaine Harris, at #1, was another Sookie Stackhouse–*True Blood* novel. Then June 2 brought Dan Brown's *Inferno* to the top to the list. *Inferno*, which traces the outlines of

Dante's poem and adds murder and intrigue, remained at #1 through June 30. *And the Mountains Echoed* by Khaled Hosseini, #2, focuses on a family in Afghanistan. *Best Kept Secret* by Jeffrey Archer was #4. In Neil Gaiman's *The Ocean at the End of the Lane*, a man recalls his childhood. The novel reached #1 on July 7. *The Inferno* was back at #1 on July 14 and July 28. *Second Honeymoon* by James Patterson and Howard Roughan was #2 on July 14. *Hidden Order* by Brad Thor was #2 on July 28. *The English Girl* by Daniel Silva reached #1 on August 4.

J. K. Rowling, writing as Robert Galbraith, had the #1 fiction bestseller on August 11 with *Cuckoo's Calling*. In the story, Cameron Strike investigates an apparent suicide. *Inferno* by Dan Brown was #2 and Daniel Silva's *The English Girl* was #3. The month of August concluded with *Cuckoo's Calling* at #2, closely followed on the list by *Mistress* by James Patterson and David Ellis. In *Mistress*, a man who has been living a split or dual existence inquires into the death of a friend. Louise Penney's *How the Light Gets In*, a novel published by St. Martin's Press, was #1 on September 15.

In the autumn of 2013, Lee Child's character Jack Reacher returned to #1 with *Never Go Back*. The story was transformed into a film with Tom Cruise in the lead role. Sue Grafton's *W Is for Wasted* was #1 on September 29. *The Longest Ride* by Nicholas Sparks was #1 on October 6, followed by Nelson DeMille's *The Quest* at #2. In DeMille's story, a journalist and an elderly priest who has escaped from jail in Ethiopia team up to search for a missing relic. In *Doctor Sleep* Stephen King brought back his character Dan from *The Shining*. As an adult with psychic abilities, he helps a threatened child. *Gone* by James Patterson and Michael Ledwidge was #3. Jhumpa Lahiri's *The Lowland* was also in the list's top five. Thomas Pynchon's *Bleeding Edge* was #6. *Storm Front* by John Sandford rose to #1 on October 27.

Early November brought Stephen King's *Doctor Sleep* to the top of the bestseller list. Elizabeth George's *Just One Evil Act* was #2. Then John Grisham appeared with his novel *Sycamore Row*. His sequel to *A Time to Kill* went to #1 on November 10. *The Goldfinch* by Donna Tartt was #2 with the story of a painting smuggled out of the Metropolitan Museum of Art. The painting is removed during an emergency incident. Tartt's novel *The Goldfinch*, which followed her top-selling book *The Secret History*, was assessed in *Vanity Fair* by Evgenia Peretz, who took up the persistent question: "But who decides what is literary art?" The article suggests that "the future of reading itself" is at stake in how we answer that question with respect to Tartt's novel ("It's Tartt—but Is It Art?" *Vanity Fair*, June 11, 2014). In the story a thirteen-year-old makes a trip to the Metropolitan Museum of Art, and a terrorist bomb goes off. In the chaos, the protagonist leaves the building with a 1654 painting known as *The Goldfinch*. *New York Times* reviewer Michiko Kakutani called Tartt's work "a glorious Dickensian novel," but Francine Prose wrote that she saw very little in it that was Dickensian in the author's use of language. In the *Paris Review* Lorin Stein asserted that Tartt deals in clichés and coats her story with "literary gentility."[2] Yet, amid the divergent reviews came appreciations of the intrigue and energy of the story.

Scott Turow's *Identical* (#4) contributed toward readers' interest in lawyers and legal thrillers at this time. Meanwhile, Wally Lamb returned to the list with *We Are Water* and Mitch Albom returned with *The First Phone Call from Heaven*. On December 1, Mitch Albom's novel went to #1, entertaining readers with a story about phone calls that are coming from heaven to a town in Michigan. Following Grisham's #2 novel was Patricia Cornwell's story of Kay Scarpetta's investigation of the murder of an MIT computer engineer. Janet Evanovich's character Stephanie Plum returned to #1 in *Takedown Twenty* on December 8. *Cross My Heart* by James Patterson was #1 on December 15. Alex Cross's family is threatened by a mad genius who wants to prove that he is the greatest and most cunning criminal of all time. In Tom Clancy's final novel, *Command Authority*, written with Mark Greaney, President Jack Ryan and his son again face the Russian problem. The Lincoln Lawyer Mickey Haller was at #3 in Michael Connelly's *The Gods of Guilt*. The same books continued high on the bestseller list the next week. On December 29, John Grisham's *Sycamore* finished the year at #1. Mitch Albom's *The First Phone Call from Heaven* was #2. *Command Authority* by Clancy and Greaney was #3. Donna Tartt's *Goldfinch* was #4. (Tartt's novel would win the Pulitzer Prize.) These books were followed by the novels by Stephen King (#5), James Patterson (#6), and Michael Connelly (#7).

2014

Imagine the busy book editor slipping into a seat on the commuter train. A hint of perfume lingers on her collar. Her briefcase is stuffed with sheaves of paper. She opens her laptop as a cell phone rings from the seat behind her. The publicist is still at his desk, five o'clock, eyes on the screen, a trickle of sweat forming on his brow, despite the AC on low in the office. A deadline is looming for the copy he must write by tomorrow. The literary agent scurries down the avenue, satisfied with the pitch she made that afternoon. She has a lunch meeting in the theater district tomorrow. Evening shadows fall even as the buildings are bathed in sunset.

Books. Pack them up. Push them. Drive them across the world on highways; fly them across the sky. The reader is waiting. The bookstore manager receives a shipment. The librarian catalogs another book and places it on the shelf. "Read me!" those books seem to cry from silent spaces, like characters come to life in an Alice in Wonderland tale.

And there is John Grisham again. The calendar turns to 2014, and *Sycamore Row* begins the year at #1. Donna Tartt's *Goldfinch* is #1 on January 19. *The Invention of Wings* by Sue Monk Kidd fictionalizes the life of the abolitionist Sarah Grimke in Charleston. In her story, Grimke is given a slave for her eleventh birthday. James Patterson has teamed with another writer, Emily Raymond, for *First Love* (#2) in which sixteen-year-old Axi Moore invites her friend on a road trip they are going to keep a secret. *Wings* and *Goldfinch* lead the list the next week. Anna Quindlen's *Still Life with Breadcrumbs* is at #3. In Quindlen's story a photographer rents a cottage in the country and has an artistic-spiritual epiphany. U.S. postage stamps now cost forty-nine cents. (Who writes letters anymore?) President Obama's State of the Union address emphasizes jobs and immigration reform. A Super Bowl game is played by the Seattle Seahawks and the Denver Broncos in the cold winter air in the New Jersey Meadowlands. *Twelve Years a Slave* is awarded best picture. The Winter Olympics begin in Russia.

In 2014, the James Patterson bestseller mill was alive and well. On March 2, *Private L.A.*, a novel written with Mark Sullivan, was #1. When a celebrity couple disappears, the series characters Jack Morgan and Justine Smith search for them. J. D. Robb's *Concealed in Death* was #1 the next weekend, on March 9. *The Undead* by Kim Harrison was another vampire novel that reached #1 on March 16. Her character Rachel Morgan is engaged in a supernatural battle. On March 21 Russia annexed Crimea. The United Nations General Assembly reacted to this. American readers escaped into Brandon Sanderson's fantasy *Words of Radiance*: #2 on March 23. Clive Cussler and Justin Scott's *Bootlegger* was #2. On

March 30, *Power Play* by Danielle Steel obtained the #1 spot with a story of male and female chief executive officers.

Missing Lion by Harlan Coben was #1 on April 6. His police detective seeks an ex-fiancée and her father's murderer. Why are online dating users now disappearing? With *NYPD Red*, with cowriter Marshall Karp, James Patterson put his third story of the year on the top of the bestseller list. *The King*, in J. R. Ward's Black Dagger series, then went to #1 on April 20. The United States issued sanctions on Russia on April 28.

Like rain, flowers, sunshine, springtime, and other inevitable features of the season, Mary Higgins Clark had another novel blossoming up in sales: *I've Got You under My Skin*. Here was the Cole Porter song title pinned like a bright corsage onto a story about a true crime television show producer who faces show participants with dark secrets. The suspense story proceeded to uncover the disturbing facts of a murder. Mary Higgins Clark's story went to #1 on April 27.

On May 4 Nora Roberts's *The Collector* became the #1 fiction book in America. *The Target* by David Baldacci replaced it in the #1 position on May 11 and remained at #1 the next week. Baldacci's team of Will Robie and Jessica Reed faces a crafty adversary. Greg Iles's *Natchez Burning* was #2. Penn Cage, a former prosecutor, investigates a crime. A doctor has been accused of killing a nurse. *Unlucky* by James Patterson and Maxine Paetro was commercially lucky on May 25. Past bestsellers by Patterson entertained a large and loyal audience. By now those readers were primed for another story. They anticipated and bought this new story featuring Lindsey Boxer and the Women's Murder Club, sending it to #1. This was James Patterson's third #1 of the year (and it was still only the month of May). John Sandford's *Field of Prey* rose to #2. In *Skin Game* by Jim Butcher, his Chicago magician-detective helps an enemy break into a vault. *Ghost Ship* by Clive Cussler and Graham Brown was #3. (Despite Cussler's adventures now being cowritten it was not likely he would keep pace with the James Patterson fiction factory.) Emily Giffin's *The One and Only* was #4.

Summer brought *Mr. Mercedes* by Stephen King to #1 at the time of the summer solstice, on June 22. One might ask if a novel like this could give a terrorist an awful idea. In King's story, a motorist drives into a crowd at a job fair. The villain then informs an ex-policeman that a worse attack is yet to come. Other novels in the top five included *Written in My Own Heart's Blood* by Diana Gabaldon and *Top Secret Twenty One* by

Janet Evanovich, which became #1 on July 6. J. K. Rowling, writing as Robert Galbraith, returned to the list with *The Silkworm* and Detective Cormoran Strike.

James Patterson's annual summer bestseller was *Invisible*. The *New York Times Book Review* described this story by Patterson and David Ellis as one in which a FBI researcher looks for the murderer who killed his sister and finds a series of other apparently unconnected cases. One reader on Goodreads writes that he got as far as three pages—the first chapter—and he gave up. "He doesn't even write his books anymore," that reader complained. *Act of War* by Brad Thor was #1 on July 27: one of those rare bestsellers where an author's title rhymes with the author's last name. Counterterrorist agent Scot Harvath is at work as the United States faces an imminent attack. Catherine Coulter's *Power Play* was #2 with a detective team: Dillon and Lacey. The detective team had by now become a common thread in bestsellers. They could be found in books by James Patterson [et al.] and seem to have paralleled the rise of the collaborative two-author book.

The Book of Life by Deborah Harkness was #1 on August 3. The story was part of what she cast as an "All Souls" trilogy with her vampire hunter protagonist. *The Heist* by Daniel Silva was #2, with Gabriel Allon working with his team of Mossad agents. Silva's novel went to #1 on August 10. *Support and Defend*, listed at #2 on that day, was written by Mark Greaney in the manner of Tom Clancy. Its protagonist Dominic Caruso was doing much of the supporting and defending. *A Perfect Life* by Danielle Steel entered the top five with the story of a television anchor who faces public revelations of her private life. Liane Moriarty's *Big Little Lies*, #1 on August 17, features three mothers with children who became friends. *Big Little Lies* found its way to television. Readers were also entertained by Lev Grossman's story of Quentin, an exiled magician, in *The Magician's Island*. It is not Shakespeare's *The Tempest* but it did sell well. It reached #2 at the same time as *The Lost Island* by Preston and Child, with their character Gideon Crew. One might wonder what it was about islands that readers were drawn toward in summertime. Maybe they wanted to go visit one?

The Long Way Home by Louise Penny, a book published by the Minotaur imprint, was #1 on September 14. In her story, Armand Ganache is seeking a neighbor's missing husband. In *Personal* by Lee Child, his protagonist Jack Reacher is assisting the U.S. Department of State to keep members of the G8 summit away from a sniper. Father Tim Kavanagh went home in Jan Karon's #2 *Somewhere Safe with Somebody Good*. *The Bone Clocks* by David Mitchell brought readers across the medieval Alps to Australia and to Shanghai. Ken Follett's *Edge of Eternity* was another development of his story of five family experiences across history.

James Patterson made two more contributions to the top of the bestseller list. *Burn* by Patterson and Michael Ledwidge was #1 on October 19. *Hope to Die*, an Alex Cross story, was #1 on December 14. Following *Burn*, Jodi Picoult's *Leaving Time* was #1 on November 2 with the story of an investigation by a psychic and a detective. John Grisham's *Gray Mountain* was #1 on November 9 and remained #1 for several weeks. *Burning Room* by Michael Connelly was #2 and slipped to #4 behind Patricia Cornwell's *Flesh and Blood* at #3. On December 7, *The Escape* by David Baldacci was #1. *Hope to Die* held the #1 spot for the next two weeks. As the year came to an end, Grisham's *Gray Mountain* returned to #1 on December 28. *All the Light We Cannot See* by Anthony Doerr was #2.

2015

Gray Mountain by John Grisham remained #1 as 2015 began. Stephen King's *Revival* rose to #2. James Patterson's *Hope to Die* was #3. Anthony Doerr's *All the Light We Cannot See* went to #1 on January 18 and January 25. It won the 2015 Pulitzer Prize. The story concerns a blind French girl and a German boy who meet in occupied France during the Second World War. The girl's father is the Museum of Natural History director, and she is introduced to Jules Verne's *Twenty Thousand Leagues under the Sea*, which she reads in braille. Coming up the list was *The Girl on the Train* by Paula Hawkins. In her story, a troubled young woman sees too much as she passes through the suburbs while on a train. On February 1 and February 8 the novel went to #1. *All the Light We Cannot See* was #2. *Saint Odd* by Dean Koontz was #3. *Private Vegas* by James Patterson and Maxine Paetro also entered the top five. *Trigger Warning* by Neil Gaiman was also in the top five.

The Girl on the Train remained #1 in March and repeatedly returned to #1 during the next few months. The novel was *USA Today*'s #1 of the year. Patterson's *NYPD Red*, *The Liar* by Nora Roberts, and Harlan Coben's *The Straight* were the #2 novels behind it on the *New York Times* and *Publishers Weekly* lists in March and April. Toni Morrison was on the bestseller list in May. John Sandford's *Gathering Prey*, *Memory Man* by David Baldacci, and *14th Deadly Sin* by James Patterson and Maxine Paetro all went to #1 for a week. So did *Radiant Angel* by Nelson De-Mille on June 14 and Stephen King's *Finders Keepers* on June 21. *The English Spy* by Daniel Silva was #1 on July 19. *Truth or Die*, a James Patterson novel with Howard Roughan, was #2.

The recently rediscovered *Go Set a Watchman* by Harper Lee became #1 on August 2. *USA Today* placed both *Go Set a Watchman* and *To Kill a Mockingbird* in its bestseller top ten for the year. Jean Louise Finch goes home to Maycomb, Alabama, to discover that her father was not as perfect as he seemed to be. *X* is what Sue Grafton called her next novel. *X* marked the spot of #1 on September 13. In that novel, the Xs lead Kinsey Millhone to secrets that revive a cold case. Harper Lee's novel was #2. *The Nature of the Beast* by Louise Penney was #3. With *The Girl in the Spider's Web* David Lagercrantz continued Stieg Larsson's characters Lisbeth Salander and Mikael Blomkvist in a new adventure. The book was #1 on September 20. *Purity* by Jonathan Franzen tells a story of college debt and a character in need of redemption. A *Star Wars* novel also rose into the top five. On September 27 the #1 novel was *Make Me* by Lee Child: another Jack Reacher story.

On October 4 the success of *Make Me* and *The Girl in the Spider's Web* continued with these books at #1 and #2. *Come Rain or Shine* by Jan Karon rose to #1 on October 11. *The Murder House* by James Patterson and David Ellis (#1 on October 18) tells the story of a murder investigation in the Hamptons. A local investigator and a New York City policeman team up to uncover the clues. *After You* by Jo Jo Mayes brought a new author to the list. In her story, Louisa Clark grieves over the death of Will Traynor, and she enters a support group. On October 25 *The Survivor* by Vince Flynn, a novel completed by Kyle Mills after Flynn's death, was #1. *The Knight of the Seven Kingdoms* by George R. R. Martin, another series of episodes in the *Game of Thrones* saga, was #2.

The last two months of 2015 were a time during which the usual suspects, the brand-name authors, again dominated the list: Nicholas Sparks, John Grisham, Stephen King. Patricia Cornwell, Janet Evanovich, James Patterson. Even Tom Clancy had a #1 book, even though he didn't write it. Clancy had died and Mark Greaney produced *Commander in Chief*, another "Tom Clancy" novel. *See Me* by Nicholas Sparks was #1 with couples with secrets in their past. *Rogue Lawyer* by John Grisham went to #1 on November 8. *Career of Evil* by J. K. Rowling as Robert Galbraith also rose into the top three. *The Bazaar of Bad Dreams* by Stephen King, a collection of twenty stories, was #1 on November 22. Toward the end of November Mitch Albom brought another distinctive title to the top five: *The Magic Strings of Frankie Presto*. This is the story of a fictional musician, one told by a narrator who is the voice of music. Frankie was an orphan in Spain in 1936 who witnessed a church burning. When he arrives in the United States, all he has is his guitar. He meets music personalities: Hank Williams, Elvis Presley, Little Richard, and the Beatles. Also appearing on the list at #6 was *Crimson Shore*, another entertaining story by Douglas Preston and Lincoln Child featuring their Agent Pendergast. John Irving's *Avenue of Mysteries* appeared on the list at #15.

On December 6, *Tricky Twenty-Two* by Janet Evanovich was #1. On December 13, James Patterson's Alex Cross returned to Statesville, North Carolina, in *Cross Justice*. On December 20, Grisham's *Rogue Lawyer* was #1, Patterson's *Cross Justice* was #2, and Mark Greaney's Tom Clancy novel *Commander in Chief* was #3. Greaney focuses on a conflict between the West and the Russian president who is behind violent outbreaks around the world. Greaney's novel was among the top bestsellers on *USA Today*'s 2015 fiction list, along with *Rogue Lawyer* and *Cross Justice*.

Nonfiction bestsellers at the end of the year included Jon Meacham's *Destiny and Power*, a study of the life of George H. W. Bush. *Killing Reagan* by Bill O'Reilly and Martin Dugard was #2. There was also book of photographs, *Humans of New York*, which reached #1. Songstress Carly Simon's memoir *Boys in the Trees* was also among the top nonfiction bestsellers.

2016

John Grisham's *The Rogue Lawyer* was #1 during the first week in January. It was the fourth consecutive year in which a Grisham novel began at the #1 position. His novels had been in the top five each January since 2011. *All the Light We Cannot See* was #2 on January 3, and James

Patterson's newest Alex Cross story was #2 on January 10. *All the Light We Cannot See* went to #1 on January 17. *The Force Awakens*, a *Star Wars* movie novel, became the #1 bestseller the next weekend on January 24. The film had been released on December 19, 2015, and was a box office smash.

My Name Is Lucy Barton by Elizabeth Strout became the #1 book on January 31. The title character writes of her childhood: "Books brought me things. They made me feel less alone." *Blue* by Danielle Steel, #1 on February 7, tells the story of a woman whose life is turned upside down and who becomes friendly with a boy. James Patterson and Marshall Karp hit #1 the next week with *NYPD Red 4*. On February 21, J. D. Robb's *Brotherhood in Death* was #1. The month of February concluded with *Morning Star* by Pierce Brown, a science fiction dystopia, at #1.

In early March, Jeffrey Archer's *Cometh the Hour* was #1. Archer tells a family story of the Cliftons and the Barringtons. *All the Light* rose to #1 on March 13. Debbie Macomber's *A Girl's Guide to Moving On* was #2. On March 20, #1 was *The Gangster* by Clive Cussler and Justin Scott, in which Isaac Bell, a detective, faces off against a crime boss in the time of Theodore Roosevelt. Readers did not only visit the past. Current news and domestic anxieties were turned into fiction. On March 27, C. J. Box's *Off the Grid* was #1 with the story of the search for a domestic terror cell. *Fire Touched* by Patricia Briggs featured Mercy Thompson, the shape-shifter.

On April 3, *Private Paris* by James Patterson and Mark Sullivan was #1. Jack Morgan is the head of a global investigation agency that investigates notable figures in France. *Property of a Noblewoman* by Danielle Steel was #2. On April 10 *Fool Me Once* by Harlan Coben was #1 in its first week on the list. Mary Higgins Clark's *As Time Goes By* followed Coben's novel at #1 on April 24. A television journalist seeks her birth mother, and there is the trial of the widow of a wealthy doctor. More #1s followed: *The Obsession* by Nora Roberts, *The Last Mile* by David Baldacci, and *Extreme Prey* by John Sandford. In late May, *The 15th Affair* by James Patterson and Maxine Paetro with the Women's Murder Club and Lindsey Boxer was #1. *The Apartment* by Danielle Steel featured four women in a loft in Hell's Kitchen in New York.

In Joe Hill's #1 *The Fireman* an epidemic causes spontaneous combustion. A nurse in New Hampshire tries to stay alive despite the infection. She is assisted by the mysterious fireman. While Joe Hill made his way on his own as a creative writer, it had by this time become known by the audience that Joe Hill was Stephen King's son. Joe Hill's novel was still on the list on June 12 when *The City of Mirrors* by Justin Cronin became #1. *The Emperor's Revenge* by Clive Cussler and Boyd Morrison, another collaborator, was #1 on June 19. Stephen King's *End of Watch* was #1 on June 26.

Summertime had often brought a Stephen King novel, or a collection of his stories. There is ample testimony that King's fiction is read avidly by both male and female readers. The next bestsellers on the list, however, indicated an apparent divide between reading by men and reading by women that had become a trend across the past decade. *End of Watch*, at #1, was followed on the list by Brad Thor's *Foreign Agent*. This was another story featuring Thor's character Scot Harvath, who is a counter-terrorism agent. Harvath seeks an informant who affected a U.S. mission in Syria. One might call that a male reader's book. The #3 book on the bestseller list was *The Girls* by Emma Cline, a book that appears to be tailored specifically for female readers. It is not the kind of book that men would ordinarily run to Barnes & Noble to get a copy of. Next on the list was Mark Grant Blackwood's *Duty of Honor*, written on the model of Tom Clancy. Clancy again gets the credit for a book he did not entirely write. One can dig into the papers left by the author and write the kind of story that Clancy would have written. "Tom Clancy" has become a marketing label, a sign that the reader can expect a suspenseful book. Clancy's books, of course, were read by many women. However, there may be something of a gender divide between readers of Brad Thor's *Foreign Agent* and Emma Cline's *The Girls*.

First Comes Love by Emily Giffin (#1 on July 17) and Danielle Steel's *Magic* (#1 on July 24) each have the feel of books marketed to female readers. In Giffin's novel, sisters overcome their differences and reconcile. In *Magic* three couples have dinner in Paris. They may be in Paris, but they could just as easily be in a more prosaic setting like their backyards in America. That is where Liane Moriarty places her characters in *Truly Madly Guilty* (#1 on August 14). Three couples have a backyard barbeque that becomes a mess. These stories are more oriented toward relationships and the home than Daniel Silva's *The Black Widow* (#1 on July 31), a spy story that ranges across the European Continent. *Bullseye* by James Patterson and Michael Ledwidge likely had a wide crossover audience of male and female readers. However, how many men read

Sweet Tomorrows by Debbie Macomber? Do these novels reinforce gender stereotypes? The separation of spheres once positioned women in the domestic sphere and men in the commercial world. That has largely changed. Many of our bestsellers today feature the strong, independent woman in the world. More conventional bestsellers of the past embraced romance, home and family, and friendly (or not so friendly) couples. Even so, many bestsellers today continue to represent a kind of wishful thinking and escapism.

The *Underground Railroad* by Colin Whitehead, a bestseller in the late summer of 2016, faces a hard reality. It is the story of a slave girl who seeks freedom. The *Underground Railroad* appears to be a favorite of reading groups at several libraries around the United States. It shot to #1 in early September 2016. The *Los Angeles Times* featured the novel as one of the "most important" books of 2016. The novel won the Pulitzer Prize in 2017. On September 18, *A Great Reckoning* by Louise Penny went to #1. In this story an instructor at a police academy is murdered. Did one of the police trainees do it? Penny's series character Armand Gamache investigates. There was continuing reader interest in the mystery/detective story. Nora Roberts was still writing stories under both her own name and that of J. D. Robb. It was J. D. Robb's *Apprentice in Death* that was #1 on September 25. Ann Patchett's *Commonwealth* was #1 on October 2. The story follows two families across five decades. The family saga, which was also at the center of Ken Follett's series of books, enables the writer to gather in a good deal of recent history as well as to explore human relationships.

The genre novel continues to dominate the bestseller list: mystery, romance, the thriller, and the family saga. In fall 2016, Harlan Coben's *Home* connected American suburban life with the mystery story, his specialty. Myron Bolitar and his friend Win trace the whereabouts of a boy who was kidnapped ten years earlier. A new name appeared on the bestseller list when Ruth Ware's *Woman in Cabin 10* reached #4 on October 9. James Patterson and Maxine Paetro hit #1 on October 16 with *Woman of God*. Nicholas Sparks's *Two by Two*, #1 on October 23, tells the tale of a single father who finds new love. *The Trespassers* by Tana French, which was among the top five bestsellers at that time, gives readers the story of how Antoinette Conway would unravel a complex case involving murders in Dublin. *Small Great Things* by Jodi Picoult (#1 on October

30) focused on a medical crisis, an African American nurse, a white supremacist, and a lawyer.

The month of November brought *Escape Clause* by John Sandford to #1. *Two by Two* by Sparks was #2. *Small Great Things* by Picoult was #3. The #4 book was *Obsidian Chamber* by Preston and Child in which Agent Pendergast has to trace the whereabouts of his ward Constance, who has been kidnapped. We follow the quirky character in his quest across the world. On November 13, John Grisham's *The Whistler* was #1. In his story, someone in Florida lets an investigator know that there is corruption being perpetrated by mob members. The world has to be set right again. Danielle Steel's *Rushing Waters* entered the list at #3. *Whistler* stayed #1 on November 20. The #2 book was Michael Connelly's *The Wrong Side of Goodbye*, in which Harry Bosch helps the police track down a serial rapist. *Night School* by Lee Child was #1 the next week. Child's series character Jack Reacher is on a case that connects him with the army, the FBI, and the CIA.

Turbo Twenty Three by Janet Evanovich was #1 as December 2016 began. David Baldacci's *No Man's Land* was #2. James Patterson's *Cross the Line* immediately shot to #1 with a story in which Alex Cross and his wife pursue villains in Washington, D.C. *Cross the Line* and Grisham's *The Whistler* each vied for #1 throughout the month. Mark Greaney, a collaborator with Tom Clancy before his passing, produced another "Tom Clancy" novel with the patriotic title *True Faith and Allegiance*, in which Jack Ryan and his son team up to oppose a secret organization. Grisham's *The Whistler* was #1 on December 18 and on December 25. It was destined for another new year #1. James Patterson's *Cross the Line* was the #2 fiction book in America. *Killing the Rising Sun* by Bill O'Reilly and Martin Dugard was the #1 nonfiction book at year's end, with an account of the American fight against the Japanese in the Second World War. Bruce Springsteen's autobiography, *Born to Run*, was on the bestseller list at #4. Much has been written about Springsteen, but this was the first book-length account of his life in his own words. He wrote it artfully, with an interesting narrative voice and style uniquely his own. The *Los Angeles Times* listed it as one of the "important" nonfiction books of the year.

2017

January 2017 brought the new presidential administration of Donald J. Trump. At the top of the nonfiction bestseller list was *Killing the Rising Sun* by Bill O'Reilly and Martin Dugard. *The Undoing Project* by Michael Lewis delved into behavioral economics. *The Magnolia Story*, at #3, emerged from an HGTV show, *Fixer Upper*. Springsteen's autobiography *Born to Run* was certainly not hiding on the backstreets. It remained at #4. *Hillbilly Elegy* by J. D. Vance, at #5, purportedly explained, at least in part, some of the populist middle America energy and economic concern that had elected Donald Trump to the White House. *Publishers Weekly* reported early in 2018 that *Hillbilly Elegy* was the #1 nonfiction bestseller of 2017. *Settle for More*, Megyn Kelly's book, written before she left Fox News for a new position at another network, was #6. Lin-Manuel Miranda and Jeremy McCarter's book on Alexander Hamilton was #7. In *All the Gallant Men*, #8, eye witness Donald Stratton recalls Pearl Harbor with writer Ken Gire. In January, *USA Today* listed *Harry Potter and the Cursed Child* as the #1 fiction bestseller of 2016. *Camino Island* by John Grisham was the novel *Publishers Weekly* recorded as the #1 bestseller in 2017. In his novel, thieves seek to steal F. Scott Fitzgerald's manuscripts at Princeton University's Firestone Library. (Of course, the vaults of *Camino Island* are figures of Grisham's fine imagination. The library at Princeton is nothing like the one described in the novel. Meanwhile, the Fitzgerald collection there is rather extensive and even expert librarians and researchers on this side of paradise are not familiar with all of it.)

Publishers Weekly continued its gauging of bestsellers and provided its wide range of book reviews. However, there were changes elsewhere. The number of lists carried by the *New York Times* were being trimmed in 2017. Book reviews editor Pamela Paul explained the changes to the Publishers Advertising and Marketing Association on March 1. Molly Wetta argued on the BookRiot website that the loss of a mass-market paperback list and attention to graphic novels was not representative of the book market. She argued against de-emphasizing digital sales.[3] Meanwhile, Amazon launched its bestseller list, to attempt to compete with the *New York Times* list. (Amazon subdivides the fiction list.) In *Slate Book Review*, Laura Miller reported that overall book sales had declined. The picture was a bit gloomy in 2017, she wrote.[4] On March 5,

Hillbilly Elegy went to #1 on most national bestseller lists. In *This Life I Live* (#2), Rory Feek, a songwriter whose wife died of cancer, tells the story of their time together. *Killing the Rising Sun* was #3. *The Magnolia Story* was listed at #4. *Big Agenda* (#5) presents the outline of a plan for the Trump administration. Of course, it was not as if Donald Trump was listening to this writer's ideas; Trump had ideas of his own. In mid-March, former president George W. Bush's *Portraits of Courage* emerged as a triumphant bestseller. The book consists of a series of paintings by President Bush of military service members, with brief biographies of the subjects of his paintings. *The Book of Joy* by the Dalai Lama and Bishop Desmond Tutu brought a message of hope to readers. They recommend embracing life's joy and sufferings and gaining a sense of peace in daily living.

With April, *Trump's War* by radio commentator Michael Savage went to #1 with Savage's assessment of the challenges that the new president faces. *Hillbilly Elegy* stayed strong at #2. Further down the list there were some interesting books. *Born a Crime* by Trevor Noah started on the bestseller list at #13. The new *Daily Show* host describes life in South Africa where he was born and issues of apartheid there. *Writer, Sailor, Soldier, Spy* at #14 sounds like a John le Carré title. It is Nicholas Reynolds's account of some of the dimensions of Ernest Hemingway's life. The book discusses Hemingway's involvement with espionage while he was in Cuba. However, Hemingway was primarily a writer. He was not a full-fledged spy, except perhaps in his imagination. Hemingway was never a soldier, although he did see war as an ambulance driver and as a war correspondent.

May brought us the Amazon charts, now listing the top twenty fiction and nonfiction books in Amazon's sales. *USA Today* was ranking 150 titles each week from online and bookstore data. *USA Today* drew upon statistics for sales at Doubleday Book Shops, Crown, Ingram, Walden Books, Hungry Mind in St. Paul, Joseph Beth in Lexington and Cincinnati, Lauriat, Scribner's, Waterstones of Boston, Tattered Cover Books in Denver, David Kidd in Tennessee, Bookland, Books-a-Million, and other booksellers.

On May 7 *The Fix* by David Baldacci rose to #1. *The Black Box* by James Patterson and David Ellis was #2. In *Anything Is Possible*, Elizabeth Strout's character Lucy Barton in rural Illinois returned to the bestseller list. James Patterson had his second bestseller on May 21 with *16th*

Seduction, written with Maxine Paetro. Reaching #1 on May 28, Paula Hawkins's follow-up to *The Girl on the Train* was *Into the Water*, a mystery about the drowning of women in a river in England. *No Middle Name* by Lee Child collected Jack Reacher stories. *Same Beach, Next Year* by Dorothea Benton Frank tells the story of two couples who become friends and visit the South Carolina coastal islands each year. On June 11, a newly discovered Michael Crichton story, *Dragon Teeth*, was #2. A college student named Johnson goes west on a scientific expedition. Two adversarial paleontologists tangle while studying fossils in 1870s Wyoming. The bones of a brontosaurus are discovered, and Johnson is chosen to deliver them across the Badlands where deadly Sioux attacks and nasty highwaymen are an ever-present threat. Wyatt Earp later makes a guest appearance. *Come Sundown* by Nora Roberts went to #1 on June 18. John Grisham's *Camino Real* shot to #1 on June 25 in its first week. *The Identicals* by Elin Hilderbrand offers the story of identical twins, separated when their parents divorced. One went to Nantucket and the other to Martha's Vineyard. *Tom Clancy: Point of Contact* kept the author's style alive years after the author was gone. A global financial catastrophe is confronted by Jack Ryan's son. Grisham's *Camino Real* remained at #1 for three weeks in July. *Murder Games* by James Patterson with Howard Roughan became Patterson's third bestseller of the year. On July 30, *House of Spies* by Daniel Silva was #1. *The Late Show* by Michael Connolly replaced it at #1 on August 6 and remained there through August 20. Debbie Macomber's *Any Dream Will Do* reached #1 on August 27.

September brought several new novels to #1: *Seeing Red* by Sandra Brown (September 3), *Y Is for Yesterday* by Sue Grafton (September 10), *Glass Houses* by Louise Penny (September 17), and John le Carré's *A Legacy of Spies* (September 24). Ken Follett took readers back to the religious wars between Catholic and Protestants in the time of Queen Elizabeth. His novel *A Column of Fire* led the fiction list on October 1. Stieg Larsson's character Lisbeth Salander appeared in another novel by David Lagercrantz. Stephen King and Owen King reached #1 on October 15 with *Sleeping Beauties*, in which women in Appalachia go to sleep and do not wake up. In *Don't Let Her Go*, Harlan Coben gives readers the story of detective Napoleon Duncan's investigation of the deaths of people who had been close to him. The *Wall Street Journal* reported the books *Sleeping Beauties* and *Don't Let Her Go* at #1 and #2, respectively.

The Cuban Affair by Nelson De Mille and Danielle Steel's *Fairy Tale* were in also top positions. That is when Dan Brown's *The Origin* jumped onto the bestseller list at #1 with another sequel to the adventures of symbologist Robert Langdon. *Publishers Weekly* listed *Origin* at #1 at the end of October.

Local or regional newspapers also recorded these books on their bestseller lists, with some variations. The *San Francisco Chronicle*, for example, placed *Exit West* by Mohsin Hamid and *Manhattan Beach* by Jennifer Egan among its list of the year's best books. The *Los Angeles Times*, in April 2018, named *Exit West* the fiction book of the year for 2017. These lists attend to the books of local authors. In 2017, the *San Francisco Chronicle* recommended *Less*, by San Francisco–based writer Andrew Sean Greer, a book that sold particularly well in the Bay Area. Greer's novel *Less* was named the Pulitzer Prize winner for fiction in April 2018. *The Color of Law* by Richard Rothstein, on segregation, and John A. Farrell's biography, *Richard Nixon: The Life*, were among its top picks for nonfiction. Farrell's study of Nixon was a runner up in the 2018 Pulitzer Prize awards for biography. The *Boston Globe* drew its list from the New England Independent Booksellers Association and designated it "Local Bestsellers." In August, *A Gentleman from Moscow* and *Manhattan Beach* held the top places. On December 13, those two novels were among the year's "best books" reviewed by the *Boston Globe*. The December 31 list of the *Wall Street Journal* had *Dog Man and Cat Kid* and *The Getaway* just ahead of Dan Brown's *Origin* and John Grisham's *Rooster Bar*. Walter Isaacson's *Leonardo Da Vinci* and Oprah Winfrey's *The Wisdom of Sundays* led its nonfiction list. Meanwhile, National Public Radio (NPR) made its choices of "The Best of 2017," selecting 350 titles. Carolyn Kellogg, named *Los Angeles Times* book editor in 2017, listed book data for 2017 on December 2. Kellogg, who served for six years with the National Book Critics Circle, also noted that Tom Hanks's short-story collection, *Uncommon Type*, was the #1 fiction book in on December 2. Pete Souza's photographs of President Obama comprised the #1 nonfiction book.

The nonfiction bestsellers of 2017 reflected a year of politics, Trump tweets, and television news commentary. Bill O'Reilly and Martin Dugard's *Killing the Rising Sun*, on World War II Japan, was joined on the list by O'Reilly's book with Bruce Feirstein, *Old School*, defending traditional values. Some critics, viewing O'Reilly's fall from grace, wondered if those values included respect for women. *A Colony in a Nation* by Chris Hayes of MSNBC looked at race relations. Chris Matthews glanced back to the 1960s for hope for today's America with his biography *Bobby Kennedy*. Other books took partisan positions on the nation's political divide. On May 7, Senator Elizabeth Warren's *This Fight Is Our Fight* was #1, and *Shattered*, an account of Secretary Hillary Clinton's presidential bid, was #2. Donna Brazile addressed Russian hacking of the Democratic National Committee. Al Franken's *Giant of the Senate* rose to #1, and soon he was a senator no more. Hillary Clinton's *What Happened* was a bestseller that looked back on the 2016 election. It continued to have a strong showing on bestseller lists into 2018.

2018

Something about adult bestseller lists may by now appear obvious. There is rapid turnover in the ratings among the books listed in them. Books dart in and out of the top positions on the lists like hotel visitors passing through a revolving door. *Fire and Fury* was all the rage for about three months in 2018. Then former FBI director James Comey's book tour lifted the controversial former FBI director's book *A Higher Loyalty: Truth, Lies, and Leadership* onto the bestseller charts. It was #2 on Amazon upon its release. Within the first week or so, more than one thousand consumer reviews appeared on the website for this book. *Publishers Weekly* and the *Wall Street Journal* listed the book at #1 on the weekend of April 28–29. However, it did not yet register on the *New York Times* list. Even with James Comey's multiple media appearances, his book was unlikely to sustain bestseller energy for more than a couple of months. Once upon a time a James Michener novel could hold the top position on the list for many months. However, during the past decade the top positions have shifted more quickly.

At the beginning of 2018, John Grisham's *The Rooster Barn* at #1 was followed on the fiction list by Dan Brown's *Origin* and James Patterson's *The People v. Alex Cross*. The *Los Angeles Times* listed *Manhattan Beach* and Tom Hanks's *Uncommon Type* atop its list. *Grant* by Ron Chernow was #1 and *Leonardo Da Vinci* by Walter Isaacson was #2 on the *L.A. Times* nonfiction list. On February 4 *The Woman in the Window* by A. J. Finn reached #1. In the novel, a woman in a Harlem townhouse may have seen a crime. *City of Endless Night* by Douglas Preston and Lincoln Child was #2. *Dark in Death* by J. D. Robb was the *Wall Street Journal*'s #1. *The Great Alone* by Kristin Hannah features a Vietnam veteran who takes his family to live in Alaska. The book was #1 on March 4. (Heavy snow across the northeast U.S. on March 7 was likely as deep as snow in Alaska.) Readers were invited to stretch across space and time. Neil deGrasse Tyson takes readers across the solar system with *Astrophysics for People in a Hurry*. The book remained high up on the bestseller lists throughout April. In *Enlightenment* (#2 on March 4), cognitive scientist Steven Pinker asserts that reason can be applied to any assessment of Western civilization and can overcome pessimistic perspectives. James Patterson produced a bestselling true crime nonfiction book. On April 1, *The Rising Sea* by Clive Cussler and Graham Brown was #1. Weeks later, on April 22, *I've Got My Eyes on You* by Mary Higgins Clark reached #1 immediately upon publication. By April 28 *The Fallen* by David Baldacci rose to #1 on the *New York Times* list and #2 on *Publishers Weekly*'s list.

Regional bestsellers reflected the national listings. On April 1 the *Los Angeles Times* listed *The Great Alone* by Kristin Hannah at #1. Meg Wolitzer's *The Female Persuasion* was #2 on its national list and #1 on its Bay Area list. *I've Been Thinking* by Maria Shriver led the nonfiction list, with the Michael Isikoff and David Corn book on the Russia, *Russian Roulette*, probe at #2. In paperback fiction, *A Wrinkle in Time* by Madeleine L'Engle was high up the list, because of a recent film release. Further down the *L.A. Times* list were some surprises: Joan Didion, James Baldwin's *The Fire Next Time*, and George Orwell's *1984*, which was at #10. The *Boston Globe* listed Richard Powers's novel *The Overstory* at #1 on April 23. Meg Wolitzer's *The Female Persuasion* was #2 on that list. Clearly that title echoed Jennifer Palmieri's address to women as #1 on the national nonfiction bestseller list cited by the *San Francisco Chronicle*. Madeleine Albright's *Fascism: A Warning* soon replaced it at #1. On April 29, the *Los Angeles Times* listed Meg Wolitzer's *The Female Persuasion* at #1 on its fiction list. Madeleine Albright's *Fascism: A Warning* was #1 on its nonfiction list. James Comey's *A Higher Loyalty* was #1 on the *Washington Post*'s bestseller list and #1 on the *Publishers Weekly* and *Wall Street Journal* national lists. *Circe* by Madeline Miller was #1 on the *New York Times* fiction bestseller list.

Biography soared to the top of the bestseller list early in 2018 with *Leonardo Da Vinci* by Walter Isaacson and *Grant* by Ron Chernow, as well as Chris Matthews's biography *Bobby Kennedy*. However, those biographies had dipped down off the *Times* list by April 15. Meanwhile, many serious readers engaged in book groups. Their reading intersected with questions about the internet and Facebook, the reliability of news media, and the war of words between the Trump administration and broadcast and print media.

Consequently, emphasis on American politics continued in 2018 on the nonfiction bestseller list. In January the top spots on the bestseller list included a book of photographs focusing on Barack Obama. There was also *Promise Me, Dad*, former vice president Joseph Biden's tribute to his son who had recently died. *Fire and Fury* by Michael Wolff shot to #1 with a gossipy tattle on the Trump administration. Similar books followed: David Frum's *Trumpocracy*; David Cay Johnston's *It's Even Worse Than You Think*; Michael Isikoff and David Corn's *Russian Roulette*, which was #1 in early April; Jennifer Palmieri's *Dear Madame President*; and James Comey's *A Higher Loyalty: Truth, Lies, and Leadership*, which began to rise on bestseller lists following its April 17 release. Meanwhile Madeleine Albright's *Fascism: A Warning* was #1 on both the *Publishers Weekly* and *New York Times* lists at the end of April.

Senator Ben Sasse of Nebraska did not write about politics in *The Vanishing American Adult* (2017). Rather, his book focused on encouraging resilience and character in children, teens, and young adults. They are a source of life, love, and energy in the present, and they are the future of America. Sasse recommended for them a reading program of great books that can instill learning, integrity, and imagination. These classics have not faded away like some bestsellers have. Classic works endure and contribute to thoughtfulness. Truly, some bestsellers entertain. Others enlighten and sustain us. Such books are not only of the past. They live on in our imaginative life as our contemporaries. Bestsellers can tell us something about our popular cultural life. Unique, classic works (including some bestsellers) reveal the human condition, broaden our perspective, and strengthen the human spirit. These dreams and voices from yesterday remain inspirations for each new beginning that we make as individuals and as a nation, for stories rich with imaginative promise are inspirations for all time.

NOTES

INTRODUCTION

1. Michael Korda, *Making the List: A Cultural History of the American Bestseller, 1900–1999* (New York: Simon and Schuster, 2001). As Korda points out, the sexy novel of one generation may seem tame and boring to a later generation (221–22). Some popular books are "extraordinary fads," Korda observes, pointing to Alexandra Ripley's sequel to *Gone with the Wind*. Her novel *Scarlett* was wildly popular for a brief time, selling 2.2 million copies according to *Publishers Weekly*. Then it was never heard from again (196). Korda's *Making the List* makes use of the *Publishers Weekly* listings, which began in 1912.

2. Laura J. Miller, "The Best-Seller List as Marketing Tool and Historical Fiction," in *Book History* 3 (2000): 286–304. See also John Bear, *The #1 New York Times Best Seller* (Berkeley, Calif.: Ten Speed, 1992).

3. Benedict Anderson, *Imagined Communities* (London: Verso, 1983), 37–38. *The Saturday Review of Books and Art* was created by Adolph Ochs of the *New York Times* in 1876 with the view that books could be treated as news. The *New York Times* hired book review editors. Saturday and Sunday literary supplements were a regular feature of newspapers that brought news of the book trade to readers in the first decade of the twentieth century. The supplement "became preeminent in terms of advertising dollars and circulation," observes Joan Shelley Rubin. See Joan Shelley Rubin, *The Making of Middlebrow Culture* (Chapel Hill: University of North Carolina Press, 1992), 40.

4. Gregory Cowles, "Inside the List," *New York Times Book Review*, June 2, 2013.

5. Leslie Howsam, *Old Books and New Histories: An Orientation to Studies in Book and Print Culture* (Toronto: University of Toronto Press, 2006), viii.

6. Howsam, *Old Books*, 5.

7. Miller, "Best-Seller List," 286.

8. Howsam, *Old Books*, 24. Elizabeth Long, *Book Clubs: Women and the Uses of Reading in Everyday Life* (Chicago: University of Chicago Press, 2003), 16–17.

9. Scott McCracken, *Pulp: Reading Popular Fiction* (Manchester, UK: Manchester University Press, 1998), 46.

10. McCracken, *Pulp*, 29.

11. Ruth Franklin, "Readers of the Pack: American Bestselling," *Book Forum*, 2011. See www.npr.org/2012/0n-writing-a-bestseller-there's-a-formula-shh.

12. Pierre Bourdieu, writing on "cultural capital," focuses on cultural knowledge of fields of study. This is not economic capital or symbolic capital. Bourdieu, *The Field of Cultural Production*, ed. Randal Johnson (New York: Columbia University Press, 1993), 7–8.

13. Martin Amis's comments appear in Michiko Kakutani, "Writers Martin Amis Admires, and He Should Know," *New York Times Book Review*, December 11, 2001, 327. This is a review of Amis's *The War against Cliché*. Martin Amis also spoke about Saul Bellow with the *Chicago Sun Times* on October 21, 2011.

14. Christine Berberich, ed., *The Bloomsbury Introduction to Popular Fiction* (London: Bloomsbury, 2015), 315.

15. Jonathan Franzen, "Why Bother? Perchance to Dream; In the Age of Images, a Reason to Write Novels." *Harper's*, April 2003, 62.

16. Robert Louis Stevenson, "A Humble Remonstrance" (1884), 3. In *Collected Works of Robert Louis Stevenson* (Oxford: Oxford University Press, 1938). (Orig. pub. 1925.)

17. Andreas Huyssen, *After the Great Divide: Modernism, Mass Culture, Postmodernism* (New York: Macmillan, 1986), vii–x.

18. Theodor Adorno, *The Culture Industry: Selected Essays on Mass Culture* (London: Routledge, 2001), 98.

19. Max Horkheimer, "Art and Mass Culture," in *Critical Theory: Selected Essays*, trans. Matthew J. O'Connell et al. (New York: Continuum, 2002), 273.

20. John Sutherland points to the "morally indignant" critic like Q. D. Leavis. Some have asked: Why bother with less than "good" books? John Sutherland, *Bestsellers: A Very Short Introduction* (Oxford: Oxford University Press, 2007), 1.

21. Rubin, *Making of Middlebrow Culture*, 143. Harry Scherman, a New York advertising man, started the Book of the Month Club in 1926. In 1927 the BOMC established a selection committee. They offered selections of books to 110,558 subscribers in 1929. Joan Shelley Rubin and Janice Radway have suggested that the word "club" recalls women's study clubs and reading circles, local groups with sociable relationships. This was the "club" for readers in a

modern world where they faced increasing anonymity. It was a way to feel like one was able to overcome the impersonal aspects of modern society. See Rubin, *Making of Middlebrow Culture*, 109.

22. Rubin, *Making of Middlebrow Culture*, 122.

23. John Sutherland, *Bestsellers: Popular Fiction of the 1970s* (London: Routledge, Kegan Paul, 1981), 3. John Sutherland recalls Robert Escarpit's sociological study. There is a "distinctive selling curve": "a fast seller that develops into a steady seller" across time (Sutherland cites Robert Escarpit, *The Book Revolution* [London: Harrap, 1966], 118). Market forces push these novels "into speedy oblivion" (Sutherland, *Bestsellers: Popular Fiction*, 7). "It is always new but never an advance," Sutherland has asserted. The bestseller author has more a "rate of production" than "an oeuvre" (Sutherland, *Bestsellers: Popular Fiction*, 8). Even so, there are historical reasons for seeing bestseller as a natural end-product of the development of the novel and the market, he says (Sutherland, *Bestsellers: Popular Fiction*, 14). Authors in America have complained about increasing materialism. Sutherland has pointed out that publishing lasted longer in Britain as a profession of gentlemen (Sutherland, *Bestsellers: Popular Fiction*, 14–15).

24. Ken Gelder, *Popular Fiction: The Logic and Practices of a Literary Field* (New York: Routledge, 2004). Foster, 2002 p. 69, is cited by Gelder, *Popular Fiction*, 88.

25. Jonathan Mahler, "James Patterson Inc.," *New York Times Magazine*, January 20, 2010.

26. Gelder, *Popular Fiction*, 100; Scott McCracken, *Pulp*, 1; Miller, "Best-Seller List," 289.

27. Raymond Williams, *Marxism and Literature* (Oxford: Oxford University Press, 1977), 24. Sarah Churchwell and Thomas Ruys Smith follow the bestseller through the methods of new historicism. Churchwell and Smith look at each era to see what there may be about certain books that appealed to the public.

28. Miller, "Best-Seller List," p.288.

29. Julianne Chiaet, "Reading Literary Fiction Improves Empathy," *Scientific American*, October 4, 2013.

30. Paula Rabinowitz, *Pulp: How Paperbacks Brought Modernism to Main Street* (Princeton, N.J.: Princeton University Press, 2014), 277.

31. Rabinowitz, *Pulp*, 1.

32. Rabinowitz, *Pulp*, xii. Rabinowitz recalls reading Boris Pasternak's *Dr. Zhivago* in the summer between sixth and seventh grade.

33. Janice Radway, *Reading the Romance: Women, Patriarchy, and Popular Literature* (Chapel Hill: University of North Carolina Press, 1984). Robert Darnton has referred to this pattern of production and distribution of print as "the

communications circuit." Robert Darnton, "What Is the History of Books? *Daedelus* 111 (Summer 1982): 65–83.

34. Radway, *Reading the Romance* (1984), 190.

35. A reader of the *Journal of Popular Romance* may see an essay on Stephenie Meyer's *Twilight* like "Deconstructing *Twilight*" (Issue 5.2) or Beth Driscoll's "Teaching Nora Roberts's *Spellbound*" (Issue 4.2). In the first issue (1.1), the lead article was "A Little Extra Bite: Dis/Ability and Romance in Tanya Huff and Charlaine Harris's Vampire Fiction" by Kathleen Miller. This was followed by "Getting a Good Man to Love: Popular Romance and the Problem of Patriarchy." Among the other articles is a review of Northrup Frye's *Notebooks on Romance* and Christina Nehring's "A Vindication of Love: Reclaiming Romance for the Twenty-First Century."

36. Michael Denning, *Mechanic Accents: Dime Novels and Working-Class Culture in America* (London: Verso, 1998), 2. Denning quotes Bishop, 1879, p. 383.

37. David S. Miall, "Empirical Approaches to Studying Literary Readers: The State of the Discipline," *Book History* 9 (2006): 291–312.

38. Darnton, "What Is the History of Books?

39. Roger Chartier, *The Order of Books: Readers, Authors and Libraries in Europe*, trans. Lydia G. Cochrane (Stanford: Stanford University Press, 1992).

40. Pierre Bourdieu, *Distinction: A Social Critique of the Judgment of Taste*, trans. Richard Nice (Cambridge, Mass.: Harvard University Press, 1984), 2. Jonathan Rose, "Rereading the English Common Reader: A Preface to a History of Audiences," *Journal of the History of Ideas* 53 (1992): 48.

41. The Marxist proposition that social being determines consciousness can be found throughout the works of the cultural theorist Raymond Williams. For Williams's reflections on what Marx referred to as superstructure, see *Problems in Materialism and Culture* (London: Verso, 1982).

I. BIRTH OF THE BESTSELLER

1. *Publishers Weekly*, January 28, 1899, p. 173.

2. Alice Payne Hackett, *70 Years of Best Sellers, 1895–1965* (New York: Bowker, 1967), 20, 87.

3. Owen Wister Journals, pp. 9–10. You can read the journal online at the University of Wyoming's scan of its Owen Wister Archive.

4. Arthur Conan Doyle, *The Hound of the Baskervilles* (London: George Newnes, 1902), 19.

5. Edith Wharton, *The House of Mirth* (New York: Penguin Classics, 2003), 497.

6. *McClure's* 47 (May–October 1915): 31.

7. *Theosophical Outlook* 5–6 (1920): 46.

8. *Publishers Weekly*, Eyes of the World; Frank Luther Mott, *Golden Multitudes: The Story of Bestsellers in the United States* (New York: Macmillan, 1947).

9. Review of *The Gentleman from Indiana*, *New York Times* (June 1900): 415.

10. Hackett, *70 Years*, 72.

11. Dennis Drabelle, "Book World: Overdue Reissue of Ernest Poole's *The Harbor*," *Washington Post*, January 13, 2012.

12. *Publishers Weekly* 1408 (January 21, 1899): 52.

13. If you looked on Google Books in summer 2018, you might see a book cover featuring John Locke the British philosopher, who is certainly not the author of *Red Planet*. Also, Winston S. Churchill's image appears on a Google Books post of one of the novels by the American Winston Churchill.

14. Martin Gilbert, *The First World War* (London: Folio, 2000), 420. Early in the 1920s, British poet Robert Graves said: "I made several attempts during those years to rid myself of the poison of war by finishing my novel but had to abandon it." Robert Graves, *Goodbye to All That* (London: Jonathan Cape, 1929), 274.

15. Sinclair Lewis, *Elmer Gantry* (New York: Harcourt, 1927), 26. Martin Light provides us insights into Sinclair Lewis's reading and of the reading habits of his character Elmer Gantry in *The Quixotic Vision of Sinclair Lewis* (West Lafayette, Ind.: Purdue University Press, 1975).

16. Lewis, *Elmer Gantry*, 37.

17. Light, *Quixotic Vision*, 104. Light gives us a description of Frank Shallard.

18. Lewis, *Elmer Gantry*, 63.

19. Lewis, *Elmer Gantry*, 177.

20. H. L. Mencken, "The Library," *American Mercury* 10 (April 1927): 506.

21. Mark Schorer, *Sinclair Lewis* (New York: McGraw Hill, 1961).

22. Paul Fussell, *The Great War and Modern Memory* (Oxford: Oxford University Press, 1975). Alfred Bonadeo, "War and Degradation: Gleanings from the Literature of the Great War," *Comparative Literary Studies* 21 (1984): 409–33. F. F. Hill is quoted by Thomas Schneider in "The Truth about the War Finally: Critics' Expectations of War Literature during the Weimer Republic," *Journalism Studies* 17, no. 4 (June 2016): 490–501. Joseph Wood Krutch's review appears in *The Nation* (1929). Also see the chapter titled "Memory" in Modris Eksteins, *Rites of Spring: The Great War and the Modern Age* (New York: Houghton Mifflin, 2000), and *All Quiet on the Western Front Study Guide* (New York: McGraw Hill, 2000), 10.

23. Schneider, "Truth about the War."

24. Schneider, "Truth about the War."

25. "The Literary Lowbrow," *Saturday Evening Post*, July 15, 1933.

26. David Blight, *Beyond the Battlefield: Race, Memory, and the American Civil War* (Amherst: University of Massachusetts Press, 2002), 1. He cites James Baldwin's comment from "Unnamable Objects, Unspeakable Crimes," 1965.

27. Hackett, *70 Years*, 159.

2. THE 1940s

1. Jonathan Rose, "Modernity and Print I: Britain 1890–1970," in *Companion to History of the Book*, ed. Simon Eliot and Jonathan Rose (Malden, Mass.: Wiley-Blackwell, 2011), 350. Rose cites the *Time* figures in *Readers' Liberation* (New York: Oxford University Press, 2018), 75.

2. The *Detroit Tribune* reprinted book two of Richard Wright's *Native Son* in vol. 20, no. 18, July 18, 1942. The article on "The Art of the Negro" appeared October 23, p. 5.

3. Adler and Robert Hutchins introduced this program in the 1930 General Honors seminar and one based in the classical trivium and the quadrivium from 1936 to 1942. Joan Shelley Rubin, *The Making of Middlebrow Culture* (Chapel Hill: University of North Carolina Press, 1992), 188.

4. Rubin, *Making of Middlebrow Culture*, 190.

5. Rubin, *Making of Middlebrow Culture*, 195.

6. Rubin, *Making of Middlebrow Culture*, 325.

7. Rubin, *Making of Middlebrow Culture*, 326.

8. Ruth Moncrief and Hans Fisher recalled their lives to interviewers for the Rutgers University Oral History Project.

9. Rubin, *Making of Middlebrow Culture*, 299. Rubin points to a comment by Judith C. Waller of NBC's Central Division that the radio show is "the hardest to write" and make accessible. Listeners tend to turn on music on radio rather than talk.

10. Rubin, *Making of Middlebrow Culture*, 305.

11. Michael Korda, *Making the List: A Cultural History of the American Bestseller, 1900–1999* (New York: Simon and Schuster, 2001), 81.

12. Rose, *Readers' Liberation*, 77–78.

13. William Sherrill's "Good Books" was in the *Detroit Tribune* on June 6, 1942.

14. "You Can Abolish Prejudice" by Carl Murphy appeared October 23, 1943, in the *Detroit Tribune*.

15. "Books for Soldiers," *Detroit Tribune*, May 15, 1943.

16. "Ottley Says New Bestseller Shows Interest in Negro Problems," *Detroit Tribune*, September 11, 1943, 19.

17. "Formal Opening of the Community Library," *Midland Journal* (March 13, 1942): 1.

18. Wayne A. Wiegand, *Part of Our Lives: A People's History of the American Public Library* (New York: Oxford University Press, 2015).

19. *The Midland Journal* printed chapter 8 of *See Here, Private Hargrove* on August 29, 1943.

20. Roland Winter's comments appear in the Rutgers University Oral History Project interviews.

21. Alvin Fagon's interview appears in the Rutgers University Oral History Project.

22. Christopher Loos, *Military History Quarterly* (2000), pp. 826–27. A. J. Liebling, "A Reporter at Large," *New Yorker*, July 1, 1944, 38. "What the G.I. Reads" was mentioned in the *Saturday Evening Post* (1943).

23. Loos, *Military History Quarterly*, 827, 829.

24. Loos, *Military History Quarterly*, 829.

25. A claim by Brazilian critics was made that *A Sucessora* (*The Successor*) (1934) by Carolina Nabuco resembled *Rebecca* and was Daphne du Maurier's source.

26. Alice Payne Hackett, *70 Years of Bestsellers, 1895–1965* (New York: R. R. Bowker, 1967), 173.

27. Bert Tryon was interviewed by the Rutgers University Oral History Project. John Berglund was interviewed on April 9, 1998.

28. John Bear, *The #1 New York Times Best Seller* (Berkeley, Calif.: Ten Speed, 1992), 23.

29. Lloyd Duncan, *Just Getting There: An Autobiography* (self-pub., Xlibris, 2006), 196.

30. Duncan, *Just Getting There*, 56.

31. Duncan, *Just Getting There*, 238.

32. Duncan, *Just Getting There*, 56.

33. Duncan, *Just Getting There*, 189.

34. Interviews with Anne Rotholz, H. Boyd Woodruff, Frieda Finkelstein Feller, Herbert Gross, and Marion Pinsdorf were conducted by the Rutgers University Oral History Project. Pinsdorf became a scholar and later a member of the board at Drew University, Madison, New Jersey.

35. John Berglund interview, Rutgers University Oral History Project. April 9, 1998.

36. Roland Winter and Robert Hoen were interviewed by the Rutgers University Oral History Project.

37. Ruth Franklin, *Shirley Jackson: A Rather Haunted Life* (New York: Scribner's, 2016).

38. Elizabeth Venant, "One for the Books: Harold Robbins, the Icon of Sleaze, Is Back—and He's as Nasty as Ever," *Los Angeles Times*, May 31, 1991.

39. In the 1950s, *The Man in the Gray Flannel Suit* (1955) criticized conformity in the very middle class that made up much of the book's reading audience. See Korda, *Making the List*, 84–85.

3. THE 1950s

1. Alice Payne Hackett, *70 Years of Bestsellers, 1895–1965* (New York: R. R. Bowker, 1967), 3.

2. John Updike, "Personal Matters," in *More Matter: Essays and Criticism* (New York: Knopf, 1999), 760.

3. Hackett, *70 Years of Bestsellers*.

4. Hackett, *70 Years of Bestsellers*.

5. David Shields and Shane Salerno, *Salinger* (New York: Simon and Schuster, 2013); Margaret Salinger, *Dreamcatcher* (New York: Scribner's, 2001).

6. Chris Kubica and Will Hochman, *Letters to J. D. Salinger* (Madison: University of Wisconsin Press, 2002), 157.

7. Kubica and Hochman, *Letters to J. D. Salinger*, 155.

8. Kubica and Hochman, *Letters to J. D. Salinger*, 151.

9. Kubica and Hochman print a letter to Salinger from Elizabeth N. Kuria, whose dissertation was "Dialectic of the Active and the Contemplative in the Religious Vision of J. D. Salinger," Indian Institute of Technology, Madras, 1988, pp.137–38.

10. On January 10, 2016, *Washington Post* writer John Kelly reflected on the Lait and Mortimer book.

11. Hackett, *70 Years of Bestsellers*.

12. Hackett, *70 Years of Bestsellers*.

13. Clive Bloom, *Spy Thrillers: From Buchan to le Carré* (Basingstoke: Palgrave Macmillan, 1990), 5.

14. Alan Elsner, "Re-reading Leon Uris' *Exodus*," *Huffington Post*, April 24, 2013, https://www.huffingtonpost.com/alan-elsner/exodus-book_b_3139291. html. At least three books have emerged in response to the concerns addressed in Uris's novel: Gordon Thomas, *Operation Exodus*; Ira Nadel's biography, *Leon Uris: Life of a Best Seller*; and M. M. Silver's *Our Exodus*.

15. Ira Nadel, *Leon Uris: Life of a Best Seller* (Austin: University of Texas Press, 2010). See Robert Cohen's review at www.JewishBookCouncil.org.

16. Nora Chahbazi, "Get Kids Reading Like Crazy," Evidence-Based Literacy Instruction: Teaching the World to Read, http://eblireads.com/kidsreading; Michael Sappir, review of *The Source*, by James A. Michener, *Did You Learn Anything?* (blog), March 6, 2012, www.didyoulearnanything.net/blog. Like other readers, he appreciated Michener's research as well as the stories he told; Betty Lytle, *The Oklahoman*, https://newsok.com/article/5530959.

4. THE 1960s

1. Jonathan Rose, *Readers' Liberation: The Literary Agenda* (New York: Oxford University Press, 2018), 80–81.

2. Alice Payne Hackett, *70 Years of Bestsellers, 1895–1965* (New York: R. R. Bowker, 1967).

3. See Rose's discussion in *Readers' Liberation*, 167–70, of the response to Rachel Carson's *Silent Spring*.

4. Hackett, *70 Years of Bestsellers*.

5. Hackett, *70 Years of Bestsellers*.

6. Chris Messenger, *The Godfather and American Culture* (Albany: State University of New York Press, 2002), 4.

5. THE 1970s

1. Charles Cumming, "*The Day of the Jackal*—the Hit We Nearly Missed," *Guardian*, June 3, 2011.

2. Stan Persky, "Re-re-reading Gore Vidal: A First Anniversary Requiem," *Los Angeles Review of Books*, July 31, 2013, 117.

3. Gore Vidal, *Burr* (New York: Random House, 1973), 13; also see Anthony Hutchison, *Writing the Republic: Liberalism and Morality in American Political Fiction* (New York: Columbia University Press, 2007).

4. Gore Vidal, *Inventing a Nation: Washington, Adams, Jefferson* (New Haven, Conn.: Yale University Press, 2003), 176.

5. Vidal, *Burr*, 13; Hutchison, *Writing the Republic*, 242.

6. Vidal, *Burr*, 522.

7. Vidal, *Burr*, 404–5.

8. The TV miniseries *The Thorn Birds* was produced by David Wolper in 1983.

9. Vidal, *United States*, 617.

10. Vidal is cited by Persky, "Re-re-reading Gore Vidal," 118–19.

11. John Bear, *The #1 New York Times Best Seller* (Berkeley, Calif.: Ten Speed, 1992), 152.

12. For these online posts see: blog.booktopia.com.au; www.artofmanliness. com, May 23, 2013.

13. Claire Croxton, *Ex-Ray* (Adams Basin, N.Y.: Wild Rose, 2014).

14. This is from a post online: "Suck It, Ken Follett," *Yellaphant* (blog), October 25, 2010, factandfiction-bridget.blogspot.com.

15. Michael Korda, *Making the List: A Cultural History of the American Bestseller, 1900–1999* (New York: Simon and Schuster, 2001), 167. The testimony of readers in the nineteenth century tells us that books were frequently passed around from person to person. The practice of passing along a hardcover book continues in our time.

16. Korda, *Making the List*, 167.

6. THE 1980s

1. Kraig L. Baker, "Are Oliver Stone and Tom Clancy Journalists? Determining Who Has Standing to Claim the Journalist's Privilege," *Washington Law Review* 69 (1994): 739–64.

2. Ted Morgan, "Higher and Yet Higher," Review of *Trump: The Art of the Deal. New York Times* (December 20, 1987).

7. THE 1990s

1. Michael Korda, *Making the List: A Cultural History of the American Bestseller* (New York: Simon and Schuster, 2001), 197–98.

2. Korda, *Making the List*, 198.

3. During his lifetime Robert Ludlum wrote the Bourne trilogy. Suspense story novelist Eric Van Lustbader, by arrangement with Ludlum, wrote *The Bourne Legacy* later, after Ludlum's death.

4. Bobbie Robinson, "Playing Like the Boys: Patricia Cornwell Writes Men," *Journal of Popular Culture* 39, no. 1 (February 2006): 95.

5. Susan S. Lanser, "(Im)plying the Author," *Narrative* 9, no. 2 (2001): 153-60.

6. Rose Lucas, "Anxiety and Its Antidotes: Patricia Cornwell and the Forensic Body," *Lit: Literature Interpretation Theory*, 2004, 207.

7. Sue Turnbull, "Bodies of Knowledge: Pleasures and Anxiety in the Detective Fiction of Patricia D. Cornwell," *Australian Journal of Literature and Society*, 1993.

8. These readers wrote letters to the editor that were published by the *New York Magazine*, January 14, 1991.

9. Sheldon Nesdale, "John Grisham Books: What Reading Order Is Best?" *Best Reading Order* (blog), December 1, 2015, https://www.bestreadingorder. com/2015/12/john-grisham-books-reading-order/.

10. Richard Eden, "John Grisham: I Tried Literature and Didn't Like It Much," *Telegraph*, September 19, 2009.

11. These reader comments appear on the Maplewood (New Jersey) Library website.

12. Peter Blauner, "King Sets Otherworldly Eye on Anti-abortion Violence," *Newsday*, October 16, 1994. Blauner is a screenwriter for the television show *Blue Bloods*. He is an exceptional crime novelist, whose most recent book is *Proving Ground* (2017).

13. Cecilia Konchar Farr, *Reading Oprah* (Albany: State University of New York Press, 2005), x.

14. Farr, *Reading Oprah*, xi.

15. Farr, *Reading Oprah*, 2.

16. Farr, *Reading Oprah*, 3.

8. THE 2000s

1. Literary agent Aaron Priest echoed the sentiments of many other people in the book industry when he said that the Harry Potter books "should not be taking space in place of bona-fide adult titles." Quoted by Rebekah Fitzsimmons in "Testing the Tastemakers: Children's Literature and Bestseller Lists and the Harry Potter Effect," *Children's Literature* 40 (2012): 78–107.

2. "The Future of Books," *Congressional Quarterly* 10, no. 24 (June 23, 2000): 545.

3. Judith Shulevitz, "Fiction and 'Literary' Fiction," The Close Reader, *New York Times Book Review*, September 9, 2001.

4. Harold Bloom, "Dumbing Down American Readers," *Boston Globe*, September 24, 2003.

9. THE 2010s

1. "Easy Writers," *New Yorker*, May 28, 2012.

2. All three reviews mentioned are quoted in the *Vanity Fair* article.

3. Molly Wetta, "The *New York Times* Bestseller Lists Have Become Even More Irrelevant," BookRiot, February 2, 2017, https://bookriot.com/2017/02/02/the-new-york-times-bestseller-lists-have-become-even-more-irrelevant/.

4. Laura Miller, "Laura Miller's Favorite Books of 2017," *Slate* (January 24, 2018), www.slate.com/topics/slate-book-review.

BIBLIOGRAPHY

Note: This bibliography consists of references utilized in this book. It does not include the bestsellers that are referred to in the text.

Adler, Mortimer J. *How to Read a Book: The Art of Getting a Liberal Education*. New York: Simon and Schuster: 1940.

Adorno, Theodor. *The Culture Industry: Selected Essays on Mass Culture*. London: Routledge, 2001.

All Quiet on the Western Front Study Guide. New York: McGraw Hill, 2000.

Anderson, Benedict. *Imagined Communities: Reflections on the Origin and Spread of Nationalism*. London: Verso, 1983.

Archer, Jody, and Matthew Jockers. *The Bestseller Code*. New York: St. Martin's, 2016.

Arnold, Matthew. *Culture and Anarchy*. Edited by J. Dover Wilson. Cambridge: Cambridge University Press, 1969.

Aubrey, Timothy. *Reading as Therapy: What Contemporary Fiction Does for Middle Class Americans*. Ames: University of Iowa Press, 2012.

Baker, Kraig L. "Are Oliver Stone and Tom Clancy Journalists? Determining Who Has Standing to Claim the Journalist's Privilege." *Washington Law Review* 69 (1994): 739–64.

Bear, John. *The #1 New York Times Best Seller*. Berkeley, Calif.: Ten Speed, 1992.

Benjamin, Walter. "The Work of Art in the Age of Mechanical Reproduction." In *Illuminations: Walter Benjamin*, edited by Hannah Arendt, 217–51. New York: Schocken Books, 1969.

Berberich, Christine, ed. *The Bloomsbury Introduction to Popular Fiction*. London: Bloomsbury, 2015.

Blauner, Peter. "King Sets Otherworldly Eye on Anti-abortion Violence." *Newsday*, October 16, 1994.

Blight, David. *Beyond the Battlefield: Race, Memory, and the American Civil War*. Amherst: University of Massachusetts Press, 2002.

Bloom, Clive. *Cult Fiction: Popular Reading and Pulp Theory*. Basingstoke, UK: Palgrave Macmillan, 1996.

———. *Spy Thrillers: From Buchan to le Carré*. Basingstoke: Palgrave Macmillan, 1990.

Bloom, Harold. "Dumbing Down American Readers." *Boston Globe*, September 24, 2003.

Bonadeo, Alfred. "War and Degradation: Gleanings from the Literature of the Great War." *Comparative Literary Studies* 21 (1984): 409–33.

Bonita, Georgianna. "*The Kite Runner*'s Transnational Allegory: Anatomy of an Afghan-American Bestseller." In *Must Read: Rediscovering American Bestsellers; From* Charlotte

Temple *to* The Da Vinci Code, edited by Sarah Churchwell and Thomas Ruys Smith. London: Continuum, 2012.

"The Book Clubs." *New Republic*, September 30, 1946, 420–21.

"Books and Radio." *Publishers Weekly*, June 26, 1948, 2607.

"Books on Forthcoming Radio Programs." *Publishers Weekly*, January 10, 1948, 139.

"Books on Radio Programs." *Publishers Weekly*, October 15, 1949, 1725.

Boorstin, Daniel J. *The Image: A Guide to Pseudo-events in America*. New York: Harper Colophon, 1964.

Bourdieu, Pierre. *Distinction: A Social Critique of the Judgment of Taste*. Translated by Richard Nice. Cambridge, Mass.: Harvard University Press, 1984.

———. *The Field of Cultural Production*. Edited by Randal Johnson. New York: Columbia University Press, 1993.

Brier, Evan. "Crimes and Bestsellers: Mario Puzo's Path to *The Godfather*." In *Must Read: Rediscovering American Bestsellers; From* Charlotte Temple *to* The Da Vinci Code, edited by Sarah Churchwell and Thomas Ruys Smith, 277–96. New York: Continuum, 2012.

Brown, Erica, and Mary Grover, eds. *Middlebrow Literary Cultures: The Battle of the Brows, 1920–1960*. New York: Palgrave Macmillan, 2012.

Cassuto, Leonard. *Hard Boiled Sentimentality: The Secret History of American Crime Stories*. New York: Columbia University Press, 2008.

Cassuto, Leonard, Clare Virginia Eby, and Benjamin Reiss, eds. *The Cambridge History of the American Novel*. Cambridge: Cambridge University Press, 2011.

Cawelti, John G. *Adventures, Mystery, and Romance: Formula Stories as Art and Popular Culture*. Chicago: University of Chicago Press, 1976.

Chahbazi, Nora. "Get Kids Reading Like Crazy." Evidence-Based Literacy Instruction: Teaching the World to Read. http://eblireads.com .

Chartier, Roger. *The Order of Books: Readers, Authors and Libraries in Europe*, trans. Lydia G. Cochrane. Stanford: Stanford University Press, 1992.

Chiaet, Julianne. "Reading Literary Fiction Improves Empathy." *Scientific American*, October 4, 2013.

Churchwell, Sarah, and Thomas Ruys Smith, eds. *Must Read: Rediscovering American Bestsellers; From* Charlotte Temple *to* The Da Vinci Code. London: Continuum, 2012.

Cowles, Gregory. "Inside the List." *New York Times Book Review*, June 2, 2013.

Croxton, Claire. *Ex-Ray*. Adams Basin, N.Y.: Wild Rose, 2014.

Darnton, Robert, "What Is the History of Books?" *Daedelus* 111 (Summer 1982): 65–83.

Denning, Michael. *Cover Stories: Narrative and Ideology in the British Spy Thriller*. London: Routledge and Kegan Paul, 1987.

———. *Mechanic Accents: Dime Novels and Working-Class Culture in America*. London: Verso, 1998.

Detroit Tribune. "The Art of the Negro." October 23, 1942.

———. "Ottley Says New Bestseller Shows Interest in Negro Problems." September 11, 1943, 19.

Doyle, Arthur Conan. *The Hound of the Baskervilles*. London: George Newnes, 1902.

Duncan, Lloyd. *Just Getting There: An Autobiography*. Self-published, Xlibris, 2006.

Eksteins, Modris. *Rites of Spring: The Great War and the Modern Age*. New York: Houghton Mifflin, 2000.

Elsner, Alan. "Re-reading Leon Uris' *Exodus*." *Huffington Post*, April 24, 2013. https://www.huffingtonpost.com/alan-elsner/exodus-book_b_3139291.html.

Ennis, Phillip H. *Adult Book Reading in the United States*. Chicago: National Opinion Research Center, 1965.

Fadiman, Clifton. *Reading I've Liked*. New York: Simon and Schuster, 1941.

Farr, Cecilia Konchar. *Reading Oprah*. Albany: State University of New York Press, 2005.

Fiedler, Leslie A. *Love and Death in the American Novel*. New York: Stein and Day, 1966.

———. *What Was Literature? Class Culture and Mass Society*. New York: Simon and Schuster, 1982.

Fiske, John. *Reading the Popular*. New York: Routledge, 2004.

Fitzsimmons, Rebekah. "Testing the Tastemakers: Children's Literature and Bestseller Lists and the Harry Potter Effect." *Children's Literature* 40 (2012): 78–107.

"Formal Opening of the Community Library," *Midland Journal* (March 13, 1942), 1.

Franklin, Ruth. "Readers of the Pack: American Bestselling." *Book Forum*, 2011.

———. *Shirley Jackson: A Rather Haunted Life*. New York: Scribner's, 2016.

Franzen, Jonathan. "Why Bother? Perchance to Dream; In the Age of Images, a Reason to Write Novels." *Harper's*, April 2003.

Fussell, Paul. *The Great War and Modern Memory*. Oxford: Oxford University Press, 1975.

"The Future of Books." *Congressional Quarterly* 10, no. 24 (June 23, 2000): 545–68.

Gates, David. Review of *The Corrections*. *New York Times Book Review*, September 9, 2001.

Gelder, Ken. *Popular Fiction: The Logic and Practices of a Literary Field*. New York: Routledge, 2004.

Gilbert, Martin. *The First World War*. London: Folio, 2000.

Graves, Robert. *Goodbye to All That*. London: Jonathan Cape, 1929.

Hackett, Alice Payne. *70 Years of Best Sellers, 1895–1965*. New York: Bowker, 1967.

Hart, James D. *The Popular Book*. New York: Oxford University Press, 1950.

Hofstadter, Richard. *Anti-intellectualism in American Life*. New York: Vintage, 1963.

Horkheimer, Max. "Art and Mass Culture." In *Critical Theory: Selected Essays*. Translated by Matthew J. O'Connell et al. New York: Continuum, 2002.

Howsam, Leslie. *Old Books and New Histories: An Orientation to Studies in Book and Print Culture*. Toronto: University of Toronto Press, 2006.

Humble, Nicola. *The Feminine Middlebrow Novel, 1920s to 1950s*. Oxford: Oxford University Press, 2001.

———. "The Reader of Popular Fiction." In *Cambridge Companion to Popular Fiction*, edited by David Glover and Scott McCracken. Cambridge: Cambridge University Press, 2012.

Hutchison, Anthony. *Writing the Republic: Liberalism and Morality in American Political Fiction*. New York: Columbia University Press, 2007.

Hutner, Gordon. *What America Read: Class, Taste and the Novel*. Chapel Hill: University of North Carolina Press, 2003.

Huyssen, Andreas. *After the Great Divide: Modernism, Mass Culture, Postmodernism*. New York: Macmillan, 1986.

James, P. D. *Talking about Detective Fiction*. New York: Knopf, 2009.

Kakutani, Michiko. "Writers Martin Amis Admires, and He Should Know." *New York Times Book Review*, December 11, 2001.

Kammen, Michael. *American Culture, American Tastes: Social Change in the Twentieth Century*. New York: Knopf, 2003.

Kelly, John. "Washington Confidential." *Washington Post*, January 10, 2016.

Klein, Kathleen Gregory. *Diversity and Detective Fiction*. Bowling Green, Ohio: Bowling Green University Press, 1998.

Korda, Michael. *Making the List: A Cultural History of the American Bestseller, 1900–1999*. New York: Simon and Schuster, 2001.

Kubica, Chris, and Will Hochman. *Letters to J. D. Salinger*. Madison: University of Wisconsin Press, 2002.

Lacy, Tim. *The Dream of a Democratic Culture: Mortimer Adler and the Great Books Idea*. New York: Palgrave Macmillan, 2013.

Lanser, Susan S. "(Im)plying the Author." *Narrative* 9, no. 2 (2001): 153–60.

Lasch, Christopher. *The Culture of Narcissism: American Life in an Age of Diminishing Expectations*. New York: Norton, 1978.

Lee, Charles. *The Hidden Public: The Story of the Book-of-Month Club*. Garden City: Doubleday, 1958.

Levine, Lawrence W. *Highbrow/Lowbrow: The Emergence of Cultural Hierarchy in America*. Cambridge, Mass.: Harvard University Press, 1988.

Lewis, Sinclair. *Elmer Gantry*. New York: Harcourt, 1927.

Liebling, A. J. "A Reporter at Large." *New Yorker*, July 1, 1944, 38.

Light, Martin. *The Quixotic Vision of Sinclair Lewis*. West Lafayette, Ind.: Purdue University Press, 1975.

Long, Elizabeth. *The American Dream and the Popular Novel.* London: Routledge, 2017.
———. *Book Clubs: Women and the Uses of Reading in Everyday Life.* Chicago: University of Chicago Press, 2003.
Loos, Christopher. *Military History Quarterly* (2000): 826–27.
Lucas, Rose. "Anxiety and Its Antidotes: Patricia Cornwell and the Forensic Body." *Lit: Literary Interpretation Theory*, 2004, 207.
MacDonald, Kate. *Middlebrow: What Mr. Miniver Read.* Basingstoke, UK: Palgrave Macmillan, 2011.
———. *Novelists against Social Change: Conservative Popular Fiction, 1920–1960.* Basingstoke, UK: Palgrave Macmillan, 2015.
Mahler, Jonathan. "James Patterson Inc." *New York Times Magazine*, January 20, 2010.
McAleer, Joseph. *Popular Reading and Publishing in Britain, 1914–1950.* Oxford, UK: Clarendon, 1992.
McCracken, Scott. *Pulp: Reading Popular Fiction.* Manchester, UK: Manchester University Press, 1998.
Mencken, H. L. "The Library." *American Mercury* 10 (April 1927): 506.
Messenger, Chris. *The Godfather and American Culture.* Albany: State University of New York Press, 2002.
Mexal, Stephen J. "Realism, Narrative History and the Production of the Bestseller: *The Da Vinci Code* and the Virtual Public Sphere." *Journal of Popular Culture* 44, no. 5 (October 1, 2011): 1085–92.
Miall, David S. "Empirical Approaches to Studying Literary Readers: The State of the Discipline." *Book History* 9 (2006): 291–312.
Miller, Laura J. "The Best-Seller List as Marketing Tool and Historical Fiction." *Book History* 3 (2000): 286–304.
Miller, Laura. "Laura Miller's Favorite Books of 2017." *Slate* (January 24, 2018), www.slate.com/topics/slate-book-review .
Morgan, Ted. "Higher and Yet Higher," Review of *Trump: The Art of the Deal. New York Times* (December 20, 1987).
Mott, Frank Luther. *Golden Multitudes: The Story of Bestsellers in the United States.* New York: Macmillan, 1947.
Murphy, Carl. "You Can Abolish Prejudice." *Detroit Tribune*, October 23, 1943.
Myers, B. R. "A Reader's Manifesto: An Attack on the Growing Pretentiousness of American Literary Prose." *Atlantic*, July/August 2001.
Nadel, Ira. *Leon Uris: Life of a Best Seller.* Austin: University of Texas Press, 2010.
Nesdale, Sheldon. "John Grisham Books: What Reading Order Is Best?" *Best Reading Order* (blog). December 1, 2015. https://www.bestreadingorder.com/2015/12/john-grisham-books-reading-order/.
New York Magazine. Letters to the Editor, January 14, 1991.
New York Times Book Review. 1943–2017.
Orwell, George. "Boy's Weeklies." In *A Collection of Essays*, 279–308. New York: Mariner, 1970.
———. "Good Bad Books" (1945). In *All Art Is Propaganda: Critical Essays.* New York: Houghton Mifflin, 2009.
Pawling, Christopher. *Popular Fiction and Social Change.* New York: Macmillan, 1984.
Perrin, Tom. *The Aesthetics of Middlebrow Fiction. Popular US Novels, Modernism and Form, 1945–75.* Basingstoke, UK: Palgrave Macmillan, 2015.
Persky, Stan. "Re-re-reading Gore Vidal: A First Anniversary Requiem." *Los Angeles Review of Books*, July 31, 2013.
Phillips, Deborah. *Women's Fiction 1945–2005. Writing Romance.* London: Continuum, 2005.
Pirsig-Wood, Ruth. *Lolita in Peyton Place: Highbrow, Middlebrow and Lowbrow Novels of the 1950s.* London: Routledge, 2013.
Price, Leah. "Reading: The State of the Discipline." *Book History*, 2004.
Rabinowitz, Paula. *Pulp: How Paperbacks Brought Modernism to Main Street.* Princeton, N.J.: Princeton University Press, 2014.

Radway, Janice. "The Book-of-the-Month Club and the General Reader." In *Reading in America: Literature and Social History*, edited by Cathy N. Davidson, 259–84. Baltimore: Johns Hopkins University Press, 1989.

———. *A Feeling for Books. Book-of-the-Month Club, Literary Taste and Middle-Class Desire.* Chapel Hill: University of North Carolina Press, 1997.

———. *Reading the Romance: Women, Patriarchy, and Popular Literature,* Chapel Hill: University of North Carolina Press, 1984. Reprint 1991.

———. "The Scandal of the Middlebrow: The Book-of-the-Month Club, Class Fracture, and Cultural Authority." *South Atlantic Quarterly* 89 (Fall 1990): 703–36.

Reisman, David, with Nathan Glazer and Reuel Denney. *The Lonely Crowd: A Study of the Changing American Character.* New Haven, Conn.: Yale University Press, 1971. Originally published 1950.

Robinson, Bobbie. "Playing Like the Boys: Patricia Cornwell Writes Men." *Journal of Popular Culture* 39, no. 1 (February 2006): 95–108.

Rose, Jonathan. "Modernity and Print I: Britain 1890–1970." In *Companion to the History of the Book,* edited by Simon Eliot and Jonathan Rose, 341–53. Malden, Mass.: Wiley-Blackwell, 2011.

———. *Readers' Liberation: The Literary Agenda.* New York: Oxford University Press, 2018.

———. "Rereading the English Common Reader: A Preface to a History of Audiences." *Journal of the History of Ideas* 53 (1992): 48.

Rubin, Joan Shelley. *The Making of Middlebrow Culture.* Chapel Hill: University of North Carolina Press, 1992.

Salinger, Margaret. *Dreamcatcher.* New York: Scribner's, 2001.

Sappir, Michael. Review of *The Source,* by James A. Michener. *Did You Learn Anything?* (blog). March 6, 2012. www.didyoulearnanything.net/blog.

Schneider, Thomas. "The Truth about the War Finally: Critics' Expectations of War Literature during the Weimer Republic." *Journalism Studies* 17, no. 4 (June 2016): 490–501.

Schorer, Mark. *Sinclair Lewis.* New York: McGraw Hill, 1961.

Schwed, Peter. *Turning the Pages: An Insider's Story of Simon and Schuster, 1924–1984.* New York: Macmillan, 1984.

Seldes, Gilbert. *The Great Audience.* New York: Viking, 1950.

Sherrill, William. "Good Books." *Detroit Tribune,* June 6, 1942.

Shields, David, and Shane Salerno. *Salinger.* New York: Simon and Schuster, 2013.

Shulevitz, Judith. "Fiction and 'Literary' Fiction." The Close Reader, *New York Times Book Review,* September 9, 2001.

Silverman, Al, ed. *The Book-of-the-Month Club: Sixty Years of Books in American Life.* Boston: Little, Brown, 1986.

Smith, Erin A. "Pulp Sensations." In *Cambridge Companion to Popular Fiction,* edited by David Glover and Scott McCracken. Cambridge: Cambridge University Press, 2012.

Stevenson, Robert Louis. "A Humble Remonstrance" (1884). In *Collected Works of Robert Louis Stevenson.* Oxford: Oxford University Press, 1938. Orig. pub. 1925.

"Suck It, Ken Follett." *Yellaphant* (blog). October 25, 2010. factandfiction-bridget.blogspot.com.

Susman, Warren I. *Culture as History.* New York: Pantheon, 1984.

Sutherland, John. *Bestsellers: A Very Short Introduction.* Oxford: Oxford University Press, 2007.

———. *Bestsellers: Popular Fiction of the 1970s.* London: Routledge and Kegan Paul, 1981.

———. *Reading the Decades: Fifty Years of the Nation's Bestsellers.* Reprint. London: BBC Books, 2002.

Tebbel, John. *The Paperback Book in America: A Pocket History.* New York: Pocket Books, 1964.

Turnbull, Sue. "Bodies of Knowledge: Pleasures and Anxiety in the Detective Fiction of Patricia D. Cornwell." *Australia Journal of Literature and Society,* 1993.

Updike, John. "Personal Matters." In *More Matter: Essays and Criticism.* New York: Knopf, 1999.

Vidal, Gore. *Burr.* New York: Random House, 1973.

———. *Inventing a Nation: Washington, Adams, Jefferson*. New Haven, Conn.: Yale University Press, 2003.

Wetta, Molly. "The *New York Times* Bestseller Lists Have Become Even More Irrelevant." BookRiot. February 2, 2017. https://bookriot.com/2017/02/02/the-new-york-times-bestseller-lists-have-become-even-more-irrelevant/.

Wharton, Edith. *The House of Mirth*. New York: Penguin Classics, 2003.

Wiegand, Wayne A. *Part of Our Lives: A People's History of the American Public Library*. Oxford: Oxford University Press, 2015.

Williams, Raymond. *Marxism and Literature*. Oxford: Oxford University Press, 1977.

———. *Problems in Materialism and Culture*. London: Verso, 1982.

Woolf, Virginia. "Middlebrow." In *Death of the Moth*, 180–84. New York: Harcourt Brace, 1942.

Worpole, Ken. *Reading by Numbers: Contemporary Publishing and Popular Fiction*. London: Comedia, 1984.

Zinsser, William K. *Revolution in American Reading*. New York: Book of the Month Club, 1966.

ARCHIVES

New York Public Library, New York, New York

Oral History Interviews, Rutgers University, New Brunswick, New Jersey

Scribner's Publishing Company Records, Firestone Library, Princeton University, Princeton, New Jersey

INDEX

ABOUT THE AUTHOR

Robert McParland is professor of English and chair of the Department of English at Felician University. He has published numerous book chapters and articles, including essays on Herman Melville, Ernest Hemingway, and Robert Penn Warren, among others. McParland is editor of *Music and Literary Modernism* (2008) and *Film and Literary Modernism* (2013), as well as author of *Charles Dickens's American Audience* (Lexington, 2010), *How to Write about Joseph Conrad* (2011), and *Mark Twain's Audience: A Critical Analysis of Reader Responses to the Writings of Mark Twain* (Lexington, 2014). McParland is also the author of *Beyond Gatsby: How Fitzgerald, Hemingway, and Writers of the 1920s Shaped American Culture* (2015), *Citizen Steinbeck: Giving Voice to the People* (2016), and *From Native Son to King's Men: The Literary Landscape of 1940s America* (2017), all published by Rowman & Littlefield.